The Symbolic Order:
A Contemporary Reader on the Arts Debate

Edited by
Peter Abbs

RoutledgeFalmer
Taylor & Francis Group

LONDON AND NEW YORK

First published 1989
By RoutledgeFalmer
11 New Fetter Lane, London EC4P 4EE

Transferred to Digital Printing 2004

Library of Congress Cataloging-in-Publication Data

The Symbolic order : a contemporary reader on the arts debate
  edited by Peter Abbs.
       p.   cm.
    Bibliography: p.
    Includes index.
    ISBN 1-85000-593-1. — ISBN 1--85000-594-X (pbk.)
    1. Arts—Study and teaching.   I. Abbs, Peter. 1942–
NX280.S9   1989
700'.7—dc20   89-32353
                                                              CIP

British Library Cataloguing in Publication Data

The Symbolic order : a contemporary reader on the arts debate. —
  (The Falmer Press library on aesthetic education).
  1. Educational institutions. Curriculum subjects:
  Arts
  I. Abbs, Peter
  700'.7'1

ISBN 1-85000-593-1
ISBN 1-85000-594-X (pbk)

Jacket design by Caroline Archer
Painting *The Vigilant One* (1984)
Oil on Canvas by Andrzej Jackowski.
Courtesy Malborough Fine Art, London.

Typeset in 10 on 12 Garamond by
Mathematical Composition Setters Ltd, Salisbury

The Symbolic Order

The RoutledgeFalmer Library on Aesthetic Education

Series Editor: Dr Peter Abbs, University of Sussex, Brighton

The aim of the series is to define and defend a comprehensive aesthetic, both theoretical and practical, for the teaching of the arts.

The first three volumes provide a broad historic and philosophical framework for the understanding of the arts in education. The subsequent volumes elaborate the implications of this comprehensive aesthetic for each of the six major art disciplines and for the teaching of the arts in the primary school.

Setting the Frame

LIVING POWERS: THE ARTS IN EDUCATION
Edited by Peter Abbs (1987)

A IS FOR AESTHETIC: ESSAYS ON CREATIVE AND AESTHETIC
EDUCATION
Peter Abbs (1988)

THE SYMBOLIC ORDER: A CONTEMPORARY READER ON THE ARTS
DEBATE
Edited by Peter Abbs (1989)

The Individual Studies

DANCE IN EDUCATION
Peter Brinson

DRAMA IN EDUCATION
Roger Hunt

LITERATURE IN EDUCATION
Edwin Webb

FILM IN EDUCATION
Rob Watson

VISUAL ARTS IN EDUCATION
Rod Taylor

MUSIC IN EDUCATION
Charles Plummeridge

THE ARTS IN THE PRIMARY SCHOOL
Glennis Andrews and Rod Taylor

Contents

Contents

Acknowledgments

Chapter 1   Earlier versions of *Aesthetic Education: An Opening Manifesto* have been published in *The Times Higher Education Supplement* (13 January, 1989) and in *The Journal of Aesthetic Education* USA 1989.

Chapter 2   *The Arts Within a Plural Concept of Knowledge* is an edited version of an Open Seminar paper given to students on the *Language, the Arts and Education* MA Course at the University of Sussex on 23 October, 1984.

Chapter 3   *Modern Philosophy and the Neglect of Aesthetics* is an abridged version of an inaugural lecture given at Birbeck College, University of London. It was published in the *Times Literary Supplement* on 5 June, 1987. Copyright Roger Scruton.

Chapter 4   *The Culture of Links* first appeared in *The Shifting Point*, Copyright 1987 by Peter Brook. Reprinted by permission of Harper and Row, Publishers, Inc.

Chapter 5   *Art, Judgment and Belief: Towards the Condition of Music* has been previously published in *Music of the Angels*, Selected and Edited by Meirion Bowen (C. Eulenburg Books, 1980). Copyright Michael Tippett.

Chapter 6   *The Education of Feeling* first appeared in the symposium *The Education of Feeling* edited by Dr Rex Gibson (Cambridge Institute of Education, 1982). Copyright Rex Gibson.

Chapter 7   *Literature and the Education of Feeling* was first published in *The Education of Feeling* (Cambridge Institute of Education, 1982). Copyright Professor L.C. Knights.

Chapter 8   *The Rationality of Feeling*. This is a revised version of a paper delivered at the Conference of the Canadian Society for Education through Art in Halifax, Nova Scotia, November 1987. It also incorporates part of a paper 'Art, Mind and Philosophy', *Journal of Aesthetic Education*, Autumn 1986.

Chapter 9   *The Father of Art History* was first given in the City of Stuttgart as the Hegel Prize Lecture and published subsequently in *Tributes*,

Ernst Gombrich (Phaidon, 1984). English translation courtesy of *Architectural Design Magazine*, London. Copyright Phaidon Press Ltd.

Chapter 10   *The Domestication of Outrage* was originally given as the second Reith Lecture in 1982 and published as part of *The Arts Without Mystery* (BBC 1983). Copyright Professor Denis Donoghue.

Chapter 11   *Approaching the End of Art* has been previously published in *The State of the Art* (Prentice Hall Press, New York, 1987). Copyright Arthur C. Danto.

Chapter 12   *Aesthetics after Modernism* was first published by Writers and Readers Publishing Cooperative Society Ltd. in 1983. It has subsequently appeared in *The Australian Scapegoat* (Western Australia Press, 1986). Copyright Peter Fuller.

Chapter 13   *The Arts in Education* first appeared in *The Parochialism of the Present* (Routledge and Kegan Paul, 1981). Copyright Professor G.H. Bantock.

Chapter 14   *Myth and Education* was first published in *The Times Education Supplement* (2 September 1977) and is published here with the permission of Ted Hughes.

Chapter 15   *Myth and Identity* has previously appeared in *On Knowing: Essays for the Left Hand*, Jerome Bruner (Harvard University Press, 1962). Copyright 1962, 1979 by the President and Fellows of Harvard College.

Chapter 16   *Individuation and the Creative Process* was first published in *The Journal of Analytical Psychology*, Vol. 28, No. 4, October 1983. It is reprinted by permission of the Peter Fraser and Dunlop Group Ltd.

Chapter 17   *The Pattern of Art-Making* was first published in *English within the Arts* (Hodder and Stoughton, 1982). Copyright Peter Abbs.

Chapter 18   *Art Worlds in Schools* by Professor Maxine Greene was first published in *The Journal of Aesthetic Education*, Vol. 21, No. 4, 1987. Copyright 1987 Board of Trustees of the University of Illinois.

Chapter 19   *Teaching Poetry* was an address delivered to a joint meeting of the Association of Canadian University Teachers of English and the Humanities Association at the University of Western Ontario London, 24 May 1978. It was first published in the Canadian Journal *The Compass* in 1979. Copyright *The Compass* Edmonton.

Chapter 20   *Purpose in Music Education* was first published as Chapter 1 of *Discovering Music* (Batsford, 1982). Copyright Professor Keith Swanwick and Dorothy Taylor.

Chapter 21   *The Arts Education and the Community* was the inaugural lecture in the Chair of Education delivered at King's College, London on 18 November 1980. Copyright Professor David Aspin.

Chapter 22   *Real Presences* was first published as a pamphlet by Cambridge University Press in 1985. Copyright Professor George Steiner.

We no longer see man against a background of values, of realities, which transcend him. We picture man as a brave naked will surrounded by an easily comprehended empirical world. For the hard idea of truth we have substituted a facile idea of sincerity. What we have never had, of course, is a satisfactory Liberal theory of personality, a theory of man as free and separate and related to a rich and complicated world from which, as a moral being, he has much to learn. We have bought the Liberal theory as it stands, because we have wished to encourage people to think of themselves as free, at the cost of surrendering the background.

Iris Murdoch
from *Against Dryness: A Polemical Sketch*

Introduction

The present volume, *The Symbolic Order: A Contemporary Reader on the Arts Debate* is the third in a series of ten related books on aesthetic education. The severe erosion and inner division of arts education in our times demand nothing less than an organized challenge of this scale.

In *Living Powers*, the first volume in the series, Peter Fuller wrote:

> The aesthetic dimension of human life extends across a wide range of human activities: and we ought to regard it as an inalienable human potentiality, as fundamental as the capacity for language. If a society cannot provide a facilitating environment within which the aesthetic potential of all of its members can find appropriate expression, then that society has failed. [1]

This defines precisely the fundamental concept at the heart of our project.

In the introduction I would like to elaborate on Peter Fuller's proposition, first, by outlining the concept of a coherent aesthetic education which informs and unifies the whole series and, secondly, by making clear the specific intentions of this symposium in relationship to the entire scheme.

The Aims of the Series

Our key word 'aesthetic' stands in need of considerable reclamation and development. Ever since the late nineteenth century when the term referred to exquisite sensations (and was related to 'the aesthete', the person who set out in pursuit of such sensations) the concept has been distorted and diminished. Raymond Williams in his *Keywords* noted that there was 'something irresistibly displaced and marginal about the now common and limiting phrase *aesthetic considerations*, especially when contrasted with practical or utilitarian considerations, which are elements of the same basic division'. [2] Our aim — the aim of the series — is to rehouse the word and make it central to educational discourse. For us aesthetic refers to *a particular form of sensuous understanding*, a mode of apprehending through the senses the patterned import of human experience. The arts, in particular, work through this aesthetic mode and it is this which gives them their fundamental intellectual unity. Through exacting perceptual and imaginative engagement, through acts of heightened and sustained bodily attention, the arts are radically involved in the quest for understanding. Their quarry is nothing less than truth, or, at least, for the revelation of some vital aspect of truth; as Milan Kundera has said somewhat extravagantly, 'the sole raison d'etre of a novel is to discover what only the novel can discover. A novel that does not discover a hitherto unknown segment of existence is immoral.... The sequence of discoveries (not the sum of what was written) is what constitutes the history of the European novel'.[3] And of what Kundera says of the novel, we would want to extend *in spirit* to all the other major art forms. The arts exist to fashion aesthetically compelling images of existence, of human meaning and human possibility. Thus, through the aesthetic we can interrogate our lives just as effectively as through any other intellectual discipline, perhaps more effectively in that the arts, at their most powerful, always remain mysteriously close to the pulse and feel of life itself.

It is in this complex of assertions that one can begin to discern a number of living and connected principles. First, that the aesthetic represents a particular category of sensuous understanding; second, that the arts cohere intellectually in that they all work through and depend upon the power and logic of aesthetic apprehension; third, that because the arts together form a generic community of understanding they must be conceived (as with the Sciences and the Humanities) as an indispensable segment of any balanced curriculum.

In *Living Powers*, the first volume in the series, we explored the various ramifications of these propositions both historically and conceptually. Our premise was that no curriculum could be considered balanced or complete which did not include each of the six major aesthetic disciplines: Art (in which we would include Design and Architecture), Drama (in which we would include all kinds of Theatre), Dance, Music, Film and Literature. However difficult it may now seem in the light of the recently nationalized curriculum, it is of the utmost importance that the conception of a unified arts curriculum is not lost sight of or whittled down. It is simply not good enough to have an imposed curriculum in which only two of the arts (the visual arts and music) are called 'foundation subjects', in which one is left somewhat ambiguous (under the title of 'English'), and in which the other three are, if not explicitly outlawed, irredeemably marginalized (namely, Drama, Dance and Film). The series exists both to question theoretically the educational status quo and yet, at the same time, to explore pragmatically what can be done within the formidable restraints of the National Curriculum.

A further major premise of the series relates to the various grammars of the arts. We believe that it is a prime responsibility of arts teachers to develop a greater awareness of the conventions, techniques and traditions of their disciplines. In *Living Powers* we put forward the notion of an aesthetic field,[4] that complex magnetic system of allusion and reference in which any individual work of art was, we claimed, necessarily constituted. The concept of an aesthetic field is close to that of a 'simultaneous order' once elaborated by T. S. Eliot. In an early essay, first published in 1917, entitled *Tradition and the Individual Talent* Eliot wrote:

> the historical sense compels a man to write not merely with his own generation in his bones, but with a feeling that the whole of the literature of Europe from Homer and within it the whole of the literature of his own country has a simultaneous existence and composes a simultaneous order. This historical sense, which is a sense of the timeless as well as of the temporal and of the timeless and of the temporal together, is what makes a writer traditional. And it is at the same time what makes a writer most acutely conscious of his place in time, of his own contemporaneity.[5]

We believe that as pupils progressively engage with the arts so they should enter more and more consciously into relationship with this simultaneous order so that they can sense the symbolic continuum of the discipline and see how their own work derives partly from it and returns to it.

In the teaching of the Arts we have often failed to create an awareness of a dynamic tradition with achieved work and a variety of genres and conventions. In *Development through Drama*, first published in 1967, Brian Way could write: 'We are concerned with developing people, not drama (and certainly not theatre)'.[6] Way's book might have been better titled *The Death of Drama* for it excluded the concept of a complex symbolic order leaving only the artistically attenuated notions of 'groups' and 'feelings', of 'sincerity' and 'trust'. In English there has been, until recently, a marked tendency to favour a kind of sociological realism and to confine work to the discussion of its most obvious social messages. Certainly, as the Kingman Report on the teaching of language stated, there has been a widespread failure to engage creatively with stylistic matters:

> Certain kinds of literary, journalistic and commercial manipulation might be studied, but the largely thematic discussions involved offered little analysis of rhetoric, choice of language, metaphor, vocabulary and other persuasive and argumentative devices. Still less were they concerned with the pleasures of crafting and ordering related to writing in precise forms, or studying literary genres.[7]

Similarly in the Visual Arts, under the pressure of Modernism, there developed a marked disposition to deny the efficacy of any tradition before 1900, while Dance, adamant about its own immediate contemporaneity, for a time automatically exiled itself from its own aesthetic field.

This brings us directly to two main targets of the series: Progressivism in education and Modernism in culture. Both of these movements in different ways, and for different reasons, served to disrupt and discredit the continuity of artistic traditions. They worked to sever the individual from the great symbolic continuum of Western Culture. In the introduction to *Living Powers*, having declared war on both these complex and labile movements, I remarked:

> Perhaps we feel that the great challenge after Modernism and Progressivism is to bring as much of the cultural past into the present to make it,

in the fundamental act of aesthetic and imaginative creation, both contemporary and deep. In practice, this means that we are suspicious of endless innovation for its own sake; of art which is only a kind of 'self-expression', of art which claims to be 'relevant' merely because it is 'of the moment' or stridently ideological in content. We are suspicious of all practices which are reluctant to acknowledge any predecessors or any need for a cumulatively acquired and tested discourse. In spirit we are cultural ecologists. We want to conserve for the arts an intricate web of symbolic connections in which the present is seen in living relationship to a past and in which the individual is seen as part of the communal culture. Modernism, in particular, erased the sense of tradition; we wish to bring it back, not as an inert acquisition, but as one indispensable element in an intricate aesthetic field. [8]

This position remains central to the series. It is out to formulate and put into practice a conservationist aesthetic. There is now a visible need for better mappings, for charts which graphically display alternative readings of our cultural history, which make visible all that high Modernist theory occluded, which stress the strong lines of continuity and play down the story of Promethean discontinuity. We need maps that disclose the field of art-making and its wealth of deposits: its traditions, techniques, its variety of exemplars. The study and practice of the arts need more scope and depth. We need to be able to stretch back to the earliest times and to be able to move down into the basic biological rhythms of our bodies and our unconscious minds; and to do both at the same time.

It is essential, however, not to be misunderstood. The demand is not for prescriptive drills or the formal teaching of the tradition. Far from it. The logic of our teaching tactics must always be in intimate relationship to the nature of the symbolism being pursued. The 'grammar' of the arts is best introduced as a necessary part of expressive and imaginative activity as it seeks formal articulation in the classroom. The task is to establish a reciprocal play between the repertoire of conventions (and achieved works) and that impulse for symbolic expression which is innate to human life. As was argued in the second volume in the series, *A is for Aesthetic*, an apprenticeship model of learning is called for. [9] The teacher enters as co-artist possessing clear lines of access to the aesthetic field. Following this model, the teacher of an arts discipline becomes, in some measure, a practitioner: the music teacher composes; the teacher of literature writes and edits; the teacher of dance dances; and all should be ready, at times, to act as creative exemplars. But there is a further related, more subtle, aspect to the notion of co-artist; the arts teacher not only initiates aesthetic activity but can also enter it directly as creative agent, to develop it and deepen it. In this way the structures and conventions can be brought to bear directly on the expressive act *within* the perceptual and imaginative search for form. It will be one of the major aims of the seven remaining volumes to articulate, in quite precise and practical terms, the application of this model across all the arts in relationship to a living tradition and the need for a repertoire of techniques. In this way, it is hoped that the series will forge a teaching methodology for the rapidly emerging, conservationist aesthetic.

Having outlined the main principles of the series it remains for me to introduce the present volume, the contemporary reader on the arts debate.

The Aims of the Symposium

The first and primary aim of this symposium is simple. It is to put teachers of all the Arts in touch with some of the most recent and some of the best writing on the nature of Art; writing by such powerful art-makers as Ted Hughes, Peter Brook and Michael Tippett; writing by such influential educationists as Jerome Bruner, Maxine Greene and Louis Arnaud Reid; writings by such seminal critics as Ernst Gombrich, Peter Fuller and George Steiner. This in itself is to foster generative conceptions and to promote a sense of connection between the arts. Such an intellectual forum is vital particularly at the present time when, with the waning of Modernism, there is a real need for new formulations, more comprehensive critiques, a greater awareness of the plurality of artistic conventions and, hence, of expressive possibilities.

Yet it would be false for me to leave the impression that the symposium is eclectic, or that it offers a representative selection of texts from the various competing schools of thought. It is not intended as a sampler of all things conceivable concerning art in our times. On the contrary, it is a highly edited reader. Texts have been selected to represent an intellectual position. If the first aim of the volume is to challenge and stimulate, then its second aim is conceptually to clarify the philosophy of the whole series. I think there can be little doubt, for example, that most of the contributing authors would, at least in principle, share the critique of Modernism and Progressivism developed in *Living Powers* and *A is for Aesthetic* and would want, again, at least in principle, to embrace the notion of art as a quest for human understanding. Indeed, some of the key essays in the symposium are directly on these themes. The book is thus simultaneously a contemporary reader *and* a broad manifesto for the series.

This brings me to a further important point. Each essay can be read in its own right for it stands squarely on its own feet; yet, at the same time, it belongs to a structured sequential argument which I would like to outline briefly.

The opening three chapters are concerned with aesthetics and with defining the nature of aesthetic experience. After the opening manifesto, Louis Arnaud Reid offers a broad view of knowledge which incorporates, radically, aesthetic understanding of the arts; while Roger Scruton examines the renewal of aesthetics within philosophy.

The next section, written by two great practitioners of the arts (Peter Brook and Michael Tippett), define the way in which art is centrally related to the quest for meaning and judgment. This is amplified in the third section by philosophers and critics (Rex Gibson, L. C. Knights and David Best) who demonstrate how this takes place within and through the power of feeling.

The fourth section opens with a new but central theme: the demise of Modernism. Here a number of distinguished art critics (Ernst Gombrich, Denis

Donoghue, Arthur Danto and Peter Fuller) outline the fallacies of Modernism or, if not the fallacies, at least the reasons for its recent disintegration. This releases, in turn, the theme of the next two sections where the need for a living and more comprehensive sense of tradition is argued for, first by G. H. Bantock in relation to the effective teaching of the arts and, then, by Ted Hughes and Jerome Bruner in relation to the deep need for mythical narratives.

At this point, having established the main elements of a more adequate aesthetic, the symposium moves to outline the nature of the process of artistic creation (Anthony Storr and myself) and some of the implications for the teaching of the arts (Maxine Greene, George Whalley, Keith Swanwick and Dorothy Taylor).

Finally, the symposium concludes with an analysis of arts education in relationship to the concept of community (David Aspin) and with a further affirmation of art as a profound and exacting quest for understanding. In his concluding essay, George Steiner writes:

> I believe that one must take the risk if one is to have the right to strive towards the perennial, never-fully-to-be-realized ideal of all interpreta-tion and valuation: which is that, one day, Orpheus will not turn around, and that the truth of the poem will return to the light of understanding, whole, inviolate, life-giving, even out of the dark of omission and of death. [10]

This passionate concern with life-giving understanding (and even the way in which it is formulated through a recasting of ancient myth) lies at the heart of this symposium and so provides its most telling conclusion.

I must now offer a brief explanation about what may be interpreted as serious omissions. I have deliberately excluded from the symposium writing of a sociological nature. Such work, committed to the ideological decoding of the arts, has its intellectual place but within the Humanities rather than within the Arts. From the point of view of this series, such a method of criticism, using exclusively discursive and political categories, by-passes the aesthetic response and misses thereby the work of art (*as art*). Such criticism raids the aesthetic field but seldom recognizes its true nature. What it discloses may well have implications for the arts which, once our main argument has been duly recognized, there will be time to consider. At the moment the primary task is to establish in an excessively propositional age the validity of the aesthetic category, although this is in no way to deny the place of critical work in the teaching of the arts.

Structuralist and post-structuralist thinking has also been omitted. Both schools, while making various contributions to the understanding of art, have yet tended to negate the aesthetic and imaginative dimension. Structuralism was guilty of a kind of reductive scientism while post-structuralism too often became engaged in a wilful obfuscation of meaning to the point of intellectual nihilism. There is no need to develop these fundamental criticisms here for they are clearly stated and elaborated in the symposium; see the chapters by Roger Scruton, Denis Donoghue and George Steiner.

Some of our readers may also be disconcerted that there are no specific essays representing the aesthetic approach to film and dance. The answer is simple; it seemed that there was none, written in the last decade, of seminal importance, to be found.[11] This defines, in part the measure of our need and it is hoped that the forthcoming volumes on Dance and Film will begin to meet it. Yet there is no insurmountable loss for most of the arguments in this volume are of a general nature and have implications for each and every arts discipline. The symposium, above all, is concerned to establish the emerging common ground of good art-making and good art-teaching.

Conclusion

The Symbolic Order: A Contemporary Reader on the Arts Debate forms the third and last volume in the first part of the series. Alongside *Living Powers* and *A is for Aesthetic*, it is intended to establish a conceptual frame for the arts in education. The next seven volumes will elaborate the implications of the philosophy for each of the arts disciplines and for the arts in the primary school. As I said at the beginning, I believe that only such a systematic response can begin to meet the crisis in arts education which now confronts us.

Peter Abbs
University of Sussex
January 1989

Notes and References

1. PETER FULLER (1987) in the Preface to *Living Powers: The Arts in Education*, Brighton, Falmer Press, p. xi.
2. RAYMOND WILLIAMS (1976) *Key Words*, London, Fontana, p. 28.
3. MILAN KUNDERA (1988) *The Art of the Novel*, London, Faber, p. 1.
4. See in particular *Living Powers*, *op. cit.*, pp. 32–6.
5. T. S. ELIOT (1917) in *Tradition and the Individual Talent* from *Selected Essays*, London, Faber and Faber, p. 14. Needless to say, we would want to disown the obvious gender bias of Eliot's formulation.
6. BRIAN WAY (1967) *Development through Drama*, London, Longman.
7. HMSO (1988) *Report of the Committee of Inquiry into the Teaching of the English Language*, p. 12.
8. From the Introduction to *Living Powers*, *op. cit.*, p. 4.
9. See in particular PETER ABBS (1989) *A is for Aesthetic: Essays on Creative and Aesthetic Education*, Brighton, Falmer Press.
10. For the full context of this passage, see the last chapter of this book, 'Real Presences', pp. 271–84.
11. Peter Brinson, for example, responding to a request for suggestions, wrote to the editor: 'I don't know of any seminal paper on aesthetic education in this decade...I recall there is nothing we turned up when we considered the matter at Gulbenkian during the last ten years.' The reader is urged to read the relevant chapters on Dance

and Film in the first volume of this series, *Living Powers*, and to await the forthcoming studies by Peter Brinson and Robert Watson.

General Note

Throughout this volume writers have used 'mankind' and, depending on the context, 'he' to refer generically to humankind as a whole. This is the traditional usage of the language and no gender bias is intended at any point.

PART I

The Renewal of Aesthetics

The three chapters in this opening section create the framework for the whole volume.

The aim of the opening manifesto is to state the broad implications of an aesthetic philosophy for the effective teaching of the arts. In the second chapter, Louis Arnaud Reid examines philosophically the nature of aesthetic understanding; while in the third chapter Roger Scruton elaborates on the deep need for aesthetic experience and places aesthetics within its broad historical framework.

Chapter 1

Aesthetic Education: An Opening Manifesto

Peter Abbs

Introduction

One of the major confusions in the teaching of the arts revolves around the word *aesthetic*. I believe it remains a crucial term for both the renewal and the unification of the arts in education, yet it is a term which is constantly misunderstood and, even, maligned. In some quarters the word 'aesthetic' has followed in the same track as the word 'academic' and denotes a certain marginality and basic irrelevance; thus as certain matters can be dismissed as being 'merely academic' so, in a similar spirit, they can be dismissed as being 'merely aesthetic'. The failure here is essentially a philosophical one and the consequences have been severe. It is high time to make the aesthetic cause not esoteric, but open and clear; open and clear to ourselves, to our pupils and students, to parents, school-governors, politicians and the society at large.

The Meaning of Aesthetic

As I stated in the Introduction, the aesthetic is most adequately conceived as a particular mode of responding to and apprehending experience. Let me put forward the argument by analogy with the mind's power of deduction. Through the ability to reason the human mind is able to isolate, explore and resolve certain aspects of its experience. Of course, we all use the deductive mode more often than we formally realize. In ordinary conversations the deductive is registered in requests for *definition* (what do you mean by that word?) by charges of *inconsistency* ('that doesn't follow', 'that's muddled') as well as by recognition of *fit* ('that follows', 'can't disagree with that'). Once it has been developed deductive analysis can become formidably powerful and, in some philosophers, an all but habitual disposition of the mind. The deductive is expressed through conceptual thinking, but it is systematically developed through the symbolic forms of logic, mathematics, dialectical and analytical philosophy. Now I want to suggest that, similarly, the aesthetic is a mode of intelligence working not through concepts but through percepts, the structural elements of sensory experience, and

3

that the arts are the symbolic forms for its disciplined elaboration and development.

The aesthetic, far from being 'esoteric', is the most basic mode of human response. The tiny child, the new-born baby, begins to mediate its world aesthetically: through touch, taste, smell, sound, feel. Nearly all the early shaping responses of human life are aesthetic in character, bringing through pleasure, pain or a diffuse sense of well-being, intimations of the nature of our common world. Long before we are rational beings we are aesthetic beings; and we remain so, though often undeveloped and unsubtle, till ultimate insensibility defines the end of individual life. For death, in the precise words of Philip Larkin, administers 'the *anaesthetic* from which none come round'.

The etymology of the word reveals that there is nothing perverse in our use of the word to denote a fundamental sensuous mode of human response and interpretation. According to the *Oxford English Dictionary* aesthetic derives from the Greek word meaning 'through the senses'. The definition runs as follows:

> of or pertaining to *aestheta* things perceptible by the senses, things material (as opposed to thinkable or immaterial) also perceptive, sharp in the senses.

Thus, consistent with its original denotations, the first use of the word *anaesthetic* in English in 1721 meant 'a defect of sensations as in Paralytic and blasted persons'. The three definitions are given as: 1) insensible, 2) unfeeling, 3) producing insensibility. Similarly, other related words: *syn-aesthetic* (feeling with) and *kin-aesthetic* (movement-feeling) record and depend upon the same matrix: of sense, of feeling and of sensibility.

It is essential also that we perceive the contiguity between sensation and feeling, of sensory experience and sensibility. Again and again the practices of our language, the inherited conjunctions and the daily alliances of our speech, suggest the intimacy of this relationship. 'To keep in touch' is both to keep in contact and to remain close in feeling. To *touch* an object is to have a perceptual experience; *to be touched* by an event is to be emotionally moved by it. To have a *tactile* experience is to have a sensation in the finger-tips; to show *tact* is to exhibit an awareness of the feelings of others. The very word 'feel' embodies the conjunction; one can feel both *feelings* and *objects* and indeed, one can do both simultaneously. Our brief analysis discloses that the aesthetic involves both the perceptual and the affective. The education of aesthetic intelligence must therefore be concerned with the development of sensation and feeling into what is commonly called sensibility.

Thus, our argument has taken us from the remote and esoteric to the ordinary and the actual, and to a number of living and connected principles. The aesthetic denotes a mode of response inherent in human life which operates through the senses and the feelings and constitutes a form of intelligence comparable to, though different from, other forms of intelligence, such as the mode of logical deduction. If these propositions stand, it becomes clear that aesthetic is a much broader category than that of the artistic; it includes all manner of simple sensuous experiences, from, say, the pleasure of tasting food to enjoying the breeze on one's face. But, at the same time, *the arts* depend on the aesthetic modality because they operate through it. The various arts comprise the differentiated symbolic forms of the aesthetic modality. The implications of such a position for the teaching of the arts and of the place of the arts in the curriculum of human understanding are many and complex; but before considering some of them I would like to give a few examples of the aesthetic at work in the making of art and in responses to it. I will allow the accounts to speak for themselves for their relationship to my argument will, I hope, be self-evident.

The German film director Werne Herzog described a moment of profound artistic realization in the making of a short documentary film as follows:

> I chose to work with a Swiss ski-jumper who did incredible things — jumping far past the limits which are considered possible without injury. Everything was working out well enough; the endless technical problems were solved; but still, for me, the film wasn't clear. Then one night the film crew, myself, and some others grabbed the skier, hoisted him on our shoulders and ran with him through the streets. His thigh was on my shoulder and I could feel the weight of him there. At that moment, the film suddenly came quite clear for me. And it came through this physical sensation. I feel everything about the films I make physically. I like to carry the reels around and feel their weight. When we are shooting I sometimes even like to touch the film itself. [1]

Defining his relationship to a play he will subsequently produce, Peter Brook, who later makes his own contribution to this volume, has written:

> When I begin to work on a play, I start with a deep, formless hunch which is like a smell, a colour, a shadow. That's the basis of my job, my role — that's my preparation for rehearsals with any play I do. There's a formless hunch that is a relationship with my play. [2]

Joseph Conrad, in a preface to one of his short stories — a preface to which Maxine Greene also alludes in Chapter 18 — wrote that the story-writer, the art-maker:

> appeals to that part of your being which is not dependent on wisdom; to that in us which is a gift and not an acquisition ... to our capacity for delight and wonder, to the sense of mystery surrounding our lives; to our sense of pity, and beauty, and pain; to the latent feeling of fellowship with all creation — and to the subtle but invincible conviction of solidarity that knits together the loneliness of innumerable hearts. [3]

And continued by defining his own artistic intentions:

> My task which I am trying to achieve is, by the power of the written word, to make you hear, to make you feel, to make you see. That — and no more, and it is everything. If I succeed, you shall find there according to your deserts: encouragement, consolation, fear, charm — all you demand

— and, perhaps, also that glimpse of truth for which you have forgotten to ask.[4]

Finally, I would like to give one example of an arts-teacher responding to Caro's sculpture *Emma Dipper*: seeing the sculpture for the first time in the Tate Gallery (1977) Janet jotted down her immediate feelings and sensations:

> It is like a drawing in the air, but it is no scribble; it has assurance, seriousness, but also playfulness. The lines give me different feelings. Their qualities are determined by their direction, colour, and thickness, but more particularly by their relation to each other. The sweeping lines are welded to uprights but don't look as if they are supported by them. There is a square opening; it provides a window through which to view the tubes, which converge, Big Dipper-like, swooping down the switch back. I almost feel a sinking, lurching feeling in my stomach; the sculpture has a bodily effect on me. It makes me aware of my ability to move; I feel a potential for movement along the lines of the sculpture. This gives me an elated feeling, but the sculpture remains static.[5]

Then some time after reflecting further on the nature of the experience Janet added:

> Later, I reflected on the nature of the 'bodily feeling'. I mentioned in my notes and think now that this did not take place in the body in the same way as the experience I had when riding on a Big Dipper. It was more akin to a mixture of anticipation and fear. In viewing the sculpture I had to 'move' through a process like day-dreaming, into a metaphorical 'space'.[6]

If we consider these testimonies, we can see that the sensation is not valued as such but rather the *apprehension* which lies within it. The film director, Werne Herzog, grasps the idea of the whole film '*through* this physical sensation'. In the case of Peter Brook the 'formless hunch', like a smell, a colour, a shadow, provides eventually the key to the structure of the play. Joseph Conrad's account brings this out well. First, he emphasizes sense experience ('to make you hear', 'to make you see'); then emotional experience ('consolation, fear, charm') and finally, 'that glimpse of truth for which you have forgotten to ask'. The sight of art brings, we might say, insight; the perception of art engenders being perceptive. As Louis Arnaud Reid will argue more fully in the next chapter, making the necessary differentiations, that difficult but indispensable word 'truth' belongs to Art as much as it belongs to Philosophy, Religion or the Humanities.

The limitations of the still dominant vocabulary of the arts become, at last, clear. Notions of art as 'therapy', 'release', 'self-expression' fall away as misleading and as trivializing; for when we talk about meaning in art, we are talking about transpersonal acts of aesthetic intelligence, and it is the nature of such acts that they belong to an open and public realm. Other fashionable notions concerning the ideological determination of art by the fixed conditions of society also break down because great art also expresses a transforming act of the mind and is able to generate new meanings and new possibilities. Art not only reflects, it also has the power to *create*, to make new, to make different, to extend, in radical ways, both perception and its artistic grammar. The languages of pure subjectivity (developed most fully by the Progressives in education) and of pure ideology (developed by the Marxists) both fail to describe adequately the nature of aesthetic intelligence and artistic creation. For us, the artist — the significant artist — is best conceived as a perceptual philosopher, as one who seeks, through the symbolic ordering of his or her sensations, understanding into the nature of human experience. Rembrandt's late self-portraits are testimonies to precisely this; they manifest the energy of reflexive consciousness to discern meaning within the sensory play of colour, texture, mood and spatial relationship. The aesthetic act is directed towards the apprehension of truth. In and through his paintings Rembrandt interrogates existence.

Such a view of the nature and value of art demands a more comprehensive definition of reason and intelligence. And there are many signs that precisely this re-defining of educational discourse is now taking place. It informs the influential Gulbenkian Report *The Arts in Schools*. It is central to the recent educational writing of Howard Gardner, as it is also central to the chapters in this book written by Rex Gibson, L. C. Knights and David Best. To correct and complement conceptual intelligence we need the notion of aesthetic intelligence and we need to see both in terms of cognition of meaning and of a balanced psyche and a balanced curriculum. Before we can reach that point, though, one further argument has to be made, and it has been implicit in our argument from the start. It is to do with the artistic structuring of the aesthetic modality. It is to do with the place of tradition and technique in the creation and appreciation of the arts.

The Centrality of the Aesthetic Field

The arts have, then, one major source in the sensory modes of human experience; they develop out of what Witkin in *The Intelligence of Feeling* called the sentient impulse. They are the expressions of our bodies, of the pulsing rhythm of the blood, of the inhalation and exhalation of breath, of the immediate delighting in sensations: in sounds, colours, textures, movements, perceptions. It is for this reason that George Whalley in his contribution to this volume (Chapter 19) urges the teacher of poetry to honour the perceptual mode. Of all the modes of intelligence that can be tabulated, the aesthetic seems the most primordial. Yet, while the arts have this source in the biological, they also have another origin, namely, in the historic world of culture and, more specifically, in the whole symbolic field of the particular arts discipline. As soon as we sing, make stories, narratives, dance, paint, we not only express and satisfy bodily rhythms we also enter into and depend upon what is symbolically available, on what has been done by previous practitioners and on how much has been effectively transmitted. Art comes out of Art, as Mathematics comes out of Mathematics. We improvise with and even extend artistic grammars but we rarely invent them; they are 'there' in the culture and it is in the transpersonal culture that art is both made and understood. The development of the sensory mode as a means of apprehending the nature of human experience depends upon the availability and range of these artistic grammars, and established narratives. This is the essential burden of G. H. Bantock's essay (Chapter 13) as it is also the central insight unifying the celebration of myth by Ted Hughes and Jerome Bruner (Chapters 14 and 15).

The point can be made by one example. When we now look at the 'child-art' fostered by the educational progressives during the 1920s and 30s, we do *not* see the unique vision of the child, although the work is often artistically very fine, we see the impressive emulation of the art of the time, either of pre-Raphaelite book illustrations or Expressionism. The 'self-expression' of the child was modelled (consciously or unconsciously) on the conventions of the art that surrounded them; thus that vogue word 'self-expression' (defined by *Chambers 20th Century Dictionary* as 'the giving of expression to one's personality as in art') did much to distort the perception of what was actually taking place in the art-room. A *unique vision* was not being created so much as *a living version* of the dominant art of the period. For many teachers still holding on to progressive theories this may seem an extremely negative and dismal interpretation. From the point of view of this chapter it is, rather, a definitive judgment, an axiom describing how things *are* — for we live in historic culture and not in self-enclosed bubbles of originality. For us this is not a negative and damning state of affairs but *potentially* a liberating judgment. What it suggests is that the innate aesthetic intelligence (like any other mode of intelligence) can be nurtured through an initiation into the forms of the symbolic discipline. It suggests — as Keith Swanwick and Dorothy Taylor make clear in their chapter on music (Chapter 20) — that in the teaching of the arts we need, with the right sense of tact and timing, to introduce the artistic grammar of expression, the tools, techniques and traditions of the art forms and a vast range of achieved work which, taken together, represent the variety of truths the art-form can 'tell' through aesthetic response. It suggests that the arts thrive best not in private cul-de-sacs but at the busy cross-roads of symbolic life.

Many art-makers have explicitly expressed their debts to tradition. Writers constantly assert that they have found their own 'voice' through the voices of others, in the very tradition of which they become, in turn, a living part. In her *Letter to a Poet* Virginia Woolf wrote to a young poet:

> Think of yourself rather as something much humbler and less spectacular, but to my mind far more interesting — a poet in whom live all the poets of the past, from whom all poets in time to come will spring. You have a touch of Chaucer in you, and something of Shakespeare; Dryden, Pope, Tennyson — to mention only the respectable among your ancestors — stir in your blood and sometimes move your pen a little to the right or to the left. *In short you are an immensely ancient, complex, and continuous character*, for which reason please treat yourself with respect and think twice before you dress up as Guy Fawkes and spring out upon timid old

ladies at street corners, threatening death and demanding two-pence-halfpenny.[7] (My italics)

This profound sense of a common symbolic order informed the whole of T. S. Eliot's work as it also informs, to take a radically different background and example, the work of the Afro-Carribbean poet Derek Walcott. According to a recent review article Walcott was encouraged by two teachers and a library:

> It couldn't afford trash. I've often wondered what would have happened if I hadn't encountered Shakespeare, Dickens — all those Faber and Dent library books — and the poets. I would set out to imitate them: I'd do one like Auden, another like Dylan Thomas — it was an apprenticeship. Walcott now teaches 'creative writing' at Boston. He'd approve the inverted commas, believing that you can't teach poetry, only 'the craft of verse ...'. His sense of poetry as a craft is connected to his passion for community and continuity. He believes in shared voices, 'a guild of poets, a craft in the best sense practised', and argues that the *modern* preoccupation with self can be reductive.[8]

Walcott's notion of 'a guild of poets, a craft in the best sense practised' expresses a sense of apprenticeship, of emulation, of continuity and development in art-making which is necessary to any arts education, whatever the art-form and whatever the age of the student.

Yet any analysis of the arts in British education would tend to show that, with great and important exceptions, this initiation into the symbolic field has not taken place. In a recent lecture Gombrich, reflecting on his own contact with art-teachers, wrote:

> When I once lectured to a teachers' training class I was firmly told in the discussion that no teacher must ever show what he personally likes since he must not influence the child. I was even told elsewhere that visits to art museums by schoolchildren were frowned upon by teachers, who alleged that the late Sir Herbert Read put freshness and originality above every other concern. But why allow oneself to be influenced by Herbert Read and not by Rembrandt? Why teach the child the words of our language but not the images of our tradition? None of us has discovered Rembrandt unaided; how can any growing mind find a point of entry into the cosmos of art without being given the opportunity?[9]

Similarly, in educational drama there has been a positive dread of theatre and the acquired conventions of dramatic expression, a virtual denial of any responsibility to the symbolic field. Even in Theatre itself, outside of the schools, there has been a provincial modernism of spirit. As Jonathan Miller expressed it: 'there's a provincialism about the English *avant-garde* that fails to see itself as part of an ancient tradition going back through Dante to Virgil'. A similar denial has characterized dance and, to a lesser extent, music; while English studies during the last three decades, has tended to confine its attention to contemporary work with a distinctive bias towards the limited genre of social realism (and concentrated on thematic discussion rather than aesthetic engagement).

If we accept the idea of a common symbolic order, if we accept the idea of a discipline having a body of distinctive works, and a range of conventions, if furthermore, we accept that creative powers and aesthetic appreciation develops in continuous contact with the whole field of the art form, then it follows that one of the art-teachers major task is to take the student into 'the cosmos of art'. Strange as it may seem, in many quarters, such a proposal smacks either of the revolutionary or the reactionary.

Above all, the position I am advocating requires a re-evaluation of our habitual interpretation of inherited culture as 'high', 'archaic', 'outmoded', 'bourgeois', 'irrelevant' etc. It entails a much more constructive and practical view; namely, that the tradition (by which I mean the sum total of past practices in a particular medium) constitutes the field in which all the art made both by the established artist and the student art-maker, operates and that, therefore, any education in that art-form must include a working knowledge and understanding of the field. It is not 'a return to tradition' so much as a return to the meaning of an arts discipline. To 'do' art is to activate the field. To talk of an initiation into the cosmos of art is, in truth, to talk of an initiation into the essence of our subject.

Conclusion

In some ways this opening essay amounts to a modest attempt to recast the last chapter of Walter Pater's *The Renaissance*. In that short curious dislocating chapter Pater defined a concept of aesthetic experience which, along with other Pre-Raphaelite formulations, did much to erode its true value. In his beautifully cadenced prose Pater wrote:

> It is with this movement, with the passage and dissolution of impressions, images, sensations, that analysis leaves off — that continual vanishing away, that strange, perpetual weaving and unweaving of ourselves .... For our one chance lies in ... getting as many pulsations as possible into the given time .... For art comes to you professing frankly to give nothing but the highest quality to your moments as they pass, and simply for those moment's sake. [10]

Unintentionally, it is a most ironic closure to a book celebrating the public and cultural achievement of the Renaissance. Life, artistic life, for the figures celebrated in Pater's book — Pico della Mirandola, Ficino, Leonardo da Vinci, Botticelli, Michaelangelo — had been anything but a high solitary pulsation before the inevitable event of death. Yet in Pater's closing manifesto the whole of cultural life is 'dwarfed to the narrow chamber of the individual mind' and the aesthetic experience is confined to solitary impressions, unstable, flickering and inconstant. In Pater, in other words, the aesthetic mode becomes locked in itself and becomes no longer an agent of understanding and transcendence; it becomes no longer part of a collective symbolic order for it serves only fleeting impressions, making them not more *meaningful* but only more *intense*. Art as sensation. The aesthetic as a flux of sensory moments doomed to extinction! How strange that a major book on the Renaissance should close on such a nihilistic note. And how much the book tells us about the intellectual current of late nineteenth-century Europe and the coming privatization of art in our own century.

Our collective understanding of the word 'aesthetic' is still bound to the writings of 'the aesthetes'; of the Pre-Raphaelites and the Bloomsbury group. In this essay I have tried, in an educational context, to undo that knot. I have wanted to affirm a number of complementary propositions. I have tried to show that the aesthetic refers to a basic modality of human intelligence and that it is enhanced and developed through the symbolic forms of the arts; I have tried to show that the arts, at their most profound and typical, are formally *heuristic* in nature and not merely hedonistic, that they apprehend meanings and values vital to our individual and communal lives and, finally, I have suggested that the arts, seen structurally, form vast symbolic orders which it is the task of arts-teachers to transmit, keep alive and relate to their students' own artistic endeavours. This conception of art moves us beyond the private and privatizing world of cultivated sensations and out into open spaces of transpersonal struggle and transcendence — those spaces which are eloquently affirmed by both David Aspin (Chapter 21) and George Steiner (Chapter 22) in their closing contributions to this volume. Such a view entails the end of Modernism and has the power to engender a more comprehensive aesthetic, with both a cultural and a biological source, for our time. Some of our best contemporary architecture already embodies the change and invites us to participate in it. It now requires a corresponding expression within the National Curriculum and within our civilization as a whole.

Notes and References

1. WERNE HERZOG I have not been able to trace the source of this fascinating quotation.
2. PETER BROOK (1987) *The Shifting Point*, London, Harper and Row, p. 1.
3. JOSEPH CONRAD in Preface to *The Nigger of the Narcissus* in *Three Great Tales* (Modern Library Paperbacks) p. VII.
4. *Ibid.*
5. JANET SANG in an essay submitted while on the *Language, the Arts and Education* MA at the University of Sussex Academic Year 1986–1987.
6. *Ibid.*
7. VIRGINIA WOOLF in her essay 'Letter to a young Poet' in *Collected Essays* Vol. 2 London, Hogarth Press, (1966) pp. 184–85.
8. DEREK WALCOTT in a review-article in *The Observer* on the publication of *The Arkansas Testament*, January, 1988.
9. ERNST GOMBRICH in *Tributes*, Phaidon, 1984, p. 89.
10. WALTER PATER in *The Renaissance: Studies in Art and Poetry*, London, Macmillan, (1904), (first edition, 1873), pp. 236 and 238.

Chapter 2

The Arts Within a Plural Concept of Knowledge

Louis Arnaud Reid

Introduction

In this chapter I wish to place the arts within a broad theory of knowledge. At the moment there is still a strong tendency in our civilization to see truth as being confined to propositional statements. Such a view is extremely narrow, works both against our common understanding and our use of language and has severely marginalized the arts. In this essay it is my intention to sketch an alternative conception of knowledge which I believe is not only more adequate to our complex experience of the world but also includes that kind of knowing which characterizes aesthetic and artistic experience. The theory of knowledge opens the way to a proper recognition of the meaning and value of the arts in civilization and to their vital place within the school curriculum.

The Nature of Propositional Knowledge

A generally, and widely accepted, account of 'knowledge' is that if one believes a proposition and the proposition is true, and one is justified in believing it true, then one has knowledge. The justification condition poses a familiar difficulty: 'how does one *know* that the justification justifies?' By further justification? And the justification of that? There is a regress; and at some point one has to say that one directly and intuitively 'sees' that the justification is a sufficient justification. If this 'seeing' or 'intuiting' is a kind of knowing, then the original account is inadequate.

The elements of 'belief' and of 'justification' in this account of knowledge (which I will, for short, call the 'propositional' account) entail of course that knowing is, in part, a function of the knowing *mind*. But mind here is functioning in a strictly limited way. The 'belief' is the belief that the propositional statement is true, and the belief that the belief is justified. This, in its context, is certainly very important. But it is also important to note that the belief is, strictly, an *intellectual* one. It would not be denied, I imagine, that in this belief feeling and conative factors are involved: if the statement is true, and one is convinced that it is true, there will be a feeling of conviction and a willingness to trust the conviction and to act upon it in a kind of faith that it is true. The feeling, conviction, faith are, no doubt, the experiences of a person. But the personal involvement of a person in his feeling and conviction that a propositional statement is true, simply *that* 'something is the case', is, in many matter-of-fact statements, very limited indeed. *If*, for the moment, we suppose that there can in some sense be 'knowledge' of art (or of other persons, or of important moral values), the involvement of the person, the 'whole' person, will be far greater and, probably, deeper and more complex. In propositional knowledge the central stresses are on clarity, truth, on the objective grounds for belief. All important, but limited.

The emphasis in knowledge of the propositional kind is indeed in its *impersonality*, on truth as statement of fact independent of mind. Though on the propositional view the relation of truth to mind is formally recognized (in the words 'belief' and 'justification') it is very easily forgotten in the stress on objectivity and fact. On the propositional view, one essential condition of there being *knowledge* is that the proposition must be true, must state the facts, that, in some perhaps metaphorical way, the statement must 'correspond' with the facts. Truth is thought to *be* a relationship between statement and fact: and if there is to be knowledge (on the propositional view) a true statement must be made. Knowledge, on this view, is made dependent on the (supposedly) independent truth of propositional statements.

I think this is a mistake, even on the assumption of the propositional account, and that if we cling to this mistake about knowledge and knowing, the way is closed to considering seriously whether the experience of art can claim in any sense to be knowledge.

Towards a Richer Concept of Knowledge

I think it is more accurate and more comprehensive to see propositional statements as the expression of something more basic, more fundamental, namely the mind's self-transcending power of being cognitively aware of a world which is not itself. I would not deny that for a great deal of knowledge it is of the utmost importance that it should be expressed explicitly in verbal statements, and that it could not be clearly grasped as knowledge without it. But the mind's transcendent power, the everyday mystery, of being able to *know*, in the wide sense of 'cognize', with infinite degrees of obscurity or clarity, — this seems basic and central. This is the *living* fact, of which statements are *one kind* of necessary articulation, deposited publicly, as it were, in an already shared language.

So, instead of making knowledge a function of the truth of propositional statements, I think we should turn it on its head and say that truth is a function, or attribute, or quality, of the mind's living cognitive apprehension of the world. Let us use the metaphor of 'prehension' or cognitive grasping. Physically, when we stretch out to grasp something we may get a firm hold of it, or we may fumble and slip. The metaphor of cognitive prehension suggests that when it is working efficiently, the character of the cognitive prehension is in some degree true and when working inefficiently in various degrees false. Truth and falsity are, I suggest, finally characters of the efficiency of the living, self-transcending, cognitive activity of mind apprehending its object. The truth of propositions is dependent on and in part derivative from that. Truth is, therefore, ultimately adverbial rather than adjectival, the character of a self-transcending mental activity rather than of a statement — however important in the realm of propositional knowledge statements may be.

One supreme advantage of this kind of view is that it opens up the way to understanding different kinds of knowing and knowledge. The propositional approach is parochial in that it accounts for only one kind of knowledge — though the 'parish' is admittedly a very large one! Direct knowledge through acquaintance and experience, direct intuition, are not in the conventional or propositional sense of knowledge, first-class citizens. I am not, of course, suggesting that those who subscribe to the propositional view of knowledge are unaware of other kinds of claims to knowledge, but only that the tyranny of the propositional *view* prevents them from being taken seriously enough.

If 'knowledge', indeed, depended on being able to say justifiably something that is true, it would discount huge areas of what we all recognize to be knowledge-claims. Apart from 'knowledge-how', now accepted i.e., the knowledge where we know how to do something but are unable to say how, there is also tacit knowledge, where we know far more than we can say. Tacit knowledge is a knowledge of things resting on an interpretive framework functioning a-critically. For example, we can have topological knowledge of a town, or we can recognize a face, or a family resemblance, without being able — either at the time, and sometimes not at all — to articulate it verbally. Then there is also the knowledge of intrinsic values: our recognition of moral, personal, and aesthetic values. There is, of course, a vast literature *about* values. But any profitable talk about them presupposes *direct experiential knowledge of them*, immediate insights, conative and affective as well as cognitive, in fact, personal insights in which these work together as a single whole. These insights can be described and shared imaginatively, but only significantly with those who have already experienced something of the same kind of thing.

Understanding the Nature of Intuition

The knowing, the cognitive apprehension, of art is essentially direct, intuitive, experiential, and not as such propositional. It can be called 'experience-knowledge'. And in so far as it is an adequate 'prehension', it will be 'true' knowledge in the sense in which I have interpreted 'true' as an adverb of cognizing. Of course, as artists, critics or philosophers of art, we continually talk about art propositionally. Such talk can philosophically illuminate the nature of art and critically aid the understanding of particular works or schools. But all such talk is empty if it is not based on direct, intuitive, first-hand cognitive experience of the works themselves. Experiential intuition is essential.

But the very word 'intuition' is anathema to many thinking people, including philosophers. It is only so, I believe, because the word is taken over (with scandalous superficiality) from a merely popular usage, which assumes it is a kind of infallible hunch, opposed to reason and reasoning, an isolated faculty of incorrigible knowledge. Simply to assume, without examination, that intuition must mean this, is irresponsible. A. R. Lacey in his *Dictionary of Philosophy* says (responsibly) of intuition: 'generally a direct relation between the mind and some object analogous to what commonsense thinks is the relation between us and something we see unambiguously in a clear light'. He adds: 'the emphasis is on the directness of the relation...'. The *Concise Oxford Dictionary*'s version is: 'Immediate apprehension by the mind without reasoning; immediate apprehension by sense; immediate insight'.

Lacey's emphasis on directness of relation between the mind and an object is acceptable. But we might question 'in a clear light'; intuitions can be vague, foggy, obscure. So, too, the dictionary's 'immediate insight' can be questioned; for intuitions can conceal misconceptions or totally erroneous assumptions. Again, 'without reasoning' is acceptable if reasoning means overt discursive reasoning; but intuition (for example logical intuition) can be 'reasonable'. And if intuition is a function of the active mind (as I think must be supposed), some time-taking process of what seems an instant 'seeing' can be assumed too. And intuition gathers into itself, as it were, much assimilated and tacit knowledge.

We can distinguish between what are often called concrete intuitions and intuition as a necessary *factor* in all knowing whatsoever. People claim to have concrete intuitions about axioms, mathematical or logical, about other persons, or have claims to moral or religious or aesthetic intuitions about particular objects of thought or experience. But to claim any of these things is different from claiming, as I will claim, that *all* knowledge contains an intuitive element or factor. It is impossible to think or perceive or imagine any complex without 'seeing' directly a relation or relations between its distinguishable parts. The content of any such intuition may be very simple: $2 + 2 = 4$; 'the cat sat on the mat'. Or it can be very complex, as when a sophisticated thinker can grasp, in a single synoptic perspective, a very complicated argument, or, in a different field, when a musician is aware intuitively of the one-in-the-many and the many-in-the-one in a very complex piece of music. But to say that there is always an intuitive *factor* in knowing anything is not, clearly, to identify knowledge with intuition. (A factor *in* knowledge could not *be* knowledge.)

In knowledge there is another factor, the truth-claim — in my terminology, *the adequacy of cognizing to its object*, an adequacy which I am assuming throughout can have degrees. (The glib assumption that mere intuition guarantees truth ignores this.) Where the cognition is of matter of *fact*, as in common sense or in science, the tests or criteria of adequacy are familiar: 'Go and look', or 'Is it consistent with other (relatively) established facts?'. Where the claim is to knowledge of *value* — for example moral value, or aesthetic or artistic value — the nature of the tests is more controversial and more difficult to establish clearly. Hence a widespread scepticism as to whether one can really talk of moral *knowledge*, or knowledge of, art. That an action is 'good' or 'right' cannot be settled merely by pointing to the fact that something has been done. That a work of art is 'good' or 'beautiful' cannot be decided by accurately describing its factual structure — even if we assume that this is ever possible. If in any sense there can be said to be objective knowledge of art-value, such description of art-structure as is possible has to be supplemented by something else, namely the *feeling* of, and for, such value. And here at once we hear sceptical cries (as we do in ethics) of 'subjectivism'.

The Primacy of Feeling in Artistic Understanding

Art-experience and knowledge of art I have already distinguished from propositional knowledge, that something *is* the case. In this latter knowledge, the cognizing of 'what is the case' may involve some subjective feeling on the part of the knower, though perhaps not always. If I enunciate some familiar fact, such as 'some apples are green', there may be, because there must be *some* interest or point in my even uttering such an obvious truth, *some* feeling in making this point: but it is negligible and unimportant. If on the other hand, an Einstein suddenly enunciates a new truth-claiming hypothesis, one can assume a great excitement, perhaps a glorious joy of discovery. Great scientists 'feel' their way towards new ideas. Excitement — sometimes terrible frustration, sometimes rapture, is a part of their total experience. But the importance, for science, does not lie in the personal experiences of value which great scientists enjoy, but in the contribution of the idea towards the enlightenment of the body of systematic science. The scientist's experience in momentous discovery is perhaps one of the great intrinsic values in human experience; but the importance for science, after the rejoicings, is instrumental to science. For science aims, as far as possible, at relatively impersonal truth. The original scientist's personal subjective life is a condition of new discovery, but not an inherent part of the relatively neutral statements of systematic science.

Whether this is true or not (and of course it is debatable), I think it is manifestly true that, in contrast, feeling *is* an inherent part of the knowledge and understanding of art, which cannot be adequately expressed in impersonal propositional statements. If art can, in *some* sense and some degree, be said to be known objectively, it will be an objectivity which can be shared between people who to some extent can share the same feelings, as well as the same 'thoughts'.

This, at once, raises again the objection that, if feeling is thus involved, the knowledge of art must be a purely 'subjective' experience. In order to meet this I shall have to say as clearly as possible what I mean by, and include in, feeling.

Feeling is the immediate awareness from the 'inside'. It refers to conscious experience in the widest and most usually accepted sense of that term. Conscious experience in human beings includes: bodily sensations, actions of various kinds, thinking, imagining, willing, having moral and aesthetic experiences, perhaps religious ones, loving, hating, coming to know and coming to terms with the external world, ourselves and other people. Feeling is the immediate awareness of, an indwelling in, that conscious life in its most inclusive sense. It is important to be aware of the distinction between feel*ing* — the participle, be*ing* immediately aware — and its content. Feeling as it actually occurs always includes both an immediate awareness and a specific content. Feeling is present throughout conscious life. But this, though I think it is true, does not mean that we are focally conscious of it all the time; usually we are not. It is, as a rule, marginal and sometimes it *seems* to be absent altogether. So I am not saying that we always feel ourselves feeling, are immediately aware of ourselves being immediately aware. Sometimes we can be; but if not, *afterwards* in retrospection we may be able to discern the factor of feeling of which we were perhaps not conscious at the time.

Now having said all this about the subjective aspects of knowing, what about 'objectivity'? To claim 'knowledge' of works of art or to say that art yields knowledge, is not to say, however important it may be, that the subjective experience of art and the enjoyment of it is all that matters. To claim knowledge of a given work of art is to claim that we know and understand, at least in some degree, the work itself, and in that degree that our knowledge of it is true, or perhaps better, valid. 'Experience-knowledge' it may be, and indeed is: but if so, it is cognitive experience of an object which is given, and it is experience which at least may claim to be true. But if this is the case, the knowledge and truth we can possess of works of art will have an objectivity which is *different* from the objectivity of scientific statements. Whereas scientific statements of fact are, relatively speaking, impersonal and neutral, statements expressing artistic judgments are, again relatively speaking, statements about what we are personally and holistically involved in. And if we talk sometimes about art in a public language which is trans-personal and in that sense to some degree neutral, the common sharing of ideas about the works themselves must always refer back to our individual felt, cognitive-conative-affective experiences of the works. Scientists, of course, have personal value-experiences too, but they are not relevant in at all the same way to the scientific statements made as are statements about a work of art to the personal experiences on which, if significant, they must be based. So the claimed objectivity of knowledge of art has to be considered on its own.

Knowing and Understanding Art

The understanding of works of art in any depth is partly conditioned by knowledge of different kinds, strictly speaking non-aesthetic, which are for the main part uncontroversial and well accepted: they could be roughly classified as *knowledge-how*, *knowledge of facts*, and *cognitive feeling for values*.

It is not necessary to enlarge on these in any detail, since they are already so familiar. I have in mind such things as general knowledge of historical backgrounds of, say, Classical or Christian arts, or of particular movements in the arts, historical or contemporary, including in this factual knowledge sensitive feeling for their value-implications. Then there is knowledge of *techniques*, in one way particularly important for working artists themselves as 'knowing-that' and 'knowing-how', but also important for discriminating appreciation. These form the background conditions or presuppositions for true artistic understanding, though none of them in themselves are sufficient, and a mere accumulation of them could simply bar the way to the aesthetic understanding of works of art.

We address a work of art as a particular, not in the sense of its being merely a particular instance of a general class (though it can, in conceptual language, also be an instance, say of Post-Impressionism), but as *this individual*. Here too, for any experienced artist or spectator, there is a complex background of knowledge, but which is of a different kind from that referred to in the last paragraph, though not cut off from it by any rigid barrier. I mean knowledge drawn from actual internal artistic experience of established works. But in immediate aesthetic response all prior experience is subject to the autonomy of *this* creation, this specific work of art. In the response a new and unique kind of knowing emerges, shaped by what went before, but not wholly determined by it.

If we consider the process of artistic making, we find that the conventional distinction between *knowing* and *making* breaks down, or is transformed in an existential unity. Knowing in the conventional sense is certainly also achieved through a constructive or making activity. Such constructions reveal our attempts to apprehend and to come to terms with independent given reality, to discover and adjust to what is already 'there'. In the creative art the constructive making is, likewise, discovery, but, paradoxically, discovery of what was not literally there before the process of creation began. In one sense the creative activity 'makes' its reality and in the making 'discovers' the new thing made. The new thing made is physical. It is an artifact. It is, for example a picture, a sculpture, a poem, a dramatic action, a dance... But, at the same time, the *raison d'etre* of art is not merely physical or factual, but imaginative exposition of *value*, the world of human life and nature seen, felt, imagined and judged by fully living persons. Art is symbolic embodiment in physically perceived forms, of unlimited ranges of meaning (of different kinds and ranges in the different arts) as apprehended by the sensitive and imaginative minds of artists, and offered to us if we will (and can) espouse it. In its symbols the riches of the physical and the spiritual are gathered in, transmuted, transubstantiated, metamorphosed, so that the division between physical and spiritual is dissolved. Meanings are drawn in and transformed in aesthetic embodiment, and, becoming embodied become localized in space and time.

The knowledge which the artist discovers through making is not properly known till the making has been completed. Of course he or she often has ideas or some tentative general plan. But the concrete final form of the work is not known, and cannot be known, beforehand. There is not even a simple *telos* to guide him, as a craftsman may have a pattern to work to or a house builder a plan. If we are talking of creation — and in spite of the commonly cheap use of this word everywhere, art-making is truly creative — we have to realize that the *telos* is changing all the time whilst the artist is working in dialogue with the medium. There is evolution whilst he works; and it is not simply the unfolding of a plan, but *creative* evolution.

On the Appreciation of Art

There is a parallel process in the experience of the *spectator* of any given art. In the experiencing of a piece of music new to us, for example, we cannot, musically, come to know and understand it till we have heard it all to its conclusion, and in fact not until we have heard it a number of times and studied it — and even then only in a high degree if we are sufficiently musical. In musical understanding 'the end is in the beginning' and throughout every flowing part. In direct aesthetic appreciation every part of the art-work is internally related to every other part and to the whole.

In considering the appreciation of art there is, of course, the problem of *interpretation*. A work of art engages the full attention and study of a person. In this act of attention, the senses, the imagination, feeling and thought are all involved with one another in intimate relationship to what is given by the specific art work. As a personal response it is and must be a private experiencing of the given object, but as *directed to the object it is self-transcending*. The focus of attention is upon the work. Yet as the work is a complex phenomenon — as apprehended by-the-spectator, the 'interpretation' is *his* or *her* interpretation. A musical score, a complex presentation with many aspects, can be 'seen' to have different musically viable interpretations by different masters. They are different because, since the musical composition is complex and has many aspects, *this* musician is bringing out certain aspects of the music, and *that* musician others. And, if we speak of an interpretation as being 'musically viable' we mean that the performer has created an artistically organic unity based on his study of the composer's given score. This is not just saying that the rendering is a good one because it corresponds exactly to the original composer's interpretation of his own music. That we do not know, unless indeed it happens that the composer is alive and is interpreting his own score. But even then — as composers have often admitted — another musician may bring out aspects of his music which the composer had not fully realized. What counts, it would seem, is that the performing musician must study assiduously the composer's works (and not only the particular work he is to play), gather the composer's musical intentions as far as he can from the written score, and then perform it in terms of his (necessarily) personal understanding. The question then of its musical 'viability' may be put in the form: 'Does the interpretative playing of this particular piece of music artistically *come off*'? The answer must come in the first place from the artistic judgment of each competently sensitive musical listener. But such judgment must be put alongside other competent musical judgments. Though there will always be healthy disagreements, the *consensus* of competent critical judgments builds up through time a critical canon, a stabilizing, but never a final authority.

It becomes clear that the objectivity of knowledge and understanding of art has to be *personally* judged. In this it can be contrasted with the objectivity of scientific knowledge and understanding. One can accept, on authority, that, to be compassionate is commonly reckoned a virtue, or that a Rembrandt self-portrait is said to be a great painting. But if one has never *felt* the goodness of compassion or the quality of Rembrandt's painting, one cannot know their intrinsic or inherent values. Knowing about bare facts involves only a small part of one's self. Knowing the value of art is a holistic involvement.

What art does is to present to the senses, mind, feeling, imagination, a new, fresh, untranslatable, individualized insight into value. What counts is that as a physically presented object, phenomenally apprehended, a work of art is experienced as the embodiment of value-meaning, to which we can repeatedly return. If it is a great work, it is significant that we should *want* to return to it again and again. A truth of pure matter of fact, once established, is over and done with. 'That's *that*!' But as a complex embodiment of value-meaning, art is known in a holistic experience and has to be 'enjoyed' in the sense that it has to be lived through, an *erlebnis* which is not necessarily all pure pleasure. As aesthetic value and as living experience, the meaning of art is not all grasped at once as a 'that's that!'. The richness of its value experience has to grow through further experience.

A Concluding Reflection

How does the functioning of emotion in art-experience differ from the functioning of emotion in life? Aesthetic emotion in the experience of art tends, like its functioning in life, to action, but to conative action rather than to overt external behaviour. In anger, one may want to hit somebody, in fear, to run away. In art-experience, contrariwise, the conative action is a reinforcement of attention to the work itself. *It is retroactive.* An acceptable account of the aesthetic is that it involves attention to something 'for its own sake' or for itself. Aesthetic attention to art is just this. The intense excitement, often the intense joy, the captivating pleasure one has in art experience is wholly inseparable from the very actively absorbed attention to the work 'for itself'.

So emotion and cognition are no longer divided in the holistic experience of art, but completely united in existential knowledge, existential knowledge of art. It is this which makes experience of the arts of such importance, in itself, throughout life, for everyone, and in education, where the very existence of the arts is more than ever now threatened. It is my hope that a richer theory of knowledge such as I have outlined in this chapter could play its part in securing a fuller recognition of the crucial importance of the arts both to society in general and to education in particular.

Chapter 3

Modern Philosophy and the Neglect of Aesthetics

Roger Scruton

The Retreat from Art and Culture

The Greeks were deeply interested in the questions of aesthetics, and their philosophers discussed them in a variety of contexts — moral, political and metaphysical. Nevertheless aesthetics, conceived as a systematic branch of philosophy, is an invention of the eighteenth century. It owes its life to Shaftesbury, its name to Baumgarten, its subject-matter to Burke and Batteux, and its intellectual eminence to Kant. Its irruption into the terrain of philosophy is one of the most remarkable episodes in the history of ideas. In Schiller's *Letters on Aesthetic Education*, the newly discovered faculty of aesthetic judgment is given the sacred task that was once laid on the shoulders of religion — the task of preparing man for his life as a moral being. In Hegel's *Lectures on Aesthetics* art is presented as the successor to religion, an all-embracing form of consciousness in which the truth of the world, at a certain point of spiritual development, is most perfectly distilled. Art, and the study of art, form the highest point to which man's self-understanding may attain, before emancipating itself from the sensuous, and passing over into the sphere of abstract concepts, philosophical reflection, and natural science — the world of *Wissenschaft*.

What Hegel said was a kind of nonsense. But what he meant was true. Or at least, true enough to serve as the starting-point for discussion. Art, culture and the aesthetic experience have been removed from the central place in philosophical speculation which they briefly occupied. In their place we find science, logical theory, and the rigour — or *rigor mortis* — of semantic analysis. This transformation in philosophy has accompanied another and larger change. The triumph of scientific thought has caused such self-doubt, such a loss of faith and simplicity, in those subjects which have had the articulation of man's self-image as their purpose, as to raise the question whether a humane education is any longer possible. At the same time, philosophy's retreat from the study of art and culture has left a vacuum. In its absence, any kind of nonsense can take root and stifle the natural growth of meaning. Here is an instance of what happens to literary criticism, when philosophy abandons it:

> Even before it 'concerns' a text in narrative form, double invagination
> constitutes the story of stories, the narrative of narrative, *the narrative of*
> *deconstruction in deconstruction*: the apparently outer edge of an
> enclosure, far from being simple, simply external and circular, in
> accordance with the philosophical representation of philosophy, makes no
> sign beyond itself, towards what is utterly *other*, without becoming
> double or dual, without making itself be 'represented', refolded,
> superposed, *re-marked* within the enclosure, at least in what the structure
> produces as an effect of interiority.

Those words occur in a book put together by a collection of staid and bewildered
American critics who, having looked in vain for a philosophy that would give sense
and direction to their enterprise, at last hit on Jacques Derrida (the author of the
passage) as the answer to their problems.[1] Their purpose was to display to the
academic world that criticism is alive and well and living in Yale, where, thanks to
Derrida, it has discovered a new method and outlook. The name of this method
(or anti-method) is deconstruction.

I do not pretend to know what deconstruction is, although apparently it tells
us that texts have neither author nor subject-matter, and that reading is
impossible. But I should like to reflect on what is implied, when those who are the
trustees of a literary tradition as deeply interwoven with life and feeling as ours has
been, should consider themselves to be studying nothing more warm or more
compromising than a 'text', and should be able to draw no more useful conclusion
from their studies than that reading is impossible. Surely something has been lost,
when those artefacts in which every possible meaning has been deliberately
concentrated should be offered to the world as 'unreadable'? Surely philosophy
has been neglectful of its duties, if it has allowed matters to proceed to such a
pass?

There are some lines of George Seferis, in which he seems to reflect on the
burden placed on the modern Greek by the classical culture which surrounds him:

> I woke with this marble head in my hands
> which exhausts my elbows, and I do not know where
> > I shall put it down:
> it fell into the dream, as I was emerging . . . .

Just such an image occurs to me, when I hear words like 'text' and 'deconstruction' on the lips of a modern critic. The work of art lies in his hands, as unbearable
as an ancient marble whose meaning he cannot fathom. Such a critic seems to be
no longer immersed in a civilization, but rather awakening from it, into a flat and
desert landscape — a 'post-cultural' world. The 'text' is a piece of dream-debris, a
burden of which he can rid himself only by analysis, or 'deconstruction'. And in
none of this does life play any part.

The collapse of English studies into deconstruction is not, in my view, the
cause but the consequence of philosophy's inertia. If literary critics now seem so
unable to appreciate the difference between genuine reasoning and empty

sophistry, it is partly because philosophy, which is the true guardian of critical thinking, has long ago withdrawn itself from their concerns. When the agenda of philosophy is so narrow and specialized that only a trained philosopher can understand it, is it then surprising that those disciplines which — whether they know it or not — depend upon philosophy for their anchor, should have slipped away helplessly into the night?

But is the cultural isolation of philosophy really so recent a phenomenon? Some would argue that, in jettisoning its links with art and literature, philosophy has returned — after a period of Romantic and post-Romantic aberration — to its traditional role in the modern world, as the handmaiden of the sciences. If we look at the first century of modern philosophy — the century of Bacon, Descartes, Locke, Spinoza and Leibniz — we see philosophical speculation arising in the wake, not of cultural and artistic endeavour, but of scientific experiment. Then as now, it was science which set the agenda for philosophy; and if modern philosophers have been so deeply concerned with logic, probability theory, linguistic analysis and the behavioural sciences, this is because those branches touch upon the frontiers of science, and address themselves to difficulties which, if they are not solved, will hamper the process of discovery. If modern philosophers have been so exercised by the 'mind-body' problem, for instance, it is largely because, until it is solved, scientists will not know what they are observing, when they study human behaviour and its causes.

On such an account, the rise of aesthetics was more of a temporary disturbance: an indentation in the smooth project of philosophical enquiry, caused by the neighbouring explosion of the Romantic movement. And Romanticism was itself the product of man's sudden and urgent need to find meaning elsewhere than in church, and in some other posture than on his knees. All revolutions in philosophy either serve to launch some new science, or else exhaust themselves in futile enquiries of which we soon grow tired. Aesthetics came into the world simultaneously with social philosophy: and the comparison between them is significant. Out of social philosophy, economics and sociology were born. But out of aesthetics — what has come out of aesthetics, if not futile enquiries of which we have now grown tired?

There is some truth in the retort. But it needs careful examination. Two features distinguish the philosophers of the seventeenth century from their modern descendants. First, they were fully integrated into the cultural life of their times; second, if they did not look to aesthetics for the source of meaning and value, it was because they were, with few exceptions, sincere believers in a benevolent God, whose redemptive purpose they read more directly in the laws of the created world.

Thus Bacon, Descartes, Locke, Leibniz and Spinoza were, despite their scientific leanings, practising participants in a literary culture. They wrote well — in the case of Bacon and Descartes, surpassingly well. Leibniz composed poetry, and Bacon essays which are as great as any in the language. Even Locke, clumsy though he sometimes was, expressed himself in a manner so succinct and vivid as to enrich intellectual discourse forever after. Consider the following passage, from the *Second Treatise on Civil Government*:

> Though the earth and all inferior creatures be common to all men, yet
> every man has a 'property' in his own 'person'. This nobody has any right
> to but himself. The 'labour' of his body and the 'work' of his hands, we
> may say, are properly his. Whatsoever, then, he removes out of the state
> that Nature hath provided and left it in, he hath mixed his labour with it,
> and joined to it something that is his own, and thereby makes it his
> property.

The simplicity of language in such a passage is one with the complexity of
thought. Each word is used with a full sense of its value, not only as a vehicle for
abstract reasoning, but as a purveyor of images. And of course the principal image
— that of the workman as mixing his labour, and therefore himself, with the thing
that he produces — has lived in the educated conscience ever since, resurging in
countless ways in the writings of Smith, Ricardo, Hegel, Marx and their modern
followers.

The second distinguishing feature of our forebears is equally important. Each
of the philosophers to whom I have referred was a believer, for whom the meaning
of the world is neither created by philosophy nor dependent upon philosophy for
its construction. Spinoza, it is true, concluded that God is identical with the
world, and therefore that many of the claims of theology are erroneous. But he at
once set out to show how a person may find peace and happiness in the very
recognition of that disturbing truth. And Spinoza's language, as he bent to this
task, became so fully alive as to convey a message well beyond the reach of abstract
argument. Even Spinoza, therefore, the most forbiddingly technical of the
seventeenth century philosophers, was able to speak directly to the heart. Goethe
records, in a moving passage of *Dichtung und Warheit*, the effect that this
solemn, mathematical prose was to exert over him:

> That wonderful utterance: 'Whosoever loves God, cannot strive that God
> should love him in return', with all the preceding sentences upon which
> it rests, with all the following sentences which spring from it, filled my
> entire meditations. To be in everything unselfish, to the highest
> unselfishness in love and friendship, was my greatest desire, my maxim,
> my rule, and so that insolent remark which follows — 'if I love you, what
> is that to you?' — was spoken directly into my heart.

The fact that the meaning intended by Spinoza was not the meaning understood
by Goethe is of small account, beside the evident force, whereby one man has
impinged through the written word upon the life and feeling of another.

Poverty of Style in Modern Philosophy

In both the respects to which I have referred — cultural participation and religious
belief — contemporary philosophy differs completely from the philosophy of the

seventeenth century. With rare exceptions, the contemporary philosopher is isolated from the surrounding literary culture, with no grasp of style or rhetoric, and with little instinct for linguistic nuances. Of course, there are philosophers with genuine literary gifts — Quine, for instance, and Strawson. And the stylistic insufficiencies of the remainder resemble those of the average practitioner of literary 'deconstruction'. Nevertheless, there is, in the idiom of modern philosophy, such a poverty of emotion, such a distance from the felt experience of words and things, as to cast doubt on its competence as a vehicle for moral and aesthetic reflection. Here is an example of what I have in mind, taken from a recent work of aesthetics:

> I start with some action A that some person P wants at time t_1 to do at time t_2. One possibility is that P believed at t_1 that he cannot perform A at t_2. Then P at t_1 has no action-plan for performing A at t_2. Alternatively, P may believe at t_1 that there is a chance that he can perform A at t_2; but there may be no action A' distinct from A such that P believes at t_1 that he might be able to perform A' at t_2 and that if he did so he might thereby generate A. In such a case, let us call the unit set, (A), P's *action-plan* at t_1 for performing A at t_2. But thirdly, there may be at least one ordered set of actions $(A_1 \ldots, A_n)$, such that P believes at t_1 that he might be able to perform A_1 at t_2 and that if he did so he might thereby generate $A, \ldots$, and believes that he might be able to perform A_n at t_2 and that if he did so he might thereby generate A_{n-1}. In such a case, let us call the $n + 1$-tuple of actions, $(A, \ldots, A_n)$, P's *action-plan* at t_1 for performing A at t_2. Let us call A the goal of that action-plan. And let us call A_n, the terminus of the plan.[2]

To understand what is so objectionable in that style, is to understand the spiritual temptation which leads people away from true philosophy into pseudo-science. The whole paragraph is a kind of fraud, an introduction of redundant terminology from set theory, in order to capture one simple fact, namely, that a plan of action involves a goal, together with the steps chosen to achieve it. Nothing is subsequently done with the technicalities, which serve merely to give a quaint appearance of rigour to banality.

The stylistic catastrophe of analytic philosophy is a subject for another occasion. I shall merely record my opinion that the alienating prose of our philosophers is due not to expertise but to idleness — to a failure to pursue a thought to the point where it speaks itself, in words of its own. (It is precisely this self-utterance of thought that we find in the passage quoted from Locke.) Style is the search for simplicity and naturalness, for the phrase which not only says what you mean, but also embodies within itself all the nuances and hesitations that would enliven the reader's judgment. Philosophy severed from literary criticism is as monstrous a thing as literary criticism severed from philosophy. In each case the result is a kind of intellectual masquerade, a phantom world of discourse, whose principal subject-matter is itself. In philosophy, as in literary criticism, the written word has largely ceased to address itself to living creatures. Only if it contains a theoretical truth, therefore — a truth to be measured by the exacting requirements of the sciences — can philosophy be justified. This partly explains the peculiar affectation of scientific language on the part of many modern philosophers — even though the real hard work of science lies beyond their competence.

The Quest for Aesthetic Value

It is the second difference between the seventeenth-century philosopher and his contemporary descendant that interests me. If we examine, from the standpoint of the historian of ideas, the episode in philosophical history to which I referred at the outset of this lecture, then we cannot fail to notice that the rise of aesthetics was simultaneous with the Romantic movement, and with the loss of confidence in revealed religion. In Kant's *Critique of Judgment* the point is already explicitly made, that the sense of God's immanence — the sense of the world as created, and of personality as shining forth from all its aspects — is to be derived from the very same faculty which has beauty as its object and judgment as its goal. It is through aesthetic contemplation that we confront that aspect of the world which was the traditional concern of theology. We cannot prove, by theoretical reasoning, that there is a God; nor can we grasp the *idea* of God, except by the *via negativa* which forbids us to apply it. Nevertheless, we have intimations of the transcendental. In the sentiment of beauty we feel the purposiveness and intelligibility of everything that surrounds us, while in the sentiment of the sublime we seem to see beyond the world, to something overwhelming and inexpressible in which it is somehow grounded. Neither sentiment can be translated into a reasoned argument — for such an argument would be natural theology, and theology is dead. All we know is that we can know nothing of the transcendental. But that is not what we *feel* — and it is in our feeling for beauty that the content, and even the truth, of religious doctrine is strangely and untranslatably intimated to us.

In Kant's third Critique we see, in remarkably explicit form, the historical meaning of that shift in emphasis which was to place ethics and aesthetics at the centre of philosophy. The *Critique of Judgment* situates the aesthetic experience and the religious experience side by side, and tells us that it is the first, and not the second, which is the archetype of revelation. It is aesthetic experience which reveals the *sense* of the world. Of course, the 'sense' turns out to be, for Kant, precisely what religion had assumed it to be. But suppose we do not accept that conclusion? Suppose we look for the meaning of the world in aesthetic experience, while reserving judgment in matters of faith? This would be to give to aesthetic interest an importance comparable to that which once had attached to religious worship. It would hardly be surprising, in that case, if aesthetics were to move from the periphery of philosophy to the centre, so as to occupy that place which, in the centuries before Bacon and Descartes, had been occupied by theology.

In the nineteenth century we do indeed find philosophers for whom aesthetics provides a central subject-matter and a central task. I think of Schiller and Hegel, of Kierkegaard, and above all of Nietzsche, whose flight towards the aesthetic followed an act of deicide unparalleled in the history of thought. And if proof is needed of the ease with which the aesthetic may replace the religious as an object of philosophical interest, it is to be found in the thought and the personality of Nietzsche. Nietzsche's philosophy arose out of art and the thought of art; it involved an effort to perceive the world through aesthetic value, to find a way of life that would raise nobility, glory and tragic beauty to the place that had been occupied by moral goodness and by faith. And of course, among philosophers, Nietzsche is one of the great stylists, rivalled among those who came after him only by Wittgenstein.

The English Literary Tradition

No such philosopher could exist in the anglophone tradition, for the simple reason that, if he did exist, he would not be called a philosopher, either by others or by himself. He would be identified as a critic or a social theorist, as an essayist or a reformer. Nevertheless, the transformation heralded in Kant's *Critique of Judgment* also took place in Britain. The search for the meaning of the world shifted from speculative theology to aesthetics, just as it had done in Germany. It is thanks to Coleridge, Arnold and Ruskin that students at a British university are now in a position to learn that there are more serious problems on earth than are dreamed of in analytical philosophy.

Nor did literary criticism lose, in our century, its place in the vanguard of the English-speaker's quest for meaning. The debates that were begun in the last century by Arnold and Newman were carried over into our times by Eliot, Chesterton, C. S. Lewis and finally — last representative of a 'great tradition' — F. R. Leavis. And it was perhaps only in the famous 'Two Cultures' debate, in which Leavis made mincemeat of C. P. Snow's suggestion that there could be a 'culture' of science, that the question which had bothered Central European writers for upwards of half a century was at last articulated in Britain.[3] The question is a philosophical one, and of the first importance. Nevertheless, it is a singular fact that it was left to a literary critic to articulate it, and a singular fact, too, that no major analytical philosopher has subsequently shown the slightest interest in what he said. It is hardly surprising, in view of this, that Leavis dismissed philosophy in general (and Cambridge philosophy in particular) as a subject which had lost contact with the human world.

I shall express Leavis's position in his controversy with Snow in my own terms. To possess a culture is not only to possess a body of knowledge or expertise; it is not simply to have accumulated facts, references and theories. It is to possess a sensibility, a response, a way of seeing things, which is in some special way redemptive. Culture is not a matter of academic knowledge but of participation. And participation changes not merely your thoughts and beliefs but your perceptions and emotions. The question therefore unavoidably arises whether scientific knowledge, and the habits of curiosity and experiment which engender it, are really the friends or the foes of culture? Could it be that the habit of scientific explanation may take over from the habit of emotional response, or in some way undermine the picture of the world upon which our moral life is founded? Could it be that scientific knowledge leads precisely in the opposite direction from a culture — not to the education of feeling, but to its destruction, not to the acceptance and affirmation of the human world, but to a kind of sickness and alienation from it, an overbearing sense of its contingency?

The question returns me to my theme. For Leavis the task of culture was a sacred task. Culture had in some way both to express and to justify our participation in the human world. And the greatest products of a culture — those works of art that Arnold had called 'touch-stones' — were to be studied as the supreme distillations of this justifying force. In them we find neither theoretical knowledge, nor practical advice, but life: life restored to its meaning, vindicated and made whole. Through our encounter with these works our moral sense is liberated, and the fine division between good and evil, positive and negative, affirmative and destructive, made once more apparent, written everywhere across the surface of the world.

To take such a view is to raise the aesthetic to the pinnacle of authority upon which Kant and Schiller had placed it. And, given his sceptical premises — his Lawrentian belief that value is not transcendent but immanent, contained in life itself — Leavis can hardly stop short of the conclusion that, whatever consolation and significance men have sought in worship, they may find it more securely in the modern world through culture. The touchstones of our culture convey to us the meanings which others have found in liturgy, ritual and prayer. It is unsurprising to find Leavis pointing to Bunyan and Blake as his authorities, or to find him extolling, as landmarks of our literary tradition, the Bible of King James, and the now vandalized liturgy of the Church of England. For it is precisely in sacred works and liturgies that the emotional memory of a civilization is recorded, and it is in the works of prophets that a language strives to its utmost towards the perception of a justifying sense.

Leavis's attack on the idea of a scientific culture has all the character of a holy war — it is a defence of the faith against the infidel, of the Israelites against the Philistines. It is interesting that the word 'philistine', used so as to denote the enemy of civilization, entered the English language from Germany, through the writings of Carlyle. The expression was coined by the German students of Schiller's day, and immortalized on their behalf by Robert Schumann. In borrowing it, Carlyle, Arnold, Ruskin and their followers entered the battle on Schiller's side. The confrontation between science and culture that we find in Leavis is foreshadowed in the conflicts between Coleridge and Bentham, between Arnold and the Philistines, between Ruskin and the immovable apparatus of Podsnappery by which he saw himself surrounded. All of them are heirs to that conception of the aesthetic which we find in Kant and Schiller, according to which aesthetic experience stands in the place of worship, our key to the moral health of humanity and to the meaning of the world.

The Primacy of Culture

In my view, the question discussed by Leavis and his forebears is not only philosophical; it is one of the most *important* of all philosophical questions. Nor has it been entirely ignored by philosophers. For one in particular — Edmund Husserl — it was central to what he called, in the apocalyptic idiom of Central Europe, 'The Crisis of the European Sciences [*Wissenschaften*]'. To put in a nutshell a thought which may or may not be contained in the tens of thousands of Husserlian pages, it is this: science has offered us a paradigm of objective knowledge. According to this paradigm, all reference to the subject of experience is to be eliminated from the description of the world. In seeking to emulate science, the various studies, even those which have man as their primary subject-matter, have tried to abstract from what is given in human experience, to purge the human subject, so to speak, from the archive of knowledge, and to achieve a kind of Stalinist history of the world, in which all persons are unpersons. The attempt, however, is fraught with paradox. For the human subject is the starting point of enquiry, and to refine him out of our science is to lose sight of the very thing that science endeavours to explain.[4]

I agree with one part of Husserl's claim. It seems to me that there are forms of understanding (*Wissenschaften*) which do not possess the objectivity of science, being derived from man's self-conception, rather than from the impersonal observation of natural processes. Nevertheless, they possess another kind of objectivity, a convergence upon a common fund of superficial truth, which entitles them to their own claims to knowledge. If philosophy has a central task, it is to protect these forms of knowledge, to anchor them once again in human consciousness, and to strike down the pretensions of science to give us the whole truth of what we are.

I draw a contrast between two modes of understanding: scientific understanding, which aims to explain the world as it is, and 'intentional understanding', which aims to describe, criticize and justify the world as it appears. The second is an attempt to understand the world in terms of the concepts through which we experience and act on it: these concepts identify the 'intentional objects' of our states of mind. An intentional understanding therefore fills the world with the meanings implicit in our aims and emotions. It tries not so much to explain the world as to be 'at home' in it, recognizing the occasions for action, the objects of sympathy, and the places of rest. The object of such an understanding is not the world of scientific theory, but the *Lebenswelt*, the world as it is revealed, in and through the life-process which attaches us to it.

This distinction explains what I have called the 'priority of appearance'. Scientific penetration into the depth of things may render the surface unintelligible — or at least intelligible only slowly and painfully, and with a hesitancy that undermines the immediate needs of human action. (Such is the case, I have argued, with the critical phenomenon of sexual desire). As agents we belong to the surface of the world, and enter into immediate relation with it. The concepts through which we represent it form a vital link with reality, and without this link appropriate action and appropriate response could not emerge with the rapidity and competence that alone can ensure our happiness and survival. We cannot replace our most basic everyday concepts with anything more useful than themselves — even if we can find concepts with greater explanatory power. Our everyday concepts have evolved under the pressure of human circumstance, and in answer to the needs of generations. Any 'rational reconstruction' — however obedient it may be to the underlying truth of things and to the requirements of scientific objectivity — runs the risk of severing the vital connection which links our response to the world, and the world to our response, in a chain of spontaneous human competence.

The concepts which inform our emotions bear the stamp of a shared human interest, and of a constantly developing form of life. Whence do they come? The answer is implicit in Leavis's attack on Snow: these concepts are the gift of a culture, being neither consciously made nor deliberately chosen but inherited. It is by the use of such concepts that the moral reality of our world is described: concepts of good and evil, sacred and profane, tragic and comic, just and unjust — all of them rooted in that one vital idea which, I would contend, denotes no natural kind, and conveys a classification that could feature in no true scientific theory of man: the concept of the person. The concepts of a culture classify the world in terms of the appropriate action and the appropriate response. A rational being has need of such concepts, which bring his emotions together in the object, so enabling him — as the Hegelians would say — to find his identity *in* the world and not in opposition to it. A culture, moreover, is essentially shared; its concepts and images bear the mark of participation, and are intrinsically consoling, in the manner of a religious communion, or an act of worship. They close again the gap between subject and object which yawns so frighteningly in the world of science.

Estrangement from the world is the poisoned gift of science. For Coleridge and his followers the same estrangement attaches to utilitarianism — that morality of the Philistine which was launched into the world by the smiling idiot Jeremy Bentham, and which has marched onwards ever since. The hostility to 'Benthamism' was inherited by Leavis, and became fundamental to his moral vision. And one can see why. Utilitarianism represents the attempt by science to take charge of our moral lives: the attempt by the objective perspective to displace the subject from his throne. The utilitarian sees the world not as it appears to the agent, but as it is in the eyes of the omniscient observer. The utilitarian moralist rises above the individual's predicament, and sees the meaning of his actions in their long-term success or disaster, freely availing himself of concepts which form no part of the individual's reasoning.

Suppose a tribesman is dancing in honour of the god of war. To the observing anthropologist, steeped in functionalist and utilitarian thinking, the dance is a means to raise the spirits, and to increase the cohesion of the tribe, at a time of danger. This description both explains and justifies. Nevertheless, it does not tell us what the dance means to the dancer. If the tribesman thinks of his dance in that way, then he is alienated from it: he loses his motive to dance, once he borrows the language of the anthropologist. His first-person reason for dancing (because the god demands it) is precisely opaque to the third-person perspective: by shutting the dancer within his dance, it abolishes the distance between agent and action. Of course, in this case, the first-person reason is founded in error: there *is* no god of war. But a culture need not be rooted in error: it may remain 'on the surface', in the way necessary to engage with our acts and emotions, and at the same time free itself from superstition. It then ceases to be a culture only, and becomes a *civilization*, sending its branches into theology, philosophy, art and law.

Even when it has launched itself, however, on the path of critical thinking, a culture cannot forswear 'the priority of appearance'. If it is to offer us the precious gift of participation it must resist the pursuit of an unobtainable objectivity. Utilitarianism fails as a moral theory because, aspiring to objectivity, it begins to justify actions in terms which remove the motive to engage in them. Utilitarianism purges our actions of their sense, by displacing the concepts under which we intend them. (Consider, for example, how the utilitarian justification of punishment erodes the will to punish, by abolishing the concept of retribution through which punishment obtains its 'sense'.)

The Renewal of Aesthetics

In our post-Enlightenment world, it is natural that we should look elsewhere than towards religion for the 'sense' of our actions. And Kant was in a way right to single out the aesthetic as, so to speak, next in line to the Eucharist, as the source of meaning. The object of aesthetic understanding is given to us in and through experience, and has no life outside the 'intuition' in which it is embodied. In aesthetic judgment, therefore, we aim to achieve the finest possible understanding of *how things seem*. All art is semblance, and (Plato notwithstanding) this is the source of its value. Art brings us to the very same point that we are brought to by religion — to an experience saturated by meaning, whose value overwhelms us with the force of law. In aesthetic experience we perceive the fittingness of the world, and of our place within it. For a moment we set aside the relentless curiosity of science, and the habit of instrumental thinking. We see the world as it really seems: in Wallace Steven's words, we 'let be be finale of seem' (although there are other emperors besides the Emperor of ice-cream). In the aesthetic moment we encounter a unity of form and content, of experience and thought. This fact, which places the meaning of aesthetic experience outside the reach of science, explains its peculiar value. In the moment of beauty we encounter directly the sense of the world; and in tragedy the most terrible things may cease to be strange to us, and cease to be so metaphysically threatening. Even the nothingness of death may be overcome. In tragedy, death is not a nothing, but a something, a part of that very order which it seems to deny. Death exists in tragedy as a pattern in the world of appearance, and is lifted free from its absurdity. (In tragedy, a man's death becomes part of his life.)

When meaning and experience are welded so firmly together, the first is secured against scepticism. The habit of uniting them in contemplation is the aim and reward of aesthetic education — of that induction into a culture which Leavis recommends. The aesthetic understanding locks our modern dancer within his dance, just as an unquestioned culture locked our warrior tribesman within his:

> O Chestnut-tree, great-rooted blossomer;
> Are you the leaf, the blossom, or the bole?
> O body swayed to music, o brightening glance,
> How can we know the dancer from the dance?

Aesthetic experience, which stands outside instrumental calculations and outside science, is therefore of the greatest practical import to beings like us, who move on the surface of things. To engage now with those distant parts of my life which are not of immediate concern, to absorb into the present choice the full reality of a life which stretches into distant moral space, I must lift that experience out of the immediate preoccupation and endow it with a meaning, in which my humanity is embodied and accepted. Hence I have a need, as a rational creature, for aesthetic experience, and for the habits and customs which engender it. No utilitarian calculation can substitute for this experience, which consists in a projection forwards of the acting self. The ability to participate imaginatively in future experiences is one of the aims of aesthetic education: without that ability, a man may have as coherent a purpose as he likes; but he will not know what it is like to achieve it, and his pursuit of it will to that measure be irrational. Failure to appreciate this point, I have argued, underlies the disaster of utilitarian and modernist architecture — an architecture which denies the priority of appearance, and denies the tradition which has formed and educated the human eye.

Conclusion

Philosophy, to the extent that it takes the study of the *Lebenswelt* as its primary concern, must return aesthetics to the place that Kant and Hegel made for it: a place at the centre of the subject, the paradigm of philosophy, and the true test of all its claims. Philosophy, I have suggested, ought to be, not the handmaiden of the sciences, but the seamstress of the *Lebenswelt*. Philosophy must repair the rents made by science in the veil of Maya, through which the winds of nihilism now blow coldly over us. And, even with the needle and thread of conceptual analysis, this labour of piety can begin.

And there is, as I remarked at the outset, a great need for it. Unless philosophy resumes its place as the foundation of the humanities, those disciplines which have the human world as their subject-matter will be exposed to intellectual corruption. Tempted now by the *fata Morgana* of deconstruction, now by sociological pseudo-science, they will wander from their purpose, in a desert of unmeaning, and dwindle into parched unwholesome remnants of themselves. The defence of humane education therefore requires the defence of philosophy. But philosophy can be defended only if it has aesthetics at its heart.

Notes and References

1. H. BLOOM *et al.*, (Eds) *Deconstruction and Criticism*, London, 1979.
2. NICHOLAS WOLTERSTORFF, *Works and Worlds of Art*, Oxford, 1980, p. 9.
3. 'Two Cultures? The Significance of Lord Snow', in F. R. LEAVIS, *Nor Shall My Sword*, London, 1972.
4. See EDMUND HUSSERL, *Die Krisis der europäischen Wissenschaften und die tranzendentale Phänomenologie*, (Ed.) W. BIEMEL, The Hague, 1976, Part 2.

PART II
Art as the Pursuit of Truth

It is central to the symposium that art is not, in essence, a 'leisure pursuit', an exercise in therapy or an act of self-expression but rather a primary quest for meaning and understanding.

In this section two distinguished practitioners of the arts define how they see the nature of this pursuit for meaning. Peter Brook describes how in his own contemporary theatre work in Paris new transcultural truths can emerge. Michael Tippett, reflecting on the nature of music, claims that all great art is involved in the formal clarification of transcendent intuitions.

Chapter 4

The Culture of Links

Peter Brook

The Meaning of Culture

I have asked myself what the word 'culture' actually means to me in the light of the different experiences I have lived through, and it gradually becomes clear that this amorphous term in fact covers three broad cultures: one, which is basically the culture of the state; another, which is basically that of the individual; and then there is a 'third culture'. It seems to me that each of these cultures stems from an act of celebration. We do not only celebrate good things in the popular sense of the term. We celebrate joy, sexual excitement, and all forms of pleasure; but also as an individual or as a member of a community through our cultures, we celebrate violence, despair, anxiety and destruction. The wish to make known, to show others, is always in a sense a celebration.

When a state genuinely celebrates, it celebrates because it has collectively something to affirm: as happened in ancient Egypt whose knowledge of a world order, in which the material and spiritual were united, could not be described or put easily into words, but could be affirmed by acts of cultural celebration.

The Bland Affirmations of State Cultures

Whether we like it or not, we must face the fact that such an act of celebration is not possible for any of our societies today. The older societies have, no doubt rightly, lost their self-confidence, and the revolutionary societies are constantly in a false position. They are trying to do after one year — or five years, or ten years — what ancient Egypt took centuries to achieve, and their brave but misguided attempts make them easy targets for scorn.

A society that has not yet truly become a whole cannot express itself culturally as a whole. Its position is no different from that of many individual artists who, though wishing and needing to affirm something positive, can only in truth reflect their own confusion and distress. In fact, the strongest artistic and cultural expressions today are often the opposite of the bland affirmations that politicians, dogmatists and theoreticians would like their culture to be. So we have a phenomenon peculiar to the twentieth century: the truest affirmations are always in opposition to the official line, and the positive statements that the world so obviously needs to hear invariably ring hollow.

The Limitations of Individualism

However, if official culture is suspect, it is necessary to look equally critically at the culture which, reacting against the inadequate forms of expression of embryonic states, strives to put individualism in its place. The individual can always turn in on himself, and the liberal wish to support that individual action is understandable; and yet one sees, when looking back, that this other culture is equally strictly limited. It is essentially a superb celebration of the ego. The total deference to the right of every ego to celebrate its own mysteries and its own idiosyncrasies presents the same one-sided inadequacy as the total deference to the right of expression of a state. Only if the individual is a completely evolved person does the celebration of this completeness become a very splendid thing. Only when the state reaches a high level of coherence and unity can official art reflect something true. This has happened a few times in the entire history of mankind.

What matters to us today is to be very much on our guard in our attitude toward 'culture' and not take the ersatz for the real. Both cultures — that of the state and that of the individual — have their own strength and their achievements, but they also have strict limitations due to the fact that both are only partial. At the same time both survive, because both are expressions of incredibly powerful vested interests. Every large collectivity has a need to sell itself, every large group has to promote itself through its culture, and in the same way, individual artists have a deeply rooted interest in compelling other people to observe and respect the creations of their own inner world.

When I make a division between individual and state cultures, this is not just a political division between East and West. The distinction between official and unofficial, between programmed and not-programmed exists within every society. Both call themselves 'culture' and yet neither of them can be taken to represent living culture in the sense of a cultural act that has only one goal: truth.

The 'Third Culture' as the Pursuit of Truth

What can one possibly mean by the pursuit of truth? Perhaps there is one thing one can see immediately about the word 'truth': it cannot be defined. In English one says in a cliché, 'You can pin down a lie,' and this is so very true that anything less than the truth takes a clear, definable form. That is why in all cultures, the moment a form becomes fixed, it loses its virtue, the life goes out of it; that is why a cultural policy loses its virtue the moment it becomes a programme. Likewise, the moment a society wishes to give an official version of itself it becomes a lie, because it can 'be pinned down.' It no longer has that living, endlessly intangible quality that one calls the truth, which can perhaps be seen in a less hazy way if one uses the phrase 'an increased perception of reality'.

Our need for this strange, added dimension in human life which we vaguely call 'art' or 'culture' is always connected with an exercise through which our everyday perception of reality, confined within invisible limits, is momentarily opened. While recognizing that this momentary opening is a source of strength, we recognize also that the moment has to pass. Therefore, what can we do? We can return to it again through a further act of the same order, which once again re-opens us toward a truth that we can never reach.

The moment of reawakening lasts a moment, then it goes, and we need it again, and this is where this mysterious element called 'culture' finds its place.

But this place can only be assumed by what to me is the 'third culture,' not the one that carries a name or a definition, but which is wild, out-of-hand, which, in a way, could be likened to the Third World — something that for the rest of the world is dynamic, unruly, which demands endless adjustments, in a relationship that can never be permanent.

Theatre as the Discovery of Relationship

In the field in which I work, the theatre, my personal experience over the last few years was very revealing. The core of our work at the International Centre of Theatre Research was to bring together actors from many different backgrounds and cultures, and help them work together to make theatrical events for other people. First, we found that popular clichés about each person's culture were often shared by the person himself. He came to us believing that he was part of a specific culture, and gradually through work discovered that what he took to be his culture was only the superficial mannerism of that culture, that something very different reflected his deepest culture and his deepest individuality. To become true to himself, he had to shed the superficial traits which in every country are seized upon and cultivated to make national dance groups and propagate national culture. Repeatedly, we saw that a new truth emerges only when certain stereotypes are broken.

Let me be quite specific. In the case of the theatre it meant a concrete line of work that had a clear direction. It involved challenging all the elements that in all countries put the theatre form into a very closed bracket — imprisoning it within a language, within a style, within a social class, within a building, within a certain type of public. It was by making the act of the theatre inseparable from the need to establish new relations with different people that the possibility of finding new cultural links appeared.

For the third culture is the culture of links. It is the force that can counterbalance the fragmentation of our world. It has to do with the discovery of

relationships where such relationships have become submerged and lost —
between man and society, between one race and another, between the microcosm
and the macrocosm, between humanity and machinery, between the visible and
the invisible, between categories, languages, genres. What are these relationships?
Only cultural acts can explore and reveal these vital truths.

Chapter 5

Art, Judgment and Belief: Towards the Condition of Music

Michael Tippett

Introduction

There is a knowledge concerning art, and this knowledge is something quite different from the immediate apprehension of works of art, even from whatever insight we feel we have gained by perceiving and responding to works of art. A simple statement such as: art must be *about* something, is innocent enough till we want to give a name to this something. Then invariably we delude ourselves with words, because with our discursive or descriptive words we cross over into the field of writing or talking *about* art. We have reversed ourselves.

This fundamental difficulty has made all discussion of art, as indeed all discussion of quality, a kind of elaborate metaphor. And since all metaphor is imprecise, the verbal misunderstandings in aesthetics have always been legion. It is only when we remain deliberately in the field of enquiry concerning the facts *surrounding* art, that we amass knowledge of the kind we expect to obtain through such intellectual disciplines as History, Anthropology, Psychology or Philosophy. We can confidently say that we have vastly increased our knowledge concerning art during the last hundred years, chiefly of course the history of art. Anthropology has added further dimensions to our sense of history as a whole, and so to the history of art. Psychology, in my opinion, will eventually make much more precise the terms with which we discuss the processes of artistic creation and enjoyment. Philosophy, in the sense in which we speak of Platonic or Christian Philosophy, has often assigned limits or directions to art considered as a social function. Yet art can be gravely endangered by extreme social systematization. Plato, for all his systematizing tendency, accepted this. Socrates says in the *Phaedrus*:

> There is a third form of possession or madness, of which the Muses are the source. This seizes a tender, virgin soul and stimulates it to rapt passionate expression, especially in lyric poetry. But if any man comes to the gates of poetry without the madness of the Muses, persuaded that skill alone will make him a good poet, then shall he and his works of

sanity with him be brought to nought by the poetry of madness and see their place is nowhere to be found.[1]

Plato names three other forms of divine madness besides the artistic, viz. the prophetic, the expiatory, and that of the lover. To understand Plato's term 'madness', we must recall the argument of the *Phaedrus* in more detail. Socrates considers first whether what we call madness might not really be of two kinds. One kind is clearly a disease — the rational mind being disordered and unamenable to the will — and even if we picture it as though the sufferer's personality has been possessed by some other and alien personality, yet this possession is unhealthy and often markedly anti-social. But the other kind might be a madness where the invading personality, though unaccountable and irrational, is yet beneficent and creative; possession not by a devil, but by a god.[2] It is this 'divine madness' of Plato's which I call the spontaneous (including the ineffable) element in art, and I think that the intuitions of Plato concerning this spontaneous element are upheld by the findings of psychology, especially depth psychology. From such psychology we have obtained a concept of apparently spontaneous psychic generation; of unconscious psychic drives and inhibitions; of, possibly, an inner psychic collectivity which is boundless and non-discrete. Yet to use the word 'concept' for such notions is, surely, a paradox. In the same way, at the point now at which this discursive essay needs to consider the immediate experience of, and the insight (if that is the right word) obtained from works of art *in themselves*, then, as has been pointed out above, this paradox reappears.

The Objectivity of Art

We must begin with the fact of works of art existing objectively and created to be appreciated. And we must accept that even if a state of mind, or an artefact arising from a state of mind, is spontaneously generated and only to be experienced immediately, or even ineffably, it is none the less a natural phenomenon, a fact of human existence. In rare experiences of this sort, such as the states of mysticism, the number of human beings to whom the experiences spontaneously come (or who have desires and techniques to induce them) is, at least in the West, small. Yet the tradition is so constant and the phenomenon so well established that we all have reasonable grounds for accepting them as factual and natural even when we can never ourselves have known them. They can clearly be spiritually refreshing; and may yet turn out to be one of man's hitherto undeveloped social qualities. For if psychosocial survival depends, as it well may do, on correctives to the present overwhelming social valuation given to material welfare, then evolutionary necessities may begin to operate, in an admittedly as yet unimaginable way, on seemingly socially valueless meditative disciplines.

While it would appear that the mystic can only render to society the refreshment received personally from mystic experiences through the quality of his conduct, the creative artist, from whatever source or in whatever medium he receives the spontaneous element, must, by the nature of his mandate, create objective works of art. These works subsist then in society independently of their creator, and many thousands of human beings receive enjoyment, refreshment, enrichment from them. This is a commonplace fact. Perhaps indeed every human being alive has experienced immediately something of this kind. Because the experience is so common and yet capable of being heightened to embody our profoundest apprehensions, it has in every age demanded intellectual understanding of itself. Modern psychology has provided new counters with which to play this age-old game.

The Nature of Art

If I now proceed to play this game in an up-to-date mode, it must be remembered that all discussion of what art *is*, or what it is *about*, is semantically imprecise. (We are probably on safer ground when we discuss what art *does*.) So it is hardly possible to proceed without the danger of misunderstanding, although our modern counters for discussion are, in my opinion, an improvement on some of those of the past, i.e. are probably semantically less equivocal.

Works of art are images. These images are based on apprehensions of the inner world of feelings.[3] Feelings in this sense contain emotions, intuitions, judgments and values. These feelings are therefore generally supposed to be excluded from scientific enquiry. I make this statement, in so far as it is true, not as an implied judgment, but solely as a fact, in order to emphasize the semantic problems of aesthetic discussion. It is not an easy matter to pass over from language used in the observation of natural objects extended outside us in space and time, to language used to discuss or describe the inner world of feelings, where space and time (at least in certain states of mind) are differently perceived altogether. Even where we succeed in such an attempt the description is always at one remove. The images which are works of art, are our sole means of expressing the inner world of feelings objectively and immediately. If art is a language, it is a language concerned with this inner world alone.

As 'inner' and 'outer' remain philosophically extremely difficult terms, so the dichotomy I have (at least verbally) established between space and time considered outside us and space and time perceived within is certainly not rigid. Hence, it often appears as though the raw material of artistic creation was obtained from observation of nature outside us, and that the creative activity resided in the organization and construction which the artist applies to this raw material. The danger of this way of considering the matter is that very quickly we come to talk of works of art as *derived from* nature, which is much too simple. It loses sight of the one absolute idiosyncrasy of art, that works of art are images of *inner* experience, however apparently representational the mode of expression may be.

This difficult matter is best set out by considering first the extreme case of space in painting. (I use the word 'extreme' because the matter is not quite the same in architecture.) And secondly the opposite extreme of time in music.

The vital fact of all pictorial works of art is that the space in the picture is always virtual, not real. The space in the room and of the wall on which the picture hangs is real. Part of the means by which a picture becomes an image of the inner world of feelings is the contrast between the real space of the wall or the room and the virtual space in the picture. Hence it is not of vital concern to the art of painting whether the virtual space is constructed by representational methods or the reverse. We accept this if we are gifted or trained to do so, without demur. We find it difficult if we consciously or unconsciously believe that art *derives* from experiences of outer nature and not, as is the basic fact, from the inner world of feelings. The representations of outer nature, if present, are always images of the inner experience, which the artist has organized.

Music and Time

At the other pole to painting music offers images of the inner world of feelings perceived as a flow. As our concept of external time is itself an equivocal one,[4] it is perhaps less easy even than with space in painting, to realize that the time we apprehend in the work of musical art has only a virtual existence in contrast with the time marked by the clock-hands when the work is performed. Works appear short or long from other considerations besides that of performance time, and our sense of performance time will be markedly modified by them.[5]

Because music is concerned not with space but time, this method of artistic creation seems to by-pass the problems of representationalism, present in some degree in all the other arts. Hence the dictum: 'all art constantly aspires towards the condition of music.' This aphorism, wrenched from its original context in an essay of Pater,[6] has nowadays been commonly used in this much looser and wider sense, precisely, in my opinion, to draw attention to this real tendency. For if the matter-of-factness of the outer world gets too much into the foreground of art, then expression of the inner world of feeling is probably correspondingly more difficult. By dispensing *a priori* with all the problems arising from expressing inner feelings through representations of the outer world, music can seem a very favoured art. This is not always a merit. Music's easiness quickly degenerates into escapism; escapism not only because music seems absolutely abstracted from real objects but also because the emotional content of music is both obvious and permitted.

Art as the Apprehension of the Inner World

To a certain degree all appreciation of art is escapism — to leave behind the world of matter-of-fact. The important question is always: escape into what? Escape into the true inner world of feelings is one of the most rewarding experiences known to man. When entry into this world is prevented, and still more when it is unsought, a man is certainly to some degree unfulfilled. Yet even escape into the simpler states of appreciation is often self-denied. Darwin wrote in his *Autobiography*:

> ... now for many years I cannot endure to read a line of poetry...I have also lost my taste for pictures and music ... My mind seems to have become a kind of machine for grinding general laws out of large collections of facts...The loss of these tastes is a loss of happiness and may possibly be injurious to the intellect, and more probably to the normal character, by enfeebling the emotional part of our nature. [7]

Darwin puts his finger unerringly on the danger. He uses the word 'machine'. In the vast social apparatus which modern science and technology demand, the person often becomes lost in a 'machine'. Eventually there arises the danger of too great mechanization of the social life in every field. [8] At this point creative artists are sometimes driven to use the shock tactics of a genius like D.H. Lawrence — or in another field, Kokoschka.

As I have already pointed out, within the dazzling achievements of the modern knowledge-explosion we must include the lesser portion of a greatly increased knowledge about art. But the contemporary explosion in the means and methods of art itself over the last hundred years is not of the same kind. The new art is not related to problems of the outer world at all but to apprehensions of the inner world. What can certainly be deduced from the contemporaneity of the two explosions, is that the psychosocial change and consequent adaptation demanded of modern man is without precedent in its totality.

It may in fact be misleading to speak of art as primarily or always responsive to social change — though in many obvious senses this is true. For art is unavoidably and primarily responsive to the inner world of feelings. And this inner world may be spontaneously generative (in the sense I attempted to define the term earlier) independently of, e.g., the social consequences of scientific technology. Or it may be attempting to restore some sort of psychosocial balance. I would say that it is all these things. Yet clearly changes (and these are constantly happening) in our ideas of human personality will be reflected in certain arts, if not necessarily in music. Music may always appear to by-pass such considerations, but literature and the drama in all their forms certainly cannot. It may be that changes in our ideas of human personality reflect changes in the inner world of feelings, and not *vice versa*. We are not yet able to judge properly what happens in this complex and interrelated field; we cannot yet be certain what is cause and what is effect.

At the present time, for example, we can only see that the knowledge-explosion in all the sciences is a challenge to psychosocial adaptation, while the violent changes in methods in all the arts are symptomatic of deep-seated changes in man's inner world of feelings.

Modern psychology is indeed beginning to produce a kind of relativity of personality, especially in personal relations. This is sufficiently far-advanced in the West (it may be nothing new for the East) for it to be satirized by a cartoonist like

Feiffer. Here is a caricatured conversation between a young couple suffering from this relativity of personality — i.e. valid uncertainty as to what is real in their notions of one another and what is projection.

> *She*: You're arguing with me.
> *He*: I'm *not* arguing with you. I'm *trying* to make a point.
> *She*: There is a difference between making a point and embarking on a sadistic attack.
> *He*: If sadism is your equivalent to impartial judgment then I admit to being a sadist.
> *She*: How *easy* to be flip when one precludes responsibility.
> *He*: How irresponsible of one so irresponsible to speak of responsibility.
> *She*: Since you *must* project your own inadequacies into a discussion of the facts I see no point in carrying this further.
> *He*: How like you to use attack as a disguise for retreat.
> *She*: Ah, but if we were not arguing as you so heatedly claim, what is it that I am retreating from?
> > *(silence)*
> *He*: I'm getting a stomach-ache.
> *She*: Me too.
> *He*: Let's knock off and go to a movie.

Behind this caricature is something real, to which art cannot be indifferent. The dénouement is also quite serious. We knock off to go to a movie. This is not merely an escape from the currently insoluble problems, it is a therapeutic necessity. We project our problems, whether of dual or multiple relationship, momentarily on to the movie — i.e. on to an objective work of art. Movies are generally works of popular art; and they are socially immensely valuable. For most of us there can be no objective examination of the constant and developing situation such as that caricatured by Feiffer, except by recourse to the movie or its equivalent; the splendid value of this recourse being that it is mostly un-selfconscious and indeed an enjoyment.

The enjoyment of popular art, in my opinion, is much more often of the same kind as the enjoyment of more serious art (though not of the same quality) than snob circles like to think. There is of course a vast mass of sentimental popular music (to take my own art) which is poor and dispiriting. But there is a great deal indeed of jazz and rock where the dissonances and distortions of the voice or the instruments, the energy and passion and often brilliant timing of the performance, combine to produce an enjoyment which is of better quality, and is also expressive of the tensions produced in man by the inner and outer changes of his life. Carried on the pulse of this music we really do renew in a limited degree our sense of the flow of life, just because this music gives hints of deeper apprehensions through its qualities of style and even form.

As the purely emotional element recedes and the formal element comes forward the music ceases to appeal to vast masses: this is always happening in the world of jazz and rock. When the limitations of popular musical harmonies, rhythms, melodies and forms are left entirely behind, as in music for the concert hall, then the public further diminishes. Yet symphonic music in the hands of great masters truly and fully embodies the otherwise unperceived, unsavoured inner flow of life. In listening to such music we are as though entire again, despite all the insecurity, incoherence, incompleteness and relativity of our everyday life. The miracle is achieved by submitting to the power of its organized flow; a submission which gives us a special pleasure and finally enriches us. The pleasure and the enrichment arise from the fact that the flow is not merely the flow of the music itself, but a significant image of the inner flow of life. Artifice of all kinds is necessary to the musical composition in order that it shall become such an image. Yet when the perfect performance and occasion allow us a truly immediate apprehension of the inner flow 'behind' the music, the artifice is momentarily of no consequence; we are no long aware of it.

Great Art as the Formal Clarification of Transcendent Intuitions

Music of course has a tremendous range of images, from the gay (and, if perhaps rarely, the comic) to the serious and tragic. On the serious side music has always been associated with religious rituals and been a favoured art for expressing certain intuitions of transcendence. That is to say, certain music, to be appreciated as it is, expects a desire and willingness on our part to see reflected in it transcendent elements, unprovable and maybe unknowable analytically, but which infuse the whole work of art. This quality in music has permitted such works as the *St Matthew Passion*, the Ninth Symphony of Beethoven, or *The Ring*.

According to the excellence of the artist, that is to his ability to give formal clarity to these analytically unknowable transcendent intuitions, these works of art endure to enrich later minds when the whole social life from which they sprang has disappeared. Hence the enduring quality of a work such as the Parthenon, even when maimed and uncoloured. And it is these formal considerations alone which enable us to set perhaps the *Matthew Passion* and the Ninth Symphony above *The Ring*. Apparent from all this is the fact that art does not supersede itself in the way science does. Methods and modes may change, and of course, in music, instruments and occasions for making music. These are the things which can make it difficult for us to appreciate, e.g. Pérotin (Perotinus Magnus) now as the great composer his period considered him to be. We may have superseded Pérotin's methods, but we have scarcely superseded his imaginative intuitions. And yet, in another sense, we have. Because the material from the inner world is never quite the same. The extreme changes in the art of the present time are, I am sure, due to more than changes in techniques.

The Place of Technique

The techniques of music have always changed from time to time with the development of new instruments, e.g. the pianoforte; and even more through the changes of social occasion and means of dissemination, e.g. the invention of the concert hall, or of radio. At the present time there are new electronic methods of producing every imaginable sound known or as yet unknown, and these methods, though they cannot supersede the older ways altogether, will certainly be added to them.

The techniques of musical composition change also. There is a wide-spread preoccupation at present with the methods of serial composition. Changes in composition technique are more the concern of the composer than of the listener, who is usually disconcerted during the period of experimentation, as with serial technique now. The deeper reasons for this constant renewal of artistic techniques are still somewhat mysterious.

The most striking novelty in music was the gradual invention of polyphony in the late middle-ages. All known music up to that time, and right up to our own time in all cultural traditions outside the European and its derivatives, had been, or is still, monodic. This means that in general the melodic line, endlessly decorated and varied, is the essential (as in India and Asia; until the invention of polyphony, Europe). Or combinations of dynamic or subtle rhythms have been used to build as unending a stream of rhythmical variation as the unending line of monodic invention (Africa, Indonesia). In both these kinds of music, harmony is incidental and secondary. But European polyphony produced the combination of many disparate lines of melody, and such a combination immediately posed problems of harmony new to music. Over the centuries these problems have been resolved in one way or another, and there have been periods of European music when the harmonic element, initially derived from the practice of polyphony, becomes primary, and what polyphony the music contains has become secondary. We are at present in a time when European-derived music has experimented to an unprecedented degree with harmony. This has been pure invention. At the same time discs, tapes and printed collections of folk-songs and dances, and discs and tapes of African, Indonesian, Indian and Chinese music, have stimulated, or been used as basis for a considerable experimentation in rhythm. The melodic element on the other hand (and the formal element in my opinion) has been secondary.

Now European polyphony has proved so powerful an expressive medium that it is mostly sweeping over the whole world and carrying away much of the indigenous traditional music with it. In this way Europe and America appear still as musical initiators for the globe. But this will not last. When the time is ripe the values of the non-European musical traditions, where they have been temporarily lost, will be rediscovered. The speed at which we are having to become industrially and politically one world would seem to be such that the problems of forging a unified expressive medium may be coming upon us faster than the European composers are as yet aware. This question may well, in my opinion, solve itself first through popular music, just because popular music is by definition and purpose music of the people. Popular music is an open music. In order to entertain it will take everything offered, from Bali to New Orleans, and whatever is successful will be amplified round the world. Popular music will become increasingly global rather than local.

Conclusion

In all the manifestations of music the enduring portion is the sense of flow, of the kind I have described above, organized and expressed formally. A wide-ranging Humanism, whether secular or religious, will always seek to extend to more and more people, through education and opportunity, the enrichment of the personality which music gives. In our technological society we should be warned by Darwin:

> The loss of these tastes (for one or more of the arts according to our predilections) is a loss of happiness and may possibly be injurious to the intellect and more probably to the moral character, by enfeebling the emotional part of our nature.[9]

These are wise and serious words. We are morally and emotionally enfeebled if we live our lives without artistic nourishment. Our sense of life is diminished. In music we sense most directly the inner flow which sustains the psyche, or the soul.

Notes and References

1. *Plato's Phaedrus:* Transl. with Introduction and Commentary by R. Hackforth, (London, 1952), p. 57.
2. MICHAEL TIPPETT, *Moving into Aquarius* (London, 1959); see esp. the chapter 'The Artist's Mandate' for a fuller discussion of this whole problem.
3. See SUSAN LANGER, *Feeling and Form* (London, 1953).
4. Cf. HENRI BERGSON, *Durée et Simultanéité* (Paris, 2nd edn. 1923); also C. G. JUNG, *Synchronicity: An Acausal Connecting Principle in The Structure and Dynamics of the Psyche* (Col. Works, transl. R. C. F. Hull, London, 1960).
5. Cf. STRAVINSKY, *Poétique Musicale* (Cambridge, Mass., 1942).
6. WALTER PATER, *The Renaissance* (London, 1873), essay on Giorgione.
7. See FRANCIS DARWIN, *The Life & Letters of Charles Darwin* (London, 1887), Vol. I, Ch. 2 (*Autobiography*), pp. 100-102.
8. Cf. TIPPETT, *Moving into Aquarius* (see note 2 above).
9. FRANCIS DARWIN, *op cit.*

PART III
The Primacy of Feeling

The arts are engaged with acts of understanding but these acts of understanding work through the feelings and through the senses. In education and in society the complex, fused, cognitive and affective nature of art is still not widely recognized and partly accounts for the low esteem of the arts in our culture.

In this section an educationist (Rex Gibson), a literary critic (L. C. Knights) and a philosopher of the arts (David Best) clarify the notion of the intelligence of feeling in relationship to the arts and, thereby, go a long way towards providing a common conception of artistic activity.

Chapter 6

The Education of Feeling

Rex Gibson

Introduction

Let me begin with three true stories:

1. In a Cambridge College, a young man, an under-chef of 20, in love with a graduate student who had recently left the College, shut himself in a storeroom 7ft by 4ft with his motor cycle, started the engine and kept it running. The following is from the coroner's inquest reported in the local paper:

   > He was left behind struggling with a part-time catering course at the local technical college that was beyond his abilities. He was, said his father...possibly dyslexic and could not cope with the written work. 'The impression I got was that he was very keen to succeed on this course he was doing in order to reveal his feelings for this girl — which perhaps he did not feel he was able to do, being an under-chef.' ...A colleague said...they talked of his worries about the written side of his course. (He) felt he could not drop it because so many people knew about it and expected him to succeed.

2. A 17 year old doing 'A' Levels was in tears about not 'doing well enough' in Maths, French and Geography. 'How's the Art going, then?' she was asked. 'Oh, there's no problem. Art is my lifeline at the moment. In fact my teacher says I'm good enough to get into Ruskin.' 'Do you *want* to?' 'Yes — but I want to prove I'm an academic success first.'

3. A group of four musicians arrived at a South London school and explained to the headteacher that they were the piano quartet who had come to perform for the pupils. 'There are nineteen other schools in the area — why pick on us?' asked the head.

In these three stories, sombre, sad and farcical respectively, feelings are central. Each stands as a sharp reminder of the many complex tensions between the demands of an academic curriculum and the insistencies of our deeply experienced, inescapable emotions. They serve too as reminders of the daunting difficulties involved in the *education* of feeling. Merely to list a few of the dozens of familiar and intensely personal emotions is to acknowledge the sheer scale or near impossibility of the task. How *can* we 'educate' love or fear, awe or guilt, joy or boredom? And isn't there more than just a smack of hubris underlying such a question, for it seems to imply that *our* feelings are 'superior' at all points to those of our pupils and their parents. But the question must be faced, for emotions are the key to most of what happens in classrooms and schools. There is thus an urgent need both to *discuss* educating the feelings and to *engage* actively in that fraught enterprise, but always with a sense of modesty, even absurdity, contingent upon our own vulnerability and the scale of the undertaking.

With that dual awareness of urgency and the need for diffidence, I shall structure my discussion of the education of feeling under four headings: Neglect, Instrumental Rationality, Some Characteristics of Feelings, Implications for Schooling.

The Neglect of Feeling

In the many curriculum documents that have poured out from the DES, HMI and other sources, there is a relative neglect of the emotions, establishing yet another curious tension between the practice of, and literature on, schooling. School life is utterly characterized by feeling. For example, no teacher of young children needs to be reminded that her job, every minute of the day, is intensely invested with feeling, and that she is vitally concerned with its expression and control. Similarly, but less obviously, as children grow older and as their teachers become more specifically concerned with their understanding of mathematics or science or history, those understandings are mediated and encouraged or denied by the feelings which accompany and contain them. But when we turn to the recent curriculum documents, the vividness and intensity, the raw, constant presence of feeling — either as a human characteristic or as a curriculum concern — seems curiously muted and played down; safely, neatly transformed into social and life skills, personal and social development. This is not to say that consideration of emotional development is omitted. It is rather to say that I find only a stifled acknowledgment of the existence and importance of feelings and of the contribution that schooling can make to their education.

This under-valuing is not just my own idiosyncratic judgment. In a major report on a curriculum area centrally concerned with the education on feeling can be found the same view:

> In the widespread discussions which have been taking place about the School Curriculum, the arts — dance, drama, music, visual arts, literature — have been given little attention. The major reports and statements from the Secretaries of State, from HMI and from the Schools Council,...have included only brief reference to them. (Gulbenkian

Report (1982) *The Arts in Schools: Principles, Practice and Provision,*
Calouste Gulbenkian Foundation, p. 3.)

To seek the roots of this neglect can be a seductive enterprise. It is all too easy
to launch into a jeremiad against industrialization, the market economy and the
corrupt state of contemporary culture; to add yet another voice to the unthinking
condemnation of modern society as hard-headed and hard-hearted, materialistic,
cynical and rotten. Those elements are there certainly, they show how easy it is to
mis-educate the feelings. The New Utilitarianism is abroad — all too often
dominant — but it is not the whole story. Each one of us knows from experience
that its balefulness is tempered and resisted in the personal encounters, common
decencies and kindnesses of daily life in and out of school. Five minutes in almost
any infant classroom reveal the evident goodness and goodwill which exist. Our
world is a sombre one but it is not uniformly black.

I shall therefore not dwell on the malformations of capitalism, or the media
or the nuclear threat; or on that embarrassment and reserve which seems so
peculiarly English and which inhibits both the discussion and expression of
emotion in public places. Rather I shall identify just one feature of schooling that
is a reflection or mediation of wider social attitudes and which acts to constrain,
distort and inhibit positive human feelings of sympathy and compassion. It is an
impulse which is deeply ingrained in personal and social life and which is
mistrustful and suspicious of talk of the education of feeling. We can call it
instrumental rationality.

Instrumental Rationality

You don't have to be committed to, or even have heard of, the Frankfurt School or
Jurgen Habermas to have experienced instrumental rationality or understand it.
Similarly, you don't have to be aware of its deep historical roots or to be versed in
Marxism or psychoanalysis. What's most important is to recognize and to resist its
presence in all aspects of education; for it is massively present in our activities and
assumptions, in our very language. [1]

Instrumental rationality signifies a preoccupation with '*How* to do it' rather
than '*Why* do it?' It represents the dissociation of reason from feeling, the
celebration of mastery, prediction, and control over nature or over others. In its
measurement of 'truth' it prefers mathematical or scientific approaches; and it
elevates 'reason' as the prime category for evaluating, judging and prescribing
human activities (i.e. what children do in classrooms). Certification and testing
assume disproportionate status. In short, instrumental rationality loses sight of the
question 'What is education *for*?' Means take precedence over ends, indeed,
become ends as details of skills, methods, techniques and measurement replace
concern for meaning, interpretation and purposes. For example, you don't have to
contract into David Holbrook's shrill tone and predilection for his own esoteric
blend of philosophy and psychoanalysis to acknowledge some truth in his finding

the Bullock Report as lacking life, as 'badly dead' (sic), as dull to read:

> It lacked touch with the child and the child's lively language. It seemed dominated by theory, and bad theory at that — of intrusions into arts subjects from linguistics, disciplines based on a physicalist psychology, even with neuro-physiology and behaviourism in the background — at a time when the essential failure of such disciplines to explain conscious-ness and experience was being widely recognised and discussed ... it marks a retreat to utilitarian approaches to language use and teaching and to a methodology and epistemology with which many are now becoming disenchanted, quite properly, as they are fallacious.[2]

Holbrook's criticism of Bullock is too sweeping, but his unease that meaning is yielding place to skills cannot be lightly dismissed. It is one of the many signs of instrumental rationality evidenced in gross and subtle forms in the 1980s: growing demands for accountability; the activities of the Assessment of Performance Unit; the unrelenting growth of examinations; legislation to impose testing of children at 7, 11 and 15; efficiency measured by non-educational criteria. Many of its manifestations seem eminently reasonable, ungainsayable: rational curriculum design, curriculum planning by objectives, a commitment to behaviour modifica-tion techniques, the importance of management and organization.

It's certainly not my intention to argue against the good sense that *is* within many of these practices; the world of schooling is too diverse, complex and contradictory a place to yield to any simple put-down condemnation. But the pattern represented in these practices cannot be ignored for (to use a very grand phrase) it represents the triumph of epistemology over being, or (less grandly) the dominance of thought over feeling. Now thought and feeling are the inseparable companions of action, but in the choice of ends the latter is the senior partner, whereas in the selection of means to achieve those ends, reason dominates.

Tiny examples of taken for granted practices in teacher education are the tips of the instrumental rationality iceberg; the impersonalization demanded in essays or dissertations ('I' gives way to 'the author'); the seminar put-down: 'but that's a value judgment' (to which the only reply should be 'of course it is!'); the transformation of children tested into 'subjects'; the beating insistence of those words which deny the interpenetration of fact and value, and which refute the subjectivity, the awkwardness and inconsistencies of which we are so aware when we examine our own personal felt experience or the institutional and historical world in which we exist. Words such as 'objective', 'disinterested', 'scientific', 'proof', 'fact' and the insistent demand to 'define your terms' (how many essays have we read — or written — which are misled by the possibilities of such linguistic precision?).

We cannot do without such language, but we must remain sharply aware that each word contains ambiguities as it implicitly denies the engagement of our feelings with what we study, how we study it, how we report it. Where such words come together most powerfully in educational studies is in that magic word 'theory': the great will-o'-the-wisp of education which all too often seeks to deny the stubbornness, quirkiness and resistances of personal and social life. In *theory's* search for neatness, for tidying up, it elevates the abstract over the concrete, the intellectual over the emotional, the impersonal over the personal, the generality over the particular instance. In education, such theory is often a sham imitation of science which diminishes and devalues as 'mere anecdote' the stories at the start of this chapter. 'Theory' becomes the tool of instrumental reason as individual experience is discounted in favour of neater, detached explanations. But that neatness and detachment are to be found neither in the world of school and classroom, nor those areas of human experience we call 'the arts'. Understanding and feeling in such spheres of our lives require a tolerance of ambiguity that instrumental reason denies.

Some Characteristics of Feeling

Let me remark on a few characteristics of feelings which have important implications for teachers. First is the very obvious point that feelings are universal and omnipresent. All people, at all ages, in all cultures share the same range and diversity of emotions. In every classroom — whatever is being 'taught' — feelings are inevitably in play and are affecting what is being learned. In every human encounter feelings pervade and underpin experience and constitute the spur to action. Teachers cannot avoid *affecting* their pupils' feelings; hence the urgency for them to consider consciously how far they are *educating* those feelings.

My second point concerns the equality of feeling. By this I mean that the distribution of feeling is of quite a different order from the distribution of intelligence. That is, however sceptical we are of the notion of IQ, however much we resist the curve of normal distribution, it is evident that some people *are* naturally better at abstract thought than others. Indeed, on any scale of achievement the Gaussian curve has clear empirical backing. Learning difficulty is not simply a matter of social construction. But my claim is that the curve of normal distribution has very little application to feeling. Self-evidently some people are kinder, more sympathetic than others, and history clearly reminds us that at certain periods significant fractions of some nations undergo huge traumatizing of moral sensitivity. But it seems equally evident that the potential for grief or love, sorrow or joy is common property. No individual, social class or occupational group has a monopoly on feeling and its 'education'. As teachers we do well to remember that in any of our teaching groups not only are there pupils who are in some ways our intellectual superiors, but even more pressingly, the claims we can make for the quality of *our* feelings in relation to those of our pupils are likely to be uneasy, provisional and qualified. In other words, what we feel, they feel — and we must be ultra-cautious in regarding *our* feelings as privileged. This brings me to my next point, the unmeasurability of feeling.

Here, I am merely drawing attention to the frequent inappropriateness of scientific methods and assumptions. To submit feelings to the techniques of science is to mistake their core and nature. We must perforce fall back on other, apparently less precise, ways of describing, analyzing and evaluating emotional experience. But this lack of measurability does not mean we do not know and cannot say valid and worthwhile things about emotions. Such a realization brings me to my next point, that our feelings show us the limits of our language. They bring home to us that language is not omnicompetent; for we know far more than we can say. It is when we try to put into words our own feelings, when we attempt to explore our inner states (states that vividly and significantly exist, have reality and are of profound consequences for action) that the gap between language and experience is starkly exposed. It is at such moments we must turn to poets and artists, not to scientists, for genuine illumination. Those understandings are rarely or never fully recoverable in written or spoken language, but it is common experience that they are nonetheless both *grasped* and valid. What we feel at Cordelia's 'no cause, no cause', or at the television picture of a dead baby in her Ethiopian mother's arms can only be hinted at through language, never fully verbalized.

We need also to remember that feeling is invariably focused on something: an object, person, event, or experience. Rarely, if at all, do feelings 'float free', unattached. We worry about *that* exam, are bored by *somebody*, are frustrated by *that* refusal, annoyed by *that* statement, respect *that* person. A child crying, a song, a television picture, are the objects of our feeling. Why stress this point? Because it raises the question of transfer of feeling: the genuine possibility of educating the emotions. To put it over-simply, schooling provides the opportunity for practising the emotions (where practising is used in the same sense as in 'doctors practising', i.e. not as activities divorced from real life). For the pupil to empathize with Hamlet (or with Rapunzel), to act out aggressive encounters, to experience compassion and affection and a concern for fairness in his or her teachers is likely to promote positive responses in other, non-school, contexts. The Nazi guards, listening to Mozart in the camps, remind us how easy it is *not* to transfer our feelings so that they apply to all human beings. The categories of apartheid, or, at a less dramatic level, school life itself, can effect their own dislocations and enforce their own rigid boundaries that human sympathy finds so difficult to cross.

Finally, we should note that feelings have puzzling relationships with time. They are processes not products: they have, in their intense here-and-now sense, a fleetingness and fugitiveness in their experience and expression. They are grasped and intuited only in their moments of experiencing, and they are incommunicable in essence to others outside the event or after it. To put it more simply: when you've had a good lesson, when you've shared a poem or play with a class, laughed at the same jokes, or when, on a school trip, you've spent a day in the outdoors together, that sense of community, that 'we-feeling', that togetherness, can't be shown to others after the event. It's done something to and for you and the children, but there's no tangible product like a tick on a sum, only traces of something left in your being and the children's, which, when recalled, are different from the experience itself. Such experiences are of the *present* to be enjoyed at the time. They are not future oriented and are not rewarded with grades or certificates. It is with this present, shared, experienced, nature of emotions in mind that we return to the question of the education of feeling.

Implications for Schooling

There seem to me to be five obvious but basic points which always require restating. They will take an infinite variety of expression in different schools. First, there must be many opportunities for the expression — indeed, overflow — of feeling provided for in the curriculum. The arts in all their forms are vital to such expression and overflow and must therefore be part of the central core of any curriculum. However, the National Curriculum which became mandatory under the Education Reform Act 1988 must give rise to unease about the place of the arts in education. English is a core subject, and music and art are foundation subjects (drama is not specified), but whether their form and content will constitute a genuine education in the arts is deeply uncertain. The example of poetry suffices. As Robert Hull and Michael Benton have, in different ways, shown, pupils need to be given time and help to resource the aesthetic choices they make in their writing and reading. Whether teachers will be able to enable such choices in the face of other curriculum demands is a doubtful prospect. (Robert Hull, 1988, *Behind the Poem: A Teacher's View of Children Writing*, Routledge; Michael Benton *et al.* (1988) *Young Readers Responding to Poems*, Routledge).

But feeling is not the exclusive preserve of the arts; all curriculum subjects as they are experienced in teacher-pupil classroom contact are heavily invested with feeling. My second point therefore is that the total ethos of school and classroom is crucial to the education of feeling. If the habitual emotional and moral character of the school or classroom is not healthy, the possibilities for positive individual affectual development are sharply reduced.[3] And that character or tone is heavily dependent on the head and teachers, on whom Martin Buber's question makes urgent, sharp demands; 'How can I hear what you are saying, when what you *are* is drumming in my ears?' The climate of classrooms and schools is compounded of the million daily interactions of teachers and pupils, and of that mundane web is the education of feeling spun.

Taken together these two points produce the third, that empathy is at the centre of the education of feeling. That doesn't just mean knowing what it's like to be the other — it means being able, however dimly and approximately, to feel what the other feels. The curriculum must provide each pupil with many opportunities for empathy; but additionally, importantly, teachers should constantly remind themselves of what it *feels* like to be a pupil, in *this* school. As one of the teenagers in White and Brockington's *Tales Out of School* complained:

> I'd be walking down the corridor and one of the teachers would say 'Hey, Masefield'. Well, that's no way to treat you is it? It ain't as if they don't know your name 'cos you've been there long enough.[4]

The fourth point then is quickly made: teachers have a duty to stand up for the common decencies of caring, concern, compassion and all those others that are given by the familiar question 'How would *you* feel if ...?' The old invocation 'do unto others as ... ' has lost not one atom of its power as a guide for action.

Fifth, the education of feeling is vitally concerned with the refining and control of emotion. To say this is not to be élitist or puritan; for it is evident that some feelings *are* better than others. What it does is to remind us of the necessary relationships of thought and feeling, hence the possibility of precision, of focusing, of emotions. It reminds us too that feeling is not simply personal and inner, but has social reference. We feel about, and for, others; but that isn't the only social point to make. Refining emotions doesn't mean that we can be superior or indifferent to industrial society; as Clive James once remarked, for every man writing poetry, there are ten men out there tightening nuts. The stance of the aesthete just won't do for it is profoundly inhuman. The arts as a retreat from the world remain just that: a retreat. They do have their own integrities, but they also engage vitally with the world around them. In this, they offer dual opportunities for the refinement and control of feelings. Through such disciplining of the emotions, sensitivity issues in action. The success of such education of feeling is manifested in practice through the qualities of relations with others. But the arts, as I have remarked, have no monopoly on such education, for refinement and control come also through mundane interactions and through direct consideration of our present, pressing, threatened and threatening society. Such consideration adds extra edge to terms like 'refinement', 'control and discipline', for a finely tempered rage may prove the more appropriate and effective response to some of the features of our precarious contemporary world.

From 1986 I've been uniquely privileged to witness how these considerations come together practically in classrooms around the country. As Director of the Shakespeare and Schools Project I've had first hand experience of how an active aesthetic can be created and shared by pupils and teachers. As students from 8 to 18 years work on the language, characters and stories of Shakespeare, I've seen vividly how an education in the arts can tap deep springs of feeling and become, intensely, lived experience. Here, the arts truly live in particular moments: inner city junior pupils celebrating in dance, music and mime the reviving to life of the 'dead' Thaisa in *Pericles*; sixth-formers imaginatively recreating Claudius' vain prayers or Ophelia's appalling plight; fifth-years around a flickering candle sharing Juliet's agonized thoughts as she prepares for seeming death. Our research shows clearly the lasting, positive effects of Shakespeare when teaching methods shake free of simple reliance on a traditional textual approach: Shakespeare as a crossword puzzle to be solved. It's when pupils are involved actively and cooperatively, in all aspects of their being: physically, intellectually, imaginatively, emotionally, socially ... that a genuine education in the arts, and of the emotions, becomes possible.[5]

Conclusion

I began with three true stories of schooling. Let me close by reminding you of an image from children's literature. In Hans Andersen's *The Snow Queen*, Kay's heart is frozen by the Snow Queen who sits in her bitter palace on the mirror of Reason, 'of all things the best in the world'. He is intent on his game, making patterns of the most elaborate kind — the Intellectual Ice Puzzle:

> Kay sat there all alone in the mile-long empty hall of ice, and gazed at the bits of ice and thought and thought till he crackled; all stiff and chill he sat; you would have though he was frozen to death.[6]

But he is saved by the ever-faithful Gerda's hot tears as in her song she reclaims him for the world of feeling. Without such compassionate aid the frozen child becomes the frozen adult who has lost contact with his feelings, who has forgotten the warmth of friendship and how to dance or sing.

Notes and References

1. See my *Critical Theory and Education* (Hodder and Stoughton, 1986).
2. DAVID HOLBROOK, *English for Meaning* (NFER, 1979) p. 10.
3. I explore the notion of school and classroom climates as 'structures' of feeling' in *Structuralism and Education* (Hodder and Stoughton, 1984).
4. WHITE and BROCKINGTON, *Tales Out of School* (Routledge and Kegan Paul, 1983).
5. The *Shakespeare and Schools* magazine, published each term, records some of the work of the Project. Details from the author at Cambridge Institute of Education. A book on the Project is in preparation.
6. HANS ANDERSEN, *The Snow Queen*.

Chapter 7

Literature and the Education of Feeling

L. C. Knights

Introduction

When I agreed to write on 'literature and the education of feeling' I was less aware than I ought to have been of the difficulties ahead. The subject was self-evidently important; for many years I had quoted with approval Coleridge's remark that 'deep thinking is attainable only by a man of deep feeling', and had referred my students to the objects he ascribed to himself in *The Friend*: 'to make the reason spread light over our feelings, to make our feelings, with their vital warmth, actualize our reason'. It was only when I started to make notes that a long-lurking difficulty surfaced. I didn't know what I was supposed to be writing about! What *are* 'the feelings' that literature is supposed to educate? Seeking the help of a wise man, I looked up 'feeling' in the index of William James's *The Principles of Psychology*, but all I found was, 'Feeling, synonym for consciousness in general'. It seemed better to turn to the great Dictionary, for as Coleridge said, 'There are cases, in which more knowledge of more value may be conveyed by the history of a *word*, than by the history of a campaign'.

From the six columns devoted to 'feel' (*v.*) and 'feeling' (*vbl.sb*) in the *NED* I want to pick out a few senses that seem to constellate round the word as we are presumably using it today. The etymology runs back through Old High German *fuolen*, to handle, to the Latin *palma*, hand, and the Sanscrit *pani*. The first meanings given for the verb are, 'to examine or explore by touch, to test or discover by cautious trial'; and I think our current use still carries a sense of immediacy of awareness, the opposite of generalized notions or stereotypes, also perhaps a connotation of the tentative and exploratory ('to feel out'). The second main group of meanings proceeds from 'to perceive, be conscious (by touch or by the senses generally)' to 'to be emotionally affected by ... to have the sensibilities excited; *esp.* to have sympathy *with*, compassion *for* (a person, his suffering, etc.)'. So here we have the action of sympathetically entering into the experience of others, as — to take an example not in the Dictionary — in Gloucester's 'superfluous and lust-dieted man,/Who will not see because he does not feel' (*King Lear*, **IV**, 1).

I think we have here some meanings that are, or should be, in our minds today. The dictionary definitions of the noun, 'feelings' ('the action of the vb.

FEEL') need not detain us, except for a comment on sense 5: 'Capacity or readiness to feel; susceptibility to the higher and more refined emotions; *esp.* sensibility or tenderness for the sufferings of others'. Perhaps we may dismiss 'higher and more refined emotions', whatever they may be, and emphasize the relations to *others*; but even here, although we recognize that 'sufferings' must come into the definition, it does not seem an adequately inclusive word. A more satisfactory definition would be, an emotionally toned awareness of the inward, individual experience of others, in its otherness and uniqueness.

We may leave further attempts at definition until we have tried to see what part literature plays in 'the education of feeling', with especial reference to the teaching of literature in schools and elsewhere. The importance of the attempt is not diminished because, as so often happens, we have to work with terms that do not admit the kind of precision that would satisfy a philosopher. Still, we can do our best to be clear.

Literature and the Extension of Sympathy

Literature certainly has to do with feelings. It does not 'communicate' the author's personal feelings to us, like sending a telegram or handing over a parcel. Nor is it quite enough to say, as Susanne Langer does in her seminal book, *Feeling and Form*, that literature finds 'presentational' symbolic forms for the living pulse of unique feelings that can only be described — distanced and generalized — in discursive modes. What it does is — in a phrase I shall come back to — to arouse something of the 'warmth and intimacy' which William James says are inseparable from our immediate feeling of self-ness, to arouse them in relation to other existences, other experiences than our own, and thereby to realize them, make them more real to us. This realization is a complicated process. It is enough to say here that the feelings in question are not mere reactions, something that we undergo, as with passions: they are active, exploratory, and (to anticipate) they are inseparable from intelligence and perception, which are certainly active and creative powers. Literature is not a code to be deciphered (though codes are involved), it is a prompting to a more lively apprehension.

A useful shorthand is the old phrase about literature extending our sympathies. It extends them to the experiences of other people, towards the non-human world, which science makes appear either alien and remote or mere stuff to manipulate, and towards our own buried or potential selves which we try to have as little dealing with as with awkward relatives.

We can only get a little further from generalizations by way of examples, and in the time at my disposal the problem of selection is almost overwhelming. Shakespeare, many other playwrights, many novelists, whatever else they may be doing, certainly invite us to share the experience of imaginary persons in imaginary situations with a more or less close relation with 'real life'; they invite us to try out different attitudes by entering into them, provisionally adopting them whilst still keeping a certain distance, and seeing what the result may be.[1] The subject of Jane Austen's *Emma* is, in fact, the awakening of a young woman by the education of her feelings: the artistry is to make us sufficiently interested in the heroine, sufficiently close to recognize her as representing one of our own potential selves, so that we do not merely observe, we live through, her successive awakenings: at the famous impertinence to Miss Bates at Box Hill, we blush as we read. And Emma of course is at the centre of a formally constructed pattern: there are many degrees of self-engrossment and openness — those inward attitudes that determine how we construct our world: from Mr Woodhouse, 'whose habits of gentle selfishness, and of being never able to suppose that people could feel differently from himself', who 'was fond of society in his own way', and welcomed 'such as would visit him on his own terms', to Miss Bates, who 'loved everybody, was interested in everybody's happiness, quicksighted to everybody's merits' (chapters I and III). It is Miss Bates who serves as the author's mouthpiece in announcing the book's almost Proustian theme. Corrected in her fancy that the unseen Mr Dixon might look like Mr John Knightley, she says, 'Very odd! but one never does form a just idea of anybody beforehand. One takes up a notion and runs away with it' (chapter XXI). But we cannot adequately deal here with extended forms such as plays and novels. I have mentioned *Emma* to suggest that it is the writer's *art* that activates and energizes our exploration of feeling, and to suggest — it comes to much the same thing — that awakened intelligence is inseparable from any 'education of feeling' that we are likely to be interested in.

As for the fuller realization of the non-human world, or more precisely of our relations with it — that seems peculiarly the province of poetry, though certainly not exclusively so (think of the description of the female whales and their young in chapter 87 of *Moby Dick*). We shall all be ready with our favourite examples. Let us take, as it were, a lucky dip and consider for a few minutes Emily Dickinson's poem, 'A narrow Fellow in the Grass':

> A narrow Fellow in the Grass
> Occasionally rides —
> You may have met him — did you not
> His notice sudden is —
>
> The Grass divides as with a Comb —
> A spotted shaft is seen —
> And then it closes at your feet
> And opens further on —
>
> He likes a Boggy Acre
> A Floor too cool for Corn —
> Yet when a Boy, and Barefoot —
> I more than once at Noon
> Have passed, I thought, a Whip lash
> Unbraiding in the Sun
> When stooping to secure it
> It wrinkled, and was gone —

Several of Nature's People
I know, and they know me —
I feel for them a transport
Of cordiality —

But never met this Fellow
Attended or alone
Without a tighter breathing
And Zero at the Bone —

The poem gives with uncommon force a blend of affectionate familiarity — the snake is 'a Fellow', like any boy in the village — and an awareness of unbridgeable distance: the snake is so inalienably *other* than anything that can be familiarized that a mere glimpse of him causes 'a tighter breathing/And Zero at the Bone'; and it is in this sense of the frightening otherness of the non-human (which nevertheless inhabits 'our' world) that the main thrust of the poem resides. But this breath-catching awe — a feeling, or cluster of feelings — about the snake — depends on the fact that the snake is not simply mentioned or gestured towards but made vividly present. It is partly a matter of shifts of tone and rhythm. The apparently casual ordinariness of the first two and a half lines is interrupted by the urgency of a question that does not stop for a formal question-mark but runs straight on into an abrupt statement quite different from the affectionate, nothing-out-of-the-ordinary tone of the opening.

You may have met Him — did you not
His notice sudden is —

The unusual word order of the last line and the ambiguity of 'His notice' force the mind to a slightly bewildered activity — the psychological equivalent of a jump of surprise: the speaker is too startled — or, we had better say these days, the poet creates a verbal image of being too startled — to put the words in conventional sequence: 'His notice sudden is' is an instantaneous apprehension not yet sorted out into formal order. And if the line means 'you notice him suddenly', it also means that the snake gives notice or serves notice (of what?) without ceremony. Of course you can feel the poem without all this fuss with minutiae: but they are there, and they have their purpose. More obvious is the exact description by means of analogies that at first seem unusual but that when assimilated seem completely natural,

The Grass divides as with a Comb —

I more than once at Noon
Have passed, I thought, a Whip lash
Unbraiding in the Sun...

It is much the same with any great poem in which some aspect of 'nature' is observed or celebrated, even though it may (and usually does) serve some further purpose such as finding form for the activities of the observing mind. In Keats' great 'To Autumn' our enjoyment is in reality a complex process of *noticing* with unusual fullness of attention as we are prompted by the poem's activators: sound ('Close bosom-friend of the maturing sun' contrasting with 'The red-breast whistles from a garden-croft'), rhythm (the impossibility of reading the opening lines quickly), imagery ('To swell the gourd and plump the hazel shells'), and so on. And all these discrete details, inter-acting among themselves, are held together in a formal pattern in which the second, central stanza that presents an apparently static, timeless moment of fullness, is flanked by a first stanza evoking the slow process of maturing, and a third — the signs of advancing autumn now present — in which that same process is seen as part of a larger order. Or, for a last example, there is Hopkins' 'The Windhover'. That poem is not of course 'about' a falcon: its subject is 'Christ our Lord', to whom the poem is addressed. But the claim made for the life of renunciation demands that the bird should exist in its own right — it isn't just 'a symbol' — and that its freedom, its autonomous life and glory should be a felt presence. And that presentness is a function of verbal artifice, that enlists new word combinations, analogies involving leaps of the mind, varied rhythms and the over-riding of line-endings (which are sufficiently there to make the jump worthwhile), and of course the bodily energy of reading words aloud with the emphasis that sense and feeling demand.

> I caught this morning morning's minion, king-
> dom of daylight's dauphin, dapple-dawn-drawn Fal-
> con, in his riding
> Of the rolling level underneath him steady air, and
> striding
> High there, how he rung upon the rein of a wimpling wing
> In his ecstacy! then off, off forth on swing,
> As a skate's heel sweeps smooth on a bow-bend: the
> hurl and gliding
> Rebuffed the big wind. My heart in hiding
> Stirred for a bird, — the achieve of, the mastery of the
> thing!

In these and a myriad other ways poetry can awaken feelings about the non-human world; if it 'educates' them, that is because the feelings are not, so to speak, raw; they are specific, subtle, organized, and in close relation with thought and perception. It is difficult to say why this is important except by invoking an intuited sense that our humanity is diminished to the extent that we fail to have such awareness, to the extent that we cut our connexions. 'You never enjoy the world aright', said Traherne, anticipating D. H. Lawrence, 'until the sea itself flows in your veins'. The most intelligible way of putting this is to say that without some such sense as it pointed to here our lives will be taken over by the practical will. No one really wants to be a robot — or to be controlled by robots. 'Long live the weeds and the wilderness yet'.

As for the third category that I mentioned earlier, the awakening and clarification of feelings towards our unacknowledged selves, that is too large a subject to be entered on here. I will merely refer you to the poems of George Herbert, Blake's *Songs of Innocence and Experience* — and the Sonnets and plays of Shakespeare. All of them would illustrate the processes of activating the reader's mind that I have touched on here.

Artistic Training as Initiation into Forms of Awareness

It will be plain that in this brief sketch I have been faithfully accompanied by the Dictionary. I said that in the many shades of meaning of 'feel' and 'feeling' the root sense of physical touch was never far away: that the feelings we are talking about have a closeness and immediacy that distinguishes them from say, notions. And in the history and ramifications of the words a central part is played by the idea of feeling *with*, of *com*passion, of *sym*pathy, both Latin and Greek keeping in view the sense of with-ness. The feelings that literature arouses are sympathies with something or other that appears as close as if it were part of ourselves — as indeed it is, or rather it becomes so in the course of successive readings, because literature doesn't simply describe, it makes us imaginatively live through whatever it is that the maker contrives to find verbal symbols for. And to repeat — what I have already said in dealing with poems involving some relation to 'nature' — the forms of symbolic presentation are virtually infinite. They range from sound, pace and rhythm.

> Absent thee from felicity awhile,
> And in this harsh world draw thy breath in pain
> To tell my story —

> Unarm, Eros! the bright day is done and we are
> for the dark —

to all the subtleties of metaphor and the forms of discursive thought. It is the variety of mental — imaginative — activities they enforce that creates the 'presentness'. And that is not a static 'state of mind'; it is a living pulse of exploratory feeling-and-thought.

We are back after all, it seems, to William James. When he is discussing 'the Consciousness of Self' he quotes a German psychologist, Horwicz:

> We may affirm with confidence that our own possessions in most cases please us better (— not because they are ours), but simply because we know them better, 'realize' them more intimately, feel them more deeply...On close examination, we shall almost always find that a great part of our feeling about what is ours is due to the fact that we *live closer* to our own things, and so feel them more thoroughly and deeply. [2]

James's point is that the self defines itself to the extent that our awareness of other people, other things, has something of the 'warmth and intimacy' that are inseparable from our immediate feeling of self-ness;[3] and later he tentatively identifies this 'warmth' with a 'feeling of pure psychic energy'. But it is Horwicz's phrase 'to "realize" more intimately' that I want to pick up. Literature continually enforces this immediacy of realization, and thereby (Lawrence's phrase about the novel) 'leads our sympathies into new places'. But I hope I have said enough to make plain that the sympathies in question are active and activating forms of awareness and knowledge.

If any of this approaches the truth it is enough to suggest why 'the education of feeling' is so important: it determines the range, power of discrimination and quality of our lives, both 'personal' and 'social'. Towards the end of *Feeling and Form*, Susanne Langer, speaking of the arts in general, says:

> Artistic training is, therefore, the education of feeling, as our usual schooling in factual subjects, and logical skills such as mathematical 'figuring' or simple argumentation...is the education of thought. Few people realize that the real education of emotion is not the 'conditioning' effected by social approval and disapproval, but the tacit, personal, illuminating contact with symbols of feeling. Art education, therefore, is neglected, left to chance, or regarded as a cultural veneer. People who are so concerned for their children's scientific enlightenment that they keep Grimm out of the library and Santa Claus out of the chimney, allow the cheapest art, the worst of bad singing, the most revolting sentimental fiction to impinge on the children's minds all day and every day, from infancy. If the rank and file of youth grows up in emotional cowardice and confusion, sociologists look to economic conditions or family relations for the cause of this deplorable 'human weakness', but not to the ubiquitous influence of corrupt art, which steeps the average mind in a shallow sentimentalism that ruins what germs of true feeling might have developed in it.[4]

More succinctly, at the beginning of his great work, *European Literature and the Latin Middle Ages*, Ernst Robert Curtius remarks, 'the greatest enemy of moral and social advance is dullness and narrowness of consciousness'.

Conclusion

I have also, I hope, said enough to show literature's part in the education of feeling; though it is not literature's part alone, of course: there are also other arts, religion, family talk and intercourse between friends. In conclusion, with an eye on the classroom and lecture hall, I would only say two things. One is that in dealing with literature the feeling of pleasure can be left to take care of itself; it is the spontaneous accompaniment of all successful intellectual-imaginative activity — success of course being a relative term; at some stage our pupils need to like 'bad' poems, that is, poems we no longer like. Let them be, show them something of the best, and wait for time and experience to tell. The second, emerging from the first, has to do with feelings in the more important sense that I have used. I began by indicating that in this area there are no certainties, not even the provisional certainties with which the scientist operates. But one thing is certain. If it is bad when the teacher makes his poetry class dull, it is something like a sin when he imposes *the* meaning that is supposed to emerge from the interplay of forces within the structure of the poem, play or novel in hand. In a lecture on 'Education' (in *Between Man and Man*) it is named by Martin Buber as 'the gesture of interference'; and it can take the form of forcing an enthusiasm or of snubbing an individual liking. Of course the teacher's zest for a work will insensibly communicate itself. But consciously his function is to point, to encourage — and to withdraw. As in all the great fields of human endeavour tact (yet another word deriving from touch) is not simply a social grace, it is a virtue.

Notes and References

1. 'The basic convention which governs the novel and which, *a fortiori*, governs those novels which set out to violate it is our expectation that the novel will produce a world. Words must be composed in such a way that through the activity of reading there will emerge a model of the social world, models of the individual personality, of the relations between the individual and society, and, perhaps most important, of the kind of significance which these aspects of the world can bear.' Jonathan Culler, *Structuralist Poetics*, p. 189.
2. WILLIAM JAMES, *The Principles of Psychology*, Dover Publications, 1950, Chapter 10.
3. 'All narrow people', he says, '*intrench* their Me, they *retract* it — from the region of what they cannot securely possess'. *Ibid*, I, 312.
4. SUSANNE LANGER, *Feeling and Form*, Routledge and Kegan Paul, 1953, pp. 401-2.

Chapter 8

Feeling and Reason in the Arts: The Rationality of Feeling

David Best

Introduction

> It is impossible to learn anything in the arts. Involvement in the arts is essentially a matter of having an experience.

Is this a typical statement by one of the many these days who regard the arts as unnecessary frills in education? One of the enemies of the arts in education? On the contrary, this is precisely what many teachers of the arts, arts-educators, and theorists of arts-education have been saying for years. That is, surprising as it may seem, in their attempt to support the case for the arts in *education*, many arts-educators continue to insist that the arts, by their very nature, cannot involve *learning* at all.

In case you think that I exaggerate, let me cite a well known and influential arts-educator who has stated explicitly that teachers who see drama in terms of learning are distorting the nature of the art form.[1] I have every reason to believe that he holds similar views about the other arts. But I do not want to criticize any individual in particular, because the conception to which I am drawing attention is widely prevalent, although it is more usually an implicit consequence of what arts-educators say and write than stated explicitly. It is part of the rampant tide of subjectivism. Even those who are beginning to recognize the educational damage done to their own case by continuing to purvey this subjectivist thesis tend to fail to see how radically they need to change their fundamental thinking.

Subjective Feeling

The root of the trouble is the largely unquestioned assumption that the creation and appreciation of the arts is a matter of subjective feeling, in the sense of a 'direct' feeling, 'untainted' by cognition, understanding, rationality. Hence the popularity of theorists such as Witkin who wrote that in order to achieve this 'pure' feeling for art, one needs to erase all memories.[2] The idea seems to be that

70

cognition, understanding and memory will prejudice and limit the capacity for direct feeling-response; that they will prevent pure artistic feelings.

I want to point out as clearly as possible how very *damaging* that is, and to argue that we need to be going in the opposite direction. Only if we recognize the crucial place of understanding and cognition can we give an intelligible account of *educating* in the arts; and only in that way can we see how individual freedom is possible.

I want to consider briefly one crucial aspect of this large and complex issue. But first let me point out that there is certainly something important which underlies what is said by theorists such as those mentioned above. What leads them, and so many others, to deny the place of cognition and learning in the arts? One important motivation behind it is well captured by D. H. Lawrence: 'Our education from the start has *taught* us a certain range of emotions, what to feel and what not to feel.'[3] Consequently we experience 'false', 'counterfeit', 'faked' feelings — 'The world is all gummy with them.' Lawrence was, of course, referring to the effects not solely of formal education, but of the whole ethos of society. The situation is perhaps even worse today, when television, the popular press, much pop music, chat shows, etc. purvey a constant barrage of cliché-emotions, and stereotyped 'norm' responses. The effect is to set as the limits of possible feelings a crude, bland, sentimental and generalized range of emotions.

It is my firm conviction that one of the most important contributions of the arts in education is precisely to resist as strongly as possible these powerful influences on our children and students towards conformist, secondhand feelings. Our aim should be to educate them to become capable of a continuously expanding range of vivid and subtly discriminated feelings, which are *their own*, firsthand, authentic.

Theorists such as Ross and Witkin are right to emphasize that crucial aspect of the arts in education. But their solution to the problem is philosophically untenable. Recognizing the danger to which Lawrence is pointing, of learning secondhand emotions, they want to reject learning and cognition altogether in arts-education. That is to throw out the baby with the bath water. What is required is not the avoidance or eradication of learning and cognition, which makes no sense anyway, but the encouragement of fresh, individual learning and cognition. Their thesis is very understandable, since it has its most powerful source in a prevalent and deeply held philosophical misconception, about which it is crucial to be clear if we are to move forward constructively in our thinking about this vital area of education.

The Myth

The misconception to which I refer, which must be recognized as such if we are to have any hope of providing an educational justification for the arts, is based on the common assumption that there is necessarily an opposition between, on the one hand, feeling, creativity and individuality, and on the other hand, cognition and reason. For instance, it is widely assumed that the arts are a matter of feeling, not of reason or cognition. This is part of one of the most widespread and damaging educational myths (henceforth the Myth), namely that the human mind is composed of two distinct realms or faculties — the Cognitive/ Rational, and the Affective/Creative. This Myth is remarkably persistent and pervasive, and is very damaging educationally, and not only to the arts. For example, it is commonly assumed that creativity is the special or exclusive province of the arts — hence, for instance, the 'Creativity Centres' in the Netherlands, which, I am told, are exclusively devoted to the arts. This prevalent misconception seems to stem from the Myth of distinct mental faculties. Yet if, for instance, the development of creative attitudes is not central to the teaching of mathematics and the sciences — and regrettably often it is not — that is an indictment of the educational policy. The point is that creativity is not in a closed mental box, along with the arts. It can and should apply to *every* part of the curriculum (and even to personal relationships). One has seen in some schools science learning which was far more creative than the arts learning. The Myth connives at an attitude to education *in general* which ought to be dead and buried. Both arts and sciences require creativity and imagination.

(The Gulbenkian Report, *The Arts in Schools*,[4] in a chapter which is supposed to offer a philosophical foundation for the rest of the Report, and despite some explicit denials, sometimes gives the impression of contending that creativity is the special province of the arts. But the Report is so confused about creativity that one cannot be sure.)

There are numerous other examples. For instance, a discussion document of the Scottish Committee on Expressive Arts in the Primary School states: 'The main curricular emphasis is still upon *cognitive* learning, with other areas — physical, emotional, affective — coming off second-best. We maintain that a better balance should be found....'[5] This clearly implies that whereas the sciences and mathematics are cognitive, the emotional and affective areas, which the document regards as primarily the province of the arts, are not cognitive. Again, the assumption is that the arts involve *feeling*, not cognition and reason.

The Myth often underlies talk of a balanced curriculum. The suggestion is that the cognitive, rational faculty of the human mind is well catered for in, for instance, mathematics and the sciences, but in order to achieve balance we need to give more time to the *non*-cognitive, affective, emotional faculty, by giving greater emphasis to the arts. But again, formulating the argument in this way is disastrous in the damage it does to the case for the arts in education.

Before continuing, let me make two points clear. I certainly do not deny that there should be a better balance achieved, by giving greater opportunity for the arts. On the contrary, what I *am* saying is that this kind of argument, common though it is, is self-defeating, in that it *destroys* the case for the arts. For how can it be seriously claimed that the arts should have a central place in the curriculum if we ourselves insist that there is no place for learning in the arts? And let us be quite clear that that is the inevitable consequence of denying the place of cognition and rationality in the arts.

Second, I hope that I shall not be misunderstood as denying the importance of feeling in the arts. Far from it. My point is that in rightly insisting on the importance of feeling, we must *not* be denying the importance of reason and cognition.

I have argued that creativity should be central in all areas of the curriculum. Equally, all areas of the curriculum should involve feeling, albeit in different ways. Of course, it is true and important that, unlike the sciences, for instance, there is a sense in which the arts, and artistic judgments, can be partly an expression of individual feeling. But it is a serious failure if education in other areas does not stimulate a feeling for a subject. Although it is often used confusedly, this underlies what is important about appeals to intuition in the arts.

Once again, my point is that here too, it is seriously mistaken to think in terms of separate mental faculties, reflected in curriculum boxes, with the arts/feeling/creativity box quite separate from the science/mathematics/cognitive/reason box.

This confused Myth is sometimes given a pseudo-scientific dress by reference to the different functions of brain hemispheres. It is said that one hemisphere is concerned with the affective/creative, the other with the rational/ cognitive. The 'balance' argument is then formulated in terms of developing each hemisphere equally, i.e. it is argued that the current and traditional emphasis in education is to develop the rational/cognitive hemisphere at the expense of the creative/affective hemisphere. (It is sad to see an example of this confused argument in the Gulbenkian Report, *The Arts in Schools*, pp. 24-5.[6]) But without even considering the philosophical confusion involved in this way of thinking, I hope that, on reflection, one can see immediately how utterly bizarre it is as an *educational* justification for the arts. It would be on a par with arguing that a justification for painting in the curriculum is that holding paint brushes develops arm muscles.

It is, as we have seen, an expression of the Myth of the Separate Faculties to assume that the arts are a matter of feeling, not of reason or cognition. It is important to recognize clearly that in that case there could be no grounds for the notion of education in and through the arts. For how can there be education if understanding or cognition have no place?

The most that could be claimed on this subjectivist view is that emotional feelings can be *induced*, as in the case of sensations such as pain. Let us be clear that this is an inevitable consequence of insisting that the arts are concerned solely with *experience*, not understanding or rationality. Moreover, this subjectivist conception cannot give sense to the crucial notions of individual freedom and integrity of feeling, on which I want to lay considerable emphasis. It can no more allow for freedom than can the feeling induced by having one's finger hit by a hammer. Yet that is how the subjectivist construes emotions, as induced effects on a passive recipient. This assumption of the essentially passive nature of emotions runs deep in empiricist philosophy, and is still prevalent in psychology and arts-education. It is certainly manifest in the assumption that artistic creation and appreciation are matters of feeling *not* cognition, and thus that the arts consist in expressing and receiving experiences, rather than progressively developing *under-*

standing. There can be no freedom, no individual artistic development, no *education*, on this subjectivist basis, but only something like conditioned responses.

There clearly has to be a far *richer* relationship between the person and the work of art, between one's emotion and the work, to make sense of education, and individual freedom. Let me emphasize again that this is not in the least to deny the importance of *feeling* in the arts. It is to point out that we need a much richer conception of what an emotional experience is than is offered by the over-simple and severely limiting subjectivist account.

Emotional Feeling and Cognition

But can such a conception be provided, which will allow in the fullest sense for a rational, cognitive content of emotional experience? That is, can a conception be provided which can show that the supposed antithesis between feeling and reason is fundamentally misconceived? I argue that it certainly can be provided, and indeed that it is a distortion to regard emotions as non-rational experiences. Hence my sub-title, for I am not really arguing even for the *close* relation of feeling and reason, but rather that artistic feelings are *rational in kind*. There is a danger of implicitly conniving in the continuance of the Myth even to speak of the *relation* between feeling and reason. It is an instance of the disease of the dichotomous mind that my arguing for the crucial rationality of involvement with the arts so frequently incurs the accusation that I ignore feelings. Because of the pervasive grip of the Myth I shall have to pursue much of the discussion in terms of it. But let me repeat that my argument is for the essentially rational character of emotional experience of the arts.

In order to bring out fully the strength of this argument, and the dangerous weakness of the subjectivist Myth, both philosophically and educationally, let us approach the issue from another direction. According to the subjectivist, an emotion is a purely private mental event which may emerge in various ways. Wordsworth captures this notion aptly: 'All good poetry is the spontaneous overflow of powerful feelings.' On this view, an emotion wells up inside and overflows into artistic expression. One might refer to this version of subjectivism as the Hydraulic Theory of the Emotions, which well up, burst out, which one dams up, or releases by opening floodgates, etc.

There are at least two major mistakes involved in the Hydraulic Theory. First, it fails to recognize that there is a logical connection between the emotion and its object. Second, on this view, no understanding is necessary to have emotional feelings. Let us consider both these points together, since they are really impossible to separate. Why do I imply that there has to be a logical connection between an emotion and its object? It is fairly generally recognized in philosophy these days that a central feature of emotions is that they are directed onto objects of certain kinds — one is afraid of X, angry at Y, joyful about Z. But the object has to be understood in a certain way. For example, my feeling is likely to be very different if I take an object under my desk to be a rope from what it would be if I believe it to be a snake. There is a logical relation between my feeling, and my understanding or cognition of the object. I am likely to be afraid if I believe it to be snake, but not if I believe it to be a rope. That is, it makes no sense to suppose that one could normally have an emotional feeling about a wholly inappropriate object. Yet, to repeat, the subjectivist Hydraulic account construes the feeling as an inner event, entirely independent of any external circumstances. On that view it would have to make sense for normal people to be terrified of ordinary currant buns. But if one understands it as an ordinary currant bun, if one has that conception or cognition of it, then no sense can be made of being terrified of it.

It can be seen, then, that the subjectivist view is based upon an over-simple conception of emotional feeling. The subjectivist construes emotions on the model of sensations. Since it is true that certain kinds of understanding or cognition are not relevant to sensations such as pain, the subjectivist assumes, wrongly, that the same is true of emotional feeling. Yet it is precisely the crucial role of cognition which distinguishes emotions from sensations. For instance, if someone were to poke me with what I believe to be a soft rubber stick, which is in fact a sharp nail, I shall have a feeling of pain, i.e. *whatever* my cognition. By contrast, if I believe an object to be a snake which is in fact a rope, I shall be afraid. That is, cognition is inseparable from emotional feelings. The significance of this point to the case for the arts in education cannot be over-emphasized. To underline it again, an emotional feeling necessarily involves cognition or under-standing of the object of that feeling. For instance, the object has to be understood as threatening or harmful in some way for one to feel afraid of it. In the case of emotions the feeling is *determined* by and inseparable from cognition.

Gavin Bolton, in his splendid book *Drama as Education* writes on p. 147: 'aesthetic meanings are *felt* rather than comprehended'; while on p. 148 he rightly insists that perhaps the major contribution of drama in education is to do with bringing about a change in a participant's *understanding* of the world.[7] It is clear evidence of the difficulty of extricating oneself from the Myth of the Two Realms that even so thoughtful and perceptive a writer as Gavin Bolton can fall into self-contradiction on two successive pages. His main emphasis is, rightly (and ahead of many other arts-educators), on the crucial changes in understanding (i.e. cognition, conception) which can be brought about by an involvement with the arts. Yet he feels so uneasy about what he takes to be the *necessary* consequence of that view, namely a repudiation of *feeling*, that he unhappily includes that too. Thus, in effect, he asserts both that the arts are essentially a matter of feeling rather than comprehension, and that the arts are essentially a matter of changing our comprehension. With 'respect, I would suggest that he does not need to disown understanding while emphasizing feeling. He can, and should, have *both*. It is only the pervasive and pernicious Myth, based on an over-simple conception of mind, which makes him feel so uneasy about the supposedly inevitable choice between feeling and reason/cognition that he includes both at the cost of self-contradiction. But he is not forced to a choice, or to self-contradiction in rightly wanting both. On the contrary, to repeat, the kinds of feeling which are the province of the arts are given *only* by understanding, cognition, rationality. They are not possible for a creature incapable of such cognition.

A more coherent philosophy of mind greatly strengthens Bolton's case — and in general the case for the arts in education.

King Lear, in mental torment, buffeted, cold, drenched while wandering without shelter in the violent storm on the heath, is suddenly brought to a sharp realization of an aspect of life of which he had never been aware in his days of power:

> Poor naked wretches, whereso'er you are,
> That bide the pelting of this pitiless storm,
> How shall your houseless heads and unfed sides,
> Your looped and window'd raggedness, defend you
> From seasons such as these? O! I have ta'en
> Too little care of this. Take physic, Pomp,
> Expose thyself to feel what wretches feel...

Was it Lear's feeling which changed his understanding, or his new understanding which changed his feeling? To put the point in either way is misleading. The example reveals not that there are two distinct but closely related mental states here, but an essential characteristic of what it is for a person to experience emotional feelings. It would make no sense to attribute to Lear that feeling without his characterizing the object of his feeling in the way he does. Thus it is clearer to say that Lear's emotional feeling is an expression of his changed understanding.

It can already be seen what a big step forward this is towards an account of the arts as in the fullest sense educational. For, by contrast with subjectivism, it can be seen that emotional feelings are cognitive in kind; they necessarily involve understanding.

Of course, this account is too brief, but I hope it is sufficient at least to vindicate my earlier claim that subjectivism has a distortingly over-simple conception of emotional feelings. More important, I hope that it has vindicated my claim that a philosophical basis *can* be provided which will allow for the cognitive character of artistic feeling.

Reason

There is another important source of subjectivism. The subjectivist who assumes the Myth of the antithesis between Feeling and Reason has a distorted and over-simple conception not only of feeling, but also of reason. I hope I have already said enough to show clearly what is wrong with the subjectivist account of feeling. But he also believes that reasons are limited to the kinds of deductive and inductive reasons which are commonly used in mathematics, symbolic logic, and the sciences. This is to fail to recognize that crucial kind of reasoning, which I sometimes call 'interpretative reasoning'. This kind of reasoning is, in fact, important in *all* areas of knowledge — not only the arts, but also, for example, the sciences. I cannot deal with it adequately here. A more complete account appears elsewhere. [8]

Before going on to explain the character and significance of interpretative reasoning, it is worth pointing out how crucial it is to Critical Studies in Art. May I add that I am delighted to see the emergence of this development in art education. I have been disagreeing for years with the strange asymmetry in the ways in which the arts are taught. Predominantly, for instance, students study literature, and there is little or no creative writing. By contrast, traditionally, students have been exclusively concerned with the creation of visual arts, to the exclusion of the development of the ability for critical appreciation (which can, of course, add very significantly to creative artistic ability). In my view there should be opportunities for *both* kinds of approach in all the arts. I should add that this kind of reasoning applies equally to the creation and appreciation of the arts.

If one thinks of reasoning solely in terms of deductive or inductive reasoning, then it is understandable that arts-educators want to deny the relevance of reasoning in the arts, and are confirmed in their conviction that reasoning is *inimical* to artistic feeling. For it is then reasonable to suppose, as it is widely supposed, that emotional feeling distorts reasoning, and conversely, that reasoning inhibits and distorts feeling. Of course, both can be true. But not necessarily. The most appropriate way to respond to the suggestion that reason is incompatible with feeling is to deny that deductive and inductive reasoning are the only or even the most important kinds of reasoning. Interpretative reasoning involves, for instance, attempting to show a situation in a different light, and this may involve not only a different interpretation or conception, but also a different evaluation. It is important to recognize that, unlike the deductive reasoning typical of, for instance, syllogistic logic, interpretative reasons do not lead inexorably to universally valid conclusions. There may be sound reasons given for different interpretations and evaluations, and there may be no way in which it is possible to resolve those differences. So my insistence on the central place of rationality in no way conflicts with that central and exciting characteristic, the creative ambiguity of art. But it does show how genuine reasoning can be used to open up new perspectives, new visions, fresh evaluations.

As I have said, this kind of reasoning is equally important in the sciences. The importance of reasons for fresh interpretations in the sciences can hardly be exaggerated. Hermann Bondi, [9] the eminent astronomer and theoretical physicist, writes: 'Certain experiments that were interpreted in a particular way in their day we now interpret quite differently — but they were claimed as facts in those days.' The point, of course, is that a major change of interpretation was required to enable scientists to see in a different light the result of their experiments. There are numerous examples one could give from the sciences. This exposes another confusion of the Myth. For the ability to use and understand interpretative reasons involves imagination, creativity. So it makes no sense to assume that reasoning is distinct from or opposed to creativity and imagination.

More obvious examples of interpretative reasoning can be seen in the ways in which we support our conflicting opinions on social, moral and political issues. Again, such reasoning does not necessarily lead to agreed conclusions. But neither is it necessarily ineffective. Reasons given for seeing a situation in a different perspective may lead us to change our opinions.

There is no need to offer more examples of the numerous ways in which reasons may be given for seeing, understanding, evaluating a situation in a particular way. It is obvious, on reflection, just how common and widespread it is. Moreover, by contrast with the assumptions of the subjectivist, such reasoning is essentially liberating, in that it opens fresh horizons of understanding, new ways of seeing the world. Indeed, we can now see that it is subjectivisim which is so narrowly limiting, for on that view one is necessarily imprisoned in feelings and thoughts which are not open to reason. The subjectivist can give no sense to the notion of recognizing the validity of different interpretations. This underlines again that it is precisely the predominant subjectivist view which is so damaging educationally. It also underlines why a revolution of thought on the philosophical foundations of the arts in education is so urgently needed.

To repeat, so far from limiting or eradicating the possibility of differences of opinion, in the arts as in other areas of human life, the very existence of interpretative reasoning *depends* upon, and is an expression of, the variety of different conceptions, interpretations, opinions.

Feeling and Reason

I have been concerned to expose as narrow, distorting and damaging to the case for the arts in education the widely accepted conception of both feeling and reason assumed by the subjectivist. We have seen that emotional feelings are not separate from or opposed to cognition or understanding, but, on the contrary, an emotional feeling is an expression of a certain understanding of the object. We have also seen that reasons are not always of the kind which lead to inevitable conclusions, but that there are very important kinds of reasons which offer new interpretations and evaluations, yet which do not compel single, definitive conclusions. The third step is to see how such reasons can be inseparably involved with feelings.

Reasons given for a change of interpretation and evaluation may change the understanding and with it the feeling. Let me give an example which I often use, although there are numerous others. At the beginning of Shakespeare's play, Othello takes Desdemona to be a purely virtuous woman whom he idolizes and loves. It is that understanding or cognition, that way of seeing her, which identifies or determines his feeling. Iago gives him reasons for a different conception or understanding of her, as unfaithful and dishonest. Othello's new conception of her involves a change of feeling, to intense jealousy and anger, as a result of which he kills her. Too late, Iago's wife, Emilia, gives Othello further reasons for recognizing that it was Iago who was treacherous, and that Desdemona was totally innocent. These reasons change his conception again, and with it his feeling to one of intense remorse. In each case Othello's feeling cannot be separated from his understanding or conception of the object of his feeling — Desdemona. His feeling could be *identified* only in terms of his cognition. And, in at least two cases, it was reasoning which changed his conception, and with it his feeling.

There are many such examples, from our ordinary lives, where reasoning for a change of understanding and evaluating a situation inevitably involves a change of feeling about it.

Feeling and reason are *not* opposed. They are interdependent. Contrast this with subjectivists such as Witkin, who writes: 'The arts stand in relation to the intelligence of feeling much as the sciences do in relation to logical reasoning.'[10] On the contrary, as we have seen, the arts involve logical reasoning as much as the sciences. Indeed, it would be impossible to *have* artistic feelings if the arts were not essentially rational.

Of course, I am not for a moment suggesting that we always, necessarily, or even usually, reason our way to a feeling about a work of art. Neither am I in the least denying spontaneous artistic feelings. My point is that such feelings are always *answerable* to reason, in that they are always, in principle, open to the possibility of being changed by reasons given for seeing and feeling about a work in different ways. To repeat, cognition and rationality are inseparable from artistic feelings, whether spontaneous or not.

Education

It may be worth pointing out that I have run together two strands in subjectivism which are usually conflated by the subjectivist anyway. (a) The first is the purely causal notion adumbrated above, where emotions are construed on the model of sensations, with induced effects on passive recipients — rather like one's finger being hit by a hammer. (b) In the second strand, the emotion is regarded as not even causally induced, since absolutely *anything* is possible. This is the common subjectivist rejection of *any* notion of appropriateness, which is assumed to be somehow restrictive. In fact, so far from allowing complete individual freedom of feeling, this notion precludes any sense to emotional freedom. Moreover, there can be no sense to education on this view.

Neither strand can allow any place for understanding and rationality, which is precisely why neither can allow for education. By contrast, the thesis for which I am arguing offers, in a substantial sense, an account of education in and through the arts, by showing the central place in artistic feeling of cognition and reason.

A more striking consequence of my argument, which is commonly over-looked, yet which offers a very strong educational case for the arts, is that a vast range of feeling is possible *only* for creatures capable of the relevant kinds of rationality and cognition. In order to bring out what I mean, and in order further to indicate just how pervasive are the damaging kinds of subjectivism which I am criticizing, let me cite the well-known and influential theorist of art-education, Elliott Eisner. In a paper entitled 'Representing what one knows: the role of the arts in cognition and curriculum'[11] (a topic on which he has subsequently written a book) Eisner commendably recognizes the crucial place of cognition with respect to the fundamental justification of the arts in education. Roughly, the justification consists in showing that art contributes centrally to mental development. But while one applauds the attempt, Eisner gets himself badly out of his depth in philosophical difficulties of which he is clearly unaware. That he is unaware of the complexities involved is made abundantly clear in his opening sentence: 'My thesis is straightforward but not widely accepted.' In fact, on the contrary, as we shall see, the conception of mind on which he relies *is* widely accepted, but on examination it can be seen to be very far from straightforward. Let me illustrate. The clearest brief statement of his thesis is in an abstract of his paper, where Eisner writes:

> Humans not only have the capacity to form different kinds of concepts, they also, *because of their social nature* have the need to *externalise* and *share* what has been conceptualised. To achieve such an end, human beings have *invented ... forms of representation* (which) are the means by which *privately held conceptions* are transferred into *public images* so that the meaning they embody can be shared. (My italics)

This is an expression of the subjectivism outlined above, for instance in the Hydraulic Theory, which regards mental phenomena, such as thoughts and feelings, as independent of their possible forms of expression. It is assumed that human beings had thoughts — 'privately held conceptions' — *prior* to language, and that they *invented* language *subsequently* in order to share these thoughts with others. But this is entirely the wrong way around. I cannot have thoughts of the relevant kind privately, unless there is already a medium (e.g. a language, an art form) in which I can *formulate* or express those thoughts. It makes no sense to suppose that such thoughts could exist if there were not already the medium of formulation.

In the quotation above, Eisner states that because of his social nature man *invented* forms of representation and communication in order to share his privately held conceptions with others. He states that, with respect to each such private thought or idea, human beings have created 'a socially arbitrary sign whose meaning is conventionally defined to convey that meaning. Thus words and numbers are meaningful not because they look like their referents but because we have *agreed* that they shall stand for them' (my italics). But since, on Eisner's view, all these conceptions are purely *private*, how could people *agree* on what words and numbers shall stand for?[12] More accurately, how could there be *words* and *numbers*? There could, on this view, only be unintelligible marks or sounds. The notion of words and numbers already implies publicly shared meanings. Although this thesis is explicitly stated by Eisner, it is worth emphasizing that such a thesis, even if not explicitly stated, is very common indeed among not only arts-educators but psychologists, linguists and many others. Hence it is worth taking the risk of repetition to make as clear as possible its fatal defects. Remember that on this thesis we are supposed to begin with each person as it were logically locked within his own mind; one's thoughts are purely private. Yet one is supposed to be able to *invent* a language which *others* can understand, in order that people can communicate with each other. But to be able to agree on meanings requires that we can *already* communicate with each other, and thus that we already have shared meanings. This becomes clear if we contrast language with a code. We can agree on the meanings of code signs only because we already have a shared language of communication in which to discuss the matter and come to agreement. Clearly it makes no sense to suppose that language itself could be invented in the same way, since, on this thesis, we are supposed to begin the enterprise without any possibility of shared meanings, and thus communication.

According to this view, no one else can ever know my private thoughts since this would require someone else's getting access to my mind to 'see' what I am thinking. And obviously I cannot *tell* others what I am thinking since, according to this thesis, there is as yet no language of communication.

The point is aptly brought out by Humpty Dumpty:

'There's glory for you!'
'I don't know what you mean by glory,' Alice said.
Humpty Dumpty smiled contemptuously: 'Of course you don't — till I tell you. I meant "There's a nice knock-down argument for you".'
'But "glory" doesn't mean "There's a nice knock-down argument for you",' Alice objected.
'When *I* use a word,' Humpty Dumpty said in rather a scornful tone, 'it means just what I choose it to mean — neither more nor less.'

The point illustrated here is that despite Humpty Dumpty's contemptuous insistence to the contrary, he inevitably has to rely upon linguistic meanings which are already there, which could not be a matter of choice or invention, in order to explain the abnormal case when he does choose or invent an arbitrary meaning for a word.

Clearly, then, language and the arts cannot be merely the overt symbolic expressions, for public communication, of purely private conceptions and feelings. It is rather the very opposite, that only because there are already linguistic and artistic forms of expression is it possible for an individual to have private thoughts and feelings of the relevant kinds. (For obvious reasons, I exclude the instinctive kinds of feelings which even an animal can have. They are not relevant to our concerns.) What gives initial plausibility to the subjectivist thesis of such as Eisner is a concentration on what appear to be simple cases like the meanings of 'dog', 'chair', 'red', and 'blue', where it might seem that one can just invent words to express one's private conceptions. (In fact, even these cases are more complex than at first appears. For instance, they depend upon the assumption that meaning is denotational, i.e., that the meaning of a word is what it names. That may be plausible for 'dog' and 'chair', but it is hardly plausible for 'if' and 'but'. However, I cannot digress to discuss that question. I have dealt with it more fully elsewhere.[13]) But there is not even initial plausibility if we consider cases such as the ability to think about, or to have feelings such as remorse or hope for, events in the distant past or future. It is obvious, even on cursory reflection, that language is a precondition of such thoughts and feelings. It would make no sense, for instance, to attribute to a dog feelings of remorse about biting the postman last week, or hope that his master will take him for a walk next week.

As I have tried to show, those who propound this subjectivist thesis inevitably have implicitly to help themselves to a notion of shared meaning *at the outset* which that thesis is explicitly denying. Such shared meaning must be presupposed to any possibility of understanding and communication. This is brought out particularly clearly when Eisner writes (pp. 18-19) that if you do not know what 'feckless' and 'mountebank' mean 'then you turn to a friend or dictionary for words whose images allow you to create an analogy.' Quite apart from the fundamental, but common, misconception of regarding the meanings of words as images,[14] it is clear that, on Eisner's view that concepts are private, it would be senseless to suggest that one should turn to a friend, since it would be impossible to understand *his* private concepts. The appeal to a dictionary reveals the misconception even more vividly, for how can one make any sense of the notion of a dictionary except where there is already a shared language? How could one understand the explanations otherwise? How could a dictionary be compiled on Eisner's view that conceptions are private? What this example shows is that, contrary to Eisner's thesis, a shared language is a precondition of communication and understanding. It certainly cannot be, as Eisner supposes, that a shared language is constructed out of numerous privately held concepts. It is not, as Eisner asserts, that '*because of their social nature* (humans) have the need to externalize and share' private conceptions. That would make sharing and the 'social nature' of man unintelligible. It is the precise opposite, namely that it is only *because* of shared language and other modes of communication that the social nature peculiar to humans is possible.

Precisely similar considerations apply to the arts, in that it is possible to express oneself and communicate only if there is already a shared artistic medium. But anyway no sharp distinction can be drawn between language and the arts, since both are part of that amalgam of social practices which together comprise a culture, and which to a large extent set the parameters of possible thought and feeling of those brought up in it.

By contrast, then, with Eisner's thesis, I am arguing that artistic feelings are necessarily *dependent* upon an understanding of the relevant art forms. Although an animal may respond to art — my neighbour's dog howls at Beethoven — it is incapable of *artistic* response precisely because of its lack of understanding. Thus, contrary to subjectivism, the Myth, and the Hydraulic Theory, it is only because we are capable of *cognition* and *rationality* that we can have artistic *feelings*.

Reason and Freedom

On the subjectivist view, I am permanently confined to the inner feelings I have. I can only impose them on other people, situations, works of art. Simone Weil points out how regrettably often we *invent* what other people are thinking and feeling. That is, we impose our feelings upon them because we have not developed the imaginative ability to move *outside* our own prejudices and preconceptions to appreciate what *they* — the *other* people — think and feel. The same is true of artistic appreciation. We need progressively to learn to enter objectively into what is expressed in the work of art, rather than imposing our feelings upon it.

I offer the deliberately provocative phrase 'the liberating emotional power of objective reasoning'. 'Objective' is by contrast with rationalization, which consists in manipulating reasons, even if unconsciously, merely to support one's subjective preconceptions. It is by coming to see objectively the characteristics of other people, situations, and works of art, that we are progressively liberated, in both understanding and feeling. No such liberation is possible on a subjectivist view, since one is confined to the feelings one has. Neither different understanding nor different reasoning can affect feelings for a subjectivist, which is precisely why he can give no account of the *educational* credentials of the arts.

Education and the Rationality of Feeling

On a subjectivist thesis, even if it made sense, the most which could be claimed for the arts (and language) is that they give the possibility of expression to thoughts and feelings which people already have. Thus there could be no sense in the notion of educating the feelings themselves. A coherent philosophical account shows that the feelings are given by conceptions implicit in the media of expression — the arts and language. Without those conceptions the feelings could not exist. Since the kinds of feelings which are involved in the arts are given only by conceptual understanding, cognition, rationality, one can learn, by means of reasons, different conceptions of art which can change one's feelings in response to it and indeed to life generally.

This opens up a far more powerful educational case for the arts. Thoughts and feelings are not immured inaccessibly in purely private minds, but are given by forms of expression in social practices. In introducing his students to the creative possibilities of the vast and continuously extending range of artistic conceptions, the arts-educator is giving them the possibility of an extended and more discriminated range of feelings. By contrast with subjectivism, this shows how the sensitive arts-educator can help his students to *develop* their individuality of thought and feeling.

In short, in learning to understand the art form one is *ipso facto* extending the range of feelings it is possible to have — i.e., not just the expression of already existent feelings, but the *feelings themselves*.

The sharp contrast between my thesis and that of Eisner is apparent. It can also be seen how much stronger is the educational case for the arts on my view. For it makes no sense to suppose that language and the arts were invented in order to express privately held concepts and feelings. It is rather that, to a very large extent, men have the concepts and feelings, and therefore the character, that they do have, *because* of language and the arts. As we have seen, an art form is not a construct out of private, individual thoughts and feelings, but a precondition of the relevant thoughts and feelings. And, given the enormously important relation of art to life, the implications for the arts in education are very considerable. For, to put it starkly, it is not that man creates language and the arts, but that, in a very important sense, language and the arts create man.

Conclusion

The subjectivist Myth of the inevitable opposition between feeling and reason dies hard. In fact, it shows no sign yet even of early symptoms of a terminal disease. We should recognize the urgent need for a revolution of thought in order to provide a sound philosophical ground for the arts in education. Accountability is demanded of all subjects in the curriculum these days. But accountability depends not only on what we do, but also on what we *say* about what we do, i.e., on the *justification* we offer for the importance of the arts in education. We need not only high quality arts, but high quality arguments for the place of the arts in the curriculum.

The common saying that the arts are a matter of subjective feeling, not of reason and cognition, is seriously damaging to the case for the arts in education. It is even more damaging that those who say it are arts-educators themselves.

We need to reject the still prevalent subjectivist clichés, and to insist that artistic feeling is itself essentially rational and cognitive.

Notes and References

1. MALCOLM ROSS (Ed.) *The Development of Aesthetic Experience*, Pergamon Press, 1982.
2. ROBERT WITKIN, 'Art in Mind: reflections on *The Intelligence of Feeling*'. (Ed.) CONDOUS, HOWLETT and SKULL, *Arts in Cultural Diversity*, Sydney: Holt, Rinehart and Winston, 1980.
3. D. H. LAWRENCE, in *Selected Literary Criticism*, ed. ANTHONY BEAL, London: Heinemann, 1955, pp. 125.
4. *The Arts in Schools*. London: Calouste Gulbenkian Foundation, 1982.
5. 'Towards a Policy for Expressive Arts in the Primary School.' Scottish Committee on Expressive Arts in the Primary School, 1984.
6. *Op. cit.*
7. GAVIN BOLTON, *Drama as Education*, Harlow, Essex, Longman Group, 1984.
8. DAVID BEST, *Feeling and Reason in the Arts*, London: George Allen and Unwin, 1985.

9. HERMANN BONDI, 'The achievements of Karl Popper', *The Listener*, Vol. 88, no. 2265, 1972, pp. 225–9.
10. ROBERT WITKIN, *op. cit.*
11. ELLIOTT EISNER, 'Representing what one knows: the role of the arts in cognition and curriculum'. *Report of the INSEA World Congress, Rotterdam*. Amsterdam: De Trommel, 1981, pp. 17–23.
12. I consider this problem more fully in *Feeling and Reason in the Arts*, Chapter 7.
13. DAVID BEST, *Expression in Movement and the Arts*, London; Lepus Books, Henry Kimpton Publishers, 1974, pp. 15–54.
14. See *Feeling and Reason in the Arts*, pp. 99–100.

Part IV

The Demise of Modernism

At the heart of this volume and the series of which it is a part is the proposition that Modernism, as a triumphant internationalist movement, is over. A number of reasons for holding such a view were given in the opening chapter of *Living Powers* (1987). In this section some of the essential evidence is provided.

Ernst Gombrich gives an analysis of the intimate relationship between the nineteenth century philosopher Hegel, the notion of the avant-garde and the idea of historicism. Denis Donoghue in his contribution diagnoses the sterile intellectualism of many modern 'works of art' and accuses modern critical theory of denying the true aesthetic and imaginative power of great art. Arthur Danto in his chapter, drawing also on Hegel, argues that 'the time for next things is past', while Peter Fuller sees that proposition as the necessary condition for a profound renewal of aesthetic activity.

Chapter 9

'The Father of Art History': On the Influence of Hegel

Ernst Gombrich

Introduction: Hegel and the Modern Study of Art

Georg Wilhelm Friedrich Hegel should be called the father of the history of art, or at any rate of the history of art as I have always understood it. We are of course accustomed to the idea that sons rebel against their fathers, and if we are to believe the psychologists, they do this because they want, and indeed need, to break away from the overpowering influence of paternal authority. I still believe that the history of art should free itself of Hegel's authority, but I am convinced that this will only be possible once we have learned to understand his overwhelming influence.

The role of the father of art history which I have assigned to Hegel is usually attributed to Johann Joachim Winckelmann; but it seems to me that rather than Winckelmann's *History of Ancient Art* of 1764, it is Hegel's *Lectures on Aesthetics* (1820-9) which should be regarded as the founding document of the modern study of art, since they contain the first attempt ever made to survey and systematize the entire universal history of art, indeed of all the arts. Hegel himself looked up to Winckelmann as one who, in his words, 'in the field of art was able to awaken a new organ and to open up totally new methods of approach to the human mind'.[1] But Winckelmann's concept of art was quite different from Hegel's. For him the essence of art lay in the Greek ideal. Just as his predecessor Vasari had written about the rebirth of his artistic ideal, so Winckelmann was concerned with the development of this exemplary art to absolute perfection. At the same time he saw his work as a *Lehrgebäude*, a theoretical treatise, aiming to demonstrate, through the example of Greek art, what beauty was. Hegel, if I may simplify for a moment, incorporated this theory into his philosophical system, but restricted its range of validity. The credit for having given classical shape to sensuous beauty still went indisputably to the Greeks, but Classicism itself only represents one phase of art, as the history of art can no more stand still than history itself.

I would like to try to formulate briefly what Hegel took over from Winckelmann and how he broadened the scope of that static system to form a universal history of art as we know it today. He found three fundamental ideas in Winckelmann which he incorporated into his own structure of ideas. The most important is the firm belief in the divine dignity of art. Just as Winckelmann in his famous hymn to the beauty of the Apollo of Belvedere is really celebrating the visible presence of the divine in a work of man, so too Hegel ultimately saw in all art a manifestation of transcendent values. It is a point of view which Plato consciously rejected, but which Neoplatonism brought back into circulation in European intellectual life, for it credits the artist with the ability to behold the Idea itself in its supernatural realm and to reveal it to others. I may perhaps call this metaphysical faith in art *aesthetic transcendentalism*, with the warning that it is not of course to be confused with Kant's transcendental aesthetics. This aesthetic transcendentalism tinged with Neoplatonism certainly appears less pronounced in Winckelmann's approach than it does in the philosophy of his friend and rival, Anton Raphael Mengs, yet Winckelmann's cult of beauty nevertheless draws its justification from there. The second fundamental idea that Hegel took over can be described as *historical collectivism*. By this I mean the role that is assigned to the collective, to the nation. For Winckelmann, Greek art is not so much the work of individual masters as the expression or the reflection of the Greek spirit, with the concept of spirit not yet quite containing the metaphysical overtones that it has in Hegel, but being much closer to Montesquieu's *Esprit des lois*. Thirdly, even in Winckelmann this consummate expression is the end result of a development, in fact of a development whose intrinsic logic is intelligible. The stages of Greek art, the progression of style, led of necessity to what Winckelmann calls the 'beautiful style', passing through the phase of the noble or austere style, and leading inevitably to decline, by making concessions to sensual pleasure. In this third instance we can talk of an *historical determinism* which explains why, for all its perfection, Greek art already bore within it the seeds of its own downfall.[2]

It is clear that this determinism is to some extent incompatible with what Winckelmann felt to be his mission: the call to emulate Greek works and to return to the Golden Age of art. This flaw in Winckelmann's doctrine was all the more evident to his German contemporaries as they were struggling to gain awareness of the independent identity of their national art. Here I am thinking primarily of Herder, but also of Schiller, whose essay, 'Über naive und sentimentalische Dichtung', aims to do justice to the Golden Age of classical Greece, without regarding it as an absolute.

The Philosophy of Progress

Those were the years in which this ancient dream of a Golden Age became unexpectedly topical. It seemed as if human reason only needed to take control of the reins to make the dream come true. I am here speaking of the French Revolution, which Hegel also regarded as virtually a cosmic event. 'For as long as the sun has shone in the firmament and the planets have revolved about it,' he says in the *Philosophy of History*,

> man has not been seen to stand on his head, that is on his thoughts, and to construct reality accordingly ... All thinking beings have celebrated this era ... an enthusiasm of the spirit filled the world with awe, as though the divine had at last come to a true reconciliation with the world.[3]

I am convinced that Hegel's philosophy, which I would like to describe as *metaphysical optimism*, can only really be understood in relation to this event. Like many of his contemporaries, he looked at the developments preceding the triumph of reason from the standpoint of this climactic event, and even in the stages of natural evolution, from dead matter through plants and the animal kingdom to man, he found confirmation of his theory that the entire historical process was a necessary development leading to the emergence of the self-knowing spirit.

Like other ideas, Hegel had certainly adopted the belief that art plays an important role in this cosmic process from his boyhood friend Schelling. The three sections on the religion of art in Hegel's difficult early work *The Phenomenology of Spirit* (1806) are on the whole couched in such abstract terms that the actual history of art plays no part in them, yet it seems to me that even here, as in the subsequent *Encyclopaedia* (1817), Winckelmann's three fundamental ideas lie behind the abstractions. For here too art is essentially theophany, the unveiling of the divine, and here too it is bound to an historical collective. In Hegel's words, 'the work of art can only be an expression of the Divinity if ... it takes and extracts ... without adulteration ... the indwelling spirit of the nation'.[4] Thus, just as aesthetic transcendentalism and collectivism are raised to the status of dynamic principles, so the logic of development in Winckelmann is elevated into universal determinism. For art also has a part to play in the self-creation of the spirit, which takes place with all the compelling force of a syllogism and thus the history of art is also seen as 'revealing the truth ... which is manifest in the history of the world.'[5]

The metaphysical optimism proclaimed in these words now necessarily carries with it a further principle, which is no less fundamental to Hegel's conception of the history of art than it is to his interpretation of all other historical events: I am talking about the principle of relativism, which in Hegel's work is a result of the dialectic. As far as the history of art is concerned, this *dialectic relativism*, which is itself again relative, only really first becomes important in the *Lectures on Aesthetics*.

The Lectures on Aesthetics

These lectures, which Hegel gave four times in Berlin, are known to us through the loving reconstruction by his student Hotho, who used Hegel's notes for his lectures as well as the notes that his students took. For this reason perhaps one ought not to weigh each word too carefully, but on the whole they bear the stamp of indisputable authenticity. Like other works of Hegel, they are hardly an easy read. The abstract presentation, of which I do not need to give examples, often becomes abstruse, but when the reader is about to lose patience he is occasionally reconciled by a passage that appears to be rooted in living experience.

Hegel had a genuine feeling for painting, and incidentally for music too, but his knowledge of the actual history of art was so scarce that he let himself be hoaxed into believing that the tomb of Count Engelbert II von Nassau in Breda was the work of Michelangelo. Nevertheless, Hegel had a clear notion of what he called the requirements of scholarship, 'the precise familiarity with the vast realm of individual works of art, both ancient and modern'. According to him scholarship in the field of art also demands, 'a wealth of historical, and also very specialized knowledge, as the individuality of a work of art is related to something individual and thus requires detailed knowledge if it is to be understood and explained.'[6] He speaks with gratitude of the achievement of connoisseurs, yet rightly recalls that they occasionally limit their knowledge of a work of art to its purely external aspects and 'have little notion' of the true nature of the work of art '... not knowing the value of deeper studies ... they dismiss them.'[7] Naturally these deeper studies were what mattered to Hegel. His aim was to prove the validity of what to him was an essential, comforting belief in universal reason, by showing that the history of art could be perceived in the terms of those steadily evolving principles which in his philosophy determine all events. Even where such an undertaking appears misguided, the reader cannot fail to be struck by the consistency with which Hegel sets about extracting the meaning allotted to every art form, to every age and to every style. This very consistency was necessary in order to help emphasize the real heart of his doctrine, namely the dialectic, which firmly anchored the metaphysical optimism in relativism.

This connection can most easily be explained by again referring to the Classicism of antiquity, which for Hegel culminated in Greek sculpture. For as an art form sculpture stands somewhere between architecture, which is still inextricably bound to matter, and painting, which represents the more advanced process of spiritualization, as its real subject is light — a thought which perhaps stems from Herder.[8]

Of course for Hegel even painting represents only a stage to be passed through before coming to music, which is an almost completely dematerialized art form, and music must in turn give way to poetry, which deals with pure meaning. The value of all the arts is again, however, relative, as 'art is far ... from being the highest form of expression of the spirit'; it is dissolved by reflection and replaced by pure thought, by philosophy, as a result of which art belongs to the past.[9]

For Hegel, therefore, the art of antiquity, as Winckelmann had perceived, certainly forms the centre-piece of the true history of art, but its perfection was confined to a limited phase of the life of the spirit, for just as long as it was still possible to represent the gods as visible beings. What precedes the art of antiquity is a less conscious stage: Oriental art. Hegel calls this pre-art (*Vorkunst*) and, following the Neoplatonist Creuzer, he attributes to it a particular form of symbolism which is not yet adequate to the spirit. [10] Hegel had the fortune, or the misfortune, to write about ancient Egyptian art just before the hieroglyphs were deciphered, and thus before the picture of Egyptian civilization was radically altered. For Hegel, Egypt

> is the land of the symbol and sets itself the spiritual task of self-deciphering the spirit, without really attaining its end. The problems remain unsolved and the solution which we are able to provide consists therefore merely of interpreting the riddles of Egyptian art and its symbolic works as a problem that the Egyptians themselves left undeciphered ... [11] As a symbol for this proper meaning of the Egyptian spirit, we may mention the Sphinx. It is, as it were, the symbol of the symbolic itself ... recumbent animal bodies out of which the human body is struggling ... The human spirit is trying to force its way forward out of the dumb strength and power of the animal, without coming to a perfect portrayal of its own freedom and animated shape. [12]

Thus an unexplained monument of art becomes for Hegel a metaphor for the spirit of the entire age. And once firm in his opinion that at that time the spirit, like the Sphinx, remained shackled to the animal, he was also able to state that:

> the Egyptians constructed their towering religious buildings in the same instinctive way in which bees build their cells ... Self-awareness has not yet come to fruition and is not yet complete in itself, but pushes on, searching, conjecturing, continually producing, without attaining absolute satisfaction and therefore always restless. [13]

It is not difficult to see how much this dramatic picture of the struggling spirit owes to the principle of the dialectic, for it essentially represents a negation of the Classical ideal which Hegel, as well as Winckelmann, saw translated into reality in the art of Ancient Greece. Yet no matter how often Hegel refers to Winckelmann in the passages concerned, he still saw, with remarkable lucidity, that the sixty years which separated him from his model had radically transformed the image of Greek sculpture. The new awareness of the sculpture of Aegina, and above all of the Parthenon, inevitably altered the emphasis. [14] In fact, Hegel is one of the first virtually to dismiss the Belvedere Apollo, with a joke taken from an English journal describing it as a 'theatrical coxcomb', and to describe the Laocoon as a late work already declining into Mannerism. [15] It may be that he did not care much for these works. He had never been to Italy and looked for reasons to explain 'why the sculpture of antiquity leaves us somewhat cold ... we feel at once more at home with painting ... in paintings we see something that works and is active within ourselves.' [16]

A crucial point in Hegel's view of history was the idea that sculpture belonged to pagan antiquity and painting to the Christian era, which he called the Romantic age. This construction rested on the coincidence that marble statues survive more easily than paintings. Hegel knew of course that the ancient Greeks held their painters, such as Zeuxis and Apelles, in no less esteem than they did their sculptors, and he was not entirely happy with this interpretation of painting as a subjective, romantic art form. But since, as he cautiously says, the inmost heart of the Greek outlook corresponds more closely 'with the principle of sculpture than with any other art ... the backwardness of painting in relation to sculpture is only to be expected.' [17] Whatever the truth may be, Hegel's efforts to examine each art form according to its ability to express certain spiritual values led him to describe the painter's medium with a clarity that has rarely been equalled, before or since, in the history of art.

For us, the notion of the 'painterly' is linked with the name of Heinrich Wölfflin, who in his *Principles of Art History* so articulately described the development of style from sculpture to painting. We should recall that Hegel too believed that the sculptural necessarily precedes the 'painterly'. Thus Hegel talks of the plastic-sculptural element in painting and describes the problems of composition in painting in a passage which could almost have been written by Wölfflin:

> The next type of arrangement still remains entirely architectural, a homogeneous juxtaposition of the figures, or a regular opposition and symmetrical conjunction both of the figures themselves and of their attitudes and movements. The pyramidal form of the group is very popular here ... In the Sistine Madonna too this type of grouping is still retained as decisive. In general it is restful to the eye because the pyramid draws together by its apex what would otherwise be a scattered juxtaposition, and gives the group an external unity. [18]

But the painter who, as Hegel says, uses all the means available to him in his art, [19] the 'painterly' painter, finds still more possibilities of development and thus, in the course of the artistic evolution that Hegel exhaustively describes, Dutch seventeenth-century painting virtually becomes an end in itself.

It would indeed be worthwhile to assemble a small anthology of the passages in which, tired of arid disquisitions, Hegel gives us his spontaneous reaction to painting. The grinding noise of his conceptual mill is silenced, giving way to a real love of the work of art. A brief example must again suffice:

> While classical art essentially gives shape in its presentation if its ideal only to what is solid, here we have, arrested and brought before our eyes, the fleeting expressions of changing Nature — a stream, a waterfall, the foaming waves of the ocean, a still life with random flashes of glasses and plates etc, the external shape of spiritual reality in the most specific situations: a woman threading a needle by the light, a band of robbers frozen in movement, the most transient aspect of a gesture, the laughing and guffawing of a peasant; in all this Ostade, Teniers and Steen are masters ... [20] But even though heart and thought remain unsatified, closer inspection reconciles us. For it is the art of painting and the painter that should delight and thrill us. And in fact if we want to know what painting is, we must look at these small pictures in order to say of this or of that master: now he can really paint ... [21]

Hegel had been to the Netherlands and was obviously filled with enthusiasm for Dutch paintings. Whereas his description of Italian art is largely based on the fundamental work by Rumohr, which had just been published, his writing here is based entirely on his own observations. There is still perhaps an ideological element in this. The Romanizing sympathies of the Nazarenes had spoiled for many the pleasure in the recently discovered, so-called 'primitive' Italian painters, whereas in Holland Hegel could enjoy the triumph of protestantism both in and through the paintings. 'It would not have occurred to any other people, under any other circumstances, to portray subjects like those that confront us in Dutch paintings as the principal content of a work of art.' Hegel finds the justification for their choice of subjects in 'their sense of a self-earned freedom, through which they have attained well-being, comfort, integrity, spirit, gaiety and even a pride in their cheerful daily life'.[22]

If we like, we can still see even in this glorification of the Dutch people a reflection of Winckelmann's idealizing of the Greeks. And as was the case with Winckelmann, it follows from Hegel's system that such a blossoming bears within it the seeds of its own dissolution. The 'colour magic' of painting brings an inevitable transition to music. When analyzing this art form, Hegel also surprises us by showing a lively enthusiasm for Mozart and Rossini, which contrasts strangely with his somewhat laboured attempts at a purely conceptual edifice.

One thing is certain. As far as Hegel was concerned, his aesthetic theory of categories formed an integral part of his total system of philosophy, for, as is stated in the *Aesthetics*,

> only the whole of philosophy can be equated with the knowledge of the universe as the *one* organic totality in itself ... within the crowning circle of this scientific necessity each single part is on the one hand a circle turning in on itself, while on the other hand it has a simultaneous and necessary connection with other parts — a backwards from which it is derived and a forwards towards which it drives itself, in so far as it fruitfully engenders an 'other' out of itself again, making it accessible to scientific knowledge.[23]

There is obviously something extremely seductive about a system like this, in which every conceivable natural, spiritual and historical phenomenon has its place, and precisely because Hegel was the last and the most consistent person to construct such a system, this philosophy did not lose its effect when the influence of his metaphysics dwindled.

Determinism in Art History

Hegel's spiritual succession is not confined to philosophers who subscribe to every definition in his *Encyclopaedia*. It is indeed well known that Karl Marx, for example, opposed to Hegel's thesis of the primacy of the spirit the antithesis of the primacy of matter, in order, to use the famous double meaning of the dialectic, both to cancel and to preserve the system (*aufheben*). His is the most influential but by no means the only attempt to secularize, as it were, the Hegelian metaphysics, without thereby sacrificing the synopsis of at least all historical events. In my essay 'In Search of Cultural History',[24] I tried to demonstrate the extent to which the leading champions of art history and cultural history in the German-speaking countries came under the spell of Hegel. The striving to 'reconstruct' the spirit of the age through art runs from Carl Schnaase, through Jacob Burckhardt, Heinrich Wölfflin, Karl Lamprecht, Alois Riegl and Max Dvořák to Erwin Panofsky. Brief as my analysis was, I neither want to nor can repeat it here. One matter however is close to my heart. I do not wish to create the impression that I lack respect for these masters. It cannot be too often repeated that the best tribute that one can pay a scholar is to take him seriously and constantly to reappraise his lines of argument. I would be the last to demand that art and cultural history should give up seeking relationships between phenomena and remain content with listing them. If that had been my aim, I would certainly not have concerned myself with Hegel. What gave me pause was not the belief that it is hard to establish such relationships but, paradoxically, that it often seems all too easy. The gigantic structure of Hegel's aesthetic can itself serve as proof of this observation. Although his virtuosity is evident, we have already seen how, in his interpretation of Egyptian art, he tried to slip from the metaphorical into the factual, and how he relegated a figure like Apelles to the verge of Greek art, to fit in with his construction of the historical sequence of the arts.

Even the professional historian succumbs easily to the temptation to *corriger la fortune*. Ultimately every historical account is, and indeed must be, selective. It is thus natural to confine oneself to what appears to be significant and to neglect that which appears less essential. Karl Popper, the great methodologist of science, has made me sensitive to the dangerous allures of these siren songs.[25] The true scientist does not seek confirmation of his hypotheses; he is primarily on the look-out for contrary examples. A theory which cannot conflict with anything has no scientific content. The danger of the Hegelian heritage lies precisely in its temptingly easy applicability. After all, the dialectic makes it all too easy for us to find a way out of every contradiction. Because it seems to us as though everything in life is really interconnected, every method of interpretation can claim success. Here it depends above all on a plausible point of departure. 'The artist must eat', we read in Lessing and since artists cannot indeed paint without eating, it is certainly possible to base a credible system of art history on the needs of the stomach.

All these attempts at interpretations often make me think of the old anecdote about the farmer who had sold a pig for 300 crowns. He is sitting comfortably in the inn with his sack of coins in front of him. He empties it onto the table and begins to count, 'One, two, three.' He gets to ten, then fifty, then a hundred and begins to yawn — 150, 180, 181. Suddenly he sweeps the money together and shoves it back into the sack. 'But what on earth are you doing?' his companions ask him. 'It's been right up to now, so the rest will be right,' the farmer replies.

I do not imagine of course that I am the first or indeed the only art historian who likes to check. On the contrary, I have often asked myself whether today, nearly one and a half centuries after Hegel's death, my polemic against certain interpretations of history is not perhaps a case of tilting at windmills. And yet I have found often enough that it is not windmills that one is charging, but real giants. I have already mentioned five of these giants by their weird names. They are *aesthetic transcendentalism, historical collectivism, historical determinism, metaphysical optimism* and *relativism*. They are all related to the mythical Proteus, since they remain constant in every metamorphosis.

Transcendentalism, the idea of art as revelation, survived in a secularized form. Though no longer the manifestation of the self-realizing spirit, the work of art is still seen as the expression of the spirit of the age, which, as it were, remains visible across its surface. The word 'expression', with its elusive ambiguity, facilitates this transition, enabling the historian to disclose the philosophy of an age, or its economic conditions, behind the work of art. What is common to both methods is the connection with collectivism. The individual work of art is seen in terms of its style, which should now be interpreted as a symptom, a manifestation of class, race, culture or the age.

Determinism now assumes an explicit, or at least implicit, key role in this method. The very essence of the Hegelian heritage lies in the *a priori* conviction that the Gothic style is a necessary result of feudalism or of scholasticism, or that all three phenomena are merely different manifestations of the same underlying principle. Now, it may well be conceded that both direct and indirect connections exist between these disparate phenomena. The question is merely to find the point at which, to use a variation on one of Hegel's favourite expressions, triviality turns into absurdity. Certainly historical determinism has found so many opponents that the question would appear to be settled, if ever a question could be settled. There is no need to make any decision here about the problem of causality, of the validity of natural laws or of free will, in order to refute the idea that the course of history follows necessary development. Thus the Nobel Prize winner from Göttingen, Manfred von Eigen, emphasized recently that we can accept the validity of the laws of nature without this being a sufficient reason to conclude that history follows an irrevocable and pre-determined course.[26] I often like to compare the multifarious influences that lie behind artistic creation with the influence that climate has on vegetation. No one will deny that this dependency exists, and the fact that the vegetation in turn influences the climate may also recommend the comparison to partisans of the dialectic. It is even possible to learn of variations in the climate from looking at the annual rings of an old tree. And yet the calculation is only of limited validity, for the mutual effect is not produced by these two factors alone; numerous other factors, which cannot be calculated in advance or reconstructed, come into play. It is worth remembering that the chance importation of a couple of rabbits into Australia nearly led to the entire land being completely stripped of vegetation. You cannot get around the reality of chance.

I know of course that in the second edition of the *Encyclopaedia* Hegel explained the famous sentence taken from his Philosophy of Law, 'Whatever is rational (*vermünftig*) is real and whatever is real is rational', to the effect that what he understood by reality was 'not the merely empirical … existence mingled with chance but the existence that is inseparable from the concept of reason'.[27] Ultimately, however, this attempt at salvage is based on a circular argument, for if chance does not concern it either. For time and time again history bears out the old proverb, '*Kleine Ursachen, grosse Wirkungen*' (small causes, great effects: tall oaks from little acorns grow) — a veritable spell which once and for all lays the ghost of historical determinism.

This really appears so obvious that we have to ask ourselves why people so often resist this insight. Maybe the power of chance hurts our self-esteem. We talk about blind, senseless or stupid coincidence and even find misfortune, both in life and history, easier to bear, if we regard it as unavoidable fate. How much easier it would be if we shared Hegel's metaphysical optimism, which tries to convince us that ultimately everything is for the best. The wish gives birth to the thought, in whatever way faith in a pre-determined happy ending to the cosmic play may be formulated. Granted that not all determinists are also optimists. Oswald Spengler, for example, who had so much in common with Hegel, prophesied the inevitable decline of the Western world. On the other hand, of course, the essential factor in metaphysical optimism is that there cannot and ought not to be any decline or deterioration which does not pave the way for a higher form of development.

I do not think I am too far wrong if I also describe this relativism as the official dogma, so to speak, of contemporary art historical teaching, in so far as it has embraced determinism. One cannot condemn that which is unavoidable, any more than a geologist can condemn the Ice Age. Certainbly it was some time before art historians came to adopt this attitude, which goes far beyond Hegel in its levelling tendency. According to Hegel there is naturally a decline, even if it does serve progress. Today it is considerd scientific to eradicate the concept of decline from the art historian's vocabulary wherever possible, so as to allot every era that was once condemned, its rightful place in the chain of development. The vindication of Gothic art in the eighteenth century was accepted even by Hegel. Later, following in the tracks of Burckhardt, Wölfflin reinstated Baroque art, Wickhoff defended Roman art, Riegl the art of late antiquity and Max Dvořák the catacomb paintings and El Greco. Walter Friedländer completely freed Mannerist art from the stigma of decline, and Millard Meiss undertook a positive evaluation of the painting of the late Trecento. At the moment we are even witnessing a revival of respect for French nineteenth-century Salon painting, which until recently was still considered to be the ultimate in kitsch.

I will by no means dispute that we have profited a good deal from all these efforts: we have cast off prejudices and have learnt to look more closely.

I am a peace-loving man and am quite prepared to let each of the five giants have his plaything as long as he limits his territorial claims. I will even concede to metaphysical optimism the reality of a form of progress which links nature with history. We have understood since Darwin that there is no   need here for a teleology; only for the cruel mechanism which eliminates the unadapted. Perhaps in the field of art too a chance mutation occasionally leads to a highly promising solution, which in turn leads to further selection. The history of art has been presented in terms of progressive evolution first in antiquity, then in the Renaissance and also by Winckelmann, and what these accounts considered as decline can admittedly also be interpreted in the relativist sense as yet another process of adaptation. But adaptation to what? After all, not every collective, not every group, makes identical demands on artists and on their standards. In connection with this, Julius von Schlosser quite rightly insisted that one should not confuse the real history of art with the history of artistic idioms or styles. [28] Certainly the history of style lends itself rather better to attempts at hypothetical reconstruction than does the phenomenon of artistic mastery. Even the master-piece cannot come into existence without the favour of fortune, but here I will willingly concede to aesthetic transcendentalism that the highest artistic achievement soars into a sphere which even in principle defies scientific analysis. [29]

The Abdication of Art Criticism

The continued topicality of the issues raised by Hegel seems to me unquestionable. But they become burning problems only in connection with the present situation in art. It is necessary here to recall the intrinsic ambiguity of the word 'history', which has also crept into the title of this lecture. Hegel, 'The Father of Art History', may be taken to refer to Hegel's relations to the historiography of art, such as I have discussed them here; but these words may also imply that Hegel influenced the development of art itself, and this, no doubt, is a much weightier question.

We must never forget that the writing of history can in its turn influence the further course of events and it is this feedback — which Hegel would probably have described as 'dialectic' — which accounts for the decisive influence of his philosophy of history. Let us recall that Hegel saw in art not only a reflection of the Divine but also an aspect of the continuous process of creation which passes through the artist. [30] The role which classical antiquity assigned most of all to the poet is therefore attributed to every true artist; he is a seer, a prophet, who is not only the mouthpiece of God but also helps God to achieve His own self-awareness.

Hegel's lectures on the philosophy of history tell us even more explicitly than do those on aesthetics how he conceived the historical role of such a divine mission. It is true that his reflections on what he called 'world historical individuals' refer more immediately to political leaders. He had, most of all, Napoleon in mind, who had overcome the French Revolution and yet preserved its achievements and whom, in a famous letter written after the battle of Jena, he described as 'this world soul'. [31] But when Hegel speaks of great men we are entitled also to include artists; in any case artists would not allow themselves to be excluded. According to Hegel it is the task of what he calls 'these business managers of the World Spirit to be aware of the necessary next step to be taken by their world, to make this step their aim and to devote their energy to this ... They

present, as it were, the next species which had already been prefigured internally.'[32]

It is obvious that it is not granted to ordinary mortals to recognize and
understand this anticipation of the future in the present. There is only one
conclusion, therefore, that they can draw from Hegel's philosophy: whatever the
World Spirit may be aiming at, it must be something new. Thus the old is being
devalued while the unknown and untried at least carries within itself the
possibility of harbouring the seeds of the future. To be rejected by his age
becomes the very hallmark of genius. The great masters must be ahead of their
time, for if they were not they would not be great masters.

Those of us who do not regard the changes of styles, of trends, and of
fashions as a revelation of higher purposes must ask ourselves how we can really
know what the future will appreciate; indeed we may even wonder why we must
assume that the next generation will necessarily have a better taste than our own.
But for those who endorse Hegel's metaphysical optimism, the process of selection
has been shifted from the present to the future. It is only future success which
counts as valid, as a true verdict, the test of the Divine Will. Any criticism of
contemporaries becomes theoretically impossible because such criticism always
incurs the danger of turning out as blasphemy in the future. All that remains for
the critic in the end is to try to see which way the wind blows. As Popper has
shown, an even more dangerous giant looms up behind metaphysical optimism:
metaphysical opportunism.

Neither Popper nor I has ever wished to assert that the philosophy of progress
in art, the theory of the avant-garde,[33] was exclusively inspired and nourished by
Hegel's philosophy. And yet I believe that it could be shown what an essential
contribution was made by the Hegelian tradition. I have drawn attention
elsewhere[34] to a remark by Heinrich Heine, who explicitly derived this consequence for art criticism from Hegel's philosophy. Heine, who regarded Hegel as
the greatest German philosopher since Leibniz, placing him above Kant, took
issue in his Paris *Salons* of 1831 — the year of Hegel's death — with the critics
who had censured a painting by Descamps because it was badly drawn. He insisted
that 'every original artist, and even more so every artistic genius, must be judged
by his own aesthetic standards ... Colours and shapes ... are no more than symbols
of the Idea, symbols which rise in the mind of the artist when the sacred World
Spirit moves it.' Heine speaks of the 'mystical bondage' of the artist, and in view
of this lack of freedom any criticism becomes arrogant pedantry.

It is true that in the field of art criticism it took a great deal of time for the
critics to admit defeat and thus to arrive at what Hegel would have called the
self-abrogation of art criticism. But every successive wave of the artistic revolution
of the nineteenth century gave a fresh uplift to optimistic relativism. The belief in
progress polarized not only the political world but also the world of art; all that
was left was the impetus of the advance and the inertia of the reactionaries. In this
constellation it was no longer the task of the critic to criticize, his mission was to
assist the good fight of the movement; he became the herald of the new epoch and
did his best to turn these prophecies into reality. Remember with what relish the

artistic manifestos of the early twentieth century indulged in apocalyptic rhetoric announcing the new dawn, the new era, the new dispensation. Here too Hegel provided the direct inspiration. Eckart von Sydow in a pamphlet of 1920 on *German Expressionist Culture and Painting*, wrote: 'We may say, with but a few qualifications, that the German Spirit has once more found immediate contact with the World Soul, as in the days of the Middle Ages.'

I do not want to be misunderstood. Such an utterance does not speak against Expressionism, merely against its metaphysical underpinning in aesthetic transcendentalism. I would even go further and admit that a metaphysical faith can indeed inspire an artist or an artistic movement. Nearly all great art is religious and the religious element in Hegel's philosophy also had its inspiring effect. I believe that the historian of the art of our century has to study Hegel much as a student of the ecclesiastical art of the Middle Ages must get to know the Bible. Only in this way can he, for instance, learn to understand the triumphant rise of modern architecture and its present crisis.

Take the words Walter Gropius wrote in 1923 in his article on 'The Idea and the Structure of the National Bauhaus': 'The attitude of a period to the world becomes crystallized in its buildings, for in these both the spiritual and material resources of the age find their simultaneous expression.'[35] Of what kind of expression he dreamt we know from the beautiful speech which he made at the opening of the first exhibition of students' work at the Bauhaus:

> Instead of sprawling academic organizations, we shall witness the rise of small, secret, and self-contained leagues, lodges, workshops, conspiracies, intent on guarding the mystery which is the core of the faith and on giving artistic shape to it until the time when these isolated groups will be fused once more into an all-embracing and vigorous spiritual and religious vision which must eventually crystallize in a great *Gesamtkunstwerk*, combining all the arts. This great communal creation, this cathedral of the future, will in turn illuminate with its radiance even the smallest objects of everyday life.[36]

I hope every reader can sense the intoxicating sweep of these words of a great architect. Intoxication, however, is so often followed by a hangover and we did not have to wait for this very long. In 1976, Sir John Summerson, one of the most outstanding critics and historians of architecture in England, on the occasion of being awarded the Gold Medal of the Royal Institute of British Architects, spoke of his beginnings in the 1930s as an enthusiastic champion of Modern architecture in England and remarked that he now finds the starry-eyed optimism of some of his articles 'nauseating'.[37] Another of the leading English critics made the frank confession in front of the same forum that during the struggle for Modern architecture he had occasionally praised works which he did not really find so very good, simply because they were modern not reactionary.[38] These confessions are worthy of the highest respect and indeed we must warmly welcome all the debates which take place today wherever architecture is being taught and practised. It is through the encountering of arguments and counter-arguments that we shall learn from the mistakes of the last few decades.

In the visual arts of painting and sculpture such a return to a critical debate will not be quite so easy, for, after all, they lack the practical criteria to which a work of architecture has to do justice. Here the critic is entirely thrown back on himself. Naturally, we must not demand that the critic should have no prejudices and no dreams of the future. But theoretically, he never has the right to operate with the slogans of 'Our Age' and even less of 'Future Ages'.

It was Immanuel Kant who insisted on the stern and frightening doctrine that nobody and nothing can relieve us of the burden of moral responsibility for our judgment; not even a theophany, such as Hegel saw in history. 'For', he writes, 'in whatever way a Being might be described as Divine ... and indeed manifest itself', this cannot absolve anyone of the duty 'to judge for himself whether he is entitled to regard such a Being as a God and to worship it as such.'[39] It may well be that Kant here demands more than is humanly possible, and yet much would be achieved if the world of art would come to see that Kant was right.

Notes and References

All Hegel's major works have been translated into English, some of them several times, and can easily be traced in the catalogues of major libraries. There is a useful selection, *The Philosophy of Hegel*, edited with an introduction by Carl J. Friedrich. Since Hegel was and remains such a controversial figure, whose writings influenced the political thought of both Marxism and Fascism, the literature pro and con his philosophy would fill a library. See also my essay 'In Search of Cultural History' in *Ideals and Idols*, Oxford, 1979.

1. AI, p. 92. I quote from the edition *Hegels Werke in zwanzig Bänden* Suhrkamp Verlag, Frankfurt-am-Main, 1970. The abbreviation AI refers to the first volume of the Lectures on Aesthetics, AII to the second volume, and so on.
2. See my lecture series, *The Ideas of Progress and their Impact on Art*, published by Cooper Union, New York, 1971 (privately circulated). Published in German as *Kunst und Fortschritt*, Cologne, 1978.
3. *Ed. cit.* p. 529.
4. *Ed. cit.*, para. 462.
5. AIII, p. 573.
6. AI, p. 30.
7. AI, p. 56.
8. I am grateful to Alex Potts for referring me to HERDER'S *Plastik* (1778).
9. AI, pp. 24–5.
10. See my 'The Use of Art for the Study of Symbols' in J. HOGG (ed.), *Psychology and the Visual Arts*, Harmondsworth, 1969.
11. AI, pp. 456–7.
12. AI, p. 465.
13. AII, p. 286.
14. In 1817 Goethe wrote to Heinrich Meyer about the Elgin Marbles: 'the continent will soon be swamped by these magnificent forms like cheap cotton goods'. See JOHN GAGE, *Goethe on Art*, London, 1980, pp. 89–94. See also: J. ROTHENBERG, *Descensus ad terram: The Acquisition and Reception of the Elgin Marbles* (Columbia University thesis, 1967), New York and London, 1977.
15. AI, p. 431, and AII, p. 434.

16. AIII, p. 17.
17. AIII, p. 20.
18. AIII, p. 68.
19. AIII, p. 99.
20. AII, p. 227.
21. AII, p. 226.
22. AII, p. 226.
23. AI, pp. 42–3.
24. In *Ideals and Idols*, Oxford, 1979, pp. 24–59.
25. K. R. POPPER, *The Open Society and Its Enemies*, London, 1945: *The Poverty of Historicism*, London, 1957; *The Logic of Scientific Discovery*, London, 1959.
26. MANFRED VON EIGEN and RUTHILD WINKLER, Das *Spiel — Naturgesetze steuern den Zufall*, Munich, 1975, p. 197.
27. I quote from KARL ROSENKRANZ, *Friedrich Georg Wilhelm Hegels Leben*, Berlin, 1844, p. 335.
28. JULIUS VON SCHLOSSER, '"Stilgeschichte" und "Sprachgeschichte" der bildenden Kunst', in *Sitzungsberichte der Bayr. Akademie der Wissenschaften, Phil.-Hist Abt*, 1935, I. See also my 'Art History and the Social Sciences', in *Ideals and Idols*, Oxford, 1979.
29. See my 'Art History and the Social Sciences', *op. cit.*
30. AI, p. 50.
31. KARL ROSENKRANZ, *op. cit.*, p. 229.
32. *Ed. cit.*, p. 46.
33. RENATO POGGIOLI, *Teoria dell'arte d'avanguardia*, Bologna, 1962. Poggioli does not refer to Hegel in this context.
34. *The Idea of Progress, op. cit.* (note 2).
35. Printed in *Manifeste*, 1905–33, Diether Schmidt, Dresden, 1964, p. 290.
36. *Ibid.*, p. 238.
37. See *Journal of the Royal Institute of British Architects*, December 1976.
38. J. M. RICHARDS, 'The Hollow Victory, 1932–1972', in the *Journal of the Royal Institute of British Architects*, May 1972.
39. *Die Religion innerhalb der Grenzen der blossen Vernunft*, II Abschn, II Teil, 4 Stück, par I, *Werke*, Berlin, 1914, Bd VI, p. 318.

Chapter 10

The Domestication of Outrage

Denis Donoghue

Introduction

It's hard, these days, to feel outrage. When the Argentinian army took possession of South Georgia and the Falkland Islands, many people felt that it was outrageous, but I think too that they were consoled to discover that they could still feel this emotion. Mary Whitehouse has made a public life for herself by specializing in outrage; not so much by collecting instances of the outrageous as by alerting herself to the sense of it, keeping it going when it would otherwise have lapsed; as it has lapsed in most people. The plain fact is that bourgeois society can accommodate nearly anything. I should say, incidentally, that I use the word 'bourgeois' as a neutral term and often a term of praise, though one is supposed to use it nowadays only for irony or contempt. To me a bourgeois liberal is one who bases his liberalism upon a commitment to the values of a family man, anxious to secure a decent future for his children. A bourgeois society approves these values and regards the occasions on which they are defeated as regrettable. A bourgeois criticism of art likes to report that images which seem wild or bizarre are not really different from the ordinary images with which we are familiar. Such criticism likes to take part in 'the rapid domestication of the outrageous' which Leo Steinberg has named as the most typical feature of contemporary artistic life.

The artistic attempts made from time to time to outrage people are hapless. We wouldn't expect much from nine-minute wonders, like Mary Kelly's display of used nappy liners or Victor Burgin's stapled photographs. But more consequential artists find it hard to stir the sense of the appalling. Diane Arbus's photographs may have been taken to remind people that thousands of lives are broken, thousands of bodies crippled, that there are people who seem to have no life but the horror of it. But when you look through a book of Arbus's photographs, you feel that what they make is a freak-show. The feeling is a temporary aberration from normality which reinforces our sense of what is normal, like the experience most people will have had on going to see *The Elephant Man*.

The most telling consequence of the domestication of outrage is that far from disturbing the security of ordinary things, it confirms it. You can make an interesting photograph of anything, however commonplace. Long before Pop Art, photography broke down the distinction between the features of art and the features of ordinary life: for that reason it was a long time before it was taken seriously as anything more than a device for recalling large occasions.

The difference between photography and the older tradition of the still life in painting is that photography, being technological, found it easy to deal with machine-made shapes. The camera turned everything, natural or manufactured, into a image, and asked you to look hard at the result. But a photograph of a car is not a car; just as there is a difference between a car and the word 'car'. The mysteriousness of art is in all art, not merely in the art of the avant-garde; it suffuses the space between the image and its reference. The difference between a great painting and the materials from which it is made is finally mysterious; 'finally' in the sense that much can be said about the painting before reaching the point at which you have to leave it to silence. But mystery is not a secret message which the critic, in principle, could discover. There are many things to be said about Brancusi's sculpture 'Endless Column', for instance, but nothing useful can be said about it on the assumption that it has a meaning it could be persuaded to disclose, or that any such meaning would exhaust it.

What remains hidden is the presence of the work, the force of its presence as distinct from the particular bits of bronze or marble or whatever it's made of. There are works of art which are present to us in something like the way in which a person may be present to us. When you love people, you don't assess their qualities, you acknowledge them without thinking of reasons or thinking that any reason would matter. So it's entirely proper to speak of loving a work of art since we extend the word from our use of it in personal life. Or at least that's a way of recognizing and celebrating what I have called its presence. The reason why modern critics are embarrassed by the mysteriousness of art is that it threatens the purity of their secular status. My evidence for this isn't particular critics but the techniques they use, the confidence they place in their sentences. They insist upon the assurance that nothing escapes their consciousness. If they sense that the work of art is indeed occult, they get away from it as quickly as possible. They keep going till they reach the artist. This displacement of interest from the work of art to the artist is nearly incorrigible.

John Berger has pointed out that the artist is no longer valued as the producer of his work, but instead for the quality of his vision and imagination as expressed in it. No longer primarily a maker of art, he is 'an example of a man, and it is his art which exemplifies him'. Now that's true, even though the work of art may command a high price.

If an artist is admired or cherished, it is for what he is, an instance of a certain kind of person. But he's also valued because he enables us to feel that we are in touch with art by seeing the artist. The resentment against mystery is mostly against its absolute difference from ourselves. It's difficult to say anything about Hans Ulrich Lehmann's 'Duets for Three Players'; it is an unwelcoming work, so the critic goes off to Lehmann himself, who turns out to be, so far as appearance is evidence, a man like any other. He can be a little different but not very different. What is unusual appears only in his music and not in the image we see of him.

The Power of Reductive Terminologies

Once on the safe ground of the artist, the critic uses any of a number of available terminologies of explanation. One of the most popular at the moment is psychoanalysis: writers such as Freud, Melanie Klein, and Lacan have provided an official vocabulary, a relatively easy set of categories, quite limited in number, at least one of which the artist may be expected to fulfil. In a recent exploit, a critic proposed to explain Henry James's work on the basis of his having been passionately in love with his brother William. James's biographer Leon Edel was so taken with this notion that he undertook to read James's entire fiction again in this light; his implication was that the new reading would be far more profound than the old one. In fact, there is no objection to the application of psychoanalytic concepts to a work of art except that the exercise seems doomed to be reductive. The psychology of the artist seeks to know him not as a special case but as an unusually clear manifestation of the ordinary. The artist is now deemed to be unusual only because he provides more evidence than other people. To be fair, any established terminology is bound to reduce its object; that is its purpose, to make sense of an obscurity by bringing to bear upon it the sense that has already been made in another way. Psychoanalysis is a dialect, a choice of privileged concepts within a language — it has the character of diction in poetry, a set of favourite words which are brought together for mutual support. But the trouble with the psychoanalytical interpretation of art is that it interprets not art but the artist: in that sense it's bound to evade the question of mystery or otherness.

Adrian Stokes, for instance, following Melanie Klein's theory about the way in which a young child's mind is formed, thought of the subject-matter of art as dominated by two experiences that have been internalized: the feeling of oneness with the mother's breast and therefore with the world; and secondly, the recognition of a separation between the child and the world, originally the mother's whole person whose loss was mourned. For Stokes, the artistic motive is the need to restore the lost loved object. He then distinguishes two forms of this motive: first, 'a very strong identification with the object whereby a barrier between self and not-self is undone'; and second, 'a commerce with a self-sufficient and independent object at arm's length'.

Now Stokes's psychoanalytic theory of art is useful. His distinction between the two forms of the artistic motive could be applied, for instance, to the experience of looking at a painting. First we try to break down the barrier between us: at a later stage we may draw back from it and try to judge it, and to do this we have to take the painting as an independent object at arm's length. But the trouble with Stokes's theory, when he applies it to particular works of art and architecture, is that the works are called upon merely to confirm the theory. If you took the theory as strictly as Stokes took it, you might still know a lot about art but you would have only one way of knowing it. And you would be so rigorous in confirming the same few axioms that you might fail to see the differences between one work of art and another. His discourse makes certain perceptions possible, but it's also restrictive, it prevents you from perceiving what lies beyond it or to one side of it.

The work of art is seen as the artist's way of dealing with compulsions which he treated otherwise when he was a child, by turning to the breast. The compulsions themselves are unconscious, but the theory accounts for them by telling a plausible story. And because a story takes place in time, it brings into time and rationality factors which otherwise would have little chance of getting there. Critics who want to escape from the mysteriousness of the work try to replace it by the intention they ascribe to the artist. Some works of art make this procedure necessary. A few years ago Robert Klein argued that it is no longer possible to judge a painting or sculpture without knowing who made it and in what spirit.

When we look at a contemporary painting in a gallery, we search for the artist's name and the title of the painting, if it has one. We do this not out of mere helplessness or curiosity but in the hope of seeing the work as the fulfilment of an intention. If we know the artist, we may happen to know his general line: if so, all the better. What Klein meant, I think, was that the work of art now persists chiefly as an indication of an intention; it is as an embodied intention that it can best be studied. We are led straight from the work to the psychology of the artist and from there to the economics of the market. To be blunt: it pays to deliver certain recognizable objects and intentions. It is comforting to be in the presence of intentions we understand because the considerations of psychology and economics aren't at all mysterious: discussion of them is easy.

The question sometimes arises whether the work exceeds the intention or merely documents it. You'll recall the incident, a few years ago, when the Tate Gallery paid good domestic cash for a work called 'Equivalent VIII', a load of bricks lain on the floor by the artist Carl Andre. Andre's intention was far more interesting than the bricks or the order in which he assembled them. He explained it in a conversation, with Edward Lucie-Smith. Referring to Turner's way with colour, he said that Turner had severed colour from depiction and then manipulated it in a condition of freedom. 'I sever matter from depiction', he said. 'I am the Turner of matter.' He meant that in choosing bricks, metal plates, or bales of hay, he chooses things that are associated with particular uses, and he diverts them from those uses so that he can give them intrinsic existence. Andre's intention is to assert that art is a system of pleasure, based chiefly upon our physical presence in a material world. It's like the theory of literature put forward by the Russian critic Boris Shklovsky, that the function of literature is to free things of their familiarity so that we can really perceive them, looking at them as if they were strange.

Normally we look at things mainly for their use; we deal with them as we deal with the wallpaper in our rooms, we would notice it only if it were gone, torn, or daubed with paint. Carl Andre wants much the same result. Looking at his bricks, we see them as such, as objects: the artist has forced us to pay attention. He doesn't claim that there is anything sacred in the bricks themselves, or even in his way of disposing them.

Andre regards the artistic event as a combination of the artist's intention and our way of receiving it. Is there anything against this? No, except that art in this sense can have no history other than that of its intention. Once we have taken the point and resolved to amend our lives accordingly, there is nothing more to do. Like any one of Andy Warhol's films, it is not necessary to see it, it's enough to understand that it is there, and why. In that respect, unfortunately, the comparison with Turner doesn't hold.

The Misplaced Cult of the Personality

Up to this point the displacement of attention from the work of art to the artistic life sounds innocent. If the work sits there, retaining its mystery, returning our stare, why shouldn't we turn aside to consult the artist, who is more likely to answer whatever questions a common discourse allows us to ask? Can't we go back to the work at any time and renew our sense of its occult power? Yes, but in practice one interest has displaced the other, precisely because an interest in the artist is easily satisfied. And there is a further consideration. Increasingly, the form in which we pay attention to anything is a result of the way in which we watch images on television. We pay attention to most things now as if they were television programmes. Now television is restless with any object which asks to be looked at slowly and patiently. The span of willing attention to an image on television is a matter of seconds, not minutes. Then a new image must be given. When such programmes as *Omnibus* and *The South Bank Show* present an artist, they run away from his works and concentrate on him, an easier subject because he is responsive, mobile, unsecretive. Instead of a work of art to be looked at, the camera gives us a man or woman, much like anybody else, so we are not affronted by seeing anything strikingly different from ourselves. Objects, when presented at all, are turned into happenings. A recent *South Bank Show* about Sir William Walton said nothing about the character or the principles of his music, but plenty about the kind of man he was. It may be that people who watched the programme have been so stimulated by the personal lore it provided that they have gone straight to his music. I can't be certain, but I doubt it. And even if it were true, it still wouldn't have provoked the right sort of attention, because they would receive the music as further illustration of a personal image.

In T. S. Eliot's *The Elder Statesman* Lord Claverton discovers that he's been freed, at last, 'from the self that pretends to be someone'. And in becoming no one,' he finds, 'I begin to live.' He begins to live, and to live in a social world, because he has given up all pretence; his privacy is not a secret self behind his disclosed appearances. But television has got people into the habit of assuming that what is there begins and ends with what they see.

The same process takes over the presentation of art. Hence the fact that the most famous artists in our time are famous as personalities rather than as makers of their work. This doesn't mean that, like Bianca Jagger, they are famous for being famous. They are artists, they have made things — pictures, films, songs. But the images they offer to the public gaze are more compelling than the works they have made. Think of the recently deceased Salvador Dali. Most people recall a crucifixion, liquefied watches, popular reproductions in the postcard-shops. But Dali's form of existence before the world made him a personality far more visible than his paintings. Allen Ginsberg became a symbol even for people who couldn't name one of his poems. Andy Warhol was far more famous as a personality than as a painter or a film director; he existed as a gesture, a snapshot from the album of the Sixties. His fame persisted not because it corresponded to any new work, but because many people approaching middle age felt nostalgic toward the decade in which they felt that they were making history. Warhol reminded them of that sentiment. It was not necessary that he should ever take up a paintbrush again.

This disproportion between artist and his work — the fact that with the connivance of the media a little work goes a long way to sustain a personality — marks a reversal of the traditional relation between the two. It was long thought a sign of success in an artist that he disappeared into his work, leaving no merely personal residue. Henry James thought that this made it extremely difficult to write a novel about a successful artist; there was not enough left over, everything had gone into the work. 'Any presentation of the artist *in triumph*,' he said, 'must be flat in proportion as it really sticks to its subject — it can only smuggle in relief and variety. For, to put the matter in an image, all we then — in his triumph — see of the charm-compeller is the back he turns to us as he bends over his work.' James felt that the good fortune of an artist would be to remain anonymous, visible in his works and not otherwise; and that his being also a person should be a matter of his privacy and reserve.

But we have now reached a situation in which privacy and reserve can be converted to visible purpose. The fact that the late Philip Larkin didn't appear on television and rarely gave readings of his poetry added to his fame. His invisibility became a nuance of visibility. A *South Bank Show* on Larkin turned his absence into an esoteric form of presence.

The urgency with which critics run from the work of art to the artist is only partly explained by the fact that the work remains mysterious and the artist doesn't. There is also undisguised revulsion against the sacred object, the original work of art. Photography is a comfortable medium because even if you see photographs which are also works of art, you're not browbeaten by their sublimity; such works are extraordinary examples of the ordinary rather than works of genius, like *King Lear*, which no one in his senses could dream that he might write. But the unique work of art is intimidating. Think of the depression of spending more than an hour in an art gallery. The aura that surrounds a masterpiece is the sign of its uniqueness, it attends our sense that there is only one of it and that any likeness is only a replica. This consideration gives the unique work its prestige, and not only in Sotheby's, but it is also the focus of a vague resentment. Few of us would really want to own a masterpiece, it would be out of place in our homes. We are happier with decent colour-reproductions, because they don't intimidate, we don't feel oppressed by them. Lithographs are acceptable because there is no original; they are all equal.

There is also a political explanation for this, asserted most vigorously by Marxist critics. Walter Benjamin has observed that history is always recited in favour of those who have won; the point of view of the defeated is never recorded. 'As in all previous history,' he says, 'whoever emerges a victor still participates in that triumph in which today's rulers march over the prostrate bodies of their victims. As is customary, the spoils are borne aloft in that triumphal parade. These are generally called the cultural heritage. There has never been a document of culture which was not at one and the same time a document of barbarism.' Benjamin's argument shouldn't make you feel guilty when you go to a gallery or a museum. For one thing, if the victors in a particular society were workers rather than princes, there is no reason to think that their triumph would be achieved and maintained without victims. A triumphal parade would still take place. One has only to attend a 'first night' in the West End or at Lincoln Center to feel that the event, whatever its artistic occasion, is also a celebration of victory. The happy few are on display to themselves and to one another.

One has the same misgiving on going to see the Kennedy Center for the Performing Arts in Washington. The building has transformed cultural life in that city, but it stands as an architectural assertion of the imperial motives that built it. Domination is inscribed in its marble. Richard Hoggart has recently asserted, following the conventional wisdom on such matters, that there is 'an almost total loss of confidence in the very idea of a higher culture to which one could and should aspire'. I would want to put it differently. Certainly the idea of accredited values, known and accepted as such whether an individual aspires to them or not, has broken down. The idea of aspiration, in anything but a careerist sense, has lapsed. But the Sydney Opera House, the Barbican, and Kennedy Center are still making assertions in favour of cultural life, even if the assertions come from an equivocal mixture of power, national pride, and a commitment to continuity. The loss of confidence has occurred, not in the decisiveness with which these buildings are built, but in knowing what should be produced in them, once they are built. What is desperately confused is the relation between cultural life and its components: the break in the circuit of attention between the work of art, the artist, the critic, and the common reader, listener or viewer is only one sign of that confusion.

The Loss of Imagination in Structuralism and Post-Structuralism

It may seem that the drift or the flight from the work of art to the artist is refuted by at least one contemporary form of criticism. Structuralists and post-Structuralists maintain that the notion of the author as the creator of his works is merely a modern consolation prize; it goes along with the prestige a bourgeois society ascribes to the individual. Roland Barthes and other critics regard as mere superstition any attempt to find the depth of the work in the psyche of the author. Instead, they replace the author by language itself, which is then studied as an impersonal system, a system that doesn't need a person to work it. The idea is that language allows for a personal intervention in the moment of writing or speaking, but the person ceases with the enunciation; nothing in language corresponds to the identity of a person or to his apparent continuity from one moment to the next. The author is at best a secretary, a scribe.

But the Structuralist thesis doesn't attribute any mystery to language as a system of signs. A critic who is interested in modern literature is not supposed to deal with it as acts of the creative imagination in the medium of a particular language. He is supposed to find that the work of art is a mere function of a compromised language, corrupted because it has been used in the exercise of power and on behalf of an ideology. The job of criticism is to document the extent to which the modern languages have been corrupted.

In turn, Structuralist readers are urged to adopt an ironic or sceptical attitude toward whatever they read; they are to know that it is poisoned. Barthes, in his later work, showed how such readers might behave themselves. They should cultivate caprice and excess, going against the grain of the writing, distrusting its rhetorical figures, reading at their own speed. In this way they retain some measure of freedom, and break the conspiracy between author, publisher, and the economy of the market which has produced the book as a commodity for sale.

It begins to appear that in Structuralism and post-Structuralism we are returned to something like the avant-garde position in relation to a society deemed to be bourgeois through and through. No wonder critics who start with these assumptions about the impersonality of language tend to lose interest in criticism and to become writers, as if to fill the avant-garde position left vacant by novelists and poets.

I often wish the Structuralists were right. It would be pleasant to give up the sense of mystery in the arts and to think that everything in the work could be explained in systematic terms. The French critics want to get rid of mystery because it sounds like theology or divinity. But I am not persuaded. The idea of a language as a system explains everything in a work of literature except what we most have to acknowledge; on that, the idea is helpless. It's at this point, and against the Structuralists, that we have to reinstate the artist: indeed, it's extraordinary that it should be necessary to say that he is the one who has made the work. What do we gain by saying that T. S. Eliot's 'Gerontion' is a work of language, or even of the English language, and that Eliot is merely its scribe? The point about a scribe is that someone else could do his work. To refuse to call the writing of 'Gerontion' a creative act performed with the collaboration of the English language is nonsense. The fact that the English language is a communal creation, the work of its speakers over many centuries, is not at all incompatible with the creative imagination we ascribe to Eliot in this instance. A linguistic system makes certain things possible, but it makes nothing actual. Nothing could ever be done if it were left to a system to do it.

Chapter 11

Approaching the End of Art

Arthur Danto

Introduction

I want to cite three propositions that occur in Hegel's monumental lectures on the philosophy of art — his *Vorlesungen uber die Aesthetik* — which has been described, by Martin Heidegger, as 'the most comprehensive reflection on the nature of art that the West possesses'. There Hegel writes:

> Art no longer counts for us as the highest manner in which truth furnishes itself with existence.

> One may well hope that art will continue to advance and perfect itself, but its form has ceased to be the highest need of the spirit.

> In all these relationships, art is and remains for us, on the side of its highest vocation, something past.

I am obsessed by the thought these propositions express, that art 'in its highest vocation' might have come to an end, and that the period we have been living through is a kind of epilogue to the history of art. At the very least this thought offers an opportunity to speculate on what one might call the philosophical history of art.

Exhausting the Possibilities of Artistic Novelty

There is a curious and rather touching passage in the *Autobiography* of John Stuart Mill, in which that philosopher responds with considerable melancholy to the thought that sooner rather than later, music will all be used up. There are only, Mill reflected, a finite number of combinations of a finite number of tones, so before too long all the melodies possible will have been discovered and there will be nothing left to compose. The augmentation of the octave by the twelve-tone scale, something Mill of course had not counted on, would but postpone an inevitable exhaustion, and the future history of music must be repetitions of all the combinations of tones that there are. Mill might have taken comfort from the fact that concert performances themselves seem infinite repetitions of the same compositions, but his concern was with creativity and the closing off of its possibility in musical composition.

Mill's argument, which I do not mean especially to examine here, anticipates a much grander cosmological speculation of Nietzsche's, to the effect that the universe itself, consisting, as he supposed it did, in a finite number of possible states, of which there can be again but a finite number of possible sequences and combinations, must finally exhaust the possibility of novelty and begin to repeat itself monotonously and eternally. This was Nietzsche's notorious theory of Eternal Recurrence, but unlike Mill (whom the thought of finitude sent into a depression uncharacteristic in a man who typified the optimism of the era) Nietzsche was exhilarated by what he thought was an immense discovery. Mill was depressed, perhaps, precisely because he was by conviction an optimist who saw his optimism limited just here, whereas Nietzsche may have been exalted because he was by nature and conviction so deeply pessimistic about the human material. Nietzsche thought Eternal Recurrence was a test, and that if we could pass this test there might be some hope for us. If we could, in the face of knowledge he presumed scientific and certain, continue to act despite having acted in just this manner countless times before in periods of the universe exactly like the present one, which itself is a phase that will return again and again and again, then one will have achieved a certain meaning in one's actions and a kind of moral strength. For the action will be seen as done for its own sake and not for any consequences it might have, for it cannot, on Nietzsche's theory, ultimately make any difference as to how the universe will be. We know, he believed, that whatever we do, we will do it again, infinitely and eternally. So there can ultimately be no different outcome.

Art in the 1970s

Since making art has often seemed to be an internally rewarding and self-contained activity, it might seem as though artmaking were a perfect example of a meaningful act in Nietzsche's view. 'Do everything you do as though you were making a work of art!' might be a form of the imperative his theory of Eternal Recurrence recommends. Now the period of artmaking I wish to discuss, that of the 1970s, seemed to many to represent that timeless circulation of the same after the same that connotes a vision not unlike Mill's or even Nietzsche's. But the malaise to which this gave rise underscored the degree to which art had been thought of by its makers as historical rather than timeless, with the imperatives being those of breaking through, making everything new, revolutionizing all that had gone before, carrying forward the history of art to new levels of achievement. And indeed, a great deal of art was made that would have made little sense but for the belief that one had achieved a historical advance by means of it. The discoveries in question had to do with the nature of art itself, for it is possible to read twentieth-century art as the collective quest for the essence and nature of art

— a reading that is confirmed by the intolerance each stage in this advance provoked when the new forms were displayed as having captured and distilled the pure being of art.

But then, in the 1970s, all this seemed to stop. Season after season passed without any of those abrupt reversals and transformations of artistic vision the art world had come to take for granted. Instead one saw the same things being done, over and over, with some slight modifications and variations. And the old puritanisms and intolerances — the charge that everything other than what one was doing was *not really art* — gave way to a sort of pluralism, which itself is a concession that one no longer believes in a truth of art. The abstractionist of the 1970s was prepared to allow realism, the minimalist resigned to allow decoration, the hard-edgers tolerated soft-edgers, the seekers after absolute flatness saw all about them the exploiters of illusory space — and if one wanted, one could paint the flaying of Marsyas or the descent from the cross or appropriate styles and images of the discarded past. Anything was permitted. Pluralism has much to recommend it, since under it one is allowed to do what one wants to do, but it is striking that when anything is allowed, a certain point in doing whatever one chooses to do is lost, and there is no question that a certain melancholy settled over the art world in those years. This is largely, I believe, because the historical presuppositions that made a given art meaningful were inconsistent with another kind of art being equally meaningful and allowed. Why even make art of the one kind if it was perfectly all right to make art of different kinds? Why stain colour fields into canvas when others were painting landscapes or making installations or doing performances?

So through the 1970s, the thought was irresistible that art might have come to an end, in the sense of having been used up. The present began to seem the way the past is always assumed to be: All the music of the nineteenth century is already composed and there is now no way to add to the music of the nineteenth century, since the whole of that history is in place. In the 1970s it was as though the whole history of the future were already in place, as though the most one could hope to do was repeat — as it were perform — a known thing. No further breakthroughs were expected, and 'the end of painting' or 'the end of art' were phrases used by critics and theorists, and indeed by artists themselves. To be sure, this might have been part of a general attitude toward culture. Certainly people spoke of the death of the novel and the end of philosophy as well, and in the field of philosophy pluralism, as in art, seemed to be inescapable. But few cultural forms had been so transformative as painting, and *its* coming to an end seemed especially dramatic. 'The problem with painting,' one commentator wrote near the end of this period (1981), 'is that by now all possible variations on neat-messy, thick-thin, big-little, simple-complex, or circle-square have been done.' How exactly like Mill this sounds!

Perhaps just because pluralism was felt as a problem, as it was in so many places where art was discussed and debated in those years, there was an unstated premise that the answer to the question of what art really is must exist among the known forms. It was only that its identification was no longer regarded as a matter of artistic discovery but of philosophical argument of a kind that no one knew how to frame. But at the same time that artists must have seen their task as increasingly philosophical in this way, the institutions of the art world continued to believe in — indeed to expect — breakthroughs, and the galleries, the collectors, the art magazines, the museums and finally the corporations that had become the major patrons of the age were also awaiting prophets and revelations. I thought at the time that there was an influential segment of the art world that rushed about the scene with Cinderella's glass slipper, but the slipper was huge and the feet were tiny. There would, even so, be ecstatic cries of 'It fits! It fits!' as one very small foot after another found it could not fill enough of the immense slipper to take even a baby-step into the historical future. And those who believed in historical closure might have said that in any case there would be no place to set one's foot, because art was walled in by its own internal logic. History was over.

So the 1970s were a kind of unstable or even a contradictory period, and the art world was the scene of conflicting beliefs about art and the history of art. All the institutions of the art world operated on the belief that art had one kind of history which may have been momentarily interrupted. But a good many artists and critics were of a different view: What others saw as interruption, they saw as exhaustion. They saw history as closed where others saw it as open and luminous.

The Visual Arts in the 1980s

All of this is meant to fill in the background of the event that really concerns me here, namely the explosive eruption, in the early 1980s, in Europe as in America, of a brash new style, Neo-Expressionism, which seemed to many to introduce a foot large and strong enough to move the glass slipper of artistic history forward a step. All at once there was something important enough for collectors to acquire — *growth* art as one might call it — art destined, in analogy with certain legendary stocks, to appreciate enormously in value over time. The art of the 1970s might have been collected by *amateurs*, in the French sense of the term: informed enthusiasts for a certain style of minimalism or realism. But as I have observed, there was a whole complex of art institutions waiting for an art of a different order, novel and big and important, a demand that had existed, perhaps even increased, through the fallow period of the 1970s when there was nothing especially to satisfy it. I was struck by the fact that in Hilton Kramer's book of critical essays, which covers the years 1972–1984, he discusses artists who already had reputations when this period began, and who merely refined a given vision without anything truly novel coming about save at the end of those twelve years with Neo-Expressionism itself. So there was almost what Marxists might construe as a contradiction in the art world between demand and supply. And here were the Neo-Expressionists to rectify the inconsistency, providing works of art that carried the look of historical importance and gave collectors something to buy which would, in no time at all, increase in value as the paintings of the Abstract Expressionists had done, or even, more astonishingly perhaps, as the irreverent works of the Pop artists had done. Jasper Johns's *Three Flags* sold for $1 million (to The Whitney Museum of American Art) in 1980. Roy Lichtenstein's comic-strip paintings bring that amount from collectors today. De Kooning's *Two Women* sold at Christies for $1.98 million in 1984 — a price which, though still the highest paid for the work of a living American artist, was certain to be overtaken. The Neo-Expressionists appeared in terms of scale and frenzy to be in this league. 'Buy before it is too late!' was the implicit imperative, and a market was made. These were not the kinds of works that were acquired by the artist's friends and a few admirers: They demanded instant acknowledgment and acquisition and they proclaimed the preemptive merit of important art almost simultaneously with their being made. It was a moment of heady effervescence, like the discovery of oil. Art had sailed out of the doldrums.

The jubilation, of course, was not universal. There was an inevitable resentment that young and flashy painters should have seized the stage, getting immense attention and reckless prices. Kramer, in his essay of November 1982, devoted to this upsurge, remarked on its 'swift and formidable presence on the international art scene.' And he explains it in a kind of philosophical way, writing that 'Change, after all — incessant and insistent change — has been the rule in the life of art as long as anyone can now remember.' But this, I think, is too weak an explanation for the kind of change it was. Even in periods of extreme stability, as in the production of statues of pharaohs or the painting of icons, there is doubtless an insidious change, and indeed for all the outward inertness, there must have been changes in the 1970s. Nothing stands quite that still in art or for that matter in life. But here was a change of a cataclysmic sort, a *discontinuous* change, a change of a different order. Changes as sharp and, as it were, punctuated, were not 'the incessant and insistent change' of art history. The question then is: What can account for the sense of a break in history, a shift in artistic direction?

Kramer is certainly aware of the shift. 'Unquestionably', he wrote, 'it represents one of the most spectacular and unexpected "divorce" cases in recent cultural history.' And 'Not since the emergence of Pop Art in the early 1970s have we seen anything of comparable consequence in the realm of contemporary painting.' There really is the resemblance Kramer notes. But my view, which requires putting forward a different sense of history than his, is that we are dealing with different kinds of cataclysms. The first of them, I want to claim, was a cataclysm internal to the history of art. The second was a kind of willed cataclysm, unconnnected with the history of art. Or, one was a real cataclysm and the other merely resembled one.

It is a complex enough matter to relate the art of a single individual to those dimensions of his or her life that explain what it expresses, but art is more than the collective biographies of individual artists, and this is especially so when we are dealing with a *movement* of art. Why, at a given moment, should so many artists, various as their biographical circumstances might be, begin to work in much the same way? To be sure, there may be one or two who happen to hit upon some novel thought and to communicate it to others — but why do these others accept it? What is there in the soil of a culture that enables the seeds of a new art to grow? Some larger concept of art history, it seems to me, is needed for there to be answers to such questions. For me, a given movement of art must be understood in terms of a certain historical necessity, and in my view, Pop Art was a response to a philosophical question as to the nature of art that had more or less energized the whole of twentieth-century painting. Abstract Expressionism, after all, had posed this question and had elicited answers of some ingenuity — painting is paint, it is the act of painting, it is an action of a certain sort, and everything else that seems to belong to the essence of art is really incidental. Pop Art put the question differently, and in its true philosophical form: Why is this art, it asked, when something just like this — an ordinary Brillo box, a commonplace soup can — is not, especially when the artwork and the real thing so exactly resemble each other as not to be told apart? This question was raised for me, vividly, in the exhibition of Andy Warhol's Brillo cartons at the Stable Gallery in 1964, and though one must resist the temptation, as a philosopher, to identify that which may have awakened one from one's own dogmatic slumber with that which may have awakened history from *its* dogmatic slumber, I cannot refrain from supposing that I grasped what art was asking about itself at that moment in 1964. Art had raised from within and in its definitive form, the question of the philosophical nature of art. All questions in philosophy have the same form: They ask why two things of an outwardly similar appearance should belong to deeply distinct philosophical kinds. Why should artworks look outwardly so like commonplace objects? Until the advent of Pop (with the dubious exception of Duchamp) artworks never had looked outwardly enough like anything else to raise the question in this form, though when art was believed to be imitation, the intuition was already there that something like this was true. The fact that this kind of question could be raised about art proved that art itself was a philosophically *important* category, which of course philosophers had in some sense understood since speculation on the nature of art had always been part of what philosophers did. It really required an indiscernibility from objects that were neither exalted nor beautiful nor pictures-que for the issue to be felt — and the banal, drab, empty Brillo box served this end magnificently.

An artist I knew loathed that Warhol show, and scribbled an obscenity in the guest-book. Years later I said to him that one difference between artists and philosophers was that artists write 'Shit' where philosophers write such things as *The Transfiguration of the Commonplace*, my own way of responding to an exhibition perceived as a problem rather than an affront.

By contrast, Neo-Expressionism raised, as art, no philosophical question at all, and indeed it could raise none that would not be some variant on the one raised in its perfected form by Warhol. On the other hand, the fact that Neo-Expressionism arose in the cataclysmic manner in which it did raised a question about the philosophical structure of the history of art that one might never have grasped had it not been for something as flamboyantly empty as this new painting style. My response to its advent was in effect: *This was not supposed to happen next.* I had that thought while working through the Whitney Biennial of 1981, in which Neo-Expressionism made such boisterous inroads. And my next thought was: *Well, if this was not supposed to happen next, what was?* And I realized, suddenly, that I was subscribing to some sort of philosophy of history, according to which art must have the history it does because it has the nature it does: There is a certain necessity, or a certain logic, in the history of art. And so I saw Pop Art as an internal event in the history of art construed philosophically. Neo-Expressionism, on the other hand, seemed but an external event, caused, perhaps by the drives of the art market and its hopes for the history of art. So though the two events really did resemble each other, just as Kramer said, they belonged to philosophically distinct histories, and represented different orders of change. And they called for different kinds of historical explanations.

The thought I wish to present is that with Warhol, art was taken up into philosophy, since the question it raised and the form in which it was raised was as far as art could go in that direction — the answer had to come from philosophy. And in turning into philosophy, one might say that art had come to a certain natural end. Neo-Expressionism was a solution to a different problem altogether, namely, what are artists to do when art is over with and where the mechanisms of the market require that something happen that looks like a continuation of the history of art? Let me now spell out some of the grounds for this difference.

The Post-Historical Period of Art

The idea that art should come to an end like this was advanced in the great work I cited at the beginning of this chapter, Hegel's *Vorlesungen uber die Aesthetik*, which he delivered for the last time in 1828, three years before his death — a very long time ago indeed — and a great deal of art has been made since Hegel last held forth in Berlin. So there is a natural temptation to say, Well, Hegel was just wrong, and drop the matter there. Philosophers have said some crazy things about the real world. Aristotle insisted, for reasons I can only guess at, that women have fewer teeth than men. In medieval representations of him, Aristotle is often depicted on all fours, being ridden by a woman with a whip in her hand. This was Phyllis, the mistress of Aristotle's pupil, Alexander. One might suppose, from his posture of erotic domination by a woman he was mad about, that Aristotle would have supposed she had more teeth than men, showing that even masochists can be sexist. In any case, one need only look in the nearest female mouth to refute that mighty thinker. Hegel himself had a proof that as a matter of cosmic necessity there must be exactly seven planets, but Neptune was discovered in 1846 and Pluto in 1930 — and if we reckon in the minor planets, of which there are more than a thousand, an argument on rational grounds that there must be seven shatters against the universe. So the claim that art must be over by 1828 sounds like another of those unfortunate thoughts philosophers have from time to time about the uncooperating world. Heidegger, whose essay on the *origins* of art appeared in 1950, was not much impressed by a refutation of Hegel based on the continuation of art since his death.

The judgment that Hegel passes ... cannot be evaded by pointing out that since Hegel's lectures were given for the last time during the winter of 1828-29, we have seen many new artworks and art movements arise. Hegel did not mean to deny this possibility. The question, however, remains: is art still an essential and necessary way in which truth that is decisive for our historical existence happens, or is art no longer of this character? ... The truth of Hegel's judgment has not yet been decided.

I suppose the simplest way to connect the possible truth of Hegel's judgment with the facts of art history since 1828 is to distinguish between something stopping, and something coming to an end. Stopping is an external matter, in that something is caused to stop when it could have continued. But coming to an end is an internal matter of pattern and consummation, when, as in a melody or a narrative, there is nothing else that can happen to cause the melody or narrative to go on. A storyteller breaks a tale off, to continue it the next night, when we learn what happens next. A novelist puts her novel aside and never takes it up again, so that though it stopped we have no way of knowing how it would have ended. Or a writer drops dead and we are asked, as with *The Mystery of Edwin Drood*, to imagine alternative endings. We all understand this difference even if we are not prepared with a good theory of narrative closure that will explain the fact that there are stories that stop *because* they have reached the end. But in such cases, though the story had ended, life goes on: A lot happens when the prince and princess live happily ever after — the king, his father, dies, so he is now ruler and she his queen, they have their children, she conducts discreet affairs with Sir Lancelot, there are border uprisings ... but still the story ended when the love toward which their destinies drove them came to mutual consciousness when they knew, each knowing the other knew, that they were meant for each other.

Hegel thought that art had come to an end in the *narrative* sense of ending, namely as an episode in a larger narrative in which art played a certain role. The story of art is the story of art's role in the grand history of the spirit. There was art before and there will be art after, but the highest vocation of art was to advance some grander matter. There was a moment when the energies of art coincided with the energies of history itself — and then it subsided into something else. If there could have been a change of that order, then it would have been change of a different order than the changes that preceded and succeeded it. So there is a question of whether there is a narrative structure to the history of art, in which case coming to an end would be almost a matter of logic, or whether the history of art is merely a chronicle, first this and then that, the record of which is so many columns of art criticism, one after the other, as in the present collection. The record of insistent change, which is all that Hilton Kramer allows, is the philosophy of history of the practising journalist, following the day-by-day events in the art world: the news, the latest, the next. So the question then is whether art has the one sort of structure or the other (which is a nonstructure); hence, whether it can come or can have come to end — or whether it can merely stop. One could imagine art stopping, as under some terrible government or during the chill darknesses of the nuclear winter when all our energy goes into keeping ourselves alive.

Now once upon a time painting was certainly thought of as narrativistic, as the progressive conquest of visual appearances. The artists sought cumulatively to present the eye with what it would receive as a matter of course from natural appearances. Gombrich's account of the history of art as a matter of making and matching is just such a story of progress. Mill's despair at the collapse of melodic possibilities implies a similar narrative for music, where perhaps the development of instruments, which allow more and more compositional possibilities, corresponds to the technical instrumentation of the painter to achieve visual equivalences by artifactual means. This must certainly have been the aim of Greek art if the severe criticisms found in Plato have any basis in practice, though the Greek artists were severely limited in what they could do by way of constructing appearances that could not be told apart, by merely optical means, from what reality itself would present. There are famous legends that confirm this goal and even record some startling successes at fooling the birds into pecking at sham and two-dimensional grapes.

In terms of this sense of the history of art, the discovery of perspective would have marked a climax, and perhaps the discovery of aerial perspective marked another. Who, unless concerned with changes in atmosphere induced by distance, would have chosen the grayed pale hues needed to register distal objects? Who even needed to register distance, unless verisimilitude was an objective? The great dramas of medieval art take place in mystical spaces, whose geometry and optics have little to do with the body's eyes. In any case, we can readily imagine this narrative coming to an end, namely with those discoveries in which, finally, the progress is achieved. Of course painting might well continue to be made, but its real history would be over with. It could not any longer have climaxes of the order of the work of Michelangelo, according to Vasari's stirring account:

> While the best and most industrious artists were labouring, by the light of Giotto and his followers, to give the world examples of such power as the benignity of their stars and the varied character of their fantasies enabled them to command, and while desirous of imitating the perfection of nature by the excellence of art ... The Ruler of Heaven was pleased to turn the eye of his clemency toward earth, and perceiving the fruitlessness of so many labours, the ardent studies pursued without any result ... he resolved, by way of delivering us from such great errors, to send the world a spirit endowed with universality of power in each art ...

This highflown and manneristic passage gives an incidental reason why imitation should have enjoyed a renaissance as a theory in the Renaissance. The artist, in imitating nature, imitates God: Artistic creativity is the emulation of divine creation. In any case, with Michelangelo, the story is over, but of course art goes on and on: halls had to be decorated, portraits executed, marriage chests embellished.

There are certain inherent limits to this progress, simply because there are certain properties of things discernible to vision that cannot be directly represented in painting. Motion is clearly one such property — an artist can represent, as it were, *the fact* that something is in motion, but he cannot imitate the motion itself. Rather, the viewer must infer that the subject shown is in movement as the best explanation of why the painting looks the way it does — the man's feet do not touch the ground, say. Here I must rather ruthlessly cut my account, but I have argued at length elsewhere that the entire concept of painting had to change when it was discovered that only through an altogether different technology could motion be directly shown, namely that of cinematography or one of its ruder predecessors. The history of art as the discovery of perceptual equivalences did not come to an end with cinema, but the history of painting so far as it was regarded as the mimetic art par excellence came to an end. The goal of history could no longer be believed attainable by painters, and the torch had been handed on. My own sense of history suggests that the history of painting took a very different turn when this was recognized. It is striking that photography presented no such challenge — it provided, rather, an ideal. But motion picture photography showed something not in principle attainable by painting, and by 1905, when we are roughly at the period of the Fauves, all the structures for narrative cinema were in place.

The very fact of the Fauves recommends the view that at some level of consciousness, artists realized that they must rethink the meaning of painting, or accept the fact that from the defining perspective of mimetic progress, painting was finished. Painters could behave archaistically just as sword-makers carry on a ceremonial trade in the era of firearms. But instead they began to reexamine the foundations of their practice, and the decades since have been the most astonishing period in the history of art. This is mainly, I believe, because the immense problem of self-definition had been imposed on painting, which could no longer acquiesce in a characterization taken for granted through two-and-a-half millennia, with some interruptions. Cinematography was immensely liberating for art, but it also changed the direction of art. Art must now, whatever else it does, come to terms with its own nature. It must discover what that nature really is. In Hegelian terms, it had reached a kind of consciousness of itself as a problem. Up to now, art had a set of problems, but it was not a problem for itself. Perhaps it had been a problem for philosophers. But now, in becoming a problem for itself, it began to attain a certain philosophical dimension. It faced that crisis of self-identity a sensitive person may face at a certain moment of her or his life, when existence can no longer be taken as given, where one can only go ahead by discovering who one is — and consciousness of that problem henceforward becomes *part* of what one is. Heidegger speaks of man as a being for whom the question of his being is part of his being. It is a profoundly philosophical moment when this becomes a matter of consciousness in one's life, and it is my claim that such a consciousness began to define art after the advent of cinematography. In rethinking its identity, art had of course to rethink the meaning of its history. It could no longer assume that its history had to be the progressive endeavour it had seemed up to then to be.

There are two theoretical responses to this problem that I know of, one of which is quite familiar today. This is a theory of art history best exemplified perhaps in the great and groundbreaking thought of the art historian Erwin Panofsky. Panofsky put forward a remarkable thesis in a no-less remarkable paper of 1927 (just a century after Hegel's prediction). Called *Die Perspektive als symbolische Form — Perspective as Symbolic Form —* Panofsky's bold thesis was that, instead of marking a certain stage in the advancing conquest of visual appearances, perspective marked a certain change in historical direction: It was a form through which its civilization began to represent the world on a symbolic level, as though optics was a matter more of meaning than mimesis. Perspective, or optical exactitude, for example, would have no meaning for an artistic tradition in which even if it were known about, its practitioners were concerned with other ways of symbolizing the world. It plays no role in the mask-making artforms of the Guro people of the Ivory Coast, whose works, concerned with magic and with dark powers, with a different intervention of art into life than optical similitude would allow, would have no use for the kind of knowledge perspective represents. For Panofsky, perspective then was symbolic of what one might call the 'Renaissance philosophy of man and world.'

It is certainly true that painting in the period after 1905 abandoned perspective, not because artists had lost the technique but because it bore no relevance to what they were seeking. Indeed, if perspective was symbolic, its rejection would be symbolic as well, and part of the meaning of the new work would be carried by its palpable absence or by distortion. And with this new symbolic form, a shift analogous to what has come to be called a 'paradigm shift' in science took place. So in Panofsky's view, there is no progress in the history of art, simply the working out of different symbolic forms until, in whatever way it takes place, some internal upheaval gives rise to a new culture and new sets of symbolic forms. Panofsky's own discipline, what he termed 'iconology,' was concerned specifically to identify those points in history at which such transformative changes took place, and to map the symbolic forms through which the new period was defined. Its art, but its art no more than anything else distinctive to it, expressed the culture as our behaviour and speech express our personality.

In any case it is clear that Panofsky's view of art history is that it has no narrative structure. There is instead just the chronicle of symbolic form succeeding symbolic form. The history of art can stop, though it is not clear that there would ever be a social life without some idiom of symbolic representation, however bleak its reality. There is no story to tell. It must have been something like this that Gombrich meant when, somewhat inconsistently with his own progressive theories of history, he suggested in his textbook on art that there is no such thing as art, only the lives of the artist.

This is one way of thinking about history of art. Hegel's is the other.

I have often said that there is no nutshell capacious enough to contain the philosophy of Hegel in the extravagance of its made totality — but in a nutshell, his thesis about history is that it consists in the progressive coming to philosophical consciousness of its own processes, so that the philosophy of history is the end of history, and internally related to its drive. Hegel congratulated history for having achieved consciousness of itself through him, for his philosophy, he supposed, was the meaning of history. This coming to consciousness proceeds by discontinuous stages, which is the dialectic of which certain theories of history make so much. So that in a way Hegel's model of history combined features of both the models I have discussed here: It is narrativistic, in that it has an end, but it is discontinuous in that there is an internal reason why there are those cataclysmic changes outwardly expressed by symbolic forms. (Panofsky's idea of symbolic forms is in fact a rephrasing of Hegel's own theory of the spirit or *Geist* of a given time.) Once more, the best example of something that exhibits this structure would be a single life, not as one event after another, say as it would be represented at a low level of biography, but as the moving from stage to stage of consciousness through growth until the person comes to understand his or her own history at some moment of maturity — after which one's life is up to oneself. Hegel, and Marx as well, supposed that once we become aware of history — or history becomes aware of itself through us — we enter the realm of freedom, no longer subject to the iron laws of development and transformation. The whole of history is the structure of a full human life writ large. It is a progress, but not a linear progress. Each stage is the revolutionization of the preceding stages, until the seeds of revolution have worked themselves out.

Now something like this structure is what I want to say is illustrated by the history of art. My sense is that with the trauma to its own theory of itself, painting had to discover, or try to discover, what its true identity was. With the trauma, it entered onto a new level of self-awareness. My view, again, is that painting had to be the avant-garde art just because no art sustained the kind of trauma it did with the advent of cinema. But its quest for self-identity was limited by the fact that it was *painting* which was the avant-garde art, for painting remains a nonverbal activity, even if more and more verbality began to be incorporated into works of art — 'painted words' in Tom Wolfe's apt but shallow phrase. Without theory, who could see a blank canvas, a square lead plate, a tilted beam, some dropped rope, as works of art? Perhaps the same question was being raised all across the face of the art world but for me it became conspicuous at last in that show of Andy Warhol at the Stable Gallery in 1964, when the Brillo box asked, in effect, why it was art when something just like it was not. And with this, it seemed to me, the history of art attained that point where it had to turn into its own philosophy. It had gone, as art, as far as it could go. In turning into philosophy, art had come to an end. From now on progress could only be enacted on a level of abstract self-consciousness of the kind which philosophy alone must consist in. If artists wished to participate in this progress, they would have to undertake a study very different from what the art schools could prepare them for. They would have to become philosophers. Much as art on one model of its history turned the responsibility for progress over to cinema, it turned the responsibility for progress over to philosophy on another model of its history. Painting does not stop when it ends like this. But it enters what I like to term its post-historical period.

In its great philosophical phase, from about 1905 to about 1964, modern art undertook a massive investigation into its own nature and essence. It set out to seek a form of itself so pure as art that nothing like what caused it to undertake this investigation in the first place could ever happen to it again. It realized that it had identified its essence with something it could exist without, namely the production of optical equivalences, and it is no accident that abstraction should be among the first brilliant stages in its marvellous ascent to self-comprehension. There have been more projected definitions of art, each identified with a different movement of art, in the six or seven decades of the modern era, than in the six or seven centuries that preceded it. Each definition was accompanied by a severe condemnation of everything else as *not* art. There was an almost religious fervour, as though historical salvation depended upon having found the truth of one's own being. It was like the strife of warring sects. That has all but vanished from the art scene today. And this returns me to the decade of the 1970s, with which I began this philosophical narrative. The 1970s were the period of relaxed toleration, a period of benign pluralism, a period of 'do as you like,' after the great style wars had subsided.

Those were the first years of the post-historical period, and because it was, as a period, so new, how could it not have been incoherent? On the one hand there was the sense that something had come to an end. On the other there was the sense that things had to go on as before, since the art world was possessed by a historical picture that called for a next thing. I am suggesting that in that sense there are to be no next things. The time for next things is past. The end of art coincides with the end of a history of art that has that kind of structure. After that there is nothing to do but live happily ever after. It was like coming to the end of the world with no more continents to discover. One must now begin to make habitable the only continents that there are. One must learn to live within the limits of the world.

Conclusion

As I see it, this means returning art to the serving of largely human ends. There is after all something finally satisfying in making likenesses, and it is not surprising that there should have been a great upsurge in realism. There is something finally satisfying in just moving paint around. Drawing pictures and playing with mud are very early manifestations of the impulses that become art. So it is not surprising that there should have been an upsurge in expressionism. These were next things, but not the kinds of next things that the art world with its view of history as demanded by the art market had in mind. So it is not surprising that there should be wild swings in that market.

It is no mean thing for art that it should now be an enhancement of human life. And it was in its capacity as such an enhancement that Hegel supposed that art would go on even after it had come to an end. It is only that he did not suppose happiness to be the highest vocation to which a spiritual existence is summoned. For him the highest vocation is self-knowledge, and this he felt was to be achieved by philosophy. Art went as far as it can have gone in this direction, toward philosophy, in the present century. This is what he would have meant by saying art reaches its end. The comparison with philosophy is not intended as invidious. Philosophy too comes to an end, but unlike art it really must stop when it reaches its end, for there is nothing for it to do when it has fulfilled its task.

Chapter 12

Aesthetics after Modernism

Peter Fuller

Introduction

A spectre is haunting Europe and America: the spectre of Post-Modernism. Western culture is undergoing a transforming shift in its 'structure of feeling'. But perhaps the image of a revolution in taste is wrong, because what is occurring in aesthetic life today is recuperative, and, in many ways profoundly conservative. Of course, this aesthetic conservatism cannot be equated with the mood of political conservatism that is infecting Western societies; indeed it may have more in common with, say, the 'progressive' conservationism of the ecological lobby, or the anti-nuclear movements, than with anything that might comfort Mrs Thatcher.

Let me cite some specific examples. Take painting. When I set out as a professional critic in the late 1960s, the history of recent art was still presented as an ever-evolving continuum of mainstream fashions. Museums, magazines and books encouraged the view that Abstract Expressionism gave way to Post-Painterly Abstraction and Pop, which are followed by Minimalism and Photo-Realism which, in turn, inevitably gave way to such non-painterly activities as Concept-ualism, 'mixed media', photo-texts, Theoretical Art, and so on. Thus in the early 1970s, the assertion of 'The Death of Painting' had become a commonplace of 'progressive' taste. Art students, for example, seemed preoccupied with the arrow of the so-called 'avant-garde' as it sped on down an ever-narrowing tunnel in which more and more of the painter's traditional concerns were shed.

Recently, however, a massive exhibition at London's Royal Academy heralded 'A New Spirit in Painting': a 'turning back to traditional concerns'. The 145 big paintings on show had all been made within the previous ten years by artists as various as Pablo Picasso, Balthus, Guston, and Hockney, and a younger generation of American, British, German and Italian painters. According to the organizers this demonstrated, 'Great painting is being produced today', and presented 'a position in art which conspicuously asserts traditional values, such as individual creativity, accountability and quality'. Thus we were told that for all its 'apparent conservatism' the work on show was 'in the true sense progressive'.

Or look at British sculpture. Back in the early sixties, when Labour leader Harold Wilson was talking about 'the white heat of the technological revolution',

Anthony Caro initiated a revolution in sculpture by going 'radically abstract'. He abandoned all reference to natural form, and jettisoned traditional sculptural materials and practices in favour of painted, prefabricated, industrial components joined together by welds. Sculpture, Caro said, could be anything: and his students at St Martin's School of Art proceeded to dissolve the art into the mere placement of unworked materials in heaps, piles, stacks, and bundles, or, worse still, such unsculptural activities as photography, events, and performance. But today, our best younger sculptors are simply refusing the history of the last twenty years; they are taking up the challenge of what had been done in sculpture before Caro's revolution and are returning to direct carving, modelling, and the making of sculptures rooted in the imagery of men, women and animals.

Inevitably, these shifts in painting and sculpture are affecting art education too. Twelve years ago, in Britain, it was officially stated in the second Coldstream report that the purpose of an education in Fine Art was not the study of painting or sculpture but the pursuit of an attitude which could manifest itself in almost any way. In the 1960s art schools had been built without even the facilities for life drawing, but mixed media, photo-based techniques, and what-have-you proliferated. Today, it is the students themselves who are demanding the right to work from the model: some are even choosing to study anatomy from the cadaver again. Similarly, of their own volition, they are flocking out into the fields, hills, and mountains of Britain, once more, armed with sketch pads and boxes of water-colours.

But this movement of taste extends beyond the Fine Arts: I well remember how, back in the late 1960s, 'mass production' was held up as the condition to which all art should aspire. Reproductions, multiples, and photographs were deemed somehow 'holier' than originals or unique objects. Today, that is changing too. John Ruskin once rejected 'the common notion of Liberalism that bad art, disseminated, is instructive and good art isolated, not so'. 'The question', he explained, 'is first ... whether what art you have got is good or bad. If essentially bad, the more you see of it, the worse for you'. We, too, are realizing that Bauhaus notwithstanding, full aesthetic expression and mechanical production are incompatible. Suddenly, in Britain, the 'arts and crafts', hidden away in fustian obscurity since the 1930s, are re-emerging on the side of the angels. In a country ravaged by recession, the craft revival — symbolized by the establishment of an official Crafts Council, with palatial new galleries — has been among the most conspicuous cultural phenomenum of the last decade.

The Shift from Modernism in Architecture

But this shift in taste is nowhere more apparent than in architecture. Sir Nikolaus Pevsner, distinguished architectural historian and author of *The Pioneers of Modern Design*, once held the view that, in our time, 'form must follow function'; he thought the International Style was the only possible path for architecture today. Back in 1961, Pevsner found himself puzzling over plans for

Sydney Opera House. At that time, he was crusading against 'The Return to Historicism', by which he meant that a few renegades were deviating from today's style to create buildings which, as he put it, 'did not convey a sense of confidence in their well-functioning'. So Sir Nikolaus raised his lance to tilt at imaginative, expressive, and decorative elements — which he regarded as anachronisms — in recent building.

But what could he say of Sydney Opera House? Pevsner had too astute an eye to reject it out of hand. And yet, of course, it could not be accommodated by any of the criteria functionalists held dear. So Pevsner was forced to suggest that maybe Utzon's sail or shell shapes were structurally necessary after all. Or, then again, perhaps opera houses were a 'special case'. 'It is at least arguable', Pevsner wrote, 'whether for so festive a building as an opera house, in so spectacular a position as the Sydney Opera House occupies, strictly functional forms would not have been too severe'. Nonetheless, such 'funny turns' by famous architects were not to be encouraged. They tempted lesser men to stray. A dangerous revolt against rationalism was seeping into architectural practice. Pevsner re-affirmed high functionalism against such deviations. 'The individual building', he argued, 'must remain rational. If you keep your building square, you are not necessarily a square.'

Twenty years on, of course, heresy reigns supreme — and not only in spectacularly positioned opera houses. No one is keeping their buildings square. Irrationalism abounds and ornamentation is flooding back. Even Philip Johnson, erstwhile originator of the International Style, is opportunistically welding bits and pieces of classical decoration onto his new sky-scrapers, just like a younger generation of self-styled Post-Modern Classicists.

Inevitably, the art of the pre-Modernist past is being re-evaluated too. Have you ever heard any one say before that William Butterfield — Victorian master of 'constructional polychromy', and architect of Melbourne and Adelaide cathedrals — was a greater architect than Mies van der Rohe? Well, you have now. And you will be hearing a lot more such judgments in the near future. The great pariahs are coming in from the cold! As a young proto-Modernist, I was taught only to revile the memory of Edwin Landseer, painter of *The Monarch of the Glen*, and Victorian doggie pictures. Similarly, Edwin Lutyens, extravagantly expressive architect to an Edwardian imperial class, was always held up to me as what was wrong in architecture until Modernism cleaned it up. As for William Burges, High Victorian designer ... well, in my youth, he was just *unspeakable*. But very recently in London you could have seen within just a few weeks national exhibitions of Landseer at the Tate, Lutyens at the Hayward, and Burges at the V & A. At roughly the same time, an exhibition of Butterfield's working drawings opened at a commercial gallery usually devoted to 'mainstream' twentieth century art. Such a line-up would have been inconceivable ten years ago.

The Aesthetic Dilemma of the Present Moment

I think it is obvious that there is much about what is going on today that I welcome; for example, the renewed interest in observation, natural form, imagination, drawing, and traditional 'painterly' and sculptural skills in the Fine Arts. I am delighted that, in British art colleges at least, pseudo-structuralist photo-texts are at last giving way to life drawing. I am also glad to see this interest in the crafts, rather than the mass-produced, and the waning of the mechanical dogmas of the International Style in architecture. All this indicates that an 'aesthetic dimension' of life which had been squashed and marginalized by modern technology and economic structure may be seeking to be born again.

But, it seems that contemporary society has a pelvic aperture of steel: at least this 'aesthetic dimension' appears crushed and warped even before it has seen the light of day. Certainly, it is having difficulty in making itself manifest in a compelling or coherent way. Thus, though the rhetoric surrounding that exhibition, 'A New Spirit in Painting', struck the right notes, most of the works actually shown (especially those by the younger generation) were, quite simply, awful. Their inflation of over-weening subjectivity certainly did not prove to me, at least, that great painting was in fact being made today. Similarly, in the crafts, however skilled and conscientious individual makers may be, their work always falls far short of the great traditions of handicraftsmanship of the past. And, as for architecture ... We have already seen and heard of enough follies (like buildings whose walls create the illusion they are crumbling), arbitrary ornament, and debased symbolic structure (e.g. houses in the shape of toy ducks, or restaurants built like hamburgers) to begin to feel a certain nostalgia for that 'rationalism' which one was once so glad to see go. So, what are we to make of the vicissitudes of the 'aesthetic dimension' in our time?

Understanding the Aesthetic Dimension

I am about to paint with a brush as broad as that of those new-spirited expressionistic painters whom I have just criticized. I need to demonstrate that this 'aesthetic dimension' was a significant potentiality of our species, but one which has been progressively menaced and emasculated in recent times. I also want to show how Late Modernism, in particular, colluded with this betrayal of the 'aesthetic dimension'. Then I will be in a position to estimate the mutant protests of the last few years against incipient 'General Anaesthesia', and to present my prognosis for 'Aesthetics after Modernism'.

Of course, this phrase, 'the aesthetic dimension', is something I have plagiarized from Herbert Marcuse's last great essay where he argued that when art is faithful to its own aesthetic form, it 'breaks open a dimension inaccessible to other experience, a dimension in which human beings, nature, and things no longer stand under the law of the established reality principle'. Thus Marcuse set himself against all manifestations of what he called 'Anti-Art' — ranging through collage, mixed media, and Dada-esque activities — which he perceived in recent Modernism. Such renunciation of aesthetic form was, he said, 'abdication of responsibility' because 'it deprives art of the very form in which it can create that other reality within the established one — the cosmos of hope'. For Marcuse, as for me, 'the encounter with the truth of art happens in the estranging language and images which make perceptible, visible and audible that which is no longer, or not yet, perceived, said, and heard in everyday life'. I want, now, to take up these themes where Marcuse left them off by asking whether we can, as it were, root this great, if threatened, human potentiality in the biology of our species.

This has been a preoccupation of my recent work. Evidently, I can't rehearse all my theories and findings here, but I want to re-iterate certain points to make my argument clear. I think it probable that, in its narrowest sense, 'aesthetic experience' is the pleasure accompanying congenitally given responses to certain auditory and visual stimuli. Such a rudimentary sense of beauty is observable among, say, birds and fishes in their responses to tunes, patterns and ornament given by nature. These proto-aesthetic phenomena always seem to be bound up with processes of identification with the species-group or material environment, and, simultaneously, with the way in which the organism differentiates itself from its environment: pattern serves the purpose of camouflage and display. In our species, however, the pleasurable response to such stimuli seems loosened from its original biological function; furthermore, sensuous impressions which give rise to aesthetic experience evoke a wide range of nuanced feelings, which merge with a labile world of symbolization, imaginative metamorphosis, and representation. Thus, whatever pure formalist painters may tell us, we can no more *reduce* aesthetic experience to instinctive response than we could reduce love to what goes on in our erectile tissues or vaginal juices.

But the aesthetic life of man differs from that of the animals in another way too. Our aesthetic experience is not just a matter of subjective response: rather it is linked to certain manipulative skills. Man, born naked, is ornamented not by nature but through his own handiwork; and he has the power to extend that process of ornamentation from his own body into the world around him. Finally, the ornamental impulse merges into the making of autonomous representations of what he has seen, dreamed, or imagined.

Now why in man, uniquely, should aesthetic life be enmeshed with symbolic transformation and expressive *work*? That is a long story I have tried to tell elsewhere. But, broadly, I believe that our capacity to make and enjoy art was a by-product of certain evolutionary changes in our species which reached a climax about forty thousand years ago. Certainly, historically, these changes were accompanied by the emergence of a higher culture: the most significant of them were the prolongation of the infant-mother relationship, and secondarily, the rapid evolution of the human hand.

Why did this extension of the infant-mother relationship prove so important for the aesthetic and cultural life of man? Well, the young of other higher animals are compelled to relate immediately to reality if they are to survive. The piglet must fight against its siblings for its place on the line of teats within instants of birth. But the human infant has not even the wherewithal to seek out the mother's breast when it feels hungry: the mother must *present* the breast, and by extension the world, to the infant, if it is to go on being.

Donald Winnicott, a leading British psychoanalyst, once explained how *subjectively* this utter dependence of the human infant gave rise to a feeling of absolute independence, of God-like omnipotence. When the infant feels hungry and the breast is presented, he experiences a 'moment of illusion': the illusion that he can create a breast, and thereby an external world, which will nourish and succour. Thus the human infant *imaginatively creates* the world to which the young of other animals are constrained to relate functionally. Only slowly does the human infant come to accept the world as existing independently of himself or his creative powers. Such acceptance, Winnicott called 'disillusion' and associated with the frustrations of weaning.

'The Reality Principle', Winnicott once wrote, 'is the fact of the existence of the world whether the baby creates it or not. It is the arch enemy of spontaneity, creativity, and the sense of Real ... The Reality Principle is an insult'. But, as Marcuse rightly saw, in art, 'human beings, nature, and things no longer stand under the law of the established reality principle'. Winnicott can help us to understand why this is so.

He points out how as the infant goes through disillusion, he begins to make use of 'transitional objects' — such things as rags, dolls, and teddy bears to which young children become attached — which belong to an intermediate area between the subjective and that which is objectively perceived. Almost as consolation for the lost capacity to create the world, the infant establishes an intermediate area of experience, or 'potential space', to which inner reality and external life both contribute. Thus the infant seeks to avoid separation by the filling in of the potential space with the use of symbols and all that eventually adds up to a cultural life. For, as Winnicott puts it, no human being is ever free from the strain of relating inner and outer reality: hence the continuing need for an intermediate area that is not challenged. The potential space, originally between baby and mother, is ideally reproduced between child and family, and between individual and society, or the world. Thus Winnicott described this intermediate area as the *the location of cultural experience*, which, as it were, provides redemption from the insult of the Reality Principle.

One way it does this is through religion which allows the illusion that if it was not our own mind which created the world, then it was, at least, some other mind, generally benevolent to ourselves. And then, of course, there is art ... Disjunctured as the human infant may be from function and necessity, the growing child (by reason of the evolution of hand and brain) manifests exceptional capacities to act on the external world. As the child abandons the illusion of omnipotence, one of his most important transitional compensations comes through *play*. Even when as an adult he is constrained to relate to reality immediately and functionally, through work, for the purposes of survival, he finds (at least if he lives in an aesthetically healthy society) that he is compensated by the persistence of a creative, imaginative, and aesthetic component in his everyday labours. As Edmund Leach, the social anthropologist, once put it: 'Each of us is constantly engaged almost from birth, in a struggle to distinguish "I" from "other" while at the same time trying to ensure that "I" does not become wholly isolated from "other". And this is where art comes in. It is the bridge we need to save ourselves from schizophrenia.' Indeed, one might say that rhythm, pattern and the decorative arts draw upon feelings of union and fusion; whereas carving, figurative painting, and the proportional arts of architecture are rather expressive of separation, and the recognition of the 'other' as an objectively perceived feature.

But we have to remember that, once, art was not a category set apart: the aesthetic dimension permeated all human skills; the potential space was held open within the everyday pursuits of ordinary men and women. But, for this to happen, the environment must be as facilitating as mother once was: in particular it must provide appropriate materials and a living stylistic tradition. Through working upon these everyone can thus simultaneously express his individuality, and affirm his identity with the shared symbolic values of the group. In this way, the insult of the Reality Principle is softened, and human creativity unleashed.

Perhaps I could clarify my concept of an aesthetically healthy society through referring to aboriginal art. In traditional aboriginal societies, we find the most rudimentary form of aesthetic activity — body painting and adornment — associated with ritual, rhythm, and the affirmation of shared religious beliefs. But we see, too, how ornamentation is extended from the body to the non-functional (except in a symbolic sense) transformation of environmental features like rocks, trees, and shells: these activities merge into pictorial representation. Nonetheless, in aboriginal culture, there are no clear boundaries between art and other forms of work. The aborigines decorate many of the things they make: naturalistic and geometric designs proliferate over paddles, spear-throwers, boomerangs, baskets, shields, message sticks — and all manner of everyday objects. Their forms are often determined not just by practical function, but also through symbolic intent, and attention to the aesthetic qualities and properties of materials used. But, as far as we know, there were no professional artists among the aboriginal tribes. Everyone participated in artistic production; or, to be more precise, art was a dimension of everyone's productive life. But this never meant that the aesthetic dimension sank to the lowest common denominator. Unevenness of ability was recognized; those who showed exceptional artistic talent tended to be specially encouraged.

The fundamental elements of the 'aesthetic dimension', then, include instinctive aesthetic sensations; and imaginative and physical work on materials and stylistic conventions as given by tradition. Through engagement with the latter, an individual's work enters into the 'symbolic order' of a society without losing its individuality. That, I think, is what Winnicott meant when he said there can be no originality except on the basis of tradition. Of course, the particular form the aesthetic dimension takes in any given society will depend on historical vicissitudes. But the problem is that in advanced industrial societies it seems almost as if 'the aesthetic dimension' has been hopelessly marginalized, and the 'potential space' — at least as the location of adult cultural experience — effectively sealed over. So what has gone wrong?

Aesthetic Experience and the Dissociation of Sensibility

I must reach for that very broad brush again, this time to do some quick history painting. I want to argue that this aesthetic crisis has its roots in the disruption of the shared symbolic order, which began in the Renaissance; and the radical change in work which was brought about by the subsequent industrial revolution. If it were permissible to psychologize historical processes, I would say that, in the Renaissance, the 'structure of feeling' changed: emphasis shifted from a sense of fusion with the world (originally the mother) towards 'realistic' individuation, and recognition of its separateness. Science began to travel along those paths which eventually led to the discovery that the world was not created by a feelingful mind well disposed to, and in effect a projection of, ourselves but was rather the chance product of natural processes. T. S. Eliot once observed that this led to a 'dissociation of sensibility' from which we are still suffering. From this time on, men and women were compelled to shift uneasily between an emotional participation in the world, and the pose that they were outside a system they could observe objectively. Predictably, in the Renaissance, the ornamental and decorative arts of fusion started their long decline; whereas mimetic and figurative arts leapt out of the decaying sub-soil of the crafts.

Soon after, these processes were accelerated by changes in the nature of *work*. I am sure no-one needs reminding that the eighteenth and nineteenth centuries, in Europe, saw the proliferation of industrial capitalism, the spread of the factory system, and the emergence of a 'working-class': these developments expunged the 'aesthetic dimension' from everyday life. The division of labour severed the creative relationship between imagination, intellect, heart and hand: in effect the 'potential space' began to shrink. The insult of the Reality Principle impinged deeper and deeper into the lives of ordinary people. There was no room for an intermediate area on production lines, at the pit-head, or in steel furnaces.

Inevitably, of course, in this situation there were those who yearned for what was being lost: John Ruskin, for example, put forward the paradigm of 'The Gothic' — which, in as far as it wasn't a purely historical category (which it never really was for him) was close to my concept of the 'aesthetic dimension', or Winnicott's idea of the 'potential space' as the location of cultural experience. Or, as John Unrau has recently put it, 'The Gothic', for Ruskin, was a mythological vision of 'what all human labour might ideally become'. Kristine Garrigan has written that for Ruskin a great masterpiece of Gothic architecture 'stands not only figuratively but also literally for the spiritually unified society in which each member's creativity however minor or imperfect is respected and welcomed'. Ruskin saw such a building not as a structural enclosure of space, but as 'a symbolic shelter for mankind's noblest aspirations'. This, of course, did not exclude individual expressive work — but rather drew it out. Thus Ruskin stressed how the Gothic system of ornament in 'every jot and tittle, every point and niche ... affords room, fuel and focus for individual fire'.

Although, in the nineteenth century, the 'aesthetic dimension' was compelled to retreat from everyday life, 'Art', of course, persisted. But it was no longer an element in man's lived relationship to his world: rather it became the pursuit of certain creative men of genius, who were set apart in the sense that they were not expected to bow to the inexorable dictates of an ever more tyrannous Reality Principle. 'The Arts in their highest province', Joshua Reynolds once said, 'are not addressed to the gross senses, but to the desires of the mind, to that spark of divinity which we have within, impatient of being circumscribed and pent up by the world which is about us'. The Arts thus became the special preserve for a dimension of imaginative creativity which had once pervaded all cultural activities. But the Artist could not, of course, penetrate deeply into the productive processes and social fabric: rather his task increasingly became the creation of the *illusion* of what Marcuse called 'other realities within the existing one'. The painter had long since ceased to be primarily the decorator of architectural space, or functional objects like pots and boomerangs: rather, with the assistance of focused perspective, he became the creator of a painted world in an illusory space behind the picture plane: a human god, in fact. Aesthetic form acquired its autonomy from, and indeed opposition too, life as lived. As Ruskin so vividly put it, 'The English school of landscape culminating in Turner is in reality nothing else than a healthy effort to fill the void which destruction of Gothic architecture has left'.

But how, even in illusion, could the Fine Artist continue to fill that void given the long, withdrawing roar of the Sea of Faith? How, without a religious iconography, could the painter appeal beyond 'the gross senses'? Ruskin tried to show how Turner had studied nature so closely because through nature he found God: but such a pantheistic solution depended upon sustaining the belief that nature *was* the handiwork of God. And, as the nineteenth century progressed, the nakedness of the shingles of the world became more and more apparent.

When it seemed that nature could no longer provide a viable alternative for the lost symbolic order, the 'aesthetic dimension' began to disintegrate even in its illusory re-incarnation behind the picture plane. Art aspired to redeem itself through submission to the Reality Principle (in naturalism, impressionism, etc.). Or, alternatively, in the aesthetic movement of the late nineteenth century, it sometimes tried to reduce itself to the pleasure to be derived from the stimulation of residual aesthetic instincts through looking at certain combinations of colour and form. Ruskin called such merely sensuous pleasure 'aesthesis' and predictably expressed contempt for 'the feelings of the beautiful we share with spiders and flies.' This was at the root of his notorious quarrel with Whistler and Modern Art 'under the guidance of the School of Paris'. But the esotericism of such movements as Symbolism could provide no consolation for the loss of a shared symbolic order. Not surprisingly, even in the nineteenth century, the artist sometimes felt himself to be menaced by a darkling plane of General Anaesthesia. As nature seemed to become drained of meaning and feeling alike, art itself seemed threatened. Significantly, as Ruskin's own religious faith waxed and waned, he found himself tormented by an obsession with a failure in nature itself; he believed he could detect an evil storm cloud and plague wind in the landscape. A grey shroud, which he associated with the blasphemous actions of men, seemed to be descending on the world portending ultimate annihilation. At such times, he could not bear to gaze even upon his beloved Turners, and he ordered them out of the house.

Others described the aesthetic crisis in different ways: William Morris predicted that the divorce of the High Arts from a living tradition of creative work in the crafts would lead to the death of architecture, sculpture, painting, and the crowd of lesser arts that belong to them. He foresaw what he called 'this dead blank of the arts'. 'If the blank space must happen', he wrote, 'it must and amidst its darkness the new seed must sprout.' I am trying to suggest that the 'dead blank' was in fact realized in Late Modernism ... and that, just possibly, what I have been calling 'Post-Modernism' is the sprouting of a new seed.

Late Modernism as the Ultimate Impoverishment of the Aesthetic Dimension

I cannot do justice to the history of Modernism here but don't worry! I'm not Robert Hughes — so I won't even try. I just want to emphasize that, however uneven its development, whatever individual triumphs there may have been on the way (and there were many) Modernism completed this draining away of the aesthetic dimension even within the arts themselves. This can be seen taking place in Late Modernism, by which I mean (roughly speaking) 'mainstream' post-Second World War art. Art severed itself from the 'cosmos of hope'; it ceased to offer 'an other reality within the existing one', or a miniature realization of the 'potential space'. Rather, it began to reflect that squeezing out of a cultural space for imagination, individual subjectivity, and expressive or affectively satisfying work. I want to illustrate my argument by saying something about two strands within the fragmented Modernist tradition: functionalist architecture, and abstract painting.

Take modern architecture: now we have seen how Ruskin rightly regarded good ornament as the means through which a building aspired to the aesthetic dimension, and entered into the shared symbolic values of the community. He also saw it as the guarantee of the creative work of the individual workman. But, of course, nineteenth century mechanization of ornamental features wrecked all this and reduced ornament to stuck on effects. At the beginning of the twentieth century, Modernist architecture arose with the credo that form should follow function, which, in effect, made the architect synonymous with the engineer, and endeavoured to sell out architecture to the 'Reality Principle'. But the pioneer Modernists had failed to recognize the distinction between the dead residue of the aesthetic dimension they were sweeping away and living ornament which as Ruskin again rightly put it is 'the principal part' of architecture as opposed to building.

Indeed, in 1908, Adolf Loos, a pioneer of Modernism, published a paper called 'Ornament and Crime' rejecting all the decorative arts (including the 'babbling' of painting) on the grounds that they were erotic and involved reproductive work. Ornament, Loos argued, was OK for children, criminals and primitive people. Children like scrawling on lavatory walls; eighty per cent of prisoners bear tattoos; 'and the Papuan tattoos his skin, his boat, his rudder, his oars; in short, everything he can get his hands on'. (Remember what I argued about aboriginal art?) But Loos claimed, 'what is natural for a Papuan and a child is degenerate for modern man'. Thus he declared, 'I have discovered the following truth and present it to the world: cultural evolution is equivalent to the removal of ornament from articles in every day use ... Don't weep!' he said. 'Don't you see that the greatness of our age lies in its inability to produce a new form of decoration? We have conquered ornament, we have won through to lack of ornamentation'. He painted a picture — if that's an appropriate metaphor — of a new Zion for modern man in which the streets of the town would 'glisten like white walls'.

Ornament wasn't just regressive. It was also uneconomic. If there was no ornament, Loos reasoned, 'a man would have to work only four hours instead of eight, for half the work done at present is still for ornamentation. Ornament is wasted labour'. Loos was especially critical of 'stragglers', i.e. 'modern men' who gave in to a liking for a little decorative stitching on their shoes, a patterned wall-paper, or frill of lace. Stragglers, he said, 'slow down the cultural progress of nations and humanity, for ornament is not only produced by criminals; it itself commits a crime by damaging men's health, the national economy and cultural development'.

The only decorative elements Loos permitted were materials deployed for their given qualities: no symbolic or expressive transformation was allowed. Similar sentiments proliferated among all the 'pioneers'; their followers implemented the anti-ornamentalist programme with the ruthlessness of converts. Modernism sought, in Lubetkin's words, to assert itself against 'subjectivity and equivocation'. Synthetic and unaesthetic materials, engineering methods, standardization, and repetitive rectilinear forms triumphed in the advance, from the 1930s onwards, of the anaesthetic International Style. 'The individual', wrote Mies van der Rohe with ominous glee, 'is losing significance; his density is no longer what interests us. The decisive achievements in all fields are impersonal and their authors for the most part unknown. They are part of the trend of our time towards anonymity'.

Now we have seen the new Zion in which the only worthwhile labour is immediately productive, ornament is banished and people inhabit not houses but 'machines for living in', and it does not work. Where, in all that dead expanse of curtain wall, is there an inch of space for symbols and values beyond the demands of function and necessity? Where, in all that cantilevering, is there any 'room, fuel and focus for individual fire'? Ruskin prophesied the hell we made for ourselves. 'You shall draw out your plates of glass', he wrote 'and beat out your bars of iron, till you have encompassed us all ... with endless perspectives of black skeleton and blinding square'.

All right, now abstract painting: I believe Modernist painting manifests a progressive *kenosis*. That's a term I've borrowed from theology: it means a voluntary relinquishment of divine power. Painters simply renounced their capacity to create illusory worlds. Thus within Modernism, perspective space and the imitation of nature fade, and there is a surge of emphasis on painting's roots in decoration and sensuous manipulation of materials, and a belief that such elements could provide a replacement for the lost symbolic order, destroyed by the decline of religious iconography, and the subsequent 'failure of nature' to provide a substitute. Some great works were produced this way. Kandinsky, for example, replaced the pathetic fallacy with the art fallacy: the belief that abstract forms and materials could palpitate with his spiritual sentiments.

But Clement Greenberg once pointed out that Kandinsky's art continued to evoke landscape and even flower subjects: 'The atmospheric space in which his images threaten to dissolve', Greenberg wrote, 'remains a reproduction of atmospheric space in nature, and the integrity of the picture depends on the integrity of an illusion'. Late Modernism was to lose all those residues of nature, and that illusion of natural space, in an attempt to use pure colour and form as the sole means for the expression of high sentiment. The greatest painter of that kind was Mark Rothko who created undulating fields of nuanced colour. 'I'm not an abstractionist', Rothko once said. 'I'm not interested in the relationship of colour or form or anything else, I'm interested only in expressing basic human emotions — tragedy, ecstasy, doom and so on.' Rothko added that people who wept before his pictures were having the same religious experience he had when he painted them. 'And if you ... are moved only by their colour relationships', he said, 'then you miss the point'.

The danger, however, was not just that the audience might 'miss the point'; the sentiment, itself, might be swallowed up by the 'negative space' Rothko was creating, leaving, as it were, a 'black hole' where once the painter had offered an alternative world. 'Art', says Hans Kung, the leading Catholic theologian, 'is seen ... no longer against a pantheistic but *against a nihilistic background*'. Kung says this raises the question of art and meaning in a wholly new and ultimate radicalness. He invokes Nietzsche's images of nihilism: 'The sea drunk up (a bleak emptiness), the horizon wiped away (a living space without prospects), the earth unchained from its sun (an abysmal nothingness).' Atheist as I am, I believe Rothko was the great master of this ultimate radicalness. In his art, he returns us to the ground of our being where we may choose extinction or re-engagement with reality in a new way. But Rothko's painting was not just a protest against the anaesthetization of contemporary 'culture': he was also a victim of that process. He chose extinction. You can see that choice in the last paintings he made before his suicide.

These pictures are grey monochromes, in which colour and pictorial space, alike, have drained away. They are not elevating expressions of despair on the threshold of death — like, say, Poussin's great grey painting of *Winter* or *The Deluge*. They, themselves, are empty, *dead*. The redeeming power of an aesthetic transformation has gone. This is what I mean by anaesthesia. In gazing at these works we think of Lear's utterance, beyond tragedy, beyond hope: 'Nothing, nothing, nothing, nothing, nothing.' In these monochromes, Rothko's high sentiments collapsed into the 'blinding square' and 'dead blank' of anti-art. Within a few months, he himself lay dead in a pool of blood on his studio floor.

After Rothko's ultimate painting, most abstract art betrayed the 'aesthetic dimension'. Either it pursued mere aesthesis, or sensuous effects — as in the 'Post-Painterly' abstraction of Morris Louis, Ken Noland, etc. Or it relinquished art in favour of the real — which, we remember, according to Winnicott was the 'arch enemy' of creativity. For example, I remember a large exhibition of 'minimal' art which came to London, from New York in 1969 — the year Rothko was painting those grey pictures. In fact, it included a Rothko as a precursor of the new 'Art of the Real' (the title of the exhibition), which included endless square monochromes and cubes, and, of course, Hal Rheinhardt's all black painting. But the attitude the exhibition expressed about art was the inverse of Rothko's. A statement in big letters on the cover of the catalogue said: 'Today's real makes no direct appeal to the emotions, nor is it involved in uplift, but instead offers itself in the form of the simple, irreducible, irrefutable object.' There we have it! Art was no longer a 'transitional object', a mediator between the real and the 'cosmos of hope', but rather a mere *thing*, indistinguishable from other phenomena. As the catalogue put it, 'The new work of art is very much like a chunk of nature ... and possesses the same hermetic otherness.' Thus, in this *reductio ad absurdum* of Modernist 'truth to materials' that creative 'moment of illusion' which good art provides was utterly extinguished; the potential space was sealed over even within the practice of painting itself. Just a few years ago, I counted up and found I knew seven painters in London who were making nothing but blank, grey monochromes. At that time it seemed that painting, too, had simply succumbed to the General Anaesthesia of our time.

The Anti-aesthetic Practices of the Mega-Visual Tradition

Of course, while ornament was disappearing from architecture, and this terrible *kenosis* of painting was taking place, new means of producing and reproducing imagery were proliferating: indeed, the Fine Arts had become only a small strand in what I have called elsewhere 'the mega-visual tradition' of monopoly capitalism. Here, I am referring to such phenomena as photography, mass-printing, bill-boards, neon signs, television, video, holography, and so on with which we are constantly surrounded. But I believe it is wrong to regard such things as the mode of the aesthetic dimension in our time: rather, like the mechanical ornament of the nineteenth century, they represent only its occlusion and eclipse.

I am sure the Victorians were right. Whatever photography may be, it is not art. A photographic image *is* mechanically processed — not imaginatively and materially *constituted*. The photograph clings to the appearances of the real, which is why it can be an excellent tool when repportage, or visual journalism, is required. But imaginative transformation of photographic materials, or images, is inimical to the practice. If the photographer tries to offer the kind of experience we get from an image of an angel or an undulating plane of colour, à la Rothko, he will certainly end up with a bad photograph. The sophisticated techniques of modern advertising, however, seem in some ways closer to the 'aesthetic dimension' than straightforward photography. There are, as it happens, angels in certain bath salt advertisements! Again, advertising takes everyday materials — like soap, beer, or tobacco — and through imagery associates them with our imaginative longings for a world transformed according to our wishes. But this is prostitution where art is love. Unlike a religion, the symbolic order within which the advertisement is articulated, is cynically displaced from deeply held feelings or values; the transformations of the real we can perceive in an advertisement occupy a shallow and attenuated 'potential space', massively impinged upon by economic interest. Who actually believes that drinking Coke rather than Pepsi will bring about peace on earth? Or that using one brand of detergent rather than another will deepen family love? But, of course, it is not just *what* is shown; it is the way the images are made that bears witness to their inauthenticity. Unlike a painting, an advertisement does not offer a paradigm of what all work might ideally become; although advertisements have displaced ornament, in no sense are they an equivalent for a true ornamental tradition through which each individual's creativity can be welcomed and realized. The advertising system is just piped spectacle, a sad travesty of what art once was.

It was, I suppose, inevitable that the anti-aesthetic practices of this mega-visual tradition would invade the anaesthetic space — the blank squares — left by the disappearance of the true arts ... That Pop Art, Conceptual Art, Political Art, video and mixed media, would swamp in over that emptiness brought about by painting's *kenosis*. Where once there was 'an other reality within the existing one', proffered through realized aesthetic form, now information, ideology, and the prostitute practices of the mega-visual world proliferate.

For example, I saw an exhibition called 'Eureka', which purported to offer a survey of contemporary Australian art. One half of it consisted of posters, installations, set-up photographs, etc. in which not the slightest residue of what I have been calling the 'aesthetic dimension' was discernible. Indeed, the imagery chosen again and again illustrated how in content, as well as in form, such work had committed itself not to the 'cosmos of hope' but rather the pornography of despair. When it comes to making a choice between looking at, say, 'art' photographs of the photographer throwing up, and Oxo's image of a family smiling blissfully around the stew-pot, then I must say I prefer the latter, even though I'm not very interested in either.

Predictably, the theorists are flooding forward to justify the spreading anaesthesia. Just as in the nineteenth century's aesthetic crisis there were those prepared to say that the aesthetic dimension in man was nothing more than instinctive response to retinal sensation, so, in the twentieth century, as that crisis deepened, there was no shortage of those — from logical positivists, to Althusserian Marxists and structuralists — happy to come forward and argue that there was *no such thing* as aesthetic experience at all. For example, a whole breed of British sociologists of art are now telling us that such words as 'artist', 'creation', 'imagination', 'work of art', etc. are just hang-overs from Romantic ideology which need to be erased in favour of such terms as 'cultural producers' and so forth. But I have tried to show you that the vocabulary of art, artists and aesthetics only appears obsolete today because a great dimension of human life and experience is presently catastrophically threatened.

Conclusion

Marcuse once argued that, in our time, the reality principle had become metamorphosed by advanced technology and monopoly capitalism into a tyrannous 'Performance Principle', which was suppressing and distorting a biologically given potentiality of our species for play, creativity, and pleasure. In my Winnicottian terminology, it might be said that today we are producing a Reality Principle, without the redemption of a 'potential space', and that is an insult to us all. I have tried to show how, as it were, the potentiality for a 'potential space' arose in our natural history, as a species; and how, after many historical vicissitudes, it is now perilously threatened. But how much hope are we justified in placing in that apparent resuscitation of the aesthetic dimension which I began by drawing your attention to: i.e. the revival of painting, sculpture, the imaginative and decorative arts, and the whole range of crafts pursuits and practices?

In one sense, it is easy to see that such phenomena represent a desperate attempt to hold open the 'potential space' in our time. But, by its very nature, the aesthetic dimension can only thrive within such a space given a socially given aesthetic *style*; good art can only be realized when a creative individual encounters a living tradition with deep tendrils in communal life. But given the present class divisions, systems of production, and, in the West, the mega-visual traditions to which these give rise, no such style exists: nor is it easy to see how it could exist. For example, in our art schools in Britain, until the changes of the last three or four years, it seemed that there were only two sorts of student: those who took as the paradigm for artistic activities the 'pre-cultural' activities of the child — and engaged in slurpy abstraction, and such like; or those who took their model from the anaesthetic practices of the mega-visual tradition, and replaced art with media studies, photo-texts, video, etc. Because society was so aesthetically sick, there seemed no avenue through which the biologically given potentiality for aesthetic production could be realized in an adult, social way, as in, say, aboriginal society, or Ruskin's concept of the Gothic. The student artist had to choose between infantilism or anaesthesia. Hence the limitations of 'The New Spirit in Painting'.

But the problem can be seen in its most extreme form in architecture now that the anaesthetic anti-style of rectilinear functionalism is under such widespread pressure. As we have seen the enabling and yet resistant forms of, say, Gothic architecture, within which the craftsman worked, sprang out of shared symbolic beliefs: but today, when the architect decides Loos was wrong, where is he to turn for his ornamental language? If he decides he wants something more than aesthesis — or sensuously attractive colours and patterns — he can *either* fall back on individual fantasy, à la Gaudi, or, alternatively, he can turn to the debased symbolic orders of advertising and spectacle. But the electric profusion of 'The Cross' at the other end of William Street in Sydney, Times Square in New York, or Piccadilly Circus in London, will never equal the level of human achievement manifest on the West front of Chartres Cathedral, nor can any number of buildings in the shape of Oxo cubes, hot-dogs, or hamburgers console us for the loss of an ornamental style rooted in sincerely held symbolic beliefs. The only other solution seems to be an eclectic borrowing from ornamental styles of the past: hence 'Post-Modernist Classicism'; but this is to use ornament with about as much sensitivity and meaning as a parrot uses words.

Neither the anaesthesia of functionalism, nor a wallowing in subjectivity, nor prostitution to the symbolic orders of advertising and spectacle, nor yet a parading of the ornamental clothes of the past can cover the fact of the crisis of the 'aesthetic dimension' in our time. Is there then no hope? Winnicott once pointed out how in an individual human subject creativity often seems almost indestructible, despite appallingly unpropitious environmental conditions. As the embryonic plant reaches for the light, creativity can twist into life and redeem the most 'hopeless' of individuals. It may be that the present aesthetic revival is the beginning of such a process within the social fabric itself. Such parallels are, I know, dangerous: but, in this case, the proposition is not entirely unsupported by sociological evidence. As I've argued elsewhere, I think there are at least grounds for hoping that the future may gave rise to a two-tier economy in which, as it were, automated industrial production will continue to develop *alongside* aesthetic production: although, of course, for the potential space to be held open in any significant way, the latter will have to be incorporated into our productive life in a much more radical way than that permitted by leisure, hobbies, or the Fine Art enclave itself. All I can say is that I had *better be* right about this. I agree with Gregory Bateson, the anthropologist, who once said that the passing of belief in the immanence of God within nature was leading men to see the world as mindless, and hence as unworthy of moral, ethical or aesthetic consideration. Although, like Bateson himself, I am an atheist, I think he got it right when he said that when you combined this alienation from nature with an advanced technology then 'your likelihood of survival will be that of a snowball in hell'. Bateson spoke of the need for a new aesthetics, rooted, as he put in, in 'an ecology of mind' — or the recognition that if nature is not the product of mind, then mind itself is in some sense the product of nature — and is therefore immanent within the evolutionary structure, and objectively discernible outside of ourselves. In the 'grammar' of the genetic instructions which inform the leaf how to grow, or the 'beauty' of the patterns on the wings of a butterfly, we see prototypes of man's highest endeavours — even if we do not believe in God. I think that the great British painter, and pioneer Post-Modernist, David Bomberg recognized this when he urged artists to seek 'the spirit in the mass'. And it may be that those who are currently seeking to re-root aesthetics in the study of nature and natural form, in ways which go beyond empiricism, and which nonetheless absolutely refuse explicitly religious connotations, are unwittingly playing their part (however small) in arresting progress towards that General Anaesthesia implicit in the development of our technological society. Of course, that Anaethesia is not just a blank grey monochrome on canvas; it is, as Ruskin foresaw, the annihilation of human life, and nature itself — something which the modern technology of nuclear war has rendered not just a historical possibility, but rather a probability. And so I would like to end by recalling the biblical words: 'Art, I believe: help thou mine unbelief.'

PART V
Art and Tradition

The demise of Modernism has given birth to the desire for a more comprehensive and historically rooted aesthetic.

In this section G. H. Bantock argues for a return after Modernism and Romanticism to a Renaissance aesthetic and considers its implications for the teaching of the arts.

Chapter 13

The Arts in Education

G. H. Bantock

Introduction

One of the best approaches to a contemporary consideration of the role of the arts in education is to see the whole problem in its historical context and evolution. There was a time when certain of the arts were very central to the whole educational system: and perhaps if we go back to that period we will be able to illumine certain of our contemporary dilemmas and difficulties.

The word 'arts' is itself somewhat ambiguous. It can refer to the artefacts, which are the products of artistic endeavour — especially, of course, to painting with which the word 'art' is very often associated. It can also be used to refer to the theory of practice explicitly articulated of some highly developed complex skill. For instance one refers to the arts and implies a body of achievements, a collection of artefacts, paintings, sculptings, musical scores, poems, novels and the like; and one also refers to the 'art' of poetry, of painting, or sculpting, and of other highly developed human activities like politics, for instance ('the art of politics') when one is using it in the theoretical sense. Indeed, I propose historically to go back to the period when the theoretical elucidation of the arts was first articulated (in post-classical Western Europe), the period of the Renaissance. It was during the Renaissance that the literary arts, at least in humanist theory, were at the very centre of educational concern. For the Renaissance was a period when artefacts were produced in very large numbers, but also when important steps were taken in theorizing about the nature of these artefacts. We can therefore not only point to the centrality of the literary arts in Renaissance education but we can also discover why they were thought to be important. Let me then first say a few words briefly about the literary arts which occupied this central position in humanist Renaissance education: what they were and why they were regarded as important. Then we can look at how gradually others of the arts came to seem of almost equal importance — painting, sculpting and so on.

The Literary Arts in Renaissance Education

In the medieval period, at school level people studied what was called the trivium, which consisted of three disciplines — grammar, logic and rhetoric. The emphasis in the medieval period was on grammar (which of course was Latin, not English, grammar), and on logic, which constituted an essential element in theological philosophical argument; the orientation of the Middle Ages towards the theological necessitated a strong stress on the science of argument. But that changed with the Renaissance. What now came to be emphasized was rhetoric, for social and political reasons, for purposes of persuasion. The new educational emphasis arose originally in Italy, where the development of the Italian city state created a need for an educated bureaucracy. This bureaucracy was to be educated in a classical tongue and particularly in that aspect of the classical tongue which came under the heading of rhetoric, derived, of course, from the classical notion of the orator.

The orator played an important political role because, as we were still in an oral age, political action could be influenced by the power of persuasive speech. So the first thing to be said about the literary arts in the Renaissance is that they were directed towards very specific social and political tasks. In a developing society, made up in Italy of small principalities but, north of the Alps, of national societies which were gradually evolving out of the feudal societies of the Middle Ages, the humanist training in rhetoric in the literary arts came to play an important, central role. These societies needed lawyers and behind the legal training there was necessarily a rhetorical training in the arts of speech. They needed ambassadors and ambassadorial functions had to be fulfilled with elegance and a certain power of eloquence. They needed men able to persuade popular assemblies of citizens in the more 'democratic' societies, or rulers in those under the guidance of prince or king. And so this training had an important central moral and political role in the life of these societies. The literary arts were accepted as providing just such a training. Stylistically they afforded models in the work of the great classical writers like Cicero. (Latin had never died, but medieval Latin had never paid the attention to stylistic purity and eloquence which the humanist did.) Secondly, in the experience of the classical past, there was thought to be important moral guidance for the elucidation of contemporary problems. The classical experience was something which arose out of an essentially political literature, for Roman and Greek writings to a very considerable extent are oriented towards politics, a politics which was sustained by the moral philosophies of the ancients, and thus, in the range of its moral possibilities should not be confused with the politicization of the modern totalitarian state. What indeed tended to happen in the Renaissance period was the gradual replacement of the Christian moral emphasis by a more humanistic classical emphasis derived from their literature. (That is a statement that needs to be regarded with some care because the humanists still remained primarily Christian; but by and large the classical experience now began to be absorbed and play a central role in the social and political life of the countries influenced by the humanistic revolution.)

Gradually, too, the other arts — painting, sculpting, architecture — began to play an increasing cultural and social role. There was a time when such arts had been regarded as servile. The medieval painter was primarily a craftsman: the

Renaissance painter, because he gradually began to theorize, and thus to lift the whole intellectual level of the work that he was doing, improved his status, until by the time we reach the high Renaissance people like Leonardo da Vinci and Michelangelo were wooed by the monarchs of Europe. (Was it not true that the Emperor Charles V himself actually bent down and picked up the paintbrush of the great artist Titian when he dropped it? What more splendid indication of the status assigned to a great artist could there be than that the Emperor himself should bend down and pick up the paintbrush of a common painter!) So, during this period artists come to improve their status enormously. From being simple craftsmen they became centrally employed in the whole business of government — as agents, one might almost say, of state prestige and propaganda. Kings and princes quarrelled, for prestige reasons, in order to get their attention. They were regarded as a means by which the state achieved fame and acclaim. So we have now a society where the arts occupied a very important and crucial role. I said earlier a 'central' role; perhaps it's just as well to remember that the scholastic philosophy still continued and therefore there were those who regarded the arts with a somewhat equivocal eye for reasons that I will reveal shortly. In general, however, they now occupied a crucially important role. And indeed if one looks at the educational theory of the Renaissance one will see that at its high-water mark it recommends making a human being as if he were himself a work of art. This is the central notion of that great book of Renaissance education, Castiglione's book *The Courtier*. The concepts which were applied to the education of the courtier are concepts which are really derived from the arts. Particularly central (this is a very important notion) is the concept of imitation. (It is important to remember that when one is talking about courtiers, one is talking about the great officers of state, people who occupied a central political role. The Cecils in this country — Queen Elizabeth's courtiers — were people who were the equivalent of prime ministers and cabinet ministers today. As they occupied that sort of role, their education was a matter of the gravest importance.) How then did one form a courtier? The central notion involved was that of imitation, as I have indicated, a word which is crucial in the whole aesthetic of the Renaissance. Imitation in what way? Castiglione indicates that the ideal courtier must learn by watching other courtiers, choose the best aspects of the behaviour of several, the best features possible to help form his own behaviour. Now this constitutes the essence of the Renaissance aesthetic; it turned to the past, to the classical experience, as I have already indicated. It chose its models from the most elegantly stylistic of the classical writers, writers like Cicero, who were regarded as the most eloquent.

There was, however, another aspect to imitation, and it is very important for the development of my argument that I make this clear. Although imitation involved very much an absorption, of a sort that nowadays we can hardly conceive, of the classical experience through its literature, at its best the Renaissance concept of imitation did not mean mere *copying*. It meant the absorption of the experience for its redeployment with a certain measure of autonomy and freedom. It meant that what the child did when he went to school, what the young apprentice did when he went into the workshop of the artist, was to learn his craft by the most careful absorption of past models. Then, if he had any real genius, he didn't become what was sneeringly referred to as an 'ape of Cicero' (i.e. a mere copyist), but was able to redeploy this tremendously detailed and careful training, with an element of what the Italians called *sprezzatura*; and this concept of *sprezzatura* is essential for the full understanding of the doctrine of imitation; both with reference to the aesthetic education of the Renaissance period and the education of the courtier. *Sprezzatura* means 'effortlessness', about the best translation one can get. It implied an internalization of previous models so detailed and precise as greatly to facilitate expression and give it an appearance of effortless ease.

I have drawn attention to the fuller implications of the notion of 'imitation' in my book, *The Parochialism of the Present*. It produced, as I have pointed out, the miracle of Shakespeare who 'never originated anything, literary types, verse forms, plots, etc. etc. and yet he is one of the most original authors who has ever lived.' We know that Shakespeare stole his plots, his characters, his words, scenes, and yet he is the most complex example of this essence of Renaissance education, this ability to absorb and redeploy in a way which makes him the greatest, most complete, and most original of writers. This paradox of an imitation that produced a profound originality is central to my theme.

The Disintegration of the Renaissance Ideal

The ultimate purpose of all this education was undoubtedly moral. The idea of the courtier was that he should learn the arts of persuasion in order to give good moral advice to his prince or king. This was the function of this essentially literary education, one which should provide a moral insight into the contemporary problems on which the courtier, the equivalent, as I have indicated, of a modern minister, had to advise his prince.

So behind Renaissance theorizing and practice were notions of truth and moral purpose. In architecture, for instance, buildings were based on notions of mathematical proportions which were supposed to reflect the fundamental harmonies of the universe. So the Renaissance accepted the notion of 'forming' or 'moulding' the child to a preordained, a pre-established pattern. As Erasmus put it, 'Homines non nascuntur sed finguntur' (men are not born but made, fashioned). That is why the disciplines of Renaissance education were so severe — they looked back to former models which were laid down for their guidance in the literature of the classics.

But in its literary form, despite their acceptance of the classical experience, there was a question that nagged at them as indeed it had nagged at some of the ancients (including Plato). Most of the literature was overtly and intentionally fictional; and someone was bound sooner or later to raise the question 'How can the fictional be real?' How can what is admittedly a fiction reveal the forms of reality, of moral truth, for instance? If one paints a picture or writes a story, however it is intended to copy or represent the real, there is a sense in which it isn't real. So though the Renaissance artist did claim to be dealing with moral reality, he was doing it through various literary or artistic devices and these devices would seem to be false to some people because they were fictional. Shakespeare placed a number of his plays in historical circumstances but the history was often not very good history. The Roman historians themselves were notoriously inaccurate in their historical accounts, as Renaissance historians discovered when they investigated. So this was a fatal flaw, this question as to how what was essentially something artificial, something fabricated, could be regarded as indicative of reality. It raised the whole question of the relationship between the artist and nature, for instance, how one interpreted the concept of the 'natural'. Renaissance writers and painters solved the problem to some extent by saying that it was natural for human beings to be artificial — that they didn't just *live* their lives but through their consciousness in a sense *made* them.

Yet obviously there were senses in which the 'artificial' couldn't be the 'natural', true to nature. It depended on one's usage of that very difficult and very complex term, the 'natural'. Clearly, there are senses of 'natural' which would seem the total opposite to the artificial — the two things are often thought to be in direct conflict. The 'natural' then is equated, with that which hasn't been made, interfered with by man — the 'real' in *this* sense. [1]

Then the very art of rhetoric itself, the very notion of persuasion opens itself to all sorts of abuses. It's all very well saying that rhetoric is for the purposes of truth and virtue, but evil men could very easily use persuasive language for their own ends. The person who explored this problem is Shakespeare, as I have indicated. 'So may the outward shows be least themselves: The world is still deceived with ornament,' says Bassanio in *The Merchant of Venice*. And there is the pervasiveness of disguise all through the Shakespearean corpus; disguise plays a crucial and important role — and disguise implies deceit.

Historically what happened was that early scientists began to explore a different conception of reality; so what came to seem to be real in behaviour was no longer this Renaissance artistic experience, but regularities noted as a result of applying quantitative mathematical techniques to observed phenomena — in other words, science. Francis Bacon wrote at the very same time as Shakespeare, and Bacon, who was the great propagandist of science, pointed out that poetry was 'feigned history' which submitted 'the shows of things to the desires of the mind whereas reason doth buckle and bow the mind unto the nature of things.' What he is in effect defining is a new difference between fact and fiction: poetry he dismisses as fictional — the realities are to be found in reason and the nature of things. And the nature of things now was revealed in their regularities, which of course provide the basis of the scientific outlook. Locke, whose thoughts on education were of the profoundest interest in the eighteenth century, went so far as to suggest that if a child had a poetic vein parents should labour to have it stifled as much as possible, for poetry was untrue to life and unprofitable into the bargain — as he put it, it is very seldom that anyone discovers mines of gold or silver on Parnassus. In any case, mixing with artists took one into bad company and thus was no place for a gentleman. (Although I said that great artists like

Michelangelo and Leonardo achieved tremendous social prestige, the ordinary average actor, painter, dancer, playwright retained a pretty lowly sort of status and did indeed down to Victorian times.)

So, we begin now to detect a very equivocal attitude towards the arts. In the eighteenth century they were no longer regarded as central to the life of the society but took on much more the function of ornament. No longer did they afford an insight into reality. Instead, they provided a source of pleasure. In their country houses gentlemen collected artefacts indicative of their elegance and taste, as a matter largely of prestige; they served for delight but did not inform the real business of living. This was increasingly administered to by developments of a technical and scientific nature. One can begin to detect the change in Rousseau's analysis of one of Aesop's fables, 'The Fox and the Crow'. This provides a perfect example of what could happen to the poetic. The story is of the fox and the crow and the cheese and how the fox got the cheese from the crow, who was holding it in his beak, by means of flattery. He thus persuaded the crow to open his beak, the cheese fell out and the fox got it. Now Rousseau analyzes this little fable (which is the sort of thing which children love) and he asked literal questions of fact about it: for example, how could the fox smell the cheese if the crow was right up in the tree? These are not the sort of questions intended in the fable. Implicit in them is a quite different view of reality, a view of reality which doesn't raise questions for children and wouldn't worry most readers of Aesop's fables; but Rousseau was judging the poetic licence of the fable and suggesting that acceptance of it implied that one was fostering in children a love of falsehood. Another progressive educationist, Maria Montessori, another 100 years further on, banished fairy-tales altogether on the grounds that they weren't true, or scientifically accurate, for this now provided the criterion of reality.

There was a reaction against this depreciation of the poetic fictional, of course. Towards the end of the eighteenth century the Romantics once more stressed the centrality of the arts, arguing that they formed a crucial part of human experience. But of course they now existed in a socially much more precarious way than during the period of the humanists. What was now emphasized was *individual* experience which hadn't received the same stress in Renaissance humanism. Humanists had regarded the arts as essentially social. The Romantics were more antagonistic to their society; they often convey a sense of being against the dominating trends and place a stress on individual experience which can very easily become eccentricity and indeed lapse into solipsism. Secondly, they tended to over-emphasize the importance of feeling. Because science depended on rationality the Romantics as a counter-blast stressed feeling: 'Oh for a life of sensations rather than thoughts,' Keats had said. This emphasis on feeling, as something over against the cognitive, induced a split in consciousness which the Renaissance, I don't think, to that extent shared. In the Renaissance there existed, at its best, an extraordinary balance of both cognition and feeling: this is certainly highly characteristic of Shakespeare and Donne.

In the Romantic period, then, there is first this concern increasingly with individual over against social experience, and, second, a broad emphasis on feeling and the primitive as opposed to the more sophisticated and the cognitive. As a result, something obviously happens to the moral aspect. The artist in his antagonistic attitude to the society can tend also to become something of an immoralist. (This was the situation which Henry James depicted in his novel *Roderick Hudson*, where James examines the position of the artist and concludes against his immoralism. Roderick Hudson himself, a young artist, is condemned because he doesn't accept the normal moral conventions of society.)

Now we must remember that it is within the ambience of the Romantic revolt that we today find our current educational dilemmas. They are particularly to be noted in the extremities of romanticism which I will term 'avant-gardism'. This has become manifest in the twentieth century in a very wide variety of different movements of an artistic and literary type. Just think of the 'isms' there are in art: Surrealism (I am not putting them in any order), Expressionism, Constructivism, Futurism, as well as op art, pop art — one could list many more. From the end of the nineteenth century there has been a continual series of movements manifesting themselves on an individualistic or small-group basis, in many cases becoming more and more extreme in their extravagant claims or in their antagonism to the bourgeois world, the world of ordinary everyday life. (Mario Praz has analyzed something of this sense of antagonism which has been implicit in the Romantic movement from the beginning in his book *The Romantic Agony*.) The Romantics have found ordinary life over-rationalistic, unwilling to give feelings its due place. The breakdown of J. S. Mill in the face of his father's excessively intellectual educational regimen lends some credence to their claims.

Now this split between the artist and ordinary society has had grave effects, artistically, as Picasso, one of the supremely great artists of the twentieth century, realized. In some respects, Picasso was the spoilt child of the twentieth century; on the one hand the twentieth century has spoilt its artists and on the other hand it has treated them with contempt. Picasso died a millionaire many times over; yet, unhappily he never really received the criticism that he should have done and therefore he degenerated too often into sheer foolishness. (The supremely foolish twentieth-century manifestation was Dadaism, a childish reaction to the First World War.) Picasso made an extremely interesting comment about the disintegration of the whole of the artistic tradition of his own times, which forms one of the very crucial and fundamental problems which the arts in education currently face:

> As soon as art had lost all link with tradition, and the kind of liberation that came in with Impressionism permitted every painter to do what he wanted to do, painting was finished. When they decided it was the painters' sensations and emotions that mattered, (that is to say in expressionism) and every man could recreate painting as he understood it from any basis whatever, then there was no more painting; there were only individuals.

That's what I have just said about the individualistic aspect.[2]

Sculpture died the same death. Beginning with Van Gogh, however great we may be, we are all, in a measure autodidacts, you might almost say primitive painters. Painters no longer live within a tradition so each of us must recreate an entire language. Every painter of our times is fully authorised to recreate that language from A to Z. No criterion can be applied to him a priori since we don't believe in rigid standards any longer. In a sense there is a liberation but at the same time it is an enormous limitation.

One remembers the story about Renoir told by his son in *Renoir My Father* by Jean Renoir, the cinema director. On one occasion Renoir was sitting with some friends in a café; they were talking about medieval painters — and one of them pointed out that they did nothing else but paint pictures of Madonnas and children. 'Ah,' said Renoir, leaning back, 'what freedom'. Once the implications of that anecdote have been grasped, the whole of the modern dilemma is revealed. As Picasso pointed out, modern freedom was at once[3]

a liberation and at the same time an enormous limitation because when the individuality of the artist begins to express itself what the artist gains in the way of liberty he loses in the way of order, and when you are no longer able to attach yourself to an order basically that's very bad.

It was just such an order that the medieval and Renaissance painter, for all his restriction of subject-matter, belonged to; and Renoir saw that such an order constituted liberty in quite a different sense from that prevailing today.

The Arts in Contemporary Education

Now let us turn to education. This much time has been spent analyzing previous artistic movements because it is within the spiritual ambience created by romantic avant-gardism and expressionism that romantic progressivism, it seems to me, became the temporary educational orthodoxy, at least among educationists. (Perhaps it had rather less impact in schools than it did among educational theorists, but it has still had a potent influence on practice during the last thirty years.) So I look upon the progressive movement as it manifested itself especially after the Second World War as coming within the spiritual ambience of the Romantic movement. This romantic progressivism, manifested in child centredness and a concern for lifting restraints and allowing self-expression, was at least an attempt to reinstate the centrality of the arts as forms of impulse release. One remembers that famous statement of Rousseau: 'The first impulses of nature are always right.' Personal artistic expressiveness was supposed to have a quasi-therapeutic value in our over-rationalistic civilization. Herbert Read, the great modern exponent of education in the arts considered that: 'The secret of our collective ills is to be traced to the suppression of spontaneous creative ability of the individual.' Yet, in the light of this historical analysis, one needs to seize upon that word 'spontaneous' and ask what it implies. Is it *sprezzatura*, the 'spontaneity' that comes from the deep absorption of previous experience or is it simply primitive impulse release? Behind the dilemma lurks one of the fundamental issues for educationists of our time.

The central concepts of romantic progressivism have been self-expression, creativity, spontaneity, and of course nature and its derivatives, 'natural', etc. 'Nature' as I have indicated is a word that should be treated with the greatest restraint and care. It's perhaps the most ambiguous word in the English language. (I believe that a history of the word 'nature' would encompass much if not most of Western thought. Arthur Lovejoy, for instance, distinguished sixty meanings in the eighteenth century.) It's a word that when one uses it one should always stop and think. What is 'natural'? Where humans are concerned, it so often implies simply an alternative form of artifice from that currently pervasive. But of course it has a basic content — I mean it's 'natural' that human beings have two eyes, a nose, a mouth, and they live by breathing: these are 'natural' basic elements, they're inescapable. It's when one gets beyond this purely physical sense, to the more sophisticated uses of the word that it becomes such an ambiguous concept. Very often, of course, it's used as an emotive approval word as a means of beating down antagonism. One says: 'It is only natural that he should do that' — sometimes as a means of excusing some quite gross piece of behaviour. This raises the issue as to what is the relationship between what is natural and what is civilized. Is it not perhaps natural for human beings to be civilized? And does this imply not simply impulse release but some degree of restraint, discipline, as an element in human achievement? Was then Rousseau right to suggest that the *first* impulses of nature are always right? Is there not a flaw at the centre of romantic progressivism in its antagonism to restraints — an antagonism that would seem to be implicit in Read's definition of spontaneous expression as 'the unconstrained exteriorization of the mental activities of thinking, feeling, sensation and intuition'.[4]

Yet there are indications of a changed orientation in art education. I have over the years been examiner for two art education courses, one ten years ago, and one whose term of duty I have just finished. Technique and discipline are returning — 'spontaneity' in its primitive sense is out. The importance of tradition is being stressed by people like Hockney who are not really members of the avant-garde, and appears in the work of sculptors like Plazzotta. There is some sort of return to more traditional modes, techniques, disciplines.

Renaissance Aesthetic Theory and the Teaching of the Arts Today

I hope now that the reason why I have spent so long on the Renaissance side will be becoming apparent because, by and large, I believe Renaissance aesthetic theory is much more soundly based than Romantic artistic theory.

The arts are ways of apprehending and exploring reality — both that of the external world and that of the internal life. They are not to be regarded as peripheral or merely ornamental, nor do they necessarily arise out of an antagonistic attitude to society — that is at best a romantic half-truth. They do not result from esoteric movements nor are they constituted simply of the strange or the bizarre. Instead they are central to us as human beings, because they are ways of exploring and apprehending the reality of our existence both in their internal manifestation of thoughts and feelings (it is important not to forget thoughts, for there are intellectual elements in all arts) and in our relations with the actual social and sensuous world around us.

I believe with Henry James that the province of art is all life, all feeling, all observation, all vision. But I also believe that the writers and artists of the Renaissance were right when they said that it was natural for human beings to be artificial. In artistic endeavour, what results is the outcome of discipline and effort, something made, not something that simply evolves, in some sense of that difficult word, 'naturally'. Art is a way of categorizing the world but it exercises a *formative* element over that categorization. This is, I think, one of the great realizations of Renaissance theorizing: we inescapably *make* our lives. Erasmus was right when he urged, 'Homines non nascuntur sed finguntur' — 'men are not born, they are made.' They may be born with certain propensities — this the Renaissance admitted. But what one does with them is the result of human culture and human artifice and is not to be assigned to primitive impulse or impulse release. Hence in education what one is involved in is the creation of human beings in the course of an educative process. What I mean is very adequately summed up by a Renaissance literary theorist, Philip Sydney, when he implied that man, in the course of his development must 'grow into another nature'. He must transcend the primitive nature of the child or the baby and he must be formed through cultural artifice. This inevitably raises problems of value, for to be human is to be involved in the value dimension. (Indeed, what we argue about as being 'natural' is often simply a device for recommending an alternative set of values.) Part of that value dimension is what emerges out of the pain and effort of artistic creativity.

In this respect we ought to pay more attention to the Renaissance concept of 'imitation'. Imitation, as I have pointed out, involved the internalization of aspects of past achievements, an essential element in creativity. We use this word 'creativity' carelessly and sometimes — though today perhaps less than we used to do — we seem to think that any manifestation of child behaviour if it's on paper somehow constitutes a manifestation of the creative. But, as our philosophers have pointed out, the essential element in the concept of creativity is some element of value; and therefore the Renaissance concept of 'imitation', with its notion of the internalization of past models as essential elements in the creative process, seems to be a very fruitful one. I think that in schools we frequently give too much liberty to children to express themselves without giving them any of the tools with which they can discipline their expression. True, the Renaissance at its worst did the opposite. Renaissance theory at its most stultifying tended to stifle all originality and degenerate into copying. But the best of the Renaissance theorists realized this, and, as I have said, did not wish to turn their pupils into 'apes of

Cicero'. They wished their artists to absorb the experience of the past in order to internalize it and to redeploy it in a genuine creative endeavour.

The view I am putting forward is very similar to the one expounded by Sir Ernst Gombrich in his book *Art and Illusion* where his famous remark 'making comes before matching' is to be found. By this he meant that in the development of artistic skill internalization of schemata of previous artists comes before the actual copying of nature, that great artists have always acquired as much by 'imitation' of past models as they have from direct copying of nature. This surely is heavily influenced by Renaissance theory. As Henry James put it, the great thing is to be 'saturated' with something — and I don't think we 'saturate' our children enough. The urge to express must be balanced by the disciplined apprehension of the public symbols in terms of which expression acquires meaning.

Thus the arts involve the *control* as well as the *expression* of the emotions. I have written on this at some length in an essay published in my *Education, Culture and the Emotions*, and also in a little book *Culture, Industrialisation and Education*. Furthermore, educating the emotions means exploring aspects of emotional life which a child, without being involved in the work of others, without absorbing a great deal from the historical artefacts of his discipline, would not be introduced to: there are whole ranges of feeling which can only come as a result of *education*. Take for instance the notion of grace, *grazia* (a central concept in both the education of the Renaissance courtier and in the painting of pictures. Leonardo was reported to have *Divinia Grazia* divine grace). Now such a notion, today, does not come 'naturally' through impulse release; it has to be learned. It is something which is acquired as a result of the study and internalization of a sophisticated culture. And so the emotions seek expression but in the form of their expression need to be disciplined by an awareness of past forms. At the same time it is possible to introduce children to new ranges of emotions, aspects they are not familiar with in our emotionally vulgar age.

Then, again, I think the arts in education raise very crucial and important moral issues. I don't mean that art should be directly didactic, for instance by teaching morality through didactic types of poetry; but the revelation through art of various aspects of the reality of the world inevitably, to my mind, carries with it a value and moral dimension, and I consider the moral implications of the arts are extremely important and very central. Consider, for instance, the incidence of bad art, by which we are surrounded, and its potential for deleterious behaviour. One only has to turn a knob, and bad art is at one's command most hours of the day and night through radio and television — and this is the art that most people absorb from their environment. The whole question and role of bad art in our society needs very careful consideration. Clearly it requires an article on its own, and it can only be raised here as an issue implicit in this crucially important matter of values. Arts of a sort are not neglected in our society; never has there been a time when there has been more art; one can get various types of dramas and plays almost any moment of the day and night one likes to turn one's television on. Yet so much of this art is of a very inferior and inadequate nature. In this respect, this indictment by Professor Susanne Langer conveys the essence of my meaning:[5]

People who are so concerned for their children's scientific enlightenment that they keep Grimm out of the library and Santa Claus out of the chimney allow the cheapest art, the worst of bad singing, the most revolting sentimental fiction to impinge on the children's minds all day and every day from infancy. If the rank and file of youth grows up in emotional cowardice and confusion, sociologists look to economic conditions or family relations for the cause of this deplorable human weakness but not to the ubiquitous influence of corrupt art, which steeps the average mind in a shallow sentimentalism that ruins what germs of true feeling might have developed in it.

Conclusion

I should like to add a final point on the subject-matter of children's art in its extended meaning. So often in current artistic creativity in schools and colleges, whether it be writing or painting, dance, etc., children and students will seek out the esoteric. This also constitutes an aspect of romanticism: they seem to want to explore the pathological or the odd or the distant, the remote or the fantastic. They write about cops and robbers — not perhaps quite so remote these days, but few of them have actually had any experience of such matters. Indeed, they don't write about them as if from actual experience, they write as if they had picked it up from the latest soap opera on the television. Again, students when they are doing their dances, often tend either to choose vast cosmic themes which they cannot in fact cope with or some quasi-pathological subject-matter. They are very much bound up with certain pathological elements in our society.

But why seek the extraordinary? Why not try to explore and transmute the ordinary, the everyday? There is in this connection a marvellous remark by Chekov. Chekov was given a short story by a friend to read. He encountered a long passage of description about the moonlight, which at interminable length described it in all its aspects. Chekov wrote back to his friend and said: 'Cut out all those pages about the moonlight, give us instead what you feel about it — the reflection of the moon in a piece of broken bottle.' That image — 'the reflection of the moon in a piece of broken bottle' — sums up for me this notion of the ability of the great, the really creative, artist to transmute the very ordinary. Moonlight and broken bottle, commonplaces of our experience — but the combination of the two sums up this ability of the artist to take the real, the everyday, the mundane, and transform it by making it symbolic of a larger whole. Some such power of compression, of transmuting the ordinary elements of real life, would prevent some of those poems which one sees too often on the walls of classrooms or the dances which too often I have to witness or the paintings of fantasy. (There may be a place for fantasy but it must be a controlled fantasy — one which gets to the essence of a situation. Some of the best examples of controlled fantasy are to be found in our fairy-tales — which, as Bruno Bettelheim has pointed out, are geared to certain fundamental realities of the human situation.)[6] Let us then try to avoid those ridiculous fantasies children indulge in — about Batman, for instance, or Superman or fantasies of a sort which make no contact with the realities of human life. After all, art will only help children come to terms with reality if we encourage them to exercise themselves on their real feelings and sensations of the world around them. In this way the arts can remain important centres of human endeavour, means through which men are enabled to make something of themselves — for remember 'men are not born, but made'. In the same way the arts don't arise as a result of untutored spontaneity, impulse release, but through the internalization of past models of greatness and the disciplined approach to creativity this involves.

Notes and References

1. Cf. WILLIAM NELSON, *Fact or Fiction: The Dilemma of the Renaissance Story-Teller*, Harvard University Press, 1973.
2. Cf. F. GILOT and C. LAKE, *Life with Picasso*, Harmondsworth, Penguin, 1966, pp. 68–9.
3. *Ibid.*, p. 69.
4. H. READ, *Education through Art*, London, Faber and Faber, 1961, p. 112.
5. SUSANNE K. LANGER, *Feeling and Form*, London, Routledge and Kegan Paul, 1953, pp. 401–2.
6. Cf. B. BETTELHEIM, *The Uses of Enchantment*, Harmondsworth, Penguin, 1978.

PART VI
The Recognition of Myth

An essential and inescapable part of our cultural
inheritance involves myth. The emergence of a conservationist aesthetic, therefore, entails a new orientation
towards all inherited mythology, including the Classical
and Biblical myths.

In the following two chapters the poet Ted Hughes
and the educationist Jerome Bruner give educational
reasons for believing in 'the Mythologically instructed
community'.

Chapter 14

Myth and Education

Ted Hughes

Plato and Myth

In *The Republic*, where he describes the constitution of his ideal state, Plato talks a little about the education of the people who will live in it. He makes the famous point that quite advanced mathematical truths can be drawn from children when they are asked the right questions in the right order, and his own philosophical method, in his dialogues, is very like this. He treats his interlocutors as children and by small, simple, logical, stealthy questions gradually draws out of them some part of the Platonic system of ideas — a system that has in one way or another dominated the mental life of the Western world ever since.

Nevertheless he goes on to say that a formal education — by which he means a mathematical, philosophical, and ethical education — is not for children. The proper education for his future ideal citizens, he suggests, is something quite different: It is to be found in the traditional myths and tales of which Greece possessed such a huge abundance.

Plato was nothing if not an educationist. His writings can be seen as a prolonged and many-sided debate on just how the ideal citizen is to be shaped. It seemed to him quite possible to create an élite of philosophers who would also be wise and responsible rulers, with a perfect apprehension of the Good. Yet he proposed to start their training with the incredible fantasies of these myths.

Everyone knows that the first lessons, with human beings just as with dogs, are the most important of all. So what would be the effect of laying at the foundations of their mental life this mass of supernatural figures and their impossible antics? Later philosophers, throughout history, who often enough have come near to worshipping Plato, have dismissed these tales as absurdities. So how did he come to recommend them?

They were the material of the Greek poets. Many of them had been recreated by poets in works that became the model and despair of later writers. Yet we know what Plato thought about poets. He wanted them suppressed — much as it is said he suppressed his own poems when he first encountered Socrates. If he wanted nothing of the poets, why was he so respectful of the myths and tales that formed the imaginative world of the poets?

He had no religious motives. For Plato, those gods and goddesses were hardly more serious, as religious symbols, than they are for us. Yet they evidently did contain something important. What exactly was it, then, that made them in his opinion the best possible grounding for his future enlightened, realistic, perfectly adjusted citizen?

Let us suppose he thought about it as carefully as he thought about everything else. What did he have in mind? Trying to answer that question leads us in interesting directions.

The Value of Myth

Plato was preceded in Greece by more shadowy figures. They are a unique collection. Even what fragments remain of their writings reveal a cauldron of titanic ideas, from which Plato drew only a spoonful. Wherever we look around us now, in the modern world, it is not easy to find anything that was not somehow prefigured in the conceptions of those early Greeks.

And nothing is more striking about their ideas than the strange, visionary atmosphere from which they emerged. Plato is human and familiar; he invented that careful, logical, step-by-step style of investigation, in which all his great dialogues are conducted, and that almost all later philosophers developed, until it evolved finally into the scientific method itself. But his predecessors stand in a different world. By comparison they seem like mythical figures, living in myth, dreaming mythical dreams.

And so they were. We find them embedded in myth. Their vast powerful notions emerge, like figures in half-relief, from the massif of myth, which in turn lifts from the human/animal darkness of early Greece.

Why did they rise in Greece and not somewhere else? What was so special about early Greece? The various peoples of Greece had created their own religions and mythologies, more or less related but with differences. Further abroad, other nations had created theirs, again often borrowing from common sources, but evolving separate systems, sometimes gigantic systems.

Those seemingly supernatural dreams, full of conflict and authority and unearthly states of feeling, were projections of man's inner and outer world. They developed their ritual, their dogma, their hierarchy of spiritual values in a particular way in each separated group. Then at the beginning of the first millennium they began to converge, by one means or another, on Greece.

They came from Africa via Egypt, from Asia via Persia and the Middle East, from Europe, and from all the shores of the Mediterranean. Meeting in Greece, they mingled with those rising from the soil of Greece itself. Wherever two cultures, with their religious ideas, are brought sharply together, there is an inner explosion. Greece had become the battleground of the religious and mythological inspirations of much of the archaic world. The conflict was severe, and the effort to find solutions and make peace among all those contradictory elements was correspondingly great.

And the heroes of the struggle were those early philosophers. The struggle created them, it opened the depths of spirit and imagination to them, and they made sense of it. What was religious passion in the religions became in the philosophers a special sense of the holiness and seriousness of existence. What was obscure symbolic mystery in the mythologies became in the philosophers a bright, manifold perception of universal and human truths. In their works we see the transformation from one to the other taking place. And the great age that immediately followed them, in the fifth century B.C. was the culmination of the activity.

It seems proper, then, that the fantastic dimension of those tales should have appeared to Plato as something very much other than frivolous or absurd. We can begin to guess, maybe, at his objective, in familiarizing children with as much as possible of that teeming repertoire.

Education and the Inner Working of Myth

To begin with, we can say that an education of the sort Plato proposed would work on a child in the following way.

A child takes possession of a story as what might be called a unit of imagination. A story that engages, say, earth and the underworld is a unit correspondingly flexible to the child's imagination. It contains not merely the space and in some form or other the contents of those two places; it reconciles their contradictions in a workable fashion and holds open the way between them. The child can reenter the story at will, look around him or her, find all those things, and consider them at leisure.

In attending to the world of such a story there is the beginning of imaginative and mental control. There is the beginning of a form of contemplation. To begin with, each story is separate from every other story. Each unit of imagination is like a whole separate imagination, no matter how many the head holds.

If the story is learned well, so that all its parts can be seen at a glance, as if we looked through a window into it, then that story has become like the complicated hinterland of a single word. It has become a word. Any fragment of the story serves as the 'word' by which the whole story's electrical circuit is switched into consciousness, and all its light and power brought to bear.

As a rather extreme example, take the story of Christ. No matter what point of that story we touch, the whole story hits us. If we mention the Nativity, or the miracle of the loaves and fishes, or Lazarus, or the Crucifixion, the voltage and inner brightness of the whole story are instantly there. A single word of reference is enough, just as you need to touch a power line with only the tip of your finger to feel its energy.

The story itself is an acquisition, a kind of wealth. We only have to imagine for a moment individuals who know nothing of it at all. Their ignorance would shock us, and, in a real way, they would be outside our society. How would they even begin to understand most of the ideas that are at the roots of our culture and appear everywhere among the branches.

To follow the meanings behind the one word *crucifixion* would take us through most of European history and much of Roman and Middle Eastern too. It would take us into every corner of our private life. And before long, it would compel us to acknowledge much more important meanings than merely informative ones, openings of spiritual experience, a dedication to final realities, which might well stop us dead in our tracks and demand of us personally a sacrifice that we could never otherwise have conceived.

A word of that sort has magnetized our life into a special pattern. Behind it stands not just the crowded breadth of the world, but all the depths and intensities of it too. Those things have been raised out of chaos and brought into our ken by the story in a single word. The word holds them all there, like a constellation, floating and shining, and though we may draw back from tangling with them too closely, nevertheless they are present. These depths and intensities remain part of the head that lives our life, and they grow as we grow. A story can wield so much! And a word wields the story.

Imagine hearing, somewhere in the middle of a poem being recited, the phrase 'The Crucifixion of Hitler'. The word *Hitler* is as much of a hieroglyph as the word *crucifixion*. Individually, those two words bear the consciousness of much of our civilization. But they are meaningless hieroglyphs, unless the stories behind the words are known. We could almost say it is only by possessing these stories that we possess that consciousness.

In those who possess both stories, the collision of those two words, in that phrase, cannot fail to detonate a psychic depth-charge.'

Whether we like it or not, a huge inner working starts up. How can Hitler and crucifixion exist together in that way? Can they or can't they? The struggle to sort it out throws up ethical and philosophical implications that could absorb our attention for a very long time. All our static and maybe dormant understanding of good and evil and of what opens beyond good and evil is shocked into activity. Many unconscious assumptions and intuitions come up into the light to declare themselves and explain themselves and reassess each other.

For some temperaments, those two words paired in that way might well point to wholly fresh appraisals of good and evil and the underlying psychological or even actual connections between them. Yet the visible combatants here are two stories.

Without those stories, how could we have grasped those meanings? Without those stories, how could we have reduced those meanings to two words? The stories have gathered up huge charges of reality, illuminated us with them, and given us their energy, just as those colliding myths of gods and goddesses in early Greece roused the philosophers and the poets.

If we argue that a grasp of good and evil has nothing to do with a knowledge of historical anecdotes, we have only to compare what we felt of Hitler's particular evil when our knowledge of his story was only general, with what we felt when we learned more details. It is just those details of Hitler's story that have changed the consciousness of modern man. The story hasn't given us something that was never there before; it has revealed to us something that was always there.

And no other story, no other anything, ever did it so powerfully, in the same way as it took the story of Christ to change the consciousness of our ancestors. The better we know these stories as stories, the more of ourselves and the world is revealed to us through them.

The story of Christ came to us first of all as two or three sentences. That tiny seed held all the rest in potential form, like the blueprint of a city. Once we laid it down firmly in imagination, it became the foundation for everything that could subsequently be built and exist there. The same is true of the story of Hitler.

Are those two stories extreme examples? They would not have appeared so to the early Greeks, who had several Christs and several Bibles and quite a few Hitlers to deal with. Are Aesop's fables more to our scale? They operate in exactly the same way. Grimm's tales are similar oracles.

But what these two stories show very clearly is how stories think for themselves, once we know them. They not only attract and light up everything relevant in our own experience; they are also in continual private meditation, as it were, on their own implications. They are little factories of understanding. New revelations of meaning open out of their images and patterns continually, stirred into reach by our own growth and changing circumstances.

Then at a certain point in our lives, they begin to combine. What happened forcibly between Hitler and the Crucifixion in that phrase, begins to happen naturally. The head that holds many stories becomes a small early Greece.

It does not matter, either, how old the stories are. Stories are old the way human biology is old. No matter how much they have produced in the past in the way of fruitful inspirations, they are never exhausted. The story of Christ, to stick to our example, can never be diminished by the seemingly infinite mass of theological agonizing and insipid homilies that have attempted to translate it into something more manageable. It remains, like any other genuine story, irreducible, a lump of the world, like the body of a newborn child.

There is little doubt that, if the world lasts, pretty soon someone will come along and understand the story as if for the first time. That person will look back and see 2000 years of somnolent fumbling with the theme. Out of that, and the collision of other things, he or she will produce, very likely, something totally new and overwhelming, some whole new direction for human life. The same possibility holds for the ancient stories of many another deity.

Why not? History is really no older than that newborn baby. And every story is still the original cauldron of wisdom, full of new visions and new life.

What do we mean by 'imagination'? There are obviously many degrees of it. Are there different kinds?

The Nature of Imagination

The word *imagination* usually denotes not much more than the faculty of creating a picture of something in our heads and holding it there while we think about it.

Since this is the basis of nearly everything we do, clearly it's very important that our imagination should be strong rather than weak. However, education neglects this faculty completely. How is the imagination to be strengthened and trained? A student has imagination, we seem to suppose, much as he or she has a face, and nothing can be done about it. We use what we've got.

We realize that imagination can vary enormously from one person to the next, and from almost nonexistent upwards. Of people who simply cannot think what will happen if they do such and such a thing, we say they have no imagination. They have to work on principles, on orders, or by precedent, and they will always be marked by extreme rigidity, because they are, after all, moving in the dark.

We all know such people, and we all recognize that they are dangerous since, if they have strong temperaments in other respects, they end up by destroying their environment and everybody near them. The terrible thing is that they are the planners, and ruthless slaves to the plan — which substitutes for the faculty they do not possess. And they have the will of desperation: Where others see alternative courses, they see only a gulf.

Of people who imagine vividly what will happen if they act in a certain way, and then turn out to be wrong, we say they are dealing with an unpredictable situation or, just as likely, they have an inaccurate imagination. Lively, maybe, but inaccurate. There is no innate law that makes a very real-seeming picture of things an accurate picture.

Those people will be great nuisances and as destructive as the others, because they will be full of confident schemes and proof, which will simply be false, because somehow their sense of reality is defective. In other words, their ordinary perception of reality, by which the imagination regulates all its images, overlooks too much or misinterprets too much. Many disturbances can account for some of this, but simple inattentiveness accounts for most of it.

Those two classes of people comprise the majority of us for much of the time. The third class of people is quite rare. Or our own moments of belonging to that class are rare. Imagination that is both accurate and strong is so rare that somebody who appears in possession of it is regarded as something more than human. We see it in the few great generals in history. Normally, it occurs patchily, because accurate perceptions are rarely more than patchy. We have only to make the simplest test on ourselves to reconfirm this. And where our perceptions are blind, our speculations are pure invention.

This basic type of imagination, with its delicate wiring of perceptions, is our most valuable piece of practical equipment. It is the control panel for everything we think and do, so it ought to be education's first concern. Yet, who has ever spent half an hour in any classroom trying to strengthen it in any way? Even in the sciences, where accurate perception is recognizably crucial, is this faculty ever deliberately trained?

Sharpness, clarity, and scope of the mental eye are all important in our dealings with the outer world, and they are plenty. If we were machines, it would be enough. But the outer world is only one of the worlds we live in. For better or worse, we have another — the inner world of our bodies and everything pertaining to it. It is closer than the outer world, more decisive, and utterly different.

So here are two worlds, which we have to live in simultaneously, and because they are intricately interdependent at every moment, we can't ignore one and concentrate on the other without accidents, possibly fatal accidents. But why can't this inner world of the body be regarded as an extension of the outer world? In other words, why isn't the sharp, clear, objective eye of the mind as adequate for this world as it is for the other, more obviously outer world? And if it isn't, why isn't it?

The inner world is not so easily talked about because nobody has ever come near to understanding it. Though it is the closest thing to us — indeed, it is us — we live in it as on an unexplored planet in space. It is not so much a place, either, as a region of events. And the first thing we have to confess is that it cannot be seen objectively.

How does the biological craving for water turn into the precise notion that it is water that we want? How do we 'see' the make-up of an emotion that we do not even feel — though electrodes on our skin will register its presence? The word 'subjective' was invented for a good reason, but under the vaguest of general terms lies the most important half of our experience.

After all, what exactly is going on in there? It is quite frightening, how little we know about it. We can't say there's nothing — that 'nothing' is merely the shutness of the shut door. And if we say there's something — how much more specific can we get?

We quickly realize that the inner world is indescribable, impenetrable, and invisible. We try to grapple with it, and all we meet is one provisional dream after another. It dawns on us that in order to look at the inner world 'objectively' we have had to separate ourselves from what is an exclusively 'subjective' world, and that it has vanished. In the end, we acknowledge that the objective imagination and the objective perceptions — those sharp clear instruments that cope so well with the outer world — are of very little use there.

By speculating backwards from effects, we can possibly make out a rough plan of what ought to be in there. The incessant bombardment of raw perceptions must land somewhere. We have been able to notice that any one perception can stir up a host of small feelings, which excite further feelings — not necessarily so small — in a turmoil of memory and association.

We do have some evidence, we think that our emotional and instinctive life, which seems to be on a somewhat bigger scale and not so tied to momentary perception, is mustering and regrouping in response to outer circumstances. But these bigger and more dramatic energies are also occasionally yoked to the pettiest of those perceptions and driven off on some journey. Now and again we are made aware of what seems to be an even larger drama of moods and energies that are hard to name — psychic, spiritual, cosmic. Any name we give them seems metaphorical, since in the inner world everything is relative, and we are never sure of the scale of magnification or miniaturization of the signals.

We can guess, with a fair sense of confidence, that all these interinvolved processes, which seem like the electrical fields of our body's electrical installations — our glands, organs, chemical transmutations, and so on — are striving to tell about themselves. They are all trying to make their needs known, much as thirst imparts its sharp request for water. They are talking incessantly, in a dumb, radiating way, about themselves, about their relationships with each other, about the situation of the moment in the main overall drama of the living, growing, and dying body in which they are assembled, and also about the outer world, because all these dramatis personae are really striving to live, in some way or other, in the outer world.

That is the world for which they have been created, the world that created them. And so they are highly concerned about the doings of the individual behind whose face they hide, because they are that individual. They want that person to live in the way that will give him or her the greatest satisfaction.

This description is bald enough, but it is as much as the objective eye can be reasonably sure of — and then only in a detached way, the way we think we are sure of the workings of an electrical circuit. For more intimate negotiations with that world, for genuine contact with its powers and genuine exploration of its regions, it turns out that the eye of the objective imagination is blind.

We solve the problem by never looking inward. We identify ourselves and all that is wakeful and intelligent with our objective eye, saying, 'Let's be objective.' That is really no more than saying, 'Let's be happy.' We sit, closely cramped in the cockpit behind the eyes, steering through the brilliantly crowded landscape beyond the lenses, focused on details and distinctions.

In the end, since all our attention from birth has been narrowed into that outward beam, we come to regard our body as no more than a somewhat stupid vehicle. All the urgent information coming towards us from that inner world sounds to us like a blank, or at best the occasional grunt, or a twinge. This is because we have no equipment to receive and decode it. The body, with its spirits, is the antenna of all perceptions, the receiving aerial for all wavelengths. But we are disconnected. The exclusiveness of our objective eye, the very strength and brilliance of our objective intelligence, suddenly turn into stupidity — of the most rigid and suicidal kind.

Scientific Objectivity and the Narrowing of Imaginative Perception

That condition certainly sounds extreme, yet most of the people we know, particularly older people, are likely to regard it as ideal. It is a modern ideal. The educational tendencies of the last 300 years, and especially of the last fifty, corresponding to the rising prestige of scientific objectivity and the lowering prestige of religious awareness, have combined to make it so. It is a scientific ideal and a powerful ideal; it has created the modern world. Without it, the modern world would fall to pieces: Infinite misery would result. The disaster is that the world is heading straight toward infinite misery, because it has persuaded human beings to identify themselves with what is no more than a narrow mode of perception. The more rigorously the ideal is achieved, the more likely it is to be disastrous: a bright, intelligent eye, full of exact images, set in a head of the most frightful stupidity.

The drive toward this ideal is so strong that it has materialized in the outer world. A perfect mechanism of objective perception has been precipitated: the camera. Scientific objectivity, as we all know, has its own morality, which has nothing to do with human morality. It is the morality of the camera. This is the prevailing morality of our time. It is a morality utterly devoid of any awareness of the requirements of the inner world. It is contemptuous of the 'human element'. That is its purity and its strength. The prevailing philosophies and political ideologies of our time subscribe to this contempt, with a nearly religious fanaticism, just as science itself does.

Some years ago in an American picture magazine, I saw a collection of photographs that showed the process of a tiger killing a woman. The story behind this was as follows: The tiger, a tame tiger, belonged to the woman. A professional photographer had wanted to take photographs of her strolling with her tiger. Something — maybe his incessant camera — had upset the tiger; the woman had tried to pacify it, whereupon it attacked her and started to kill her. So what did that hero of the objective attitude do then?

Jim Corbett's stories about tigers and leopards that eat human beings describe occasions when such an animal with a terrifying reputation was driven off its victim by some other person, or by a girl who beat the animal over the head with a digging stick. But this photographer — we can easily understand him because we all belong to this modern world — had become his camera. Whatever his thoughts were, he went on taking photographs of the whole procedure while the tiger killed the woman. The pictures were there in the magazine, but the story was told as if the photographer were absent, as if the camera had simply gone on doing what any camera would be expected to do, being a mere mechanical device for registering outward appearances.

The same paralysis comes to many of us when we watch television. After the interesting bit is over, what keeps us mesmerized by that bright little eye? It can't be the horrors and inanities and killings that jog along there between the curtains and the mantelpiece after supper. Why can't we move? Reality has been removed beyond our participation, behind that very tough screen, into another dimension.

Our inner world of natural impulsive response is safely in neutral gear. Like broiler killers, we are reduced to a state of pure observation. Everything that passes in front of our eyes is equally important, equally unimportant. As far as what we see is concerned, and in a truly practical way, we are paralyzed.

Even people who profess to dislike television fall under the same spell of passivity. They can free themselves only by a convulsive effort of will. The precious tool of objective imagination has taken control of us there. Materialized in the camera, it has imprisoned us in the lens.

In England, not very long ago, the inner world and Christianity were closely identified. Even the conflicts within Christianity only revealed and consolidated more inner world. When religious knowledge lost the last rags of its credibility, earlier this century, psychoanalysis appeared as if to fill the gap. Both attempt to give form to the inner world, but with a difference.

When it came the turn of the Christian Church to embody the laws of the inner world, it made the mistake of claiming that they were objective laws. That might have passed, if science had not come along, whose laws were so demonstrably objective that it was able to impose them on the whole world.

As the mistaken claims of Christianity became scientifically meaningless, the inner world that it had clothed became incomprehensible, absurd, and finally invisible. Objective imagination, in the light of science, rejected religion as charlatanism, and the inner world as a bundle of fairy tales, a relic of primeval superstition. People rushed toward the idea of living without any religion or any inner life whatsoever as if toward some great new freedom — a great final awakening. The most energetic intellectual and political movements of this century wrote the manifestos of the new liberation. The great artistic statements have recorded the true emptiness of the new prison.

The inner world, of course, could not evaporate just because it no longer had a religion to give it a visible body. A person's own inner world cannot fold up its spiritual wings, shut down all its tuned circuits, and become a mechanical business of nuts and bolts, just because a political or intellectual ideology requires it to. As religion was stripped away, the defrocked inner world became a waif, an outcast, a tramp. Denied its one great health — acceptance into life — it fell into a huge sickness, a huge collection of deprivation sickness. And this is how psychoanalysis found it.

The small piloting consciousness of the bright-eyed objective intelligence had steered its body and soul into a hell. Religious negotiations had formerly embraced and humanized the archaic energies of instinct and feeling. They had conversed in simple but profound terms with the forces struggling inside people and had civilized them, or attempted to.

Without religion, those powers have become dehumanized. The whole inner world has become elemental, chaotic, continually more primitive, and beyond our control. It has become a place of demons. But of course, insofar as we are disconnected from that world anyway, and lack the equipment to pick up its signals, we are not aware of it. All we register is the vast absence, the emptiness, the sterility, the meaninglessness, the loneliness. If we do manage to catch a glimpse of our inner selves by some contraption or mirrors, we recognize it with horror — it is an animal crawling and decomposing in a hell. We refuse to own it.

In the last decade or two, the imprisonment of the camera lens has begun to crack. The demonized state of our inner world has made itself felt in a million ways. How is it that children are so attracted toward it?

Every new child is nature's chance to correct culture's error. Children are most sensitive to the inner world, because they are the least conditioned by scientific objectivity to life in the camera lens. They have a double motive, in attempting to break from the lens. They want to escape the ugliness of the despiritualized world in which they see their parents imprisoned, and they are aware that this inner world we have rejected is not merely an inferno of depraved impulses and crazy explosions of embittered energy. Our real selves lie down there. Down there, mixed up among all the madness, is everything that once made life worth living. All the lost awareness and powers and allegiances of our biological and spiritual being are there. The attempt to re-enter that lost inheritance takes many forms, but it is the chief business of the swarming cults.

Drugs cannot take us there. If we cite the lofty religions in which drugs did take the initiates to where they needed to go, we ought to remember that here again the mythology was crucial. The journey was undertaken as part of an elaborately mythologized ritual. It was the mythology that consolidated the inner world, gave human form to its experiences, and connected them to daily life. Without that preparation a drug carries its users to a prison in the inner world as passive and isolated and meaningless as the camera's eye from which he or she escaped.

Objective imagination, then, important as it is, is not enough. What about a 'subjective' imagination? It is only logical to suppose that a faculty developed specially for peering into the inner world might end up as specialized and destructive as the faculty for peering into the outer one.

Besides, the real problem comes from the fact that outer world and inner world are interdependent at every moment. We are simply the locus of their collision: two worlds, with mutually contradictory laws, or laws that seem to us to be so, colliding afresh every second, struggling for peaceful coexistence. And whether we like it or not, our life is what we are able to make of that collision and struggle.

What we need, evidently, is a faculty that embraces both worlds simultaneously. A large, flexible grasp, an inner vision that holds wide open, like a great theatre, the arena of contention, and that pays equal respects to both sides — that keeps faith, as Goethe says, with the world of things and the world of spirits equally.

This really is imagination. This is the faculty we mean when we talk about the imagination of the great artists. The character of great works is exactly this: that in them the full presence of the inner world combines with and is reconciled to the full presence of the outer world. And in them we see that the laws of these two worlds are not contradictory at all: They are one all-inclusive system; they are laws that somehow we find it all but impossible to keep, laws that only the greatest artists are able to restate.

They are the laws, simply, of human nature. People have recognized all through history that the restating of these laws, in one medium or another, in great works of art, are the greatest human acts. They are the greatest acts and they are the most human. We recognize these works because we are all struggling to find those laws, as an individual on a tightrope struggles for balance, because they are the formula that reconciles everything and balances every imbalance.

So it comes about that once we recognize their terms, these works seem to heal us. More important, it is in these works that humanity is truly formed. It has to be done again and again, as circumstances change, and the balance of power between outer and inner world shifts, showing everybody the gulf.

The inner world, separated from the outer world, is a place of demons. The outer world, separated from the inner world, is a place of meaningless objects and machines. The faculty that makes the human being out of these two worlds is called divine. That is only a way of saying that it is the faculty without which humanity cannot really exist. It can be called religious or visionary. More essentially, it is imagination that embraces both outer and inner worlds in a creative spirit.

The Place of Myth and Legend in the Curriculum

Laying down blueprints for imagination of that sort is a matter of education, as Plato divined. The myths and legends, which Plato proposed as the ideal educational material for his young citizens, can be seen as large-scale accounts of negotiations between the powers of the inner world and the stubborn conditions of the outer world under which ordinary men and women have to live. They are immense and at the same time highly detailed sketches for the possibilities of understanding and reconciling the two. They are, in other words, an archive of draft plans for the kind of imagination we have been discussing.

Their accuracy and usefulness, in this sense, depend on the fact that they were originally the genuine projections of genuine understanding. They were tribal dreams of the highest order of inspiration and truth, at their best. They gave a true account of what really happens in that inner region where the two worlds collide. This has been attested over and over again by the way in which the imaginative people of every subsequent age have had recourse to their basic patterns and images.

But the Greek myths were not the only true myths. The unspoken definition of myth is that it carries truth of this sort. These big dreams become the treasured property of a people only when they express the real state of affairs. Priests continually elaborate the myths, but what is not true is forgotten again. So every real people has its true myths. One of the first surprises of mythographers was finding how uncannily similar these myths are all over the world. They are as alike as the lines on the palm of the human hand.

Plato implied that all traditional stories, big and small, were part of his syllabus. Indeed the smaller stories come from the same place. If a tale can last, in oral tradition, for two or three generations, then it has either come from the real place or found its way there. The small tales are just as vigorous educational devices as the big myths.

There is a long tradition of using stories as educational implements in a far more deliberate way than Plato seems to have proposed. Rudolf Steiner has a great deal to say about the method. In his many publications of Sufi literature, Idries Shah (*The Way of the Sufi*, 1969) indicates how central to the training of the sages and saints of Islam are the traditional tales. Sometimes they are no more than small anecdotes, sometimes lengthy and involved adventures such as were collected into the Arabian Nights.

As I pointed out, using the example of the Christ story, the first step is to learn the story, as if it were laying down the foundation. The next phase rests with the natural process of the imagination.

The story is, as it were, a kit. Apart from its own major subject — obvious enough in the case of the Christ story — it contains two separable elements: its pattern and its images. Together they make that story and no other. Separately they set out on new lives of their own.

The roads they travel are determined by the brain's fundamental genius for metaphor. Automatically, it uses the pattern of one set of images to organize quite a different set. It uses one image, with slight variations, as an image for related and yet different and otherwise imageless meanings.

In this way, the simple tale of the beggar and the princess begins to transmit intuitions of psychological, perhaps spiritual, states and relationships. What began as an idle reading of a fairy tale ends by simple natural activity of the imagination as a rich perception of values of feeling, emotion, and spirit that would otherwise have remained unconscious and languageless.

The inner struggle of worlds, which is not necessarily a violent and terrible affair, though at bottom it often is, is suddenly given the perfect formula for the terms of a truce. A simple tale, told at the right moment, transforms a person's life with the order its pattern brings to incoherent energies.

While the tale's pattern proliferates in every direction through all levels of consciousness, its images are working, too. The image of Lazarus is not easily detached by a child from its striking place in the story of Christ, but once it begins to migrate, there is no limiting its importance. In all Dostoevsky's searching adventures, the basic image, radiating energies that he seems never able to exhaust, is Lazarus.

The image does not need to be so central to a prestigious religion for it to become so important. At the heart of *King Lear* is a very simple little tale — the Story of Salt. In both of these we see how a simple image in a simple story has somehow focused all the pressures of an age — collisions of spirit and nature and good and evil and a majesty of existence that seem uncontainable. But it has brought all that into a human pattern, and made it part of our understanding.

Chapter 15

Myth and Identity

Jerome Bruner

Introduction

We know now a new origin of the faint hissing of the sea in the conch shell held to the ear. It is in part the tremor and throb of the hand, resonating in the shell's chambers. Yet, inescapably, it is the distant sea. For Yeats, it would have been a reaffirmation of his proper query:

O body swayed to music, O brightening glance,
How can we know the dancer from the dance?

And so with myth. It is at once an external reality and the resonance of the internal vicissitudes of man. Richard Chase's somewhat cumbersome definition will at least get us on our way: 'Myth is an aesthetic device for bringing the imaginary but powerful world of preternatural forces into a manageable collaboration with the objective (i.e., experienced) facts of life in such a way as to excite a sense of reality amenable to both the unconscious passions and the conscious mind.'[1]

That myth has such a function — to effect some manner of harmony between the literalities of experience and the night impulses of life — few would deny. Yet I would urge that we not be too easily tempted into thinking that there is an oppositional contrast between *logos* and *mythos*, the grammar of experience and the grammar of myth. For each complements the other, and it is in the light of this complementarity that I wish to examine the relation of myth and personality.

The Externalizing Powers of Myth

Consider the myth first as projection, to use the conventional psychoanalytic term. I would prefer the term 'externalization' better to make clear that we are dealing here with a common process found in connection with works of art, scientific theories, inventions in general — the human preference to cope with events that are outside rather than inside. Myth, insofar as it is fitting, provides a ready-made means of externalizing human plight by embodying and representing them in storied plot and characters.

What is the significance of this externalizing tendency in myth? It is threefold, I would say. It provides, in the first instance, a basis for communion among men. What is 'out there' can be named and shared in a manner beyond the sharing of subjectivity. By the subjectifying of our worlds through externalization, we are able, paradoxically enough, to share communally in the nature of internal experience. By externalizing cause and effect, for example, we may construct a common matrix of determinism. Fate, the full of the moon, the aether — these and not our unique fears are what join us in common reaction. Perhaps more important still, externalization makes possible the containment of terror and impulse by the decorum of art and symbolism. Given man's search for art forms, it must surely be no accident that there is no art of internal feeling or impulse. We seem unable to impose what Freud once called the artifice of formal beauty upon our internal sensations or even upon our stream of seemingly uncontrolled fantasy. It is the fact of fashioning an external product out of our internal impulses that the work of art begins. There is no art of kinaesthesis, and, mindful of Aldous Huxley's fantasies, it is doubtful whether the titillation of the 'feelies' could ever become an art form. Sharing, then, and the containment of impulse in beauty — these are the possibilities offered by externalization.

Of the economy provided by the externalized myth, little need be said. Dollard and Miller, looking at the psychotherapeutic process, have commented upon the importance of sorting and 'labeling' for the patient'.[2] That is to say, if one is to contain the panicking spread of anxiety, one must be able to identify and put a comprehensible label upon one's feelings better to treat them again, better to learn from experience. Free-floating anxiety, as Freud's translators have vividly called the internal terror that seems causeless to the sufferer, cries for anchoring. Therapy, with its drawn-out 'working through,' provides an occasion for fashioning an anchor of one's own. So too with hope and aspiring. In boundless form, they are prologues to disenchantment. In time and as one comes to benefit from experience, one learns that things will turn out neither as well as one hoped nor as badly as one feared. Limits are set. Myth, perhaps, serves in place of or as a filter for experience. In the first of the world wars, the myth of the fearless soldier forced a repression of the fear one felt in battle. The result, often enough, was the dissociation and fugue of shell-shock. A quarter century later, a second world war, governed by a different concept of mythic human drama, had provided a means of containment through the admission of human fear. The case books of the two wars are as different as the myths that men use to contain their fears and fatigue. The economical function of myth is to represent in livable form the structure of the complexities through which we must find our way. But such representation, if it is to be effective, must honour the canons of economy that make art.

Let me illustrate my point by reference to Homer, particularly to the madness of Ajax in the *Iliad*. Recall the occasion of the death of Achilles and the determination of Thetis that the bravest man before Ilium shall have her slain son's arms. Agamemnon must make the fateful decision, and it is Odysseus and not Ajax who receives the gift of Hephaestus-forged armour. Ajax is lashed by human anger and a craving for vengeance in a proportion to match his heroic capacities. But before these impulses can be expressed, there is an intervention by Athene: Ajax is struck mad and slaughters the captive Trojan livestock, cursing Agamemnon, Odysseus, and Menelaus the while, in a manner that would be described today as a massive displacement of aggression. It is Athene, then, who saves Ajax from a more direct expression of his fury and saves the Greeks from a slaughter of their leaders. Again we have the ingenious and rational intervention of the gods, a formal working out of internal plight in a tightly woven and dramatic plot. It is much as E. R. Dodds has suggested in examining the containment of irrationality in Greek myth. The clouding and bewildering of judgment that is *ate*, or the seemingly unnatural access of courage that is *menos* — both of these sources of potential disruption of natural order are attributed to an external agency, to a supernatural intervention, whether of the gods or of the Erinys.

> I suggest that in general the inward monition, or the sudden unaccountable feeling of power, or the sudden unaccountable loss of judgment, is the germ out of which the divine machinery developed. One result of transposing the event from the interior to the external world is that the vagueness is eliminated: the indeterminate daemon has to be made concrete as some particular personal god.[3]

These were the gods that the Greeks shared, by virtue of whom a sense of causation became communal, through the nurturing of whom an art form emerged. The alternative, as Philip Rahv comments in discussing the governess in *The Turn of the Screw* and the chief protagonist in *The Beast in the Jungle*,[4] is to give up one's allotment of experience. If one cannot externalize the demon where it can be enmeshed in the texture of aesthetic experience, then the last resort is to freeze and block: the over-repression and denial treated so perceptively by Freud in *The Problem of Anxiety*.

The Dramatic Form of Myth

What is the art form of the myth? Principally it is drama; yet for all its concern with paeternatural forces and characters, it is realistic drama that, in the phrase of Wellek and Warren, tells of 'origins and destinies'. As they put it, it comprises 'the explanations a society offers its young of why the world is and why we do as we do, its pedagogic images of the nature and destiny of man.'[5] Ernst Cassirer senses a proper antinomy when he notes that the myth somehow emphasizes the facelike character of experience while at the same time it has the property of compelling belief. Its power is that it lives on the feather line between fantasy and reality. It must be neither too good nor too bad to be true, nor may it be too true. And if it is the case that knowing through art has the function of connecting through metaphor what before had no apparent kinship, then in the present case the art form of the myth connects the daemonic world of impulse with the world of reason by a verisimilitude that conforms to each.

But there is a paradox. On the one side we speak of myth as an externalization; on the other we speak of it as a pedagogic image. This is surely a strange source of instruction! But it is precisely here that the dramatic form of myth becomes significant, precisely here where Gilbert Murray perceived the genius of Homer and the Greeks: 'This power of entering vividly into the feelings of both parties in a conflict is ... the characteristic gift.'[6]

I revert for a moment to a consideration of the human personality, to the nature of the vicissitudes that are externalized in myth. It is far from clear why our discordant impulses are bound and ordered in a set of identities — why one pattern of impulse is the self-pitying little man in us, another the nurturing protector, another the voice of moral indignation. Surely it is something more than the sum of identifications we have undertaken in the course of achieving balances between love and independence, coming to terms with those who have touched our lives. It is here that myth becomes the tutor, the shaper of identities; it is here that personality imitates myth in as deep a sense as myth is an externalization of the vicissitudes of personality.

Joseph Campbell writes:

> In his life-form the individual is necessarily only a fraction and distortion of the total image of man. He is limited either as male or as female; at any given period of his life he is again limited as child, youth, mature adult, or ancient; furthermore, in his life-role, he is necessarily specialized as craftsman, tradesman, servant, or thief, priest, leader, wife, nun, or harlot; he cannot be all. Hence the totality — the fullness of man — is not in the separate member, but in the body of the society as a whole; the individual can be only an organ.[7]

But if no man is all, there is at least in what Campbell calls the 'mythologically instructed community' a corpus of images and identities and models that provides the pattern to which growth may aspire — a range of metaphoric identities. We are accustomed to speaking of myth in this programmatic sense in reference to history, as when Sorel invokes the general strike of all workers as a dynamic image, or when Christians speak of the Second Coming for which men must prepare themselves. In the same sense, one may speak of the corpus of myth as providing a set of possible identities for the individual personality. It would perhaps be more appropriate to say that the mythologically instructed community provides its members with a library of scripts upon which the individual may judge the play of his multiple identities. For myth, as I shall now try to illustrate, serves not only as a pattern to which one aspires but also as a criterion for the self-critic.

The Types of Mythic Plot

Take as an example the myths that embody and personify man's capacity for happiness. They are not infinite in variety, but varied enough. An early version is the Greek conception of the Five Ages of Man, the first of which is the happy Age of Gold. As Robert Graves tells it:

> These men were the so-called golden race, subjects of Cronus, who lived without cares or labour, eating only acorns, wild fruit, and honey that dripped from the trees ... never growing old, dancing, and laughing much; death to them was no more terrible than sleep. They are all gone now, but their spirits survive as happy genii. [8]

This is the myth of happiness as innocence, and in the Christian tradition we know it as Man before the Fall. Innocence ends either by a successful attempt to steal the knowledge of God or by aspiring to the cognitive power of the gods, *hubris*. And with the end of innocence, there is an end to happiness: knowledge is equated with temptation to evil. The issue appears to revolve around the acquisition and uses of knowledge.

I will oversimplify in the interest of brevity and say that from these early myths there emerge two types of mythic plot: the plot of innocence and the plot of cleverness — the former being a kind of Arcadian ideal, requiring the eschewal of complexity and awareness, the latter requiring the cultivation of competence almost to the point of guile. The happy childhood, the good man as the child of God, the simple ploughman, the Rousseauian ideal of natural nobility — these are the creatures of the plot of innocence. At the other extreme there are Penelope, the suitors, and Odysseus. In Murray's words:

> Penelope — she has just learned on good evidence that Odysseus is alive and will return immediately — suddenly determines that she cannot put off the suitors any longer, but brings down her husband's bow, and says she will forthwith marry the man who can shoot through twelve axeheads with it! Odysseus hears her and is pleased! May it not be that in the original story there was a reason for Penelope to bring the bow, and for Odysseus to be pleased? It was a plot. He [Odysseus] meant Eurycleia [the old maidservant] to recognize him [by his scar], to send the maids away, and break the news to Penelope. Then husband and wife together arranged the trial of the bow. [9]

Again and again in the Greek myths there are cleverness, competence, and artifice — Herakles, Achilles, Odysseus, Perseus — wherever you look. It is the happy triumph of clever competence with a supernatural assist. And yet there is also the ideal of the Age of Innocence. So too in the later Christian tradition and in our own times. The manner in which superior knowledge shows itself changes: the ideal of the crafty warrior, the wise man, the interpreter of the word of God, the Renaissance omnicompetent, the wily merchant, the financial wizard, the political genius. If it is true that in some way each is suspect, it is also true that each is idealized in his own way. Each is presented as satisfied. New versions arise to reflect the ritual and practice of each era — the modifications of the happiness of innocence and the satisfaction of competence.

The manner in which man has striven for competence and longed for innocence has reflected the controlling myths of the community. The medieval scholar, the Florentine prince, the guild craftsman, as well as the withdrawn monastic of Thomas à Kempis and the mendicant of St. Francis — all of these are deeply involved with the myths of innocence and competence and are formed by them. Indeed, the uncertainty in resolving the dichotomy of reason and revelation as ways to know God reflects the duality of the myth of happiness and salvation. It is not simply society that patterns itself on the idealizing myths, but unconsciously it is the individual man as well who is able to bring order to his internal clamour of identities in terms of prevailing myth. Life, then, produces myth and finally imitates it.

A Closing Remark: Myth and the Novel

One may ask whether the rise of the novel as an art form, and particularly the subjectification of the novel since the middle of the nineteenth century, whether these do not symbolize the voyage into the interior that comes with the failure of prevailing myths to provide external models toward which one may aspire. For when the prevailing myths fail to fit the varieties of man's plight, frustration expresses itself first in mythoclasm and then in the lonely search for internal identity. The novels of Conrad, of Hardy, of Gide, of Camus — paradoxically enough — provide man with guides for the internal search. One of Graham Greene's most tormented books, an autobiographical fragment on an African voyage, is entitled *Journey Without Maps*. Perhaps the modern novel, in contrast to the myth, is the response to the internal anguish that can find no external constraint in myth, a form of internal map. But this is a matter requiring a closer scrutiny than we can give it here. Suffice it to say that the alternative to externalization in myth appears to be the internalization of the personal novel, the first a communal effort, the second the lone search for identity.

Notes and References

1. *Quest for Myth* (Baton Rouge: Louisiana State University Press, 1949).
2. J. DOLLARD and N. E. MILLER, *Personality and Psychotherapy* (New York: McGraw-Hill, 1950).
3. *The Greeks and the Irrational* (Boston: Beacon Press, 1957), pp. 14–15.
4. *The Great Short Novels of Henry James* (New York: Dial Press, 1944), Introduction.
5. RENÉ WELLEK and AUSTIN WARREN, *Theory of Literature* (New York: Harcourt, Brace, 1942), p. 180.
6. *The Literature of Ancient Greece* (Chicago: University of Chicago Press, 1957), p. 43.
7. *The Hero with a Thousand Faces* (New York: Meridian Books, 1956), pp. 382–383.
8. *The Greek Myths* (Baltimore: Penguin Books, 1955), p. 36.
9. *The Literature of Ancient Greece, op. cit.*, pp. 39–40.

PART VII

Art and the Creative Process

All vital teaching of the six major arts disciplines must largely depend upon a sensitive understanding of the creative process, the nature of the dynamic process through which works of art are made.

In this section Anthony Storr, taking the influential formulations of Carl Jung as his focus, examines the psychological nature of the creative act, while Peter Abbs, also beginning with an example of frustrated creative activity from the life of Jung, considers the structural phases of the creative act in relationship to art and the arts curriculum.

Chapter 16

Individuation and the Creative Process

Anthony Storr

Introduction

It is the purpose of this paper to affirm that, although Jung seems to have denied it, the individuation process and the creative process are closely analogous. Both artists and scientists are concerned with bringing about new syntheses, and with integrating opposites; and the state of mind which artists and scientists describe as conducive to new discovery is the same as that which Jung advocated for active imagination. In order to demonstrate this, it is necessary to recall some of Jung's fundamental hypotheses about mental health, mental illness, and the development of personality.

Jung's Concept of the Personality

At the time when Jung was writing his doctoral dissertation, 'On the psychology of so-called occult phenomena', psychiatrists were fascinated by the observations of Morton Prince and Pierre Janet on cases of so-called 'multiple personality'; and it will be recalled that the subject of Jung's dissertation was his fifteen-year-old cousin, Hélène Preiswerk, who claimed to be a medium, controlled by a variety of personalities who spoke through her. Before Freud's concept of repression became widely employed, the term used to describe such phenomena was 'dissociation'; and Jung, who had studied under Pierre Janet in Paris, continued to think of personality as being capable of dissociation into a number of subsidiary personalities, any of which could temporarily take over the executive rôle. Although Jung later accepted the idea of repression in the Freudian sense of making the unacceptable unconscious, and indeed provided experimental proof of repression with his word-association tests, he continued to think and write in terms of dissociation. For example, he referred to complexes as 'splinter psyches' which appear in personified form in dreams; and I believe that it is Jung's continued employment of the concept of dissociation which accounts for his personification of various aspects of the psyche as 'shadow', 'animus', 'anima', and so on. However this may be, the concept of dissociation was certainly valuable as applied both to hysteria and to schizophrenia. An hysterical patient, for example, might behave as if she were two or more different persons, who had no cognizance of each other; and it was obvious that the cure of this type of neurosis depended upon making the divided selves conscious of one another and, by bringing them into direct relation with each other, creating a new unity of personality.

In schizophrenia, the personality was fragmented into many parts, rather than into two or three, as in hysteria; and, because that part of the personality which we call the ego was overwhelmed, the schizophrenic lost contact with reality in a way in which the hysteric did not. Jung describes the schizophrenic as being 'split into a plurality of subjects, or into a plurality of *autonomous complexes*' (Jung[9], para. 498). It may be assumed that it is the extent of fragmentation which makes integration difficult or impossible in such cases.

If dissociation and fragmentation are characteristic features of mental illness, it follows that integration and cohesion are likely to be distinctive aspects of mental health. In Jung's scheme of things, this is so; and Jungian analysis is directed toward achieving a better balance and interrelation between the various parts of the psyche. For the purpose of my argument, I want to emphasize the point that Jungian analysis was not aimed at ridding the patient of symptoms as one might rid the body of bacteria. Indeed, neurotic symptoms, in Jung's view, were often valuable pointers to the patient's one-sidedness and lack of balance. Jung sometimes said of an individual; 'Thank God he became neurotic!', meaning by this that neurosis had compelled the person concerned to take stock of himself and re-examine his values and his way of life. In Jung's view, the psyche, like the body, was a self-regulating system. When the system became unbalanced, because the individual was straying too far from his own true path, compensatory forces would be set in motion to restore equilibrium. The idea of compensation and self-regulation runs right through the whole of Jung's writings. It is an integral part of his view of dreams, of his theory of psychological types, and of his conception of neurosis as an expression of one-sidedness.

However, it would be too simple merely to equate neurosis with dissociation and lack of balance, and psychic health with integration and equilibrium. Personality, in Jung's view, is an achievement, not merely the absence of gross dissociation:

> The achievement of personality means nothing less than the optimum development of the whole individual human being ... A whole lifetime, in all its biological, social and spiritual aspects, is needed. Personality is the supreme realisation of the innate idiosyncrasy of a living being. It is an act of high courage flung in the face of life, the absolute affirmation of all that constitutes the individual, the most successful adaptation to the universal conditions of existence coupled with the greatest possible freedom for self-determination (Jung[10], para. 289).

The picture Jung paints is of an ideal; and I need hardly stress the point that no human being ever reaches it. But I do want to emphasize that Jung's concept of mental health is neither static nor negative. He does not think of the ideal mental state as merely an absence of neurotic symptoms, or even as the ability to love and work, as Freud conceived it. Nor does he think of it as something once and for all attained. In Jung's view, the achievement of optimum development is a lifetime's task which is never completed; a journey upon which one sets out hopefully toward a destination at which one never arrives. In his paper, 'The transcendent function', written in 1916, Jung writes:

> There is a widespread prejudice that analysis is something like a 'cure', to which one submits for a time and is then discharged healed. That is a layman's error left over from the early days of psycho-analysis. Analytical treatment could be described as a readjustment of the psychological attitude, achieved with the help of the doctor. ... The new attitude gained in the course of analysis tends sooner or later to become inadequate in one way or another, and necessarily so, because the constant flow of life again and again demands fresh adaptation. Adaptation is never achieved once and for all (Jung[13], paras 142–143).

One implication of this point of view is that there are always opposing forces within the psyche; that conflict is an inescapable part of the human condition. When conflict becomes so extreme as to cause obvious distress to the individual or to those in his milieu, we speak of neurosis or psychosis. But none of us is ever entirely free of conflict, however normal we believe ourselves to be. As one of my teachers used to say: 'The normal man is a very dark horse'.

One source for Jung's conception of human nature was certainly Schopenhauer. As an adolescent Jung steeped himself in philosophy. He found himself particularly in tune with Schopenhauer because of the philosopher's sombre picture of the world. 'Here at last', wrote Jung, 'was a philosopher who had the courage to see that all was not for the best in the fundaments of the universe' (Jung[14], p. 71). Schopenhauer, himself profoundly influenced by Kant, thought that space and time were human, subjective categories imposed upon reality which compel us to perceive the world as consisting of individual objects. This *principium individuationis*, as Schopenhauer named it, prevents us from seeing reality as a seamless whole. Schopenhauer considered that individuals were the embodiment of an underlying Will which was outside space and time. Jung also believed that there was a realm outside space and time from which individuals became differentiated. Borrowing the Gnostic term, he referred to this realm as the pleroma. In the *Septem Sermones ad Mortuos* he wrote: 'We are distinguished from the pleroma in our essence ... which is confined within time and space' (Jung[15], p. 8). Within the pleroma, there is no differentiation between opposites like good and evil, light and dark, time and space, or force and matter. It is the *principium individuationis* which compels distinctiveness. Schopenhauer's conception of the Will and Jung's conception of the unconscious are clearly similar; and Schopenhauer would have entirely appreciated Jung's remark at the beginning of his autobiography: 'My life is a story of the self-realization of the unconscious' (Jung[14], p. 17).

The very existence of individuals, therefore, implies loss of an original unity and differentiation into opposites. We cannot conceive of a person who does not himself enshrine opposites. We cannot conceive of an individual without contrasting him with other individuals. As John Macmurray put it: 'The unit of personal existence is not the individual, but two persons in personal relation' (Macmurray[18]). Moreover, the nature of thought and language is such that human beings are bound to categorize things as opposites; that is, all human statements are antinomian. I cannot, for example, assert that this room is dark without contrasting that state with potential lightness. We are caught by the opposites and cannot escape their trap.

I suggest that what Jung wrote about the process of the development of personality is closely paralleled by what is known of the process of creation in the arts and sciences.

Creativity and the Union between Opposites

I am not asserting that making a scientific discovery and creating a work of art are exactly equivalent. As Leonard Meyer has pointed out in his essay, 'Concerning the sciences, the arts — *and* the humanities', scientists discover something which is already there, like the double helix, whereas the artists create something which has never previously existed (Meyer[19]). Scientific hypotheses are not works of art, and works of art are not scientific hypotheses. Nevertheless, science and art share certain aims, notably the aim of seeking order in complexity, and unity in diversity. Often, both scientific discovery and artistic creation are concerned with bringing about a new union between opposites. I shall give two examples, one from science, and one from music.

My first example is Newton's discovery of the law of universal gravitation. The Newtonian synthesis was based upon the discoveries of Kepler, who had been able to describe the motions of the planets around the sun, combined with those of Galileo, who had described the laws of motion of objects upon the earth. Until Newton, these two sets of laws had seemed to be quite separate. When Newton made the leap of imagination which led him to suppose that gravity was a universal force which acted at enormous distances, he combined the discoveries of Kepler and Galileo in such a way that the motions of bodies upon earth and bodies in the heavens could be seen to obey the same universal laws. The Law of Gravitation, which states that 'every body attracts every other with a force proportional to the product of their masses and inversely proportional to the square of the distance between them', has been described as the greatest generalization achieved by the human mind. In order to prove his law, Newton had to show that the path of the moon round the earth could be accounted for by the interaction of the gravitational force upon it which he supposed the earth to be exerting, together with the centrifugal force of the moon, the formula for which had already been discovered by Huygens. Newton's mathematical ability enabled him to do this. He then computed the sun's attraction on the planets, and demonstrated that their orbits, which Kepler had described, but for which he could not account, complied with the same law. Newton left a diagram which anticipates the possibility of artificial satellites by showing that increasing the velocity of a projectile will eventually result in its circling the earth at the same velocity for ever.

Here is a classic example of scientific discovery being concerned with the union of opposites: Kepler's laws and Galileo's laws being both reconciled and superseded by a principle which was both superior to both and yet comprehended both. Is not this closely parallel with what Jung describes as the 'transcendent function'?

My other example is one of the late works of Beethoven. Those of you who are familiar with the last quartets will be familiar with the so-called 'Grosse Fuge', which was originally written as the last movement of the quartet in B flat major, Opus 130, but which Beethoven's publisher insisted upon publishing as a separate work, thus requiring Beethoven to write a new finale to the quartet, which was actually the last work he finished. Here is what Martin Cooper has to say about the Grosse Fuge in his book *Beethoven: The Last Decade*:

> The Grosse Fuge is unique. The contrapuntal ingenuity of the music, which might suggest an affinity with J. S. Bach's *Kunst der Fuge*, is in reality secondary. What grips the listener is the dramatic experience of forcing — for there is frequently a sense of violence in this mastery — two themes which have, by nature, nothing in common, to breed and produce a race of giants, episodes, or variations that have no parallel in musical history ... It is clear that the ability to conceive such a work argues certain definite psychological traits — a huge fund of aggression, in the first place, and an instinctive resentment of restriction in any form — and a 'philosophy of life' (something quite different from the intellectual systems of professional philosophers, for which Beethoven had little or no understanding) based on the struggle for self-development on the one hand and self-mastery on the other. In this sense the Grosse Fuge is one of the most personally revealing of Beethoven's works; but, as always, he reveals himself in purely musical terms and it is almost as though his 'personality', which determined the form and moulded the details, can be withdrawn from the finished work, just as the wooden mould can be withdrawn from the completed arch (Cooper[2], pp. 388–389.)

The Grosse Fuge is an extreme example of combining and transcending opposites; but even the simplest kind of music is composed of contrasting elements. A single line of melody, for example, leaves the tonic, ventures forth, and then returns home from whence it came; two steps in opposite directions, brought together by the form of the melody.

Another parallel to what Jung wrote in his paper 'The transcendent function' can be found in what a composer writes about the process of composition. Aaron Copland, in lectures he gave at Harvard which are published as *Music and Imagination*, wrote:

Why is it so important to my own psyche that I compose music? What makes it seem so absolutely necessary, so that every other daily activity, by comparison, is of lesser significance? And why is the creative impulse never satisfied; why must one always begin anew? To the first question — the need to create — the answer is always the same — self-expression; the basic need to make evident one's deepest feelings about life. But why is the job never done? Why must one always begin again? The reason for the compulsion to renewed creativity, it seems to me, is that each added work brings with it an element of self-discovery. I must create in order to know myself, and since self-knowledge is a never-ending search, each new work is only a part-answer to the question 'Who am I?' and brings with it the need to go on to other and different part-answers (Copland[3], pp. 40–41).

This statement seems closely parallel to Jung's remark, already quoted, that 'the constant flow of life again and again demands fresh adaptation. Adaptation is never achieved once and for all' (Jung[13], para. 143).

I conclude, therefore, that the process of individuation, as described by Jung, and the process of creation as described by Copland and many others, have in common that they are both concerned with making new syntheses out of opposites, and that they are both journeys which are characterized by stops on the way, like stations on a railway journey but which never finish at an ultimate destination. Even Newton's synthesis, which lasted for 250 years, was finally superseded by Einstein.

Jung and Freud on the Status of Art

I think it remarkable that Jung never seems to have associated the creative process with individuation in any direct fashion. In fact, he might be said to have repudiated the notion. Let me remind you of a passage in his autobiography. Jung writes, in the chapter entitled 'Confrontation with the unconscious':

When I was writing down these phantasies, I once asked myself, 'What am I really doing? Certainly this has nothing to do with science. But then what is it?' Whereupon a voice within me said, 'It is art'. I was astonished. It had never entered my head that what I was writing had any connection with art. Then I thought, 'Perhaps my unconscious is forming a personality that is not me, but which is insisting on coming through to expression'. I knew for a certainty that the voice had come from a woman. I recognised it as the voice of a patient, a talented psychopath who had a strong transference to me. She had become a living figure within my mind.

Obviously what I was doing wasn't science. What could it then be but art? It was as though these were the only alternatives in the world. This is the way a woman's mind works.

I said very emphatically to this voice that my phantasies had nothing to do with art, and I felt a great inner resistance. No voice came through, however, and I kept on writing. Then came the next assault, and again the same assertion: 'That is art'. This time I caught her and said, 'No, it is not art! On the contrary, it is nature', and prepared myself for an argument. When nothing of the sort occurred, I reflected that the 'woman within me' did not have the speech centres I had. And so I suggested that she used mine. She did so and came through with a long statement (Jung[14], p. 178).

Later, Jung goes on:

What the anima said seemed to me full of a deep cunning. If I had taken these phantasies of the unconscious as art, they would have carried no more conviction than visual perceptions, as if I were watching a movie. I would have felt no moral obligation towards them. The anima might then have easily seduced me into believing that I was a misunderstood artist, and that my so-called artistic nature gave me the right to neglect reality. If I had followed her voice, she would in all probability have said to me one day, 'Do you imagine the nonsense you're engaged in is really art? Not a bit.' Thus the insinuations of the anima, the mouthpiece of the unconscious, can utterly destroy a man. In the final analysis the decisive factor is always consciousness, which can understand the manifestations of the unconscious and take up a position towards them (*Ibid.*, pp. 179–180).

In his book, *A Secret Symmetry*, Aldo Carotenuto identifies the 'talented psychopath' with Sabina Spielrein, the patient with whom Jung became emotionally involved, and who later became a Freudian analyst (Carotenuto[1]). However, Carotenuto gives no evidence for his supposition. He alleges that Jung was trying to separate himself from Sabina Spielrein by the year 1909; and the passage from Jung's autobiography refers to the year 1914, by which time he had already embarked on his long relationship with Toni Wolff. It is, I agree, unlikely that Jung would have referred to Toni Wolff as a 'talented psychopath'; but whichever lady it was that suggested that what Jung was engaging in was art, it is hard to understand why he repudiated her with such vehemence. For, although his phantasies were, admittedly, rather crude products of the unconscious, they could legitimately be regarded as the raw material of art, requiring conscious refinement before they could be shaped into something coherent. I would suppose that both Wagner and Tolkien worked with rather similar material. Why should Jung say that, if he had regarded his phantasies as art, they would have carried no more conviction than visual perceptions as in a film? Is Jung revealing that his conception of art is that it is escapist? It sounds remarkably like it. In 1914, Jung could hardly be said to have emancipated himself from Freud's influence, and Freud was notably ambivalent about the artist's activity, affirming that artists were in advance of ordinary people in their knowledge of the mind, but at the same time, introverts who had transferred their interest to the wishful constructions of phantasy, and turned away from reality.

I have examined Freud's attitude to art in a paper published in *The New Universities Quarterly* in which I showed that Freud seemed to think of aesthetic form as order *consciously* imposed upon chaotic, or at any rate, unorganized, phantasy derived from the unconscious (Storr[22]). This dichotomy is far too simple. As Anton Ehrenzweig[5] and other writers like Marion Milner[20] have demonstrated, the need to impose order is itself unconsciously determined. It is virtually impossible to look at three dots, for instance, without making them into a triangle — as the Gestalt school of psychology discovered; and this is not something we deliberately set out to do. One of the reasons that new discoveries are hard to make is that it is difficult to break established perceptual modes (*Gestalten*) as Thomas Kuhn has shown in his book *The Structure of Scientific Revolutions* (Kuhn[17]). But we get satisfaction from perceiving a new order; the 'Eureka' phenomenon, as it has sometimes been called. Freud, tied to his concept of a pleasure principle that was wholly sensual, did not allow that mastery, the sense of achievement which we get from discovering or imposing order, could be a genuine source of pleasure.

Jung goes on to denigrate art still further. In a later passage Jung reveals that, toward the end of World War I, he had another letter from 'that aesthetic lady' in which she again asserted that the phantasies arising from the unconscious had artistic value and should be considered art. Jung wrote:

> The letter got on my nerves. It was far from stupid and therefore dangerously persuasive. The modern artist, after all, seeks to create art out of the unconscious. The utilitarianism and self-importance concealed behind this thesis touched a doubt in myself, namely, my uncertainty as to whether the phantasies I was producing were really spontaneous and natural, and not ultimately my own arbitrary inventions. I was by no means free from the bigotry and hubris of consciousness which wants to believe that any half-way inspiration is due to one's own merit, whereas inferior reactions come merely by chance, or even derive from alien sources. Out of this irritation and disharmony within myself there proceeded, the following day, a changed mandala: part of the periphery had burst open and the symmetry was destroyed (Jung[14], p. 187).

In this passage, Jung is asserting that, if his phantasies were anything to do with art, they must be rated as his own arbitrary invention, whereas if they were what he calls 'spontaneous and natural' products of the unconscious, they could not be anything to do with art.

The Integrating Powers of Aesthetic and Scientific Creation

I find it difficult to understand this distinction. Both artists and scientists attribute their inspirations and discoveries to a source beyond conscious striving. Most discoveries are made when the creative person is in a state of reverie: a condition halfway between waking and sleeping. This is, of course, the very state which Jung recommends for the process of 'active imagination', in which the phantasies which he calls 'spontaneous and natural' are deliberately encouraged. What then, are the 'arbitrary inventions' that Jung both links with art and also despises? I think it is possible that he is referring to those inferior products of the imagination which can indeed be dismissed in Freudian terms as no more than wish-fulfilling phantasies. Romantic novels, of the kind written by Barbara Cartland or published by Mills and Boon, come into this category. So do the James Bond phantasies of Ian Fleming, and most pornography. Such daydreams, which all of us have indulged in, come from 'the tops of our heads', our egos, and have none of the depth which the kind of phantasies subserving art or scientific discovery possess. It is characteristic of this superficial stuff that it is quickly noted, and as quickly forgotten, and can hardly be rated as art. On the other hand, the great creators recognize, and over and over again describe, that the ideas which come to them in reverie are far from arbitrary inventions; and arise from a source which they cannot control, but with which they have to put themselves in touch. Jung's notion of individuation was of a spiritual journey; and the person embarking upon it, although he might not subscribe to any recognized creed, was nevertheless pursuing a religious quest. By paying careful attention to the unconscious, as manifested in dream and phantasy, the individual comes to change his attitude from one in which ego and will are paramount to one in which he acknowledges that he is guided by an integrating factor not of his own making.

But this is just what the greatest artists do. The composer, Josef Haydn, for instance, when inspiration failed him, said: 'But if I can't get on, I know that I must have forfeited God's grace by some fault of mine, and then I pray once more for grace till I feel I'm forgiven' (Hughes[8], p. 47).

Darwin, in *The Descent of Man*, wrote: 'The Imagination is one of the highest prerogatives of man. By this faculty he unites former images and ideas, independently of the will, and thus creates brilliant and novel results' (Darwin[4]).

One of the best examples of creative inspiration taking place independently of the will is furnished by Wagner, who describes how the orchestral introduction to the Rheingold came to him. You will remember the remarkable nature of this piece, of which the first 136 bars are based upon the triad of E flat, sounding without interruption. Wagner had been ill with dysentery, and was staying at Spezia in Italy. He writes:

After a night spent in fever and sleeplessness, I forced myself to take a long tramp the next day through the hilly country, which was covered with pinewoods. It all looked dreary and desolate, and I could not think what I should do there. Returning in the afternoon, I stretched myself, dead tired, on a hard couch, awaiting the long-desired hour of sleep. It did not come; but I fell into a kind of somnolent state, in which I suddenly felt as though I were sinking in swiftly flowing water. The rushing sound formed itself in my brain into a musical sound, the chord of E flat major, which continually reechoed in broken forms; these broken chords seemed to be melodic passages of increasing motion, yet the pure triad of E flat major never changed, but seemed by its continuance to impart infinite significance to the element in which I was sinking. I awoke in sudden terror from my doze, feeling as though the waves were rushing high above my head. I at once recognised that the orchestral overture to the Rheingold, which must long have lain latent within me though it had been unable to find definite form, had at last been revealed to me. I then quickly realised my own nature; the stream of life was not to flow to me from without, but from within (Wagner[23], p. 603).

Jung tells us that he painted his first mandala in 1916, just after completing the *Septem Sermones ad Mortuos*. He drew a great many during the years between 1918 and 1920. Jung felt that mandalas represented a union between opposites, expressions of the self, the totality of the personality. At the same time, he realized that he 'had to abandon the idea of the superordinate position of the ego' (Jung[14], p. 188), as he puts it. Many people tend to think that the appearance of mandalas during analysis is an indication that the patient's progress toward individuation is far advanced. This may be so: but they often forget that Jung noted that mandalas occur as compensatory phenomena in conditions of dissociation and disorientation. Jung gives as examples children between the ages of eight and eleven whose parents are about to be divorced, schizophrenics whose view of the world has become confused, and adults who as the result of treatment of neurosis, are confronted with the problem of opposites (Jung[11], para. 707). Ernst Gombrich in *The Sense of Order* wrote:

> I have never found it easy to come to terms with Jung's psychology with its mixture of mystical and scientific pretensions. All the more do I find it necessary to put on record that I have myself experienced the vision described at the end of this paragraph. Even in the life of a cloistered academic there are moments when difficult decisions have to be made — for instance whether or not to move to another cloister. It was during such a crisis that I wavered a good deal, but when I went to bed at the end of the day on which I had at last made up my mind, I vividly saw in front of my eyes what is called a hypnagogic image, the visual experience that can precede sleep. I remember it as a regular flower bed with a group of tulips in the centre. It was certainly accompanied by that feeling of harmony and peace described by Frieda Fordham.
>
> I still would not be inclined to concede that this experience provides evidence for Jung's interpretations of a collective psyche. My bias prompts me rather to seek the explanation in that sense of order which is the subject of this book. Order can serve as a metaphor for order, particularly in the context of alternatives. What I experienced was the contrast between the dithering oscillations of my former state of uncertainty and the balance I had at last regained by a firm decision. ... There is no need to assume that our dreams and visions draw on a collective pool of

archetypes. What may be part of our psychological make-up is rather the disposition to accept degrees of order as potential metaphors of inner states (Gombrich[7], pp. 246–247).

Jung does not mention anywhere, so far as I know, the research into children's drawings conducted by Rhoda Kellogg, a nursery-school teacher from California, in spite of the fact that he once met her. Somewhere towards the end of the third year of life, children begin to produce drawings which Kellogg named 'combines'; that is, patterns in which two opposites, like cross and circle, square and triangle, are combined into a single pattern. Howard Gardner, a psychologist from Harvard, in his book on children's drawings, *Artful Scribbles*, writes:

> Mandalas are the examples, *par excellence*, of a combine. Not only are mandalas visible in many combines, but, more important, mandalas seem to represent a central tendency of 'combining behaviour': the simplest and most balanced diagrams, when combined with one another, produce mandala-like forms. ... Both Carl Jung and Rhoda Kellogg find the mandala inevitable — Jung because it is unequivocally encoded in our nervous system and uniquely suited to resolve our existential dilemmas, Kellogg because it is the natural outgrowth of the drawing sequence through which every normal (and many abnormal) children will pass, a sequence marked by a search for order and harmony (Gardner[6] p. 43).

And so, mandalas should not be regarded simply as the end-point of the process of individuation; but also as symbols of uniting opposites, of the search for order and harmony, a search which manifests itself from the earliest years. Jung, in his commentary on *The Secret of the Golden Flower*, wrote that he became interested in what he called the individuation process because he was confronted by patients whose fundamental problems were insoluble unless violence was done to one or other side of their natures. Jung describes how such patients 'outgrow' their problems by reaching a new level of consciousness. 'Some higher or wider interest appeared on the patient's horizon, and through this broadening of his outlook, the insoluble problem lost its urgency. It was not solved logically in its own terms, but merely appeared in a different light, and so really did become different' (Jung[12], para. 16).

Jung is making an important point here. When patients come to accept, let us say, those aggressive or sexual aspects of themselves which had been repressed or dissociated, the crudely unacceptable elements decline, because the intensity of the impulse is diminished when brought into consciousness and allied with the total personality. A young person may, for instance, harbour murderous impulses toward his parents which he has repressed. But when these murderous feelings are brought into relation with the rest of his personality and can perhaps be seen in the light of a need to separate from parents whom he also loves, his murderous feelings become transmuted into differentiation and self-affirmation. Instead of a dissociated shadow, a balance between opposites takes place; and this is symbolized by the archetype of synthesis, the mandala.

It is my contention that this recurrent attempt at synthesis takes place throughout life, from the earliest stages onward. It may be more evident in certain types of person. Howard Gardner tells us that, early in life, his drawing children could be divided into what he names as 'patterners' and 'dramatists'. Patterners 'analyse the world very much in terms of the configurations they can discover, the patterns and regularities they encounter ... they spend little time re-enacting familiar scenes in play and they engage in relatively little social conversation'. Dramatists, on the other hand, engage in 'pretend play, in story-telling, in continuing conversation and social interchange with adults and peers. For them, one of life's chief pleasures inheres in maintaining contact with others and celebrating the pageantry of interpersonal relations. ... Our patterners, on the other hand, seem almost to spurn the world of social relations, preferring to immerse (and perhaps lose) themselves in the world of (usually visual) patterns' (Gardner[6], p. 47). Patterners would appear to be introverts; perhaps potentially obsessional; whilst dramatists seem extraverts who, if neurotic, might develop hysteria.

It is tempting to speculate further, and suggest that, if creatively gifted, the dramatists will become novelists, playwrights, or representational painters: whilst patterners will turn to science, abstract painting, or music. Whether these early characteristics detected in differing types of drawing remain permanent features and do in fact reflect basic differences in personality remains to be proven.

The creatively gifted show, in their works, recurrent attempts at new syntheses which strive to include elements which have been previously omitted or which only later obtrude themselves. Sometimes these attempts are unsuccessful. Einstein, the greatest scientist since Newton, provides one of the saddest examples. C. P. Snow, in his posthumous book *The Physicists*, writes:

> After his brilliant explanation of gravitation in his General Theory of Relativity back in 1915, Einstein had spent the rest of his life in an attempt to formulate a theory which would cover *all* the forces of nature at once. At first his unified field theory needed to combine gravitation and electromagnetism under the same set of equations. By the 1930s there was the nuclear force to include. In the 1950s, the physicists knew there were two types of nuclear force, very different in character and strength. A unified theory must cope with four forces. For all his efforts, Einstein had no success ... Einstein's tremendous instinct for physics had sadly gone astray, and led him up a blind alley for the last forty years of his life (Snow[21], pp. 132–133).

In my own opinion, some of Beethoven's last quartets are exploratory attempts at new syntheses which do not reach that rounded perfection of form attained in some of his earlier works; broken mandalas, if one likes to use that analogy. Joseph Kerman refers to the B flat quartet — the one for which he wrote the Grosse Fuge as the original finale — as 'the most problematic of all his compositions', and speaks of it as 'harassing him to the last' (Kerman[16], p. 374). Beethoven had broken away from conventional sonata form, of which he was a supreme master, increasing the number of movements, and interrupting the flow of the music with surprising interpolations and sudden contrasts. In another passage, referring to the same quartet, Kerman writes: 'Force jostles with whimsy, prayer with effrontery, dangerous innocence with an even more dangerous sophistication' (*Ibid.*, p. 304). No wonder Kerman names the chapter in which the B flat quartet is discussed together with its far more coherent neighbour, the C sharp minor quartet Op. 131, 'Dissociation and Integration'.

Why is it that man seems doomed to be always striving toward unity, but never destined to find it? As I see it, this divine discontent is part of his special biological endowment, and one which has enabled him to develop potentialities far beyond those of his animal cousins. Creatures that are perfectly adapted to their environments are rigidly governed by sets of instinctive responses. At first sight, this seems admirable. The key of the environment fits the lock of the creature to perfection. But suppose that the environment changes? Creatures which cannot flexibly adapt are doomed. We have seen the havoc that man himself has wreaked upon wildlife by his use of chemical fertilizers and the like; but environments change without human intervention, from Ice Age to temperate, and from temperate to tropic. Man has been able to adapt to all these changes just because he is not rigidly programmed; not closely adapted by nature to any one type of environment. It is this lack of rigid adaptation which increases the exploratory drive in man which can be discerned, to a lesser extent, in other animals. The more an animal can discover about a new environment, the safer it becomes for him, as those of you who have taken a dog to a new house will have already observed. Man's urge to master and understand the world is an elaboration of this drive, which takes the form of constructing scientific hypotheses which impose order and pattern upon the maze of phenomena, and thus bring more and more of the external world under man's control. But, as we all know, scientific hypotheses are never complete. There are always elements which do not fit, and which spur on the scientist to construct new theories which will comprehend still more of reality within a single scheme. Lack of unity is therefore adaptive in that it spurs discovery.

Whereas the scientist is orientated toward discovering unity in the external world, and to this end, has to be as objective as possible, the artist is endeavouring to find unity within, and to make sense and coherence out of his subjective experience. The lack of order which he finds when he looks inward is a mirror of the lack of order he discerns when he looks outward. In R. D. Laing's phrase, we are all 'Divided Selves'; though the degree of this division varies widely. I think that it is this which motivates our search for unity, for the Utopian harmony which we never achieve; and which accounts for the phenomenon that, although each effort at synthesis may be marked by a new mandala, that mandala will always break down and require us to seek another to replace it.

Summary

Mental illness is characterized by dissociation of the personality: mental health by integration.

Although extremes of dissociation and fragmentation are only seen in neurosis and psychosis, lesser degrees of division within the personality are an inescapable part of the human condition. Even the healthiest person never achieves complete integration.

Conclusion

The creative process, whether in the arts or in the sciences, is concerned with synthesis, with bringing about new unions between opposites. It is closely parallel with what Jung described as happening during the course of the development of personality.

The process of individuation has many features in common with the creative process, including the state of mind which Jung described in connection with active imagination. Mandalas symbolize new syntheses; but each mandala represents a step on a never completed journey rather than a permanent solution. The same is true of scientific hypotheses and works of art.

Notes and References

1. CAROTENUTO, A. (1982) *A Secret Symmetry*, New York, Pantheon.
2. COOPER, M. (1970) *Beethoven: The Last Decade*, Oxford University Press.
3. COPLAND, A. (1952) *Music and Imagination*, Oxford University Press.
4. DARWIN, C. (1871) *The Descent of Man*, London, Murray.
5. EHRENZWEIG, A (1963) *The Hidden Order of Art*, London, Weidenfeld and Nicholson.
6. GARDNER, H. (1980) *Artful Scribbles*, New York, Basic Books.
7. GOMBRICH, E. (1979) *The Sense of Order*, Oxford, Phaidon.
8. HUGHES, R. (1962) *Haydn*, London, Dent.
9. JUNG, C.G. (1928) 'Mental disease and the psyche', *Coll. Wks*, 3.
10. JUNG, C.G. (1934) 'The development of the personality', *Coll. Wks*, 17.
11. JUNG, C.G. (1955) 'Mandalas', *Coll. Wks*, 9, 1.
12. JUNG, C.G. (1957) 'Commentary on *The Secret of the Golden Flower*', *Coll. Wks*, 13.
13. JUNG, C.G. (1958) 'The transcendent function', *Coll. Wks*, 8.
14. JUNG, C.G. (1963) *Memories, Dreams, Reflections*, London, Collins and Routledge and Kegan Paul.
15. JUNG, C.G. (1967) *Septem Sermones ad Mortuos*, London, Watkins.
16. KERMAN, J. (1967) *The Beethoven Quartets*, Oxford University Press.
17. KUHN, T. (1962) *The Structure of Scientific Revolutions*, Chicago University Press.
18. MACMURRAY, J. (1961) *Persons in Relation*, London, Faber and Faber.
19. MEYER, L. (1974) 'Concerning the sciences, the arts — and the humanities', *Critical Inquiry*, I, 1. University of Chicago Press.

20. MILNER, M. (1971) *On Not Being Able to Paint*, London, Heinemann.
21. SNOW, C. P. (1981) *The Physicists*, London, Macmillan.
22. STORR, A. (1976) 'Freud and art', *New University Quarterly*.
23. WAGNER, R. (1911) *My Life*, London, Constable.

Chapter 17

The Pattern of Art-Making

Peter Abbs

Introduction: The Impulse to Symbolize

In his autobiography *Memories, Dreams, Reflections* Carl Jung briefly states why, as a pupil, he was unable to respond to his art classes:

> I was exempted from drawing classes on grounds of utter incapacity. This in a way was welcome to me, since it gave me more free time; but on the other hand, it was a fresh defeat, since I had some facility in drawing, although I did not realise that it depended essentially on the way I was feeling. I could draw only what stirred my imagination. But I was forced to copy prints of Greek gods with sightless eyes, and when that wouldn't go properly the teacher obviously thought I needed something more naturalistic and set before me the picture of a goat's head. This assignment I failed completely, and that was the end of my drawing classes. [1]

Jung's case is representative of so many individuals who later when the springs of the art-making process were unexpectedly released found, to their great satisfaction, that they actually had an ability to express their feelings in the very medium from which they had once been formally excluded or judged as wanting by their teachers.

It is deeply ironical that Jung who as a child sat for hours in front of the paintings at the Klein-Huningen parsonage, 'gazing at all this beauty', and who was later to restore the place of the gods to the human imagination could not respond to the prints of the Greek gods in his drawing classes. Yet, as he indicates, the reason was simple enough; no feeling was released and without feeling there could be no creative act, only a sterile imitation. Like so many teachers of the expressive disciplines, Jung's teacher had found a way of developing certain mechanical skills which by-passed the expressive task altogether.

The Five Phases of Art-Making

Impulse is the pulse of art-making, rooted in the body and moving outwards. To exclude impulse is to exclude the very source of art-making. For it is impulse which bears the energy necessary for the creation of new symbols. Within impulse there is a desire for reflection, a desire for an image which will hold, comprehend and complete. This desire is buried in the body, bound into our instincts, an innate propensity. Art is the life of the body, projected, developed and taken into consciousness.

The art-making process, thus, begins with an impulse which taken into a particular medium struggles to develop itself, to give shape to itself, to recognize its latent meanings. It is not, as has often been claimed, a question of emotional discharge or of displacement of emotion or of some therapeutic release. Such phrases presuppose an essentially negative view of emotion. It is rather a question of following through an impulse in order to comprehend its meaning. It is to do with passionate reflection. What we are describing is a process which has a fair chance of culminating in knowledge, in the cognition of human nature and an evaluation of that nature. Art is, thus, an epistemological activity, one of the most subtle agents we have for the realization of the perennial injunction: 'Know thyself and be thyself'. In the English tradition, John Stuart Mill fleetingly recognized the philosophical importance of art when in a letter to Carlyle he wrote:

> for it is the artist alone in whose hands Truth becomes impressive and a living principle of action.

> ... the poet or artist is conversant chiefly with such (intuitive) truths and that his office in respect to truths is to declare them and to make them impressive. ...By him alone is real knowledge of such truths conveyed. [2]

And it was, later, Collingwood who in the closing paragraph of *The Principles of Art* gave such a magnificent defence of the arts in their power to keep consciousness true:

> The artist must prophesy not in the sense that he fortells things to come, but in the sense that he tells his audience, at risk of their displeasure, the secrets of their own hearts. His business as an artist is to speak out, to make a clean breast. But what he has to utter is not, as the individualistic theory of art would have us think, his own secrets. As spokesman of his community, the secrets he must utter are theirs. The reason why they need him is that no community altogether knows its own heart; and by failing in this knowledge a community deceives itself on the one subject concerning which ignorance means death. For the evils which come from that ignorance the poet as prophet suggests no remedy, because he has already given one. The remedy is the poem itself. Art is the community's medicine for the worst disease of mind, the corruption of consciousness. [3]

At the same time as we recognize this philosophical dimension to the arts we must not forget that art-making is a wholly natural activity, an astonishing outgrowth of instinct. Its blossom may open out in consciousness but its roots are down deep in affective impulse, in muscular and nervous rhythms, the beat of the heart, the intake and release of breath, patterns of perception, unconscious coordination of the limbs, the obscure, fluctuating, dimly sensed movements of the organism, in the preconceptual play of the psyche.

The release of impulse, then, forms the first phase of the creative process. There is a stirring of the psyche which through expression desires clarification and integration. The second phase of the movement can be discerned when the impulse grapples with a particular medium for its full representation and in the encounter develops further its own nature. As we know, this can be a prolonged activity with its outcome uncertain. Only occasionally does the material in the hands of the maker shape itself immediately to the pattern of the informing impulse. It is worth noticing here that the word 'medium' to denote expressive form or materials remains somewhat deceptive as the word too easily suggests (as in its spiritualist use) an open space through which a force passes, a neutral passage for the vehicles of creative intention. But in the expressive disciplines the medium is not simply neutral, open or passive. The medium has its own inner propensities, its own laws, its own history. It allows and forbids. It invites and resists. It may or may not yield the authentic representation we seek. The impulse can be lost in the material, can be betrayed by the material, or, at high moments, taken to an expected consummation. Certainly, the second phase of the art-making process is the most problematic of all.

Let us consider a little more carefully the relationship between impulse and medium, taking language as our example. The words the writer uses to convey his experience are not his own; they have been inherited; they belong to the culture and he relies on them to make his personal meanings communal. The words carry distinct qualities, deposits built up over the centuries, condensations of collective responses to experiences, wise responses, foolish responses, responses more-or-less adequate, responses wholly inadequate but nevertheless recorded and passed on. *The language is not a neutral medium*. It can ensnare the writer. How often, for example, do we write about a particular feeling only to admit 'But that isn't it at all. That is another state of mind, not mine'? The habits of the established language take over the impulse and confer upon it an alien sense. And yet how tempting it can be to accept the given formulation because, while it may feel wrong, *it sounds right*. It sounds so acceptable because it has been safely established as a language pattern. Because it conveys what has been commonly established, it takes an extraordinary amount of stubbornness to resist the false meaning that has appeared to crystallize within an emerging impulse. The spontaneous work of art is frequently no more than the gushing forth of unconsciously assimilated clichés and platitudes. In such cases the medium is, paradoxically, in tyrannical control and the original impulse submerged, almost from birth, in the miasma of received opinions. Nevertheless it is also true that, at other times, the words can take the writer deeper than he anticipated so that the impulse is given a depth and resonance which is, at once, infallibly right and yet seems to possess so much more than the initial upsurge of feeling promised. Here, in contrast, the language richly contributes to the expression of the original impulse giving it a quality and meaning it could not have had prior to expression. Just as there is no neutral impulse, so there is no neutral medium; the encounter between the two demands the most refined discrimination. Only by loving and hating and coming to know his medium can the art-maker hope to discover the full import of his impulses and thus make patent the latent self, the self which longs to be.

The way artists describe this phase of art-making is revealing. We read accounts which dramatize the aggressive nature of the act; thus we hear of the artist's *struggle*, his *wrestling* with the materials, his *attacking* the canvas, of his *dominating* or *subduing*, *manipulating* or *capturing* his subject-matter; of his *forging* a language; but we also hear of artists who gently *allow*, who *coax*, who *submit to*, who quietly *attend* to, let *unfold*, become *receptive channels for*. In the creative act both masculine and feminine dispositions are called for. Sometimes, the art-maker has to listen passively to the material or receive the impulse. At other times, he must actively convert the invisible throb of impulse into the visible language of art. The difficulties have been well caught by T. S. Eliot:

> Words strain
> Crack and sometimes break, under the burden,
> Under the tension, slip, slide and perish
> Decay with imprecision, will not stay in place
> Will not stay still.[4]

In this second phase of art-making the individual is striving to embody his experience, to make it not only personal but also representative. He moves from first approximations, from notes and highly-charged fragments, towards that which is progressively more shaped, more completely expressive. As the work develops, so his critical judgment comes more fully into play. He begins to discard, to select, to consider, to evaluate. Dryden described the process succinctly when he referred to one of his plays:

> Long before it was a play, when it only was a confused mass of thoughts, trembling over one another in the dark; when the fancy was yet in its first work, moving the sleeping images of things towards the light, there to be distinguished, and then either chosen or rejected by the judgement.[5]

Towards the end of this second phase of art-making, the critical judgment, which has to be in abeyance or severely inhibited in the first stages of creative work, slowly comes into its own. This coincides with a subtle but distinct shift in attention from a preoccupation with immediate approximate expression to a preoccupation with final representative form. As the work moves towards completion the art-maker will frequently consult with an imagined audience, constantly seeking its advice: 'How does this bit look?' 'Should it be this way round?' 'Is the reference too obscure?' 'Does it go on too long?' 'Is it finished?' It is as if a continuous inner dialogue is taking place between the artist and critic, between the creative subject and the sympathetic onlooker. And through this often harrowing interrogation, the work, if all goes well, attains its definitive shape. In some circumstances, of course, the critical voice is not only inside the art-maker, it is also out there, in the close friend, a fellow artist, a guiding tutor. But the common concern for an outside viewpoint suggests a truth about art-making which needs stressing: it is not only a personal activity it is also impersonal and has a communicative and communal intention. Art is a public category. What is made by the art-maker, and particularly that which is made well, requires the recognition of a community. On the one side, the art-maker, if his work is to mature, needs an audience; he needs its regard, it appreciation and its criticism. He needs to know whether he has achieved representative form, whether he has succeeded in capturing the essential truth of the human impulse. On the other side, the community for its health and wholeness, needs to attend to the truths which the art-maker, defiantly or tentatively, holds up for its reflection.

Thus, the art-making process does not end when the paints are returned to their boxes, the pen put down, the plaster and clay droppings swept into the corner; these actions only mark the ending of one crucial sequence. The next sequence, of equal importance, takes the artefact into the world in search of that audience the art-maker has already imagined and addressed in the heat of the creative art. In fact, an analysis of the entire process of art-making discloses a characteristic movement from subjective to objective, from self to other, from private to public, from self-expression to representative embodiment. Here we can begin to see how the Progressive's insistence on 'self-expression', the Cambridge School's emphasis on 'discrimination' and the Socio-Linguist's concern for 'audience' represent partial truths which can be given their full meaning only when they are brought into relationship with the whole complex pattern of art-making. Dislocated from this broad context, however, they can become dangerously misleading. 'Self-expression' may be valuable in the initial stages of art-making but it does not convey the ultimate goal of the activity for it excludes both the principles of representative embodiment and of a transpersonal communication. Art has much to do with 'self' and with 'expression', but it also has much to do with discipline, form, structure, objectivity, community and cultural inheritance. 'Discrimination' likewise is an essential element but only in its fitting place. Too much discrimination, too soon, and the source of authentic art dries up. The art-maker, in Dryden's words, must first freely invite 'the confused mass of thoughts, trembling over one another in the dark' into consciousness before he can begin coherently to select and shape. First indiscriminate expression ('self-expression'); then discriminate making ('representative embodiment'). It is similar with the need for an 'audience'. Art may be consummated in its electric transmission to an audience, but before this can happen the art-maker needs a protected space, an enclave, without ideological pressure, in which he can give mankind's confused mass of struggling impulses a habitation and a name:

> That girls at puberty may find
> The first Adam in their thoughts,
> Shut the door of the Pope's chapel,
> Keep those children out.

There on that scaffolding reclines
Michael Angelo.
With no more sound than the mice make
His hand moves to and fro.
Like a long-legged fly upon the stream
His mind moves upon silence. [6]

The art-maker serves an audience but to serve it well he must serve, first, a deeper impulse in his own nature. As Collingwood rightly declared he is not an entertainer, not a magician, not a propagandist. And the art-maker must be constantly on his guard against an audience that might seduce him into any one of these three pseudo-roles. Yet, as Yeats insists, the artist labours for the illumination of others, for the enlargement of consciousness. As we have seen, there is a reciprocal relationship of need between the art-maker and his audience.

The fourth phase of the art-making process, then, takes what has been made (and judged as sufficiently representative by the maker) into the community. The work calls for presentation, for performance. The painting or sculpture needs exhibiting, the poetry needs disseminating, the music needs playing. Such presentations can demand creative energy of the highest order. Indeed, in the case, say, of musical performance, the performers become co-authors of the work. The performer has to re-create the artefact, enter it with his own personality, relive it and embody it for a living audience. It is a healthy sign that we have recently begun talking about 'the performing arts' for such a description italicizes the public face of art and rightly suggests that the performer is an artist in his own right. His activity too is central to our conception of the expressive disciplines. It is his function to bring the truth of the emotion as determined by the art home to the society. Through presentations (exhibitions, publications) and through performances (concerts, recitals, dance, theatre, public readings) the art-work is taken out into the world until, at best, it enters the imagination of the human race.

The response of the audience and, particularly, of the immediate audience is also an essential part of the art-making process. If the performer is co-author of a work so, to some extent, is the audience. An audience, as we all know from first-hand experience, can 'bring out' or 'freeze' a performance. A collaborative audience is all but a necessary condition for good art. The audience is not just a hollow receptacle or the terminal station on the long route of art-making, although in an age of mass-culture, this so easily happens. A mass audience cannot contribute to any process, nor can the instant electronic communication to millions of distracted individuals nurture the arts. When the art-maker addressed the audience of his imagination, it was a united audience, an engaged audience, an identifiable audience possessing passion, intelligence and disarming honesty. It must be so because he needs to learn from it. So it should be with the audience 'out there' — it needs to be intimate, collaborative and forthright. Without such an audience art can quickly deteriorate into consumer fodder (as with most books, most music, most film, most theatre, most art) or solitary masturbation. Without such an audience art becomes what we largely have, an-artism. The final stage of the art-making process lies with the audience, in their response to and evaluation of the art that has been produced. Do the forms embody the secrets of their own hearts? Does the art delight, disturb, reveal the enduring lineaments of the psyche? Does it tell the human truth, however darkly strange and demanding? Or is it sham? Ego writ large? Mere cosmopolitan flash? Or is it caught in the very platitudes from which individuals struggle to free themselves, looking at art for the wider meaning? Without a discriminating audience, the integrity demanded by the earlier art-making phases is liable to falter and fail.

Art-Making inside the Aesthetic Field

Our account of art-making discloses five essential phases which can be schematically delineated in spiral motion as follows:

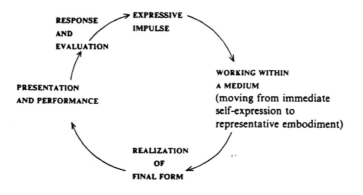

The phases placed in such a schematic spiral relationship represent an idealized sequence. It has not been my intention to plot the separate itineraries of each art-form (the differences emerging from the marked differences between the media) but rather to point to the common nature of the journey. Later I want to register certain qualifications about the application of such a schema to the teaching of the arts, but at this point I want now to take the argument a stage further by placing the foreground of the creative process against the general background of cultural mimesis through which the art-maker absorbs, uses and learns from all that exists in the culture, and through a continuous assimilation, masters and transforms. We need, in other words, to see the five phases of art-making as working within an endless dialectic between inherited form and emergent process.

The artist is not an autist. He creates out of his impulses but he can only create through his culture. Let me give one example. For decades Van Gogh has been the stereotype for the manic genius, the solitary creator of an individual vision. Yet this stereotype is hopelessly out of relationship with the actual truth of Van Gogh's life. This is not the place to make the argument in detail but any cursory acquaintance with the letters of Van Gogh reveals a man immersed in culture. Not only does he warmly discuss the literary work of Tolstoy, Dickens, Zola, Carlyle, Maupassant, Whitman, George Eliot, Shakespeare and Goethe, he also shows the keenest appreciation of innumerable painters: of, for example, Monticelli, Daumier, Gericault, Delacroix, Millet, Rembrandt, Rousseau, Courbet and Giotto. He encounters certain Japanese prints and his work immediately absorbs the influence. Writing to Theo in 1888 about the painting of his bedroom he claims 'it is coloured in free flat tones like Japanese prints'. He sees Gauguin's work and, again, it has an immediate effect on the form of his own work. The original painter sees himself in traditional terms. From Saint-Rémy, a year before his death, he writes to his brother (who represented the only community he ever had): 'When I realize the worth and originality and the superiority of Delacroix and Millet, for instance, then I am bold to say — yes, I am something, I can do something. *But I must have a foundation in those artists*, and then produce the little "which I am capable of in the same direction"' (my italics). The art grows out of the culture as well as out of the deep impulses of self: the two are inextricably intertwined. Identity without culture is a definition of autism. Culture without identity defines the closed totalitarian state. Furthermore, in Van Gogh we find an example of a man who is driven to suicidal despair because he cannot find a living community for the culture he has made.

The creative process takes place inside a specific aesthetic field where the forms of the past are constantly recreated and recast. As we claimed earlier, the seed of impulse must be sown into the rich humus of culture, or, at least, the richest we can manage. It was the fallacy of the Progressive School to posit a 'pure' individual who was 'naturally' creative and who, as it were, created works of art merely by breathing. The notion of 'self-expression' as an absolute aim derives from an indulgent and insupportable view of human nature. To create we have invariably, to imitate. Poesis requires mimesis. We need to know what others have done and how they have done it. In teaching the arts, therefore, we need to grapple with the historical dimension of culture-making but always in terms of living impulse and existential need. In this way the culture grows into the child, the child into the culture; the present roots itself into the past, the past flows, renewed, into the present. In an earlier chapter Professor Bantock outlined the implications of mimesis for the teaching of all the arts. Here I raise it to suggest the encompassing framework within which and through which individual creativity operates and develops. The notion of mimesis raises a further problem about art-making for we live in a society where the dominant forms of culture are corrupt, designed not to reveal but to conceal, not to illuminate but to exploit. Such a condition makes the teaching of all the arts problematic. Nevertheless the principle of mimesis holds. We have no choice but to engage with contemporary forms in an attempt to turn them into fresh material for revelation and embodied insight. We must throw the junk of the consumer society into the furnace of the imagination in order to transmute, in order to create forms which correspond more closely to the authentic impulses of our children and adolescents. The existing metaphors of our society demand, even more than the traditions we receive from the past, the habits of creative mimesis. The danger is that we become corrupted by the very symbolism we seek to transform. Sinking so low, we cut our chances of flying high. Nevertheless if we are to transcend consumer-culture, we must first penetrate it. To leave it out of account in our teaching, is to leave its power untouched and unchecked.

The creative act does not take place in a vacuum. The symbol is the *sine qua non* of all the expressive disciplines and in the symbol the self and the community struggle to meet.

Implications for the Teaching of the Arts

I want now to consider the value of the concepts I have developed in this chapter for the teaching of the expressive disciplines. It is hoped they go some way towards providing a common language across the arts and, through the language, a shared understanding. I think they enable us to see where our teaching in the arts often goes wrong. Used with great sensitivity they also provide tools for an analysis of classroom practice. I want first to make some general reflections about the arts in schools and then, draw the chapter to a close by making a number of qualifications about the art-making schema.

Jung's art-teacher was no exception. Innumerable teachers then and now demand creative work without ever releasing an expressive need, a generative impulse in their pupils. In English, for example, a title can be simply announced or scribbled on the board and the class are expected, within a certain allocated time, to provide an animated story or poetic narrative. There is often no attempt to free an impulse, sufficiently urgent to break through the enclosing walls of platitudes and dreary commonplaces. In most of the expressive disciplines, teachers fail to stimulate in their students a prolonged experimental encounter with the medium, do not encourage a professional sense of work in process; do not convey the sense that revision may well constitute the messy path to vision. There is also often a grudging attitude to wastage, a cramped narrow, restrictive view as regards materials. The following remarks by an art-teacher to his students reveal the generous exploratory spirit of good arts teaching (though in some teaching contexts the hectoring almost bullying tone might be dangerously amiss):

> Take a look at her. Sitting there like a great, fat, rolling Buddha! Bloody marvellous, she is. And look what you've made her. Call that drawing? Puny, little scratches. Scrap it. Get yourself a decent sheet of paper. Pin it on the wall ... and a pot of black ink and brush. Then go at it. Get into her. Make her alive. Stop caring. All right, you make a mess of it. Take another sheet. Have another go. But for Christ's sake, give it all you've got ...[7]

Many teachers just fail to take their students through any formative experience.

As Witkin pointed out in *The Intelligence of Feeling*, one of the reasons for this failure is that teachers having started a creative activity are reluctant to intervene; they stand nervously on the side lines isolated from the activity, inwardly praying that they will not be called into the ring. But it is important that the teacher is able to enter the creative act, to know what stage the pupil may have reached and therefore what kind of problems he is likely to be engaging with. At times, the pupil may require technical help and then it is essential that the teacher can introduce the required technique in such a way that it bears upon the informing impulse. As an English teacher I have looked through innumerable exercise books full of stories which each time have merely received some minimal remark: 'Good', 'Poor', 'An improvement', 'Excellent'; remarks given without any indication as to what elements make it good (and how they could be developed further) or what elements make it weak (and how they could be re-handled). It must lead the pupil to conclude that, after all, creative work is only a fancy label for another exercise in which neatness, number of words and a certain plausibility count.

It is also the case that many teachers in the arts fail to envisage the class, the school and the neighbourhood as the obvious community for the art-work. Too often the original poem lies like a crushed butterfly caught between the pages of some drab exercise book, the sensitive sketch lies lost beneath a dusty pile of sugar-paper, the unusual play goes unrecorded and unperformed. How many English departments, even when they have ready access to cheap xeroxing or printing machines, bring out with some degree of regularity novels, essays, poems, reviews selected from their pupils' work? How many art departments arrange exhibitions in local cafes, post offices, libraries and other public or private institutions? How many even ensure that the best art and sculpture form an inescapable part of the school environment? How many music departments compose music, let alone perform it at school assembly or in local arts festivals? And yet, as we have seen, the art-maker requires an encompassing context for the development of his work.

The schema I have put forward in this chapter may be valuable in identifying areas which are being neglected in the teaching of the expressive disciplines. Through a rapid series of observations and questions I have tried to indicate where some of the weaknesses lie. Ultimately, the problem is a pedagogic one — for sensitive teaching of the arts should imaginatively meet the various demands of each phase. Yet it is clear from discussions and interviews that many teachers have a very truncated understanding of the art-process and so inevitably do harm when teaching, substituting mechanical imitation for emotional representation, craft for art, clever know-how for authenticity of response, competitive competitions for communal exhibitions. Yet a significant minority of teachers do have an excellent grasp of the intrinsic value of aesthetic activity and teach with acumen and delight.

The Need for a Dynamic Synthesis

The dynamism of concepts resides in their power to open up actuality; they urge us to envisage an articulate sequence rather than a random series of instants, allow us to conceive a living totality rather than a disconnected mass of fragments.

I have been very conscious of trying to hold opposed but complementary forces together, that of the individual and that of the community, that of process and that of production, that of originating impulse and that of surrounding and received culture. I contend that our life is lived in the centre of these tensions and that any adequate theory of aesthetics must include both sides, must keep the painful, renewing dialectic in motion. Again and again, art-discourse and educational discourse slacken the tension by choosing one side at the expense of the other. The society is made dominant or the individual; the product is made dominant or the process. The history of drama teaching, like the history of dance, is split into factions which affirm a commitment to either expression or technique, process or production. It would be wrong not to observe the integrity which underlies many of these time-worn divisions, but it would also be foolish not to observe that, invariably, the factions *understood together* make up the essential meaning of the discipline. For art is both to do with the individual and with the society; with expression, representation, and communication. It is only by struggling for the synthesis of all the key elements that we can arrive at a more comprehensive understanding and, thereby, a fitting pedagogy.

Some Vital Qualifications

I am anxious that the schema is not crudely imposed upon the living rhythms of experience. I want, therefore, to register a number of further reflections and qualifications.

Firstly, as a schema it cannot possibly describe the unique process by which any individual creation is made or begin to suggest the delight, fear and trembling which attends its making. All it purports to do is to define conceptually the characteristic spiral pattern of art-making.

Secondly, although I have referred to impulse as the origin of the creative act it is nevertheless clearly the case that art-making can be initiated by simply playing with the medium (feeling the clay, making sounds, listing arbitrary words, limbering up with the body). In such instances the medium itself generates an expressive impulse which then turns back onto the medium with a sudden directed energy. Here, then, we find a new variation: medium → impulse → grappling with the medium → approximate form → realization of final form, etc. Such a variation, however, in no way denies the generative importance of impulse.

Thirdly, the impulse and the symbol often seem to emerge simultaneously. Thus we do not always experience a discreet impulse followed by a symbolic form. The symbolic form often seems to reside within the impulse. The thought and the word, the feeling and the image are experienced together. Although this is true, nevertheless, the distinction can be conceptually discerned. We can, for example, all recognize when words are being used to fill a vacuum and when they are serving the energy of a creative impulse. Such impulses, rooted in the affective, give birth to art; that such impulses may be immediately experienced as sound, shape, imagery confirms my earlier notion that art is a biological activity and in no way negates the later *conceptual* delineation of art-making.

Fourthly, the emphasis placed on performance and evaluation must not be allowed to distort the first vulnerable exploratory stages of art-making. The intention is not to promote an artificial simulation of emotion for the pleasure of an amused audience but rather to create genuine art-making within a living community. It might well be that for a number of terms a particular class might concentrate entirely on the first phases of art-making; might, at times, concentrate only on the generation of approximate forms, of images in process. In certain cases, the teacher alone may have to represent the attentive audience and the quality of the creative work may depend entirely upon this protected, unconditionally trusted, single relationship. When it comes to performance to a larger community, it is of the utmost importance that this too is seen as a living process, demanding perhaps different imaginative qualities than the initial creation and often calling for a different kind of emotional integrity. We may want to restore theatre to the drama-process but we want to exclude, at all costs, the 'theatrical'. We do not want show-biz, simulation or ego-trips. We want art and the challenge of art. And we want that art to penetrate as deeply as it can into both the individual *and* the community.

Fifthly, my account has not described in any detail the differences engendered by the various media, e.g. drama, unlike expressive writing, has a strongly communal and communicative nature from the start. I have consciously emphasized *the similarities* in the process in order to establish the common ground.

Finally, the schema is no more than a schema. It cannot determine the details of teaching. If it reveals an underlying pattern in the arts, teachers must in the creative act of teaching work out what this means for their own expressive discipline. It may provide a general framework, it cannot provide a detailed programme.

Conclusion

My main intention has been to delineate the common ground between the expressive disciplines. I have argued that the arts are not ends in themselves but epistemological tools for the clarification of experience. I am advocating, then, not art for art's sake but for meaning's sake. Art is one of the enduring means for representing (for oneself and for others) those truths latent within our experience, those meanings which are, as it were, curled up inside the seeds of impulse. In exposing the origins of the creative act we found ourselves becoming aware of the bodily sources of art, begun to see art as, in certain ways, the symbolic elaboration of emotional and instinctual energies, an elaboration, however, which always takes place within a society and a culture. Yet it is imperative that we do not slip into the reductive fallacy, of explaining meaning in terms of origins, of confining the nature of art to physiology. Rather we have to cultivate a phenomenological understanding of art-making, seeing it in terms of highly complex human experience and such an approach points to the transformational nature of expressive symbolism. Through art-making and art-responding we extend our existence. We become more than we could ever have rationally anticipated. Art has its roots in instinct (hence its power) and its blossom in consciousness (hence its educative importance). It is because the expressive disciplines are centrally preoccupied with *the sensuous embodiment of representative meaning* that we refer to them as forming an epistemic community. And once we have made a connection between art and knowledge we can then demonstrate that no school which excludes the arts can be fully involved in the task of educating.

I have also suggested that the conception of art developed here, while including the insights of the Progressives, goes well beyond them. We have found ourselves taking their concepts and placing them in a much broader context. While retaining the concept of 'self-expression' we have had to develop the restraining concept of representative form; while wanting to affirm self-realization we have, at the same time, insisted on collaborative community and cultural heritage. We have struggled to deepen the notion of creative impulse by conferring on it an urge to meaning, an innate desire for reflection, a cognitive disposition.

It has been my aim to describe in the arts a common rhythm, a cumulative sequence moving from self to community back to self, in an endless dialectical motion. Our new ground is that of creative mimesis in which the self struggles to become itself within its own culture, dynamically conceived.

Notes and References

1. JUNG, C., *Memories, Dreams, Reflections*, Fontana, 1967.
2. MILL, J. S. in letters to Carlyle dated July 1832 and July 1833 reproduced in *Mill's Essays on Literature and Society*, edited by Schneewind, Collier Books, 1965.
3. COLLINGWOOD, R. G., *The Principles of Art*, Oxford University Press, 1958.
4. ELIOT, T. S., *Four Quartets*, Faber and Faber, 1944.
5. DRYDEN, quoted in LANCELOT LAW WHYTE *The Unconscious Before Freud*, Tavistock Publications, 1962.
6. YEATS, W. B., 'Long-legged fly', from *Collected Poems*, Macmillan, 1933.
7. CARO, A., Quoted in *The Guardian*.

Part VIII

The Teaching of the Arts

Subsequent volumes in this series will examine the teaching of each of the major arts disciplines in relation to the philosophy of this symposium. The aim of this section is merely to indicate, with some specific examples, the dynamic and disciplined mode of teaching which is envisaged.

In the first chapter Maxine Greene outlines some of the general conditions and values which are necessary for what she calls an emergent curriculum for the teaching of the arts. The following two chapters demonstrate what is entailed in the active teaching of an aesthetic discipline; George Whalley describes the teaching of poetry, Keith Swanwick and Dorothy Taylor, the teaching of music. In stance and spirit, though of course not in content and detail, the accounts represent the way to teach any aesthetic discipline, perceptually and dynamically. When George Whalley talks of 'the ability to hold cognitive activity in the perceptual mode with looped excursions into the conceptual' he describes the approach to arts teaching perfectly.

Chapter 18

Art Worlds in Schools

Maxine Greene

Introduction

Even with a consciousness of the seriousness of arts curricula in these days, and the complexities in the discussion of them, one cannot but feel some sense of carnival, some sense of openings when people come together to explore their experiences in the arts. And, indeed, they cannot *but* tap their own experiences; none of us can. Our arguments for the arts' centrality in schools, for raising the school windows to the art worlds outside, are grounded in our own encounters, many of which have permanently changed our lives.

The Arts in a Contemporary Context

Because I am an unreconstructed New Yorker and because these words were originally articulated in my city, I am moved to begin with a rendering of the New York experience that sheds a kind of light on what I said above. The beginning of Herman Melville's *Moby Dick* comes back to me, those sentences about the 'insular city of the Manhattoes, belted round by wharves as Indian isles by coral reefs.' He went on to say that 'commerce surrounds it with its surf.' And then:

Right and left the streets take you waterward. Its
extreme down-town is the battery, where that
noble mole is washed by waves and cooled by breezes,
which a few hours previous were out of sight of land.
Look at the crowd of water-gazers there.[1]

He was not only describing or depicting the city where he once had lived. He was bringing into being a transfigured city, a created world, offering to readers his vision of people 'of week-days pent up in lath and plaster — tied to counters, nailed to benches, clinched to desks' — reaching outward towards the sea, towards another space, an alternative reality. You know what a work of art can do when it comes to making us reach out that way, break free of the counters, benches, desks of the ordinary.

Those Melville was rendering — many of those we teach — seek possibilities of expansion and significance no one can ever entirely predefine. The several arts in their multiplicity and mystery hold such potentials; but they can be realized only if we find ways of tapping the range of human capacities too often left dormant when persons are conceived mainly as human resources for the building of a technological society, or if they are thought of as passive spectators, members of an audience or crowd. 'With the arts,' wrote Denis Donoghue, 'people can make a space for themselves, and fill it with intimations of freedom and presence.'[2] Martin Heidegger, earlier, wrote that the arts 'make space for spaciousness';[3] they often open worlds. Openings, beginnings, initiatives, new understandings, more intense engagements: these, I think, are our shared concerns.

Who does not welcome the attention now being given to the arts in education and nourish the hope they will never again be treated as frivolous, decorative, purely of 'right-brain' significance? At once, even as I say that, I am sharply aware that our discussions are taking place within a context of technicism, of product and achievement orientation, of proposals that often treat education as a means to the end of achieving economic competitiveness and military supremacy in the world. Yes, the arts are flourishing, according to all appearances. People line up for the cultural events that are the great museum exhibitions: the Van Gogh show, the Miró show, the Matisse show, Cindy Sherman's photographs, Richard Serra's sculptures, Henry Moore's. Regional theatres proliferate; students study Bournonville ballet in the middle west as well as in New York: balletomanes are multiplying, as are aficionados of extremely 'modern' dance; there are large audiences for musical performances, especially if Isaac Stern or Itzak Perlman or Rampal or Bernstein or Previn is playing. There is a huge diffusion of the arts, as television introduces larger and larger audiences to serious drama, opera, dance, the great symphonies.

None of this testifies to a high level of aesthetic sophistication or even to a high level of enjoyment. The temper of the time is consumerist, passive, uncritical, careless, often uncaring. The schools are accused of insufficiency when it comes to the fundamental literacies. Publics are convinced, somehow, that, 'since research has told us what works,' we are in need of applying the tools of technical rationality to teaching. If we do, it is assumed, the young will be effectively prepared for success in the advanced technological society to come. There is talk of critical thinking, much talk of 'cultural literacy'. But there is boredom; there are addictions all around; there are drop-outs; there are the doubts and fears evoked by the Chernobyl and the Challenger disasters. And at once, without surcease, there are the voices of the evangelists and the audiences saying 'yes' to Jesus and the promise of Armageddon. There are the other voices presenting cost-benefit formulations, lulling with unreadable calculations. There are silences in the spheres that ought to be public spheres where people can come together in speech and action, out in the open, to identify common concerns. I do not need to go on about homeless people, hungry children, broken families, and the erosion of support systems. It is only that I find it hard to consider rationales for art education and aesthetic education without having a context in mind or without naming the context as I see it. If we do not think about it now and then, if we confine ourselves to talk of 'cultural formation', we are likely to forget our distinctiveness as people committed to the arts. Denis Donoghue, whom I quoted earlier, wrote that 'the arts are on the margin, and it doesn't bother me to say they are marginal. ... I want to say that the margin is the place for those feelings and intuitions which daily life doesn't have a place for, and mostly seems to suppress.'[4]

Even as we work to incorporate and incarnate the arts in curricula, I believe we ought to cherish that special marginality. Certain current proposals respecting art programmes (certain so-called 'action plans') extend the definition of the arts so much that schoolpeople are never challenged to confront the peculiar role of the artistic-aesthetic in human lives. Other programmes, emphasizing the *basic* character of art education, are prone to justify it by summoning up the pragmatic or utilitarian arguments of the education reports. The arts, they suggest, can contribute to the intellectual power required by this country, or to the productivity being demanded, or to the cultural literacy that is supposed to bind us together, or to the disciplinary emphases that are to enhance academic rigour and overcome shiftlessness, relativism, 'soft' electives, and the rest. I shall not even mention those that stress the vocational relevance of the arts first of all.

Too many questions are tamped down; the more we gain a spurious security, the more we respond to outside demands. I am reminded of a question posed by the poet Holderlin in an elegy, a question to which Heidegger referred in his discussions of the arts: 'And what are poets for in a destitute time?'[5] I think we should ask: 'And what are artists for? What are the arts for? What are art and aesthetic education for?' You might not want to call this a destitute time, but you might agree to call it a troubled time, for all the appearances of well-being, for all America feeling good about itself, for all the resurgent patriotism, and for all the light before the golden door. Nonetheless, it is important to live in it fully, to be *interested* in our projects and our lived worlds. Young people have to be interested in this fashion if they are to pose questions with respect to their lives, renew their worlds as the days go on, try to keep them alive in time. For this to happen, they have to be enabled to break with confinement in the domains of popular culture, mass entertainment, televised realities, and private cynicism or hopelessness. Offered concrete and significant alternatives, windows through which to see beyond the actual, they may refuse their own submergence in the typical and the everyday. They may raise challenges to the taken-for-granted and begin to look at things as if they could be otherwise. In my view, this is the ground for learning to learn. I am convinced that it is not only the thought of *having* more that moves the young to reach beyond themselves; it is the idea of *being* more, becoming different, experiencing more deeply, overcoming the humdrum, the plain ordinariness and repetitions of everyday life.

Artists are for disclosing the extraordinary in the ordinary. They are for transfiguring the commonplace, as they embody their perceptions and feelings and understandings in a range of languages, in formed substance of many kinds.

They are for affirming the work of imagination — the cognitive capacity that summons up the 'as if', the possible, the what is not and yet might be. They are for doing all this in such a way as to enable those who open themselves to what they create to see more, to hear more, to feel more, to attend to more facets of the experienced world.

I think of Joseph Conrad saying (in the Preface to *The 'Nigger' of the Narcissus*) that the artist

> appeals to that part of our being which is not dependent on wisdom; to that in us which is a gift and not an acquisition ... to our capacity for delight and wonder, to the sense of mystery surrounding our lives; to our sense of pity, and beauty, and pain; to the latent feeling of fellowship with all creation — and to the subtle but invincible conviction of solidarity that knits together the loneliness of innumerable hearts.[6]

Is it not at least conceivable that such an appeal may make palpable and visible such parts of being in the young? That it may bring to the surface what many of them have never suspected, much less known? Conrad went on:

> My task which I am trying to achieve is, by the power of the written word, to make you hear, to make you feel, to make you see. That — and no more, and it is everything. If I succeed, you shall find there according to your deserts; encouragement, consolation, fear, charm — all you demand — and, perhaps, also that glimpse of truth for which you have forgotten to ask.[7]

I think it is possible to say as well 'by the power of paint, by the power of musical sound, by the power of the body in movement'; but I also think we need to acknowledge that the task (Conrad's task, Cézanne's task, Mozart's, Balanchine's) cannot be achieved if persons have not been empowered to be personally present to their works — if they cannot notice what is there to be noticed, if their awareness is not informed.

The Arts Foster Human Freedom

I am concerned about what can be done to make such discriminating presentness more likely in the lives of the young. When I ponder it, I cannot disentangle my preoccupations with it from my other overriding concerns for critical reflectiveness, moral sensitivity, craft, care, and even the struggle against nuclearism. I am afraid of somnolence, you see, and carelessness, and impassivity, and lack of concern. Sometimes, thinking back to Albert Camus's great novel, I associate all that with what he called the 'plague',[8] a metaphor for indifference, abstractness, and for the incapacity to 'take the side of the victim in times of pestilence.' Lately, I have been associating it with what the Czech novelist, Milan Kundera, calls 'kitsch',[9] meaning anything that stops people from thinking, from confronting their lives, I believe that education, among other things, should be a means of arousing persons to wide-awakeness, to courageous and (I would add) resistant life.

To open people to the arts and what they may (or may not) make possible for them is to make a deliberate effort to combat blankness and passivity and stock responses and conformity. And, yes, the empty verbalizations and chit-chat that build folding screens against reality. I realize there are no guarantees, that there is an 'unregenerate Adam' in each of us, that release and arousal do not always lead to humane action or convictions of solidarity. But it is crucial for me to hold in mind the fact that works of art, when faithfully perceived, when attentively read, address themselves to persons in their freedom. And persons, as has been pointed out, are centres of choice and valuation. They are capable of intention and agency; they can take initiatives and embark on new beginnings in what they perceive as an open world. I cannot conceive of a teacher committed to educating rather than training who does not posit his/her students as persons who can be provoked to choose to learn, to choose to become, with all the risks that that entails. And of course there are risks: we cannot determine where free persons, acting on their freedom, will go. This seems to be especially relevant to art education and aesthetic education; since, obviously, choosing is involved if a person moves into an aesthetic encounter of any kind. I cannot conceive of *imposing* an aesthetic experience on a student, of manipulating him/her into having one, anymore than I can conceive of having an aesthetic experience in a state of bland, uninformed receptivity.

The Nature of Aesthetic Attention

Like Louis Arnaud Reid, Mikel Dufrenne, and John Dewey as well, I cannot separate the subject from the object when I ponder aesthetic encounters. I find it impossible to imagine aesthetic qualities — the textures of sound, the shimmer of light, the heavy sadness of spoken words — without someone experiencing them, attending to them for what they are. Nor can I imagine an aesthetic experience being wholly subjective, happening apart from the live presence of an aesthetic object or event, in some private interior space. Reid wrote:

> On the one hand, there is the physical picture with its physical surface which we attend to. We attend to it, and in the way which is called aesthetic, and the aesthetic quality of the picture would not exist except in relation to the body-and-mind of someone perceiving it. ... The physical picture is the physical basis without which there would not be this particular aesthetic experience. It is through the appearing-of-the-physical-object-to-a-specator-looking-at-it-in-a-certain-way that the aesthetic quality comes into being. [10]

Perceived in a certain way, distanced in a certain way from the commonplace and the habitual, the physical work *is*, as it were, transmuted into an aesthetic object by and for an attending consciousness. A living human being must choose himself/herself in relation to it, allow his/her energies to move out to the work, to achieve it in his/her experience, to order its particularities and gradually realize it as a whole. What is important is the event, the situation out of which the aesthetic object emerges. It is not *there*, hanging on the wall; it is not *here*, in the attending mind. The situation is created by the transaction, by the grasping of a consciousness — drawn to a Cézanne painting, say, by a stir, a quiver of feelings, held rapt for a time as it intuits its presence — vaguely, at first, as landscape — as line, colour, shape. There is tacit awareness at work, and then a gradual focusing on images like mountain, tree, overarching sky. The more the beholder knows about picturing, about paint and canvas, the more he/she sees, the more details, the more appearances emerge. Apprehending it as a depiction rather than a representation of an actual mountain, noticing what there is to be noticed, the beholder may be able to see *into* the images revealed, see meanings condensed in symbolic forms. Taking time, he/she may single out the strokes of violet paint that model and give shape and contour to the transfigured mountain, watch the form of it jut forth against the pictorial plane, grasp the shifting perspectives that make its many profiles somehow visible, feel the touch of the textured sky, the play of light. When this occurs, it may be possible for the beholder to take his/her own journey through a world that discloses what he/she may never have suspected, much less seen. The poet Rilke, wondering at a Cézanne painting, spoke of the conflict between Cézanne's continual *looking* and his effort to appropriate and make personal use of what he received *through* looking — a discord in some way visible in his painting, one that may affect not only an individual's way of attending but his/her way of grasping the phenomenal world. The more becomes visible, the wider becomes the ground over which imagination can play, shaping, ordering the particularities into a never completed whole. This may become an occasion for the ordinary, the taken-for-granted to show its hidden abundance — for imagination to move to the unexpected, for the individual to discover that there is always more in experience and more to experience than can ever be predicted. To realize that is to be acutely conscious of possibility, of windows opening in experience — to understand that there is always more for personal use, for appropriation by the live consciousness of a person fully present to the world.

I might say similar things about encounters with other art forms, different though the languages are, and even though (as Nelson Goodman says) they are untranslatable into one another.[11] The point I want to make has to do with the disclosures that become possible when we focus upon actual encounters. I grant the importance of 'instruction in the concepts and processes intrinsic to the subject of art,' but primarily as such instruction informs and provokes the perceiving and imagining that bring works of art alive.

There is no question but that engagement with the medium concerned has a focal role to play. In many senses, the effort to learn the languages of music and dance and the visual arts is self-justifying. And it is unarguably valuable for persons to discover the multiple ways there are of expressing and articulating what is felt and perceived and even known, to summon up stored images, to find new images that carry meaning. Obviously, this involves more than free-floating creativity. Knowledge of many sorts is involved. I think of Vincent Van Gogh writing to Theo about the laws of proportion, of light and shadow, of perspective 'which one must know in order to be able to draw well; without that knowledge, it always remains a fruitless struggle and one never brings forth anything.' And I think about him saying, 'The question was — and I found it very difficult — how to get the depth of color, the enormous force and solidity of that ground. And while painting it I perceived for the first time how much light there was in that darkness, how was one to keep that light and at the same time retain the glow and depth of that rich color?' I am struck by the significance of his saying that 'while painting it I perceived it for the first time';[12] because it suggests to me how the very act of painting and the struggle with the vehicles at hand themselves open up features of the surrounding world, certainly something we all want to do — as we want to provide opportunities for children to explore the language of imagery, to seek their own symbols, to use intelligences too often ignored.

At the Lincoln Center Institute for the Arts in Education, where I have worked and tried to do philosophy for a decade, and in its related institutes around the country, we strive for an interplay between explorations of the media of the various art forms — the body in motion; spoken and written language; sound; paint, clay, paper — and apprehension of actual performances, exhibitions, texts. At the institutes, professional artists work initially with classroom teachers on all levels to initiate them into the disciplines, the languages, the modes of artistry, the craft that identify their particular art forms. The presumption is that teachers involved that way in learning to learn — with a clear sense of norm, of standard, of how an art form *ought* to be pursued — are not only prepared to work productively with artists when they come to their schools; they are in a better position to communicate to their students, at appropriate levels, some awareness of concepts and processes, many learned from practising artists, many discovered in the heightened awareness they themselves have gained with regard to dance, theatre, music, visual forms, even literature. Numbers of them have discovered what they never suspected about the play of energy in space and time, the shaping of sound, the patterning of stage movement, the forms of dialogue, the colours of voices, the interplay of lights and colour — the stuff, the many-faceted stuff out of which works of art are made. To move with a professional dancer or choreographer and, in doing so, to be introduced to the language of dance is to be provided a means of exploring the raw materials with which Petipa and Balanchine and Graham began, and at once of exploring one's own body and others' bodies in motion. It may be to discover *what is entailed* by exerting energy in a given space and period of time, by making patterns with gesture and movement, by creating visual metaphors with fingers, hands, shoulders, legs. And this enables people to notice more, as it enables them to apprehend dance on stage with tacit and bodily awareness that cannot but feed into the consciousness of attending and bring content to the words used for describing dance. If consciousness is indeed embodied consciousness, if a person present to a work of art is present as both body and mind, it becomes particularly important to introduce people to what it feels like to apprehend with newly discovered bodily capacities and with minds empowered to pay heed to designs, diagonals, shifts and shimmers and turns.

Whether teachers are improvising with a drama teacher after a performance of *The Glass Menagerie*, say, or *Death of a Salesman*, setting scenes, writing dialogue, becoming acquainted with the choices that have to be made as the script is interpreted and reinterpreted, relating speech to gesture, finding out how an illusioned world can be brought into persuasive being on a stage — whether they are inventing themes and melodies for percussive instruments and inscribing what they hear on musical staffs, the better to think by means of music the next time they listen to a Bach fugue or a Beethoven quartet, the more they are discovering about the works being performed — and about themselves attending to those works.

Of course various critical approaches can help in the process of uncovering, most particularly if criticism is used to provide perspectives on what is being experienced, to elucidate, to point out, to disclose. And, yes, it helps if teachers — and, in time, their students — can take several points of view towards a given work of art — attending to it as artefact, perhaps, in the cultural history of drama or music, viewing it in terms of style, seeing it as expressive or mimetic or in terms of their own responses, seeing it as a significant form, complete unto itself. Each mode of criticism provides a grid; each selects out certain dimensions for attention; no one exhausts the meanings of a work or identifies all its possibilities. Think of the multiple ways in which the 'new expressionism' can be read — of the differing ways in which the Klimt and Shiele paintings at the Vienna 1900 show can appear, depending on the critical point of view. Consider the exhibit of primitive art some years ago and what the discovery of 'affinities' made visible — or the ways in which we have learned to encounter the African pieces or the doorposts, masks, and relics from the Pacific islands in the Michael Rockefeller wing at the Metropolitan Museum.

An Emergent Curriculum for the Teaching of the Arts

I think in terms of expansion, of new connections in experience, of a sedimenting or a layering of meanings, a thickening, if you like, a growing density of texture as persons allow their past experiences to feed into their present ones, as more and more is known. I think of Dewey, saying in *Art as Experience* that experience becomes conscious only when meanings derived from earlier experiences enter it. 'Imagination,' he wrote, 'is the only gateway through which these meanings can find their way into a present interaction.' [13] He meant that present experience only becomes fully conscious when what is given is extended by meanings drawn from what is absent, what can be summoned up imaginatively. Reading *Moby Dick* again, quoting from it as I did, I am somehow aware that I am grasping the text this time with the help of meanings funded from past readings and past experiences as well. For example, my reading about a 'damp, drizzly November' in Ishmael's soul and his desire to move off, to save his own life, is informed by memories of some of my Novembers and my desires to confront my own White Whale. And I am conscious of the reason water-gazing means so much to me, why the image of water-gazers evokes multiple images (drawn from past experience) of persons in search, persons reaching out to possibility. There is always a gap, Dewey said, between the here and now of a present interaction and past experiences. 'Because of this gap, all perception involves a risk; it is a venture into the unknown.' As my present reading of *Moby Dick* is assimilated to past readings and past experiences, it somehow makes me rewrite my own life story, makes me see what I have never seen, recognize what I have never noticed in the themes of my own life. If it did not defamiliarize in that fashion, if my present reading only confirmed what I have always known, the resulting experience would have been routine and mechanical. My imagination would not have gone to work; I would not be wondering, questioning, re-experiencing even now, reaching beyond where I am. Realizing how much the novel (even the paragraph I read) have made me see, I can only deeply agree that a work of art operates imaginatively by concentrating and enlarging immediate experience, by expressing the meanings imaginatively evoked. Pondering this, I think again about making works of art accessible in such a fashion to diverse young persons of different ages and with different biographies — and about the ventures into the unknown we can encourage as we provoke them to learn to learn.

It strikes me that my own sequential mastery of aesthetic and literary concepts, my own acquaintance with American history and the history of the arts in America, my reading of the many criticisms of *Moby Dick* — for all that they have contributed to my store of knowledge — cannot account for the moments of heightened consciousness I lived through in rereading *Moby Dick* these past few days. I question, for that reason and others, the notion of a sequential curriculum when it comes to informed appreciation of art forms. A spiral, perhaps, in Jerome Bruner's sense, an emergent curriculum, perhaps, but not a curriculum modeled after those in the traditional disciplines, where the primary goal is to initiate the young into the distinctive symbol systems associated with the so-called 'forms of life' and the criteria governing their public expression.

Of course we need to introduce students to the symbol systems associated with the various arts; but we want to do so (or so I believe) to enhance their capacity to see, to hear, to read, and to imagine — not simply to conceptualize, or to join the great 'conversation' going on over time. For Nelson Goodman, whose work focuses on symbol systems and who regards the aesthetic experience as basically cognitive, the experience involves

> making delicate discriminations and discerning subtle relationships, identifying symbol systems and characters within these systems and what these characters denote and exemplify, interpreting works and reorganizing the world in terms of works and works in terms of the world. Much of our experience and many of our skills are brought to bear and may be transformed by the encounter. The aesthetic 'attitude' is restless.

searching, testing — is less attitude than action: creation and recreation.[14]

Process, action, not mainly conceptualization; the consummation, the culmination is in experience rendered conscious and increasingly informed. Yet, art history has a part to play in informing it, if some knowledge of past context, past conventions, and cryptograms can help persons engage, say, with an El Greco and, later, with a Francis Bacon or an Edvard Munch. What is involved in encountering those straining, aspiring El Greco faces — and, then, Bacon's figures at the Crucifixion and Munch's *The Scream?* Heidegger has provided a cautionary word where this is concerned.

> Well, then, the works themselves stand and hang in collections and exhibitions. But are they here in themselves as the work they themselves are, or are they rather here as objects of the art industry? Works are made available for public and private art appreciation. Official agencies assume the care and maintenance of works. Connoisseurs and critics busy themselves with them. Art dealers supply the market. Art-historical study makes the works the objects of science. Yet in all this busy activity, do we encounter the work itself?[15]

Teachers of the art of literature have had experiences, as you well know, with abandoning the work of art in the study of social contexts, biographies, literary history; and, indeed, it is and has been extraordinarily difficult to do an adequate historical study of any art form and, at once, take time for aesthetic encounters with particular ones. In the domain of literature, the reaction to the loss of the work of art is to be found in the movement called the New Criticism, where the literary work was conceived as an autonomous universe, sufficient unto itself, to be analyzed and examined and explored for purely aesthetic values, untrammelled by sociological or psychological or historical associations. In the past period, there has been a mounting critique of pure formalism in literary teaching and literacy criticism — and a rising interest in what is sometimes called 'reader reception', in interpretation, in teaching in such a fashion that readers will be empowered to *achieve* diverse works as meaningful within their own experience. Emphasizing the necessity for a book to be read and to engender responses in human beings for it to be meaningful, Wolfgang Iser speaks of the two poles — the artistic and aesthetic — of the literary work. The artistic pole is the text; the aesthetic is the realization accomplished by the reader.

> In view of this polarity, it is clear that the work itself cannot be identical with the text or with the concretization, but must be situated somewhere between the two. It must inevitably be virtual in character, as it cannot be reduced to the reality of the text or to the subjectivity of the reader, and it is from this virtuality that it derives its dynamism. As the reader passes through the various perspectives offered by the text and relates the different views and patterns to one another he sets the work in motion, and so sets himself in motion, too.[16]

Not only does that draw our attention to the important fact that imaginative literature must be included among the arts as we think of arts curricula; it makes very much the same points as have been made above about the aesthetic encounter where other kinds of art forms are concerned. We are left with open questions with respect to arts curricula and whether, indeed, they can or should be discipline-based. I understand the need to counteract the view that instruction in many of the arts (although not literature) is nonacademic and nonsystematic; I understand the desire for 'scope, sequence, and accountability.' I am not convinced, however, that 'acquisition of art concepts and skills' will lead to the experiences of expansion I have described, or to the 'creation and recreation' of which Goodman speaks, or to the kind of encounter that sets beholders or listeners or readers 'in motion' — breaking with the fixed and the ordinary, transforming their lived worlds. I think there may be other ways.

I want to allow for water-gazing. I want to allow for the sound of a 'blue guitar' — which, as in the Wallace Stevens poem, does not 'play things as they are.' Yes, it is a metaphor for imagination, for the unpredictable, for possibility. The guitarist sings at the end: 'You as you are? You are yourself. The blue guitar surprises you.'[17] I want to see a curriculum that allows for the risks of which Dewey spoke — and for surprise.

Conclusion

I have spoken my piece on the arts, if not on love, and settled nothing. I think of the end of Plato's *Symposium* and that remarkable upward movement rendered by Socrates — towards what? — towards the essence of beauty, the essence of love, the stars. Not believing we will find the essence of an art curriculum today, I choose to conclude with another image of someone moving upward, against all prediction, breaking with ordinary sequences and certainly with calculations, but ending with a reassuring word. It is by Anne Sexton, and it is (appropriately) in a collection called *New York Poems*. It is entitled 'Riding an Elevator into the Sky' and begins with a fireman's warning not to book a room over the fifth floor in any New York hotel, and a comment taken from the *New York Times* saying that the elevator always seeks out the floor of the fire and automatically opens and won't shut. And then:

> Many times I've gone past
> the fifth floor
> cranking toward,
> but only once
> have I gone all the way up.
> Sixtieth floor:
> small plants and swans bending
> into their grave.
> Floor two hundred:
> mountains with the patience of a cat,
> silence wearing its sneakers.

Floor five hundred:
messages and letters centuries old,
birds to drink,
a kitchen of clouds.
Floor six thousand:
the stars,
skeletons on fire,
their arms singing.
And a key,
a very large key,
that opens something —

some useful door —
somewhere —
up there.[18]

A key. A useful door. That is why we are here.

Notes and References

1. HERMAN MELVILLE, *Moby Dick* (Berkeley: University of California Press, 1979), p. 3.
2. DENIS DONOGHUE, *The Arts without Mystery* (Boston: Little, Brown and Company, 1985), p. 129.
3. MARTIN HEIDEGGER, *Poetry, Language, Thought*, trans. Albert Hofstadter (New York: Harper and Row, 1971), p. 45.
4. DONOGHUE, *The Arts without Mystery*.
5. HEIDEGGER, *Poetry, Language, Thought*, p. 91.
6. JOSEPH CONRAD, Preface, *The Nigger of the Narcissus*, in *Three Great Tales* (New York: Modern Library Paperbacks, n.d.), p. vii.
7. CONRAD, 'Preface,' p. ix.
8. ALBERT CAMUS, *The Plague* (New York: Alfred A. Knopf, 1948).
9. MILAN KUNDERA, *The Unbearable Lightness of Being* (New York: Harper and Row, 1984), pp. 254 ff.
10. LOUIS ARNAUD REID, 'Aesthetics and Aesthetic Education,' in *The Study of Education and Art*, ed. Dick Field and John Newick (London: Routledge and Kegan Paul, 1973), p. 168.
11. NELSON GOODMAN, *Languages of Art* (Indianapolis: Hackett Publishing, 1976).
12. W. H. AUDEN, *Van Gogh, Selected Letters Revealing His Life as a Painter* (Greenwich, Conn.: New York Graphic Society, 1961), p. 300.
13. JOHN DEWEY, *Art as Experience* (New York: Minton, Balch, 1934), p. 272.
14. GOODMAN, *Languages of Art*, pp. 241–2.
15. HEIDEGGER, *Poetry, Language, Thought*, p. 40.
16. WOLFGANG ISER, *The Act of Reading* (Baltimore: Johns Hopkins University Press, 1980), p. 21.
17. WALLACE STEPHENS, 'The Man with the Blue Guitar,' in *The Collected Poems* (New York: Alfred A. Knopf, 1964), p. 183.
18. ANNE SEXTON, 'Riding an Elevator into the Sky,' in *New York Poems*, ed. Howard Moss (New York: Avon Books, 1980), pp. 247–8.

Chapter 19

Teaching Poetry

George Whalley

Introduction

My purpose is modest. I simply wish to ask what could conceivably be meant by
the shorthand phrase 'teaching poetry', and why such an undertaking could be
considered to be of more than common importance in education. I shall say a little
about knowing and thinking. I may be a little theoretical at times. I ask you to be
patient.

'To teach' has a disagreeably aggressive sound to it, but I let that pass. Do we
teach poetry, or do we teach students? It seems safe to suggest that 'to teach' is
either 'to cause somebody to know something' or 'to cause somebody to know how
to do something'. I conclude from the prevalence of such phrases as 'to acquire
knowledge', 'to contribute to the fund of knowledge', 'to work at the fringes of
knowledge', etc., that we are very inclined to think of 'knowing' as the gathering
of reliable pieces of 'information' — largely perhaps because we tend to think of
'knowing' as the analogy of seeing. If we are provided with suitable visual
equipment (the supposition seems to go), we can see what is visible. There is a
seeing subject and a visible object; the relation between the two is (so to speak)
instrumental. Good results depend upon good visual equipment and clear
conditions for observation; results improve as the instrumental errors are adjusted
and the lighting approaches the optimum. Both these conditions, it follows from
the analogy, can to some extent be prepared ahead of time. Again, we commonly
think (analogically) of seeing-with-the-mind's-eye; sometimes we call it 'intuition' (in which we perceive clearly at a glance), sometimes we call it 'understanding' (in which we see-through something complex and grasp the scheme of its
inner relations and workings). The usual preface to a statement arising from, or
affirming, either kind of knowing is 'I know that...', even though sometimes the
statement may prove to be incorrect. Some philosophers have even stated that if
we cannot say distinctly *what* is known, there is no knowing. But I'm not so sure.

When the object known begins to lose clear definition as an entity, the verb
'to know' loses its affirmative clarity and changes its meaning. When I say 'I know
that person' I am most likely to mean 'I've seen that person before' or 'I know that
person's name'. If I say 'I know that poem' I probably mean 'I can tell you its title

and who wrote it'. In both cases I am then dealing in items of verifiable information, in themselves more or less trivial. If the intent is more profound, the inflexion changes: 'I *know* that person' (meaning 'I know him through and through; he has no secrets from me'), or 'I *know* that poem' (meaning 'I am thoroughly acquainted with the poem — or with that piece of music or the work of the writer'). I have then moved into an area in which the object cannot be fully accounted for by any number of statements in the form 'I know that ...'; not only does verification of points of detail become difficult, but the unity of conception tends to dissolve in a multiplicity of descriptive detail. Yet, as the word 'intuition' implies, I *can* mean something genuine — and something different in quality and extent from an accumulation of verifiable detail — when I say 'I know that person' or 'I know that poem.'

This is a very crude way of saying that there are different orders of knowing; and that what is knowable or to be known is the exponent of the quality of knowing required to encompass it — that is, that the nature and status of the knowable not only invokes the process of mind required to know it, but also that it leaves in the product of the knowing the marks of that nature and status. At the level of veridical information this involves no difficulty. But when the object-to-be-known passes out of the range of sensory or logical verification, we find that our minds can easily short-circuit the difficulty by assigning to what-is-to-be-known a nature and status that makes it readily knowable; that is, we work from the answer to the question instead of from the question to the answer.

I suggest that because poetry lies at a profound meeting-point of two extremely complex variables — life and the mind — poetry may well tax our cognitive ingenuity rather severely.

The Nature of Poetry

The distinctive marks of poetry are, in part, at least: precision, economy, multivalency, the condition of music. Poetry is a necessary and inevitable mode of utterance. Like all works of imagination, poems are entities of direct appeal. Given our natural capacity for the integrative and energetic state called 'imagination', and granted our gift of language — our most specifically human endowment — it would be surprising if reading and listening to poetry were not the most natural thing in the world. I suggest, therefore, that if we are using literature as an educational instrument, we should always begin with poetry; for poetry is not a sub-species of literature (as prose fiction is, or drama) but the prototype of whatever in language we call 'imaginative' or 'symbolic'.

'In art as in life there are no classes for beginners' — and with poetry there don't have to be any classes for beginners. Nor can there be, because there is no such thing as elementary or rudimentary poetry — there is only poetry more or less clearly defined. In order to establish the peculiar *feel* of poetry, we must always begin with highly developed and complex examples of the art. That at least will accustom the ear to the tune and shapeliness of the thing. There are other advantages. We can also establish confidence that even 'difficult' poetry is directly accessible (even though not immediately intelligible) to an untrained reader — as music is accessible to listeners untrained in the art of music. We can also establish the fact that we can *experience* poetry without fully understanding the poem. Until a poem is in some sense experienced, it does not exist in the mind; nothing relevant to the poem can be done with it. An elaborate expository or analytical reconstruction of the 'meaning' of the poem cannot substitute for direct perceptual experience at the outset; and it is unlikely to serve well as an introduction for a responsive activity that best arises from innocence of intent and is free from anxiety about 'meaning'.

Poetry seems to have a double nature: as a substantial thing to be grasped primarily by the senses; and as a complex mental event. Whether or not a poem records a mental event that *actually* occurred in the poet who made it, it certainly is itself a complex mental event standing on its own feet, and capable of regenerating in a reader (or listener) a mental event corresponding in some way to itself in quality, power, and configuration. As an 'event' a poem presents itself to us directly, and invites us to enter into it and partake of its activity; there's nothing else we can *do* with it. The *substance* of a poem, on the other hand, the fact that it can present itself to us as a solid presence (like Coleridge's nightmares, 'a foot-thick reality') arises not so much from the physical circumstance that it is printed on a page or uttered on the air; it arises rather from the fact that it is made in language, that it presents itself as having certain formal and temporal limits and patterns accessible only to the ear and (by synaesthetic transfer) to the sense of touch; through these perceptual relations it induces refined and subtle patterns of 'feeling' (or psychic energy). By 'experiencing' a poem I mean paying attention to it as though it were not primarily a mental abstraction, but as though it were designed to be grasped directly by the senses, inviting us to 'function in the perceptual mode'. Poetry can and does make its primary engagement through the senses as much when a poem demands strenuous conceptual activity as when it is as purely musical as the specific music of language will allow.

Poems have *substance* — that is, they have the qualities that make them not presences only, but *physical* presences — in virtue of being made of words, of language organized dominantly according to metaphorical or symbolic relations. Our bond with language is primarily through the sense of *hearing*, a radical sense that, like touch, but unlike sight, does not readily evoke the conceptual processes of abstraction and generalization. For educational purposes it is essential that poems be actually heard and listened to, whether as actually spoken aloud or as literally heard when reading in silence. The proper and discreet speaking of poetry provides a double physical bond: we not only hear, but also feel — in the musculature of tongue, lips, throat, and face — the physical articulation of the words, the shape, mass, movement, impulse of the thing. In my own experience, most students looking at poetry need deliberately to subdue their cerebral anxiety. The first lesson is to engage the senses; not as an agreeable adjunct to other more intellectual delights, but as the necessary means to hold the mind in the perceptual mode, to keep the habits of abstraction and generalization in their place. Once the senses are engaged all sorts of reflective activities are possible. If that has *not* happened we cannot expect much beyond a feeble pastiche of what is thought to be scholarly behaviour.

That such an elementary point should be worth making draws attention to some curious (but tacit) assumptions we seem commonly to make about the stuff we are working with. We seem to assume that if we can postulate an external cause for an event, we can understand and interpret that event. But sometimes we assign ridiculous 'causes' — self-expression, the desire to communicate, a hunger to declare the position of man in a hostile world, and so on. In fact, the central preoccupation of a poet is to *make* poems, to construct stable and patterned word-things. These things-made arise from life, certainly, and reflect back upon life, but they are not 'about life'. They are incorrigibly made in words, the words becoming unaccountably solid and tactual under the fingers of the mind. Paul Valéry has some very penetrating things to say about how and why poems get made. A poet, he says, is distinguished by the ease with which he enters the poetic state — 'a mysterious apparatus of life that has as its function to compose all differences, to make what no longer exists act on what does exist, to make what is absent present to us, to produce great effects by insignificant means'. A poet is 'an individual in whom the agility, subtlety, ubiquity, and fecundity of this all-powerful economy are found in the highest degree'. And a poem: 'a kind of machine for producing the poetic state of mind by means of words'. Again, the universe of poetry is a harmonic universe: in it 'resonance triumphs over causality'. The cause is intrinsic to the poem and can be discerned only within the poem. And 'If I am asked what I "wanted to say" in a certain poem, I reply I did not *want to say* but *wanted to make*, and that it was the intention of *making* which *wanted* what I *said*'. (In support of this last, I think of Hopkin's *Wreck of the Deutschland*, or Valéry's *Le Cimitière Marin*, or of those four lines of a Wyatt sonnet that were important in shaping Auden's rhythms.)

If the end of our endeavour is to know poems — not simply to know-about them — then the beginning and end of our work, the essence of it, will be to induce that quality of knowing appropriate to the psychic events that we call 'poems'. But it is clear to me that if we actually attempt to 'teach poetry' we shall end up in one or several of the plausible evasions that are the hazard of our profession; either teaching how to 'interpret' poems, by extracting the 'meaning' as though it could be separated out from the physical body of the poem, as though 'interpretation', like many other analytic procedures, were an end rather than a means; treating the poem as a puzzle to be solved; teaching how to classify a poem so that the awkward uniqueness of the individual poem can be dissolved into generalized discourse upon the category to which the poem is alleged to belong, teaching analytical 'approaches' and 'techniques', providing checklists of symptoms to watch out for (vowel sounds, irony, ambiguity, metaphor, paradox, etc.); and so on. Admittedly all these — and many more — will at some time be essential to the student of literature, but not at the beginning, and not indiscriminately. All of them are pretty blunt-edged tools, and can easily encourage presumptions and habits of mind not altogether appropriate to a delicate and heuristic enterprise.

The Discipline of Heuristic Reading

Now I must speak for myself — not expecting that my views are either exclusively my own, or of any great originality. I can only hope that those who share them will take pleasure in hearing them repeated. What we must *teach* from the outset is the discipline (*disciplina*) of 'heuristic reading'; the end is the cultivation of heightened and informed awareness. Everybody has to do his own knowing; the best we can do is to train our students in how to get-to-know. Beyond that we shall want to show them (as best we can) how to sustain reflection upon a poem, how to develop confidence in their own perceptions and recognitions, how to test the accuracy of their perceptions, and what to do if reflection becomes blocked in tautology or in some gross disproportion between the tone and mass of the poem and the tone and depth of our cognitive response to it.

For some years children have been taught in school to read rapidly by eye. The first thing then is to make sure that a student can actually hear what he is reading; for if he cannot hear, he will not be aware of the rhythmic declaration of the energy and intricacy of the poem — the life, that is: nor will he be able to enter into the harmonic universe of the poem and be able to sense the dynamics or discern the drama, the trajectory of pure action traced out by the whole poem. Then — and always — anything that helps to cultivate a rich and subtle sense of language is of value; not only the multiple meanings of words, but their sounds and histories, and the way — in that activity in which the senses reverberate with each other — words can assume a physical and tactual quality, having configuration, mass, texture, translucence, intrinsic energy, active function; and how in a poem words typically assume manifold, even conflicting, simultaneous meanings. The sense of language, and the cultivation of sensibility, the ability to hold cognitive activity in the perceptual mode as the root of the operation, with looped excursions into the conceptual (abstractive and generalizing) processes always returning to the physical actuality and presence of the poem itself — these can all develop together, and are probably best drawn from a serious and minute study of poems of high quality, rather than from theoretical or generalized descriptions examined in the absence of actual poems. (In the study of poetry the integrity of the particular is paramount. The illuminating function of trying to categorize a poem is to be able to see in what precise respect the poem does not match the assumed category).

Once a student stops looking only for 'meaning', and engages the ear in the activity of the poem, the poem will begin to present a contoured shape rather than a plane surface of uniform emphasis; it will present itself as a patterned activity, shapely and self-consistent, with nodes of force that initiate and guide complex mental activity. (These patterns of force are often at variance with the surface 'meaning' and logical progress of the matter.) Altogether this encourages confidence in 'the gift of seeing more than one knows'. This phase of the work is largely carried out in the state called 'contemplative', the mind gazing. This 'synthesis' is the way of finding out what is what in a poem.

I can see three advantages in separating this phase out, deliberately and markedly, by strong imperatives *against* 'interpretation' and against 'thinking *about*' the poem. (Indeed it may be useful to advise students to sublimate their habit of thinking about by telling them not to expect a poem to *mean* anything more specific than we expect of a piece of music; this throws the emphasis upon listening.) The three advantages are: (a) The student becomes increasingly aware of a changing quality of relation between himself and the poem; his presumption that he is a knowing *subject* and the poem a knowable *object* has changed into a cognitive *relation*, dominantly perceptual, in which the initiative begins to shift from himself as knower to the poem as capable of directing the process of getting-to-know — a process (as I suggested) that is very much like getting to know a person. (b) Instead of the reader dominating and commanding the poem, the poem begins to command the reader's attention and to establish a hierarchy of relevance — the sense of a centre and a periphery. Instead of telling the poem to 'get-known', he finds that the poem is somehow vicariously making him over into its own shape and dynamics. (c) As the obsession with 'meaning' dwindles, the reader becomes aware of the poem as a harmonic system in which many kinds of resonance begin to be discernible, that these resonances are by no means all auditory, that to a great extent they actually constitute the substance of the poem.

All this can come about without any prior knowledge about poetry or about forms of verse, metrics, philology, or theories of analytical procedure. The poetry comes in through the porches of the ear. Inasmuch as most of this, as far as possible, is conducted in the perceptual mode, the experience of the poem is largely in terms of 'feeling' (psychic energy as distinct from 'emotion'). Clearly *this* is not what the kids used unprettily to call a 'gut response'; for the feeling is not only generated by the poem, but it is also controlled — with increasing fineness — by the poem itself (the substance of the poem being defined largely in terms of feeling). So the 'sense of fact' and the 'sense of relevance' begin to develop. The *facts* of a poem are the substantial centres of attention as presented to us — things that certainly happen, and that happen at a perceived level of quality and energy. The sense of relevance is simply a matter of being able to discern what goes with what, what is more important than what; it is associated with a sense of proportion, relation, fittingness — the same sense of 'rightness' that (unaccountably) guides the poet in his making.

The first engagement is by Tom Piper's whistle: the poem calls out to us, arrests and holds our attention. This is also the way an object in the outside world — something seen or heard — will command a poet's attention and, usually by being named or found a physical body in words, will become the germ around which a symbolic event grows. At first, by quietness and submission, a reader will seem to merge with the poem, and so can treat the poem as a 'self-unravelling clue' (which is what Coleridge says 'method' is); but the sign of a maturing cognitive process is the way the poem separates itself from the reader, becomes a 'thing out there', unchanged by enquiry, distinct and separate, with a life of its own — certainly not a projection of ourselves. As the poem moves away from us, we are aware that we are no longer merely 'experiencing' the poem; we are getting-to-*know* it as it becomes less and less like ourselves. What seemed at first little more than an intriguing encounter with a dark stranger becomes cause for a careful and faithful tracing out of the nature of the poem's existence, the universe it represents, or simply what it is and how it lives. The perceived contouring of the poem, its pattern of forces, allows us to separate out our own 'errors and ignorances' from the real issues and questions raised by the poem itself. We can then venture a little analysis.

This is the crucial phase in reflective enquiry. In order to remove the element of accident or the merely personal, to confirm and consolidate the cognitive experience, we will seek to analyze complex impressions, loosen them into their elements so that we can see them more clearly. But unless our analysis is guided by a firm perceptual grasp of the whole complex, the poem itself somehow accepting and adjusting whatever we offer to it, we shall probably find ourselves constructing a surrogate poem as a plausible substitute for the true poem. Unfortunately it is towards the construction of such fantasy poems that much of our formal school and university training prepares us. The result can be, for the thinker, very satisfactory: it is a way of dispensing with the unmanageable uniqueness and strangeness of the poem by converting it into something differently constituted, and because we have made it ourselves (a little slyly) it will be utterly familiar.

Coming back to the beginning again, we are very much inclined not to recognize how profoundly the quality of our thinking is affected by the state of mind we bring to the thinking. If we imagine that we are not changed by what we know, if we imagine that we are knowing-machines that are not modified by their own knowing, our attempts to get-to-know can become aggressive and can destroy what we thought we wanted to know. The adjustment of the mind to a complex and delicate task is not primarily the selection of certain procedures or techniques, but rather the assumption of *discipline* — the quiet and submissive preparation of the mind for its task. Not only the temper of the mind needs to be adjusted, but also the 'colour'. Hence the immense importance of delight, wonder, affection, respect — opening the mind, making it alert, sensitive, receptive, hesitant to impose itself. The more intimate one's sense of what language is doing and can do in a poem, the more exact our appreciation of the complex and fugitive activities of mind involved in the making of a poem, the more inclined we are to feel delight, wonder, respect. This is an instance of the way that what we know can extend our ability to know further; the first knowing is not directed as a technical weapon towards the poem — it has imparted the tone and clarity that allows the mind to function appropriately in a task that cannot be forecast and for which therefore we cannot make specific and deliberate preparation. Yet the attitudes of mind that I suggest are fruitful (and a matter of virtue to attain to) are the very qualities that 'technical analysis' tends to dismiss as interfering with 'objectivity' and 'rigour'.

The only name I can think of for the process I have been describing (a phrase introduced by Alex Corry some years ago) is 'reflective enquiry'; and the theory of such an activity could be called 'heuristics' — the business of searching out something that is at once familiar and unknown, according to rules of search that are determined largely by the quarry, not by the hunter; and as the quarry is uncatchable (though knowable), the process will establish an intimate bond between the hunter and the hunted until it is not certain which is the quarry and which the hunter. This reversal of apparent causal sequence is not uncommon in human affairs; even psychologists have noticed it. If all goes well, you get something like a reverse Pavlov effect: the dog eats its dinner and the doctor rings the bell.

Suppose we have (by 'teaching') trained a person to be a 'good reader'. He would have a fine ear, a rich and subtle sense of language, a copious store of learning gathered so affectionately and so promiscuously that it had all become like housemates, cherished but half-forgotten, reverberant to the lightest touch of association. He would be capable of clearing the line of vision by getting his own ignorances, preferences, and fantasies out of the light so that (by grace or luck) it is the poem and not himself he's looking at, and so would be capable of sustained reflection over the poem, not seriously troubled by the fact that there can be no end to his reflection (unless he has chosen a poem so trifling that it will not support much reflection). Then what? What can he *do* with these marvellous capacities?

It may be that it is precisely at this point we fail to see that we have, as far as direct commerce with poems is concerned, fulfilled our task. What comes next is either not our business as teachers, or else it is almost entirely beyond our influence; for the next phase, if separable, is what we *do* with our knowing. We are all very inclined (as teachers) to try to make over our students into our image; as most of us are primarily scholars (rather than poets), we try to make our students over into scholars. No reflection over poems can proceed far without sound and comprehensive scholarship; but scholarship by itself will never produce the qualities of a fine reader — even though scholarship cannot get very far unless it is informed by an alert sense of what is going on in the body of its chosen material. The crux, from a paedagogic point of view, is in the body of literature itself, the stuff it is made in — language, words. At some point thinking must achieve body and articulation by being worded — another clue must be paid out for unravelling — not simply in order to 'record' what has happened in the thinking, but as a means of defining, of sustaining and illuminating our own enquiry, the sustaining of our thinking. As the making of a poem is always a process of discovery, so the wording-out of reflection becomes itself a process of discovery; and this goes well or ill according to the precision and fertility of the wording itself. Hence the immense importance of teaching precision in choosing and applying special terms — not merely for purposes of accurate definition, but in order to keep the line of vision clear, to keep the mind in sharp focus so that the glimpse of a fruitful possibility can be traced analytically to its most remote consequences. Hence the need to be wary of inflated, honorific, and vogue terms, of catch-phrases that make the head nod slowly in impassive approval like certain Chinese figures without ruffling the surface of the brain-pan. Where better can one learn the functional virtues of a fine precision in words than in poetry itself? or where better study the crucial implications of that precision as the condition under which alone symbolic activity can occur — not least in the 'other harmony' of prose? If, like myself, you see the end of good reading (? criticism) to be heightened and informed awareness, the question for written or spoken 'reflective enquiry' is not simply whether a record of that awareness will be a 'contribution to knowledge', but whether it will make somebody else more aware, with a refreshed capacity for knowing, the perceptions purified, the object of enquiry placed intact in the mind of the reader as matter for further enquiry and further delight. In this way, literature itself becomes an *instrument* of enquiry, showing us how far a question can be pursued, to what self-revealing end a glimpse of a possibility can lead.

To expect all our students to engage in such an activity is probably an unreal and unreasonable hope. For a great many students the best that can be hoped for is that they will have become better, that is, more perceptive, readers, that through their contact with us they will (as Frost says of the good reader of a good poem) have suffered an immortal wound and will never get over it. That would be no trivial accomplishment. A few certainly will take up the clue, the scent, the pursuit; and of those a smaller few will succeed beyond any reasonable expectations. But we need to be clear, in setting exercises and encouraging certain ways of speaking and writing, what the exercise is meant to achieve. If we are inviting students to venture into an area of discourse unfamiliar to them, we need to be sure that there are excellent examples of the art available for study (that is, for listening to); otherwise we get imitations of allegedly learned articles that are themselves too often, alas, no better than lifeless parodies of both genuine scholarship and genuine reflective enquiry. The limits of behaviourism are obvious and sombre.

The Place of Levity in the Teaching of Aesthetic Disciplines

One of the great advantages of working at literature is that it engenders something of the devil-may-care, jackdaw mentality that makes poets objects of our scholarly envy and indignation. We learn from literature to develop a sense of humour, to feel an instinctive disrespect for grave formulations that purport to provide a fulcrum to move the whole universe of literature. We find that some of the more fruitful (though limited) methods of analytical enquiry need little or no theoretical or philosophical underpinning; they are clever paedagogic devices that sometimes and in some cases put us on a right track, and work well if we don't press them beyond their limits. (And yet where would the calculus be without the clever deceit of $\frac{dx}{dy}$) We find that certain theories, catch-phrases, axioms, thoughtless epigrams thrown out by artists themselves — the tune of this man's way of thinking, or the translucence of that man's prose — are of value (is it disreputable to admit this?) not as dogmas or as technical directions, but as talismans which quieten and dispose our minds; objects the contemplation of which clear our vision, relax our nerves, tempt us to dangerous enterprises. If we take any of these devices too earnestly we endanger the delicate heuristic poise of our minds.

For the mind is (in one sense) a symmetrical integrative energy system, complete in itself and constantly completing itself. Like any energy system, the mind seeks equilibrium and repose by the swiftest means available. Take the example of what Gabriel Marcel calls 'reflection'. To be looking for something you care about induces a specific state of mind, characterized by certain dynamics that cannot be induced otherwise. The essential functional element is 'concern'. If I am looking for some *thing* that I care about and already know — something lost (say) that I care about — I am not looking for the thing but for the whereness of the thing. The urgency of my search, the induced activity of mind, is a direct function not of the intrinsic value of the thing but of my concern for it. When I have discovered the whereness, the activity of the mind relapses into composure. Correspondingly, if I seek to know a poem (or to know it better), and approach it through a formula for finding it or a formula for recognizing it, my mind is orientated by the formula, and achieves penetrating power by being concentrated in that way. But if it is the fulfilment or matching of the formula I am looking for, that is certainly where the search will end — in the tautology of what I started with, not in a fresh discovery of what, not-knowing, I set out to get to know. If, however, our intent is set upon knowing the poem, and we are prepared to use for what it is worth any promising device, means, formula, or incantation, then we stand some reasonable chance of finding what we are looking for. Beforehand we can never be certain that any preconceived method will 'work': the poem has to decide that.

We have to be a little quizzical and light-hearted about ourselves too; because we are well aware that the fact that we knew something once does not mean that we know it for good and all — not because we can forget and do forget, but because we may not be lucky enough to pick up the clue again. The authentic values lies not in the *product* of the knowing, but in the act and process of knowing, and in how we handle that knowing. Usually, I think, we cannot remember the act of knowing itself; what we remember is that that act occurred and what it felt like; and we may be more or less confident that we can recover the act, or that we can regenerate an even more valuable act of knowing in the presence of the same objects of our reflection. By grace, through patience, and through a curious combination of passive attention and alert response, we are certain that we can enter into the universes of poems, and that these are new worlds that for all their strangeness are recognizably our worlds; that if we can read perceptively and are learned enough and innocent enough to respond deeply and richly to something conceived in a mind more copious, daring, and agile than our own, then our relation with poems will surely sustain and nourish reflection, and may now and then bring us, through the necessary articulation that alone sustains thinking, to see something worth seeing and to say something that may be worth remembering — if only as a talisman. Most valuable, if the integrity of the poem is of primary concern, is the way this kind of reflection reverses (as it were) that habitual reconciliatory movement of the mind from the particular to the general, from the less to the more, which is a spontaneous resolution to equilibrium (so that there's no more work to be done). Reflective enquiry shows us how to think from the more to the less, from the generalized to the particular; and this, when luminous, evokes the otherwise unattainable recognition of the universal. In this too we re-enter the universe of the poet — our birthright if we have a clue to it. It would be disingenuous, however, not to repeat a remark of Valéry's on the 'marvellous economy needed for the beginnings of Poetry'.

> If one knew a little more about it, one could hope in consequence to form a fairly clear idea of the poetic essence. ... A little metaphysics, a little mysticism, and much mythology will for a long time yet be all we have to take the place of positive knowledge in this kind of question.

The same goes for reflective enquiry, for sustained thinking.

I have been speaking of a propaedeutic, not a system nor a whole programme. I would do or say nothing to diminish the importance of profound learning, of skill in analysis guided to remote consequences, of the capacity for sustained, even ruthless, logical sequence, for that elegance in exposition that is the crown both of mathematics and of music. I would however encourage a little self-mockery in supposing ourselves capable of undertaking work of such alarming educational possibilities and of such a subtle privacy. Because poetry is the heart and prototype of all literature, we must be prepared at all stages to lose the thread.

As far as the teaching of poetry is concerned, probably the best we can do — each in his own way — is to find out how to bring our students into the presence of poems. We must also find ways of preventing them from aborting their acquaintance by short-circuiting their mental activity into thinking about something else, and so bringing their minds to rest. The most valuable thing we can do, I think, is to allow students to *witness* the heuristic processes I have been speaking about and the quality of sustained reflection; to encourage them to gain confidence in the accuracy of their own perceptions and their own judgments; to encourage them to engage all their faculties, especially at the level of perception, and so to advance towards a disciplined — that is, submissive — adjustment of themselves to the inexhaustible business of getting-to-know; to encourage in them, by example, confidence that their own perceptions and judgments can be tested against the consistency of the poem; to demonstrate that the quality of an idea depends upon the quality of the mind that holds it, that the quality of an enquiry depends not so much upon technical skill as upon fineness of discrimination and quality of intelligence. We need also to make clear the hazard that our desire to understand and to unify brings us into; how the phase of analysis is always in danger of losing us by attaching us to a plausible will-o'-the-wisp; and how, if we are to move out of the area of mere accident, we must take that risk over and over again — with the confidence of a person walking a tight-rope with no net under him.

George Whalley

Conclusion

Above all, in an age bemused by the specious beguilements and expectations of parascientism, by attempts to represent all human action — no matter how lyrical or inventive — as the products of Newtonian machines of no great sophistication, it is the business of poetry — and our professional business — to affirm and enjoin a way of mind that is specifically human, inventive, and daring, a way of mind that can include everything the mind can encompass and every way the mind has of working; and to spread that infection with all the subversive and light-hearted zest that poetry makes us heir to.

Chapter 20

Purpose in Music Education

Keith Swanwick and Dorothy Taylor

Introduction

One of the most urgent tasks for teachers of music, especially those teaching music in schools, is to find some kind of basis on which to build a worthwhile and purposeful musical curriculum. A lack of purpose communicates itself to pupils in school, especially those in secondary schools, and makes music appear to be an aimless and rather arbitrary subject which varies enormously from school to school and teacher to teacher. The rediscovery of purposefulness is therefore a prime need at this time. However, along with a sense of purpose must go the flexibility required for different groups of children, different types of school and widely differing teacher strengths and weaknesses.

Making a Curriculum

There are several different ways of setting about the task of making a music curriculum. The most common way, and the least structured, is for teachers to amplify their own enthusiasms, to notice which of these seem to be accepted by classes and to work on this. Unfortunately the result of this approach is a kind of 'rag-bag' of activities where any sense of purpose is very weak. There will inevitably be many flat spots during the time given over to music, if this curriculum model prevails, due to the arbitrary selection of activities.

A second way of constructing a music curriculum is to identify particular skills and concepts and to develop these through appropriate activities. Unfortunately, this often results in second-hand activities where music itself becomes subordinate to teaching something else. For example, we might find ourselves choosing particular tunes, not for their musical quality but because they illustrate some point of notation or because they are examples of a particular style or composer or because they develop certain rhythmic skills. The most highly organized and systematic of such courses would be something along the lines of the Kodály system of carefully graded material. However, we ought to remember that Kodály was a composer of considerable stature and it is not surprising that the Kodály

Choral Method contains a wealth of satisfying music, even though much of it was composed for didactic reasons.

The approach to curriculum building advocated is one which stays very close to first-hand musical experience for the teacher and the pupils. We are taking as a basic assumption the view that music education is essentially about developing what might be called musical *appreciation*. By this we do not necessarily mean using records or tapes of music along with details and information about the composer or the work itself but rather the ability, and it *is* an ability, to perceive what is going on in music and to respond to it with enjoyment and possibly delight. Whatever our pupils do out of school and when leaving school, we would want them to respond to a wide range of music in a positive and lively way. They may or may not be actively concerned in the world of amateur music-making, or become composers or professional performers. They may find their way into types of music that may not have featured very large in the school curriculum but we would hope that the work in school has developed the sense of the value of music and some glimpse of its power to engage us, to speak to us, and at the highest level to move us profoundly.

If we can accept that the main objective of all music education is to enable people to appreciate music, that is to value music as a life-enhancing experience, then we have not only the best possible basis on which to build a curriculum but also the only really satisfactory justification for music education that exists. We all recognize that human needs are not fully met by the provision of physical and material well-being. People need to make sense of their lives, to find living a rich and worthwhile experience. Evidence for this can be seen in the pervasive myths, rituals, ceremonies and artistic activities that are powerfully present in all cultures, whether in the East, in the Third World or in the Western tradition. Music, along with the other arts, satisfies a basic human need to make sense of life and to engage in rich experiences. Music is not an alternative to living but an enhancement of life. The role of a music teacher is therefore to develop the ability to respond to music in the fullest possible way across the widest range of experiences. Only the exceptionally gifted teacher can manage this intuitively and without prior thought, and it is impossible to conceive of any other profession that relies entirely on such exceptional gifts. However, most of us are 'good enough' teachers if we think out clearly what we are about and test what actually happens against some form of yardstick, noticing when we succeed and, perhaps more important, when we fail. Only in this way can we be said to be truly professional. In a quite frightening way teachers stand between pupils and music, sometimes acting as a window or an open door but at other times functioning only as an impediment, blocking off access to music itself.

Music and Knowing

It may be that much of our difficulty comes from not recognizing the different kinds of knowledge that are involved in musical experience. This is not as complicated or academic as it may sound. For example, it is very necessary at times for us to *know how* to do things, to operate a lathe, to spell a word, to translate a passage, to put our thoughts into a structured form, to manipulate a musical instrument, to use musical notation. Knowing how to do things is essentially the use and development of particular skills. The second most commonly understood kind of knowledge is *knowing that*. For example we may know that 2 + 7 makes 9 or that Manchester is 200 miles from London or that 'avoir' is the verb 'to have', or that Beethoven wrote nine symphonies, or what a note-row is. A further way of knowing is sometimes called knowledge by acquaintance, or in other words *knowing him, her or it*. For example, we may know Renoir's painting *The Rower's Lunch*, or know a friend or pupil, or know a city. This is the most important kind of knowing for music teachers. In music it is the specific knowledge of a particular musical work, the one we are listening to or the one we are composing or performing. For example, we might know *how* to manipulate technically a musical instrument and we might know *that* the piece we are playing is by Bartok but we would also need to know the piece *itself* and become aware of its particular character — its expressive quality and its structure — the way in which one part relates to another. The fourth way of knowing we might call knowing *what's what*, knowing what we really like, what matters to us; in other words — what we value. In case this seems somewhat theoretical let us consider a practical example. A child learning to play on the piano an easy piece by Bach, may be able to cope with the skills involved in playing the right notes at the right time. In other words she will know *how*. But she may also know *that* it is by Bach and may have some idea of what it is to play Bach in an appropriate style. However these kinds of knowing are by themselves insufficient. The pupil will also have to know *it*, the piece itself, the way in which the phrases are shaped, the way in which each note relates to each other note, the form determined by the cadences and something of the expressive potential of the piece which might be achieved by a choice of a particular speed and levels of loudness at different times. However, even if she knows how, knows that, and knows it she may well say 'But I don't like it'. In other words, the piece does not count as a valued experience. It does not fit in to the pupil's idea of *what's what*, but at least she will have reached a point where she can choose on a basis of experience.

The same kind of analysis can be applied to any musical activity in classrooms. For example, a class may play a twelve-bar blues improvisation at a fairly low level of skill (with very little know-how) but communicate the expressive qualities of the piece (knowing it). At the same time they may have more or less information about this particular musical form (knowing that) and may vary from individual to individual as to whether they find it of value or not (knowing what's what). Or again, when a small group is composing using a note-row the members might be very skilful in handling the instruments and the row, achieve a good sense of structure in the composition, be well-informed about serial techniques but find the activity boring — that is to say of little value for them. 'Knowing' is quite complicated and it is difficult for us to understand what is involved at times. It may be helpful therefore to keep these four rather crude categories in mind and we shall return to them later on. There is obviously a good deal of linking between them and for most pupils it will probably be true to say that if they achieve some skills, along with relevant information, while getting to grips with actual music (knowing it), then there will be a strong tendency to enjoy and value the activity. After all, we all tend to 'like what we know' as well as 'know what we like'.

Merely knowing how to do things or knowing something about music is no substitute for knowing music itself and finding enjoyment in the experience. Yet a tremendous proportion of teaching in music is devoted to knowing how or knowing that, while very little attention is given to knowing it, the music itself, partly because it is very difficult to find an appropriate language in which to discuss what happens in music itself. It is certainly not possible to come to the fourth way of knowing (knowing what's what) through direct teaching or persuasion. The way in which we value things has a great deal to do with our own personal development as human beings, our age, our social attitudes, the type of personality we are and the previous experiences we have undergone along with all the associations with music that have been built up. We can however do a great deal more than we often manage to achieve in the development of a vocabulary, a workshop language that enables us, where necessary, to talk with one another about music itself. Knowing *it* is our real goal and our language must serve this aim.

The Elements of Music

Basically, as we hinted earlier, there are two elements to be taken into account. All music has *expressive character* or quality. That is to say, it is more or less active or fluid or angular or stationary, more or less dense or heavy, driving forward or holding back. Music can be spiky or flowing, smooth or cutting, expanding or contracting. Most of these and other expressive elements will not be revealed in traditional or any other form of notation. They are brought out by the manner of performance or develop in the aural imagination of the composer. Some conductors have the gift of communicating through gesture, the kind of weight and size, the ebb and flow of the music that makes it meaningful, that gives it expressive character. The second element is the *perceptible structure* of the music that is being experienced as composer, performer or listener; fundamentally the relationship between different materials and ideas. This involves the awareness of the significance of change, recognition of the scale on which events take place, a sense of what is normal in a particular context and what is surprising or strikingly different. We shall call the perception of these elements *musical understanding*. Because this is such an important concept we must consider it further at this point.

Musical Understanding

Musical understanding obviously depends to some extent, on various kinds of skill and information, but it goes beyond these and is able to be described in terms of structure and expressive character in the following way:

1. *Structure*: the relationships of part to part and part to whole. Structural understanding implies more than labelling musical forms such as Ternary or Rondo. It involves perceiving the way in which one idea follows another and what the effect of repetition is or how strongly contrasted parts of the music are. There can be no musical understanding away from *particular* pieces of music, whether we compose, perform or listen to them.

Repetition and contrast are the main features of musical structure and the most easily understood. All other structural devices are derived from these. The following are examples of this:

Repetition	*Contrast*
ostinato	change of figure
motif	extension, fragmentation
theme	middle section, episode
tonic key	transposition, modulation, chromaticism
beat	off-beat, syncopation
'air'	variation
recapitulation	development
fugue subject	augmentation, diminution
note-row	inversion, retrograde motion
'natural' sound	electronic distortion

These kinds of repetition and contrast can be identified in conventional musical forms such as binary structures in simple songs; binary short movements in Bach, Handel, Purcell; extended binary movements as in Scarlatti piano Sonatas; the extension of binary to simple sonata form, as in the first movement of Mozart's *Eine Kleine Nacht-musik*, or in simple variation form, rondo, fugue, or the contrasts and similarities of pitch, timbre and levels of loudness in a work such as Berio's *Sequenza V*.

2. *Expressive character*: mood, atmosphere, changing levels of tension and resolution, display of feeling or emotion, impression, dramatic and operatic devices. Expressive character is most obvious in opera, oratorio and programme music and in the works of 'Romantic' composers where there is some connection with nature, the composer's life, literature or stories. However, even the 'purest' music, such as a Bach Fugue or Invention has a clear character that can be grasped or missed by the performer, or listener. It may be bold, lilting, resolute, flowing, march-like, lively, solemn, etc. The expressive character of music can be explored in many simple ways, for example, by varying the speed and loudness of a well-known song or by composing a short piece (perhaps in a group) using only three notes but controlling the speed and loudness and texture (two or more notes at once) to achieve a building up of tension.

Expressive character is determined by such things as pitch register, pitch intervals, phrase shapes, *tempi*, rate of acceleration or retardation, degree of smoothness or detachedness, accentuation, metre, density of texture. It is important that children explore these things for themselves, making choices in performance and composition, as well as identifying them in other people's music. When recorded music is used it is best to find pieces that are strongly characterized, especially for younger children, not too long and with some changes of character that can be identified and discussed. Several listenings will be required to attain the necessary familiarity to identify the more subtle aspects of the particular character of any piece of music. The range of styles ought to be as wide as possible including the traditional works but including also different kinds of ethnic, folk and pop music, and the music of contemporary composers. It is better to discuss rather than tell classes what to expect. We can ask 'What is it like?' and 'How is it done?' For this reason heavily pre-scripted works, such as *Peter and the Wolf*, have less educational value.

Bearing in mind that what we have called Musical Understanding is central to music education, it becomes obvious that this understanding can only result from direct contact with music as *composer, performer* and *listener*. Alternative activities, such as copying down notes on the lives of great composers, or answering questions on instruments of the orchestra, or undertaking a project from resource books on acoustics or opera should always be related to direct musical experience in one of the three central activities.

When we perform, compose or listen to music we are not of course necessarily conscious of expressive character and structure as separate entities. However, because teachers stand between music and other people, and because it is essential to develop helpful ways of talking about music with one another, we shall find it useful to bear in mind expressive character and structure as two sides of a single coin. Our own critical faculties will be sharpened, and, in the best sense of the

word, a teacher will often be functioning as a kind of *critic*, acutely perceiving what is happening and responding to it in an appropriate way. We should at least be able to ask good questions. What would it be like if you left out this section or made it longer? What would happen if we took more time over making this crescendo? What difference does it make if the lower instruments play louder and the higher ones quieter?

We can see what happens if we take as a simple example the well known Jewish round *Shalom Chaverin* (on page 242).

What Would Happen If?

What would happen if we sang this tune as a brisk march? What would it be like if we sang it with a heavy accent on the first beat of the bar as though it were a work song or a stomping dance? How would it be if we sang it very quietly, smoothly and slowly, as though it were a distant memory gently coming back to us? If we were teaching this song to a class we might well want to raise these kinds of questions and find words like 'heavy' or 'driving' or 'holding back' or 'gentle' to describe the expressive character of particular performances. We might also want to explore the structural elements by having the second alternate phrases sung by different sections of the class to point up the answering function of these phrases, or to compare the 'unfinished' quality of the second phrase with the stronger finality of the last. The fusion of expressive and structural elements is felt in the movement out and up towards the middle of the tune and the retracting, returning movement to the end. The sense of arrival and finality can be enhanced by repeating the figure several times, the sound gradually dying away.

So much is now open to us. The class might get into small groups and choose their own way of performing the song, bringing out its expressive possibilities — like a march, a dance, a lament, flowing, spiky, heavy, light. Or they might compose a free texture of sound that has the same kind of structure — statement followed by response. Or using a few notes of a mode or scale they might compose and perform their own tune with a 'going away' and 'coming back' to the home-note. Or the words can be taken and used as sound materials for a voice composition: each of the nine syllables has its own special sound and fascinating pieces can be composed using just three or four of these.

The richness of possibilities stems from knowing *it*, the round itself. Knowing *how* has played its role incidentally; knowing how to pronounce the words, how to sing in tune and in time. Knowing *that* may also take its place; knowing that the song has a Jewish context, that it is in $\frac{2}{4}$ time, that it is in the Aeolian mode, though all this seems less essential than knowing how. Ultimately though, both these ways of knowing stop short of the experience and possibilities of this song, this particular 'it'. Only when we begin to think about its expressive and structural elements does a world of implications open up for us. Instead of being driven into dead-ends of skills and information *for their own sake*, the road ahead becomes open with a multitude of alternative ways leading off in various directions. Teachers and pupils are all learners, exploring the possibilities generated by an encounter with a particular tune.

Discovery

What we are advocating then is that all encounters with music ought to have about them an element of *discovery*. The problem is that for many of us elements of discovery and the excitement of discovering are buried beneath knowledge that has been acquired in other ways and at other times. Many children, let alone teachers, are ready to give up the effort of discovering and put in its place an acceptance of received information. We all too easily sell our birthright of natural curiosity in exchange for the comforting certainties of the familiar. Effective teaching depends in part upon the recognition of this and requires us to structure carefully what we do, to maximize the potential for truly musical encounters in the classroom. Our book *Discovering Music* (Swanwick and Taylor, 1982) gives some ideas for developing this approach in a purposeful rather than an aimless and careless way.

One of the bonuses of adopting the notion of discovery as central to music teaching, is that it cuts across all kinds of arguments and problems that have perplexed people for many years. Discovery can happen whether we are composers, performers or in audience. Discovery can happen whether the music we are handling belongs to the classical tradition, the East, jazz, pop, rock, reggae or the many shades of contemporary music. We can rediscover something we thought we already knew or open up a totally unexplored territory. To get on the inside of this experience it is important for teachers too to feel a sense of curiosity and discovery frequently and powerfully. Too often we are content with the second-hand and the second-rate. We use course-books or other people's ideas mechanically and sometimes blindly. We set our pupils tasks that are unmusical, unexciting. We become dulled and stale by repetition. The procedures we are suggesting here may help to rejuvenate teaching and to give it direction, purpose and imaginative quality.

Because teaching is demanding and complex we need a fundamental, simple and powerful set of working principles. The first of these stems from the discussion so far. We must be true to music, that is to say we must provide our pupils with experience of the stuff itself, knowledge of *it*, the integrity of the particular. The second principle has to do with what motivates pupils as people, with the mainsprings of human behaviour, the dynamic forces that propel us all.

Motivation

Basically and naturally and in the beginning everyone wants to learn, to achieve mastery, to develop. Unfortunately this natural impulse is often stunted by pressures exerted by teachers and schools. Children are put through an incredible series of 'educational' hoops: heavy timetables, rigorous social and academic demands, days spent switching from the thought processes of one subject to another and yet again another. We impose a whole range of extrinsic reasons for learning, that is to say not to do with the quality of the experience itself but with success in tests, examinations, in the achievement of good reports and so on. Yet surely we ought to be searching for the deep wells of human motivation that spring out of the qualities of the activities themselves. The stick and the carrot may be necessary at times but they should never be regarded as fundamental. We can gain insights here from the thinking of one of our most influential psychologists, Jerome Bruner.

> The will to learn is an intrinsic motive, one that finds both its source and its reward in its own exercise. The will to learn becomes a 'problem' only under specialized circumstances like those of a school, where a curriculum is set, students confined and the path fixed. The problem exists not so much in learning itself, but in the fact that what the school imposes often fails to enlist the natural energies that sustain spontaneous learning — curiosity, a desire for competence, aspiration to emulate a model, and a deep-sensed commitment to the web of social reciprocity. [1]

This passage has about it a certain 'ring of truth' and we would do well to consider the implications for teaching and learning in music.

If we are to tap those natural sources of energy then every learner has to become *involved* and active. So much music teaching seems concerned with handing out information. How often do we ask children what they notice in music rather than tell them what they should 'know' about it? How frequently is there note-taking rather than discussion — a dialogue of discovery? Music is especially unsuited to this approach. Coming to musical perceptions, making choices and decisions in composition and performance, recognizing the preferences of oneself and other people; these are much more central to musical experience than providing 'correct' answers. How are we to engage in music education unless we provide frequent opportunities for the development of these elements? Long ago the Greek philosopher Socrates saw this clearly. The ultimate and ever-present objective in teaching is to guide the learner to the point where he sees things for himself, one could say, to a point where teachers become redundant. This affirms that learning in music ought to be a succession of discoveries linked with a feeling of personal mastery, thus drawing on what Bruner calls curiosity and a desire for competence. Because these discoveries take place alongside other people, especially in the peer group of a school class, the 'commitment to social reciprocity' of which Bruner speaks is also engaged. There is a substantial difference between the competition of tests, examinations and reports, and the stimulation of the achievements of others along with the sympathy engendered by any difficulties experienced by them.

The 'aspiration to emulate a model' is also part of the fabric of peer-group interaction. There are important implications here for the development of small group work.

The teacher him or herself of course is a crucial model and this demands that whatever is done should be done, as far as possible, in a way that is true to music, totally musical. The teacher is much more than a benevolent ring-master as he directs, guides and shares discovery with his pupils. In demonstrating his *own* curiosity, desire for competence, admiration for good models, and commitment to the group, a powerful motivating force is released.

A Model of Musical Knowing

Finally, we need to clarify ways in which pupils become active in music and the roles they play. These have been discussed in *A Basis for Music Education* (Keith Swanwick, 1979) but it may be helpful now to remind ourselves of the model suggested in that book. There are five parameters of musical experience — three of them directly relating to music and two more having supporting and enabling roles, easily remembered by the device C(L)A(S)P

C	Composition	formulating a musical idea, making a musical object
(L)	Literature studies	the literature about music
A	Audition	responsive listening as (though not necessarily in) an audience
(S)	Skill acquisition	aural, instrumental, notational
P	Performance	communicating music as a 'presence'

This way of identifying the activities relating to music has proved helpful in many ways. For example, it reminds us of the centrality of *Audition*, that particular kind of listening when we are really *understanding* music and not just spotting tunes, or dominant sevenths or identifying composer or performers. It also picks out the three clusters of activity when we directly relate to music; composition, audition and performance. Observations made in large numbers of classrooms suggest that teachers spend most time trying to improve skills or adding to knowledge of literature studies, more time than they in fact predict or estimate. Some teachers have found it helpful to prepare for or to analyze their teaching along the lines of these five parameters, bearing in mind that we often move very quickly from one to another and that one kind of activity relates to the others.

There can however be some confusion between an activity, what is *done* and what is acquired *through* the activity, what is *learned*. For example, someone might be playing tennis, that would be the activity, but she may, as a result of playing tennis, improve her service or come to watch the ball better or even come to realize what a difficult game it is to play well! These things would be what is *learned* and such changes in levels of skill and attitude would still persist when the particular game was over. The improved service would still exist in a future game (provided it was not too far in the future!) and the learned attitude about the difficulty of the game could be a topic of conversation when not playing and would certainly influence the play on subsequent occasions. The instance of tennis is particularly apt. A recent report on tennis in Britain concludes that too much emphasis has been placed on isolated skills, such as serving or using a backhand and not enough emphasis has been placed on a *feeling* for the game, developing a sense of competition, determination, flexibility and total involvement. In other words, isolated skill practice may not bring about *understanding* of what tennis is really about. We might find parallels in music, an emphasis on skills (scales) or on factual knowledge of one kind or another in the area of Literature Studies.

We have tried to indicate earlier in this chapter what we mean by *musical understanding*. This must surely be at the heart of our teaching though we would still look for certain learning of skills and information (from now we shall call the area of Literature Studies *information*). Once we have identified particular areas in which we expect or hope that learning will take place we can then begin to be more precise about our objectives as teachers. The sharpest and clearest way of formulating objectives is to preface every statement we make about our music curriculum with the phrase 'the pupils should be able to ...'. These will be the learning outcomes of the particular activities and it is vital that we realize that activities themselves may not bring about learning, a fact that sometimes escapes us and gives rise to classroom practice that could hardly be said to be education in any real sense of the term.

We need to register here that doing things is not the same as learning things. The following illustration may make this clear. The three columns in the following diagram represent the three areas where we can formulate teaching and learning objectives. They are, *Understanding, Skills* and *Information*. Information relates, of course, to what we have previously called Literature Studies. The activities we have in mind are mainly in the areas of Composition, Performance and Audition (active listening) relating to the round *Shalom Chaverin* which we examined earlier.

Objectives: the pupils should be able to:

Understanding	Skills	Information
Perform in class and smaller groups with the character of a march, a work-song, a lament.	Sing back each phrase accurately; sing the whole tune from memory.	
Choose *one* instrument to enhance the effect; identify phrases that 'reach out' and those that 'draw back'.	Recognize differences of loud/soft and smooth/detached; beat in $\frac{2}{4}$ time to the music at different speeds.	Say what *Shalom Chaverin* means and what language it is.
In small groups compose and perform a short piece using the sounds 'Sha', 'Lom', 'Averin', choosing the order, the speed and levels of loudness to make an interesting and expressive composition.	Demonstrate ensemble skills, starting together, listening to each other.	Explain and demonstrate what an accent is.
Suggest titles that describe the compositions of other groups.		

These are not just 'activities' but are demonstrations of abilities which are 'taken away' and can be extended in the future.

Conclusion

To summarize, we are advocating an approach to music education which emphasizes the following:

1. Delight in music, a rich appreciation is our aim.
2. Discovery is central to musical activities and the crucial questions are: What is it (like)? and What happens if ...?
3. Through the activities of composition, performance and listening we shall be looking for the development of skills, information, musical understanding and valuing, with *understanding* as central.
4. Teaching and learning should be so organized as to draw on the natural energies of motivation common to everyone.

Any ideas and suggestions should be regarded only as examples and must be approached in a sufficiently flexible way so as to meet the individual settings of teachers in terms of resources, personal strengths and particular pupils.

Each teacher will need to explore for him or herself what is possible but this does not mean that anything goes. We shall have before us two challenging questions which must be asked about any classroom activity. *Is it musical?* This implies that we are beyond mere skills and information and that what we have called 'musical understanding' is taking place. *Is there a sense of achievement?* This involves a sense of going beyond where we were before and discovering music for ourselves as should the pupils for themselves. We may not always succeed in this but if we are not prepared to try there seems little point in bothering with music in school at all.

Notes and References

1. JEROME BRUNER, (1966) *Towards a Theory of Instruction*, Harvard University Press, p. 127.
2. KEITH SWANWICK and DOROTHY TAYLOR, (1982) *Discovering Music*, Batsford.

PART IX

Art and the Community

The arts have an indispensable creative role in modern society. The development and refining of aesthetic intelligence is essential not only to the well-being of society but to the very survival of civilization.

In this penultimate chapter David Aspin gives an impassioned defence of the central place of the arts in any balanced curriculum, of their crucial importance to the community and to an informed sense of civilization which supports both curriculum and community.

Chapter 21

The Arts, Education and the Community

David Aspin

Introduction: The Definition of the Arts

I have taken as my theme 'The Arts, Education and the Community' but I think I must preface my remarks with one important qualification. 'The Arts', as we are all aware, can be used in a number of different senses, and I must make plain which of them I have in mind here.

'Arts' in the sense of the 'artes liberales' (those branches of study, such as the humanities, social studies, history, philosophy and the rest that befitted a 'free man') is not what I mean here. Nor do I mean 'The Arts' in the sense in which it is used by Aristotle when he talks of the 'productive' Arts or Crafts that aim at and are used for completing the works of nature. I do not mean what Bach presumably had in mind when he wrote 'The Art of Fugue'; nor what hi-fi enthusiasts mean when they praise products as representing the 'state of the art'; nor the kind of cunning wizardry or stratagems that is implicit in Prospero's address to his staff to 'Lie there, my Art!' I employ 'The Arts' here in a sense similar to that distinguished by Aristotle when he wrote of the 'Mimetic Arts' — those, in which an imaginary world of thought and feeling is created — what we call the 'Fine Arts'. By 'The Arts' here I mean what the Arts Council means by the Arts: literature, poetry, painting, music, sculpture, drama and the dance. And what I am interested in is the problem of establishing whether there are any arguments that might be used to justify the inclusion and retention on the curricula of our schools of an education in those activities, the practice and products of which are so prized by our society as adding beauty and quality to the environment in which its members live and as being apt to enrich and dignify their lives. This problem is particularly of moment now, when the current climate of increasing financial restriction is becoming inimical to any sorts of activity or excellence other than those of an industrial, technical or commercial kind, and when, in consequence, starkly utilitarian concerns have come increasingly to predominate in and be determinative of the curricular content of our community's educating institutions.

There is a line in one of the *Odes* of Horace that serves as a daunting antinomy to such an undertaking on the part of those who love the Arts and wish to see them become more widely known and understood:

> Odi profanum vulgus et arceo[1] (I hate the mass of the uninitiated and keep them at a distance).

The sentiment implicit in this verse is a familiar one: the artist is a different sort of being, operating on a higher level and in a distant world of thought and feeling, apart from the mundane preoccupations and concerns of ordinary mortals. The poet viewed thus is an inhabitor of the citadel of culture, the bulwarks of which have to be defended again the uncomprehending assaults of philistines and barbarians. In some people's eyes, artists enjoy the same sort of status as that of Hegel's 'World-historical individuals' or Nietzsche's Superman — and it is only those who, in Horace's words, can leave behind a 'monument more enduring than bronze'. True understanding of the work of the artist, viewed in this way, can only be achieved by like people; it cannot be achieved by the generality of the common herd; it can only be displayed to them. Something like a 'pearls before swine' attitude permeates this tradition — which we may call the 'Roman' approach to the arts — and it is, for that reason, daunting to those who seek, by means of education, to get people on to the inside of the citadel.

There is another, equally powerful, tradition in the arts, however, that we may call the 'Athenian'. It stretches from the time of Pericles to the present day. According to this view of things, it is part of the greatness of man that he alone of all creatures can enrich his existence and the environment in which he lives by creating and furnishing it with works of Art, the constant exposure to and contemplation of which can evoke and be a vehicle for the expression of the sublime in every man and can thus give to all a vision of beauty that can be a source of pleasure and joy for ever — an 'everlasting possession'.[2] This was surely the spirit of the creators of that paradigmatic *Gesamtkunstwerk* — the complete artistic experience — the great Dionysiac festival at Athens. For Dionysus was determined to encourage each and every man to achieve an 'identification with the Divine', in stark contrast to the injunction of the Apolline tradition that ordinary human beings must only 'think mortal thoughts'.

These two traditions are still to be observed in the practice and dissemination of beliefs about the arts today. Those artists whose endeavours exemplify the preconceptions of artistic ideologies such as social realism or community involvement are recognizably heirs to the Athenian tradition; other artists of the 'high culture' or iconoclastic kind can be seen as inheritors of Roman thinking about the nature and purpose of Art. The differences between such protagonists are, of course, crucial, since for us, a judgment in favour of either determines the model of Art that will be dominant in our appraisals of those objects presented or capable of being seen as 'works of Art'. There is more to the debate than this, however; for the model of aesthetic judgment to which we adhere and we employ as adults will also be, as crucially, a function of those preconceptions in accordance with which we will have been educated. Thus the question for us is sharper and more to the point: to which of these traditions should educators adhere in their attempts to inform and direct their pupils? For it is clear that their answer to this question will also determine the character and purpose of the educational experiences they devise for them. Thus the future of the Arts in our society depends not only on their dissemination but upon the ways in which this is done and for what purposes. As Edward Bond remarks: 'teaching about art is as important as creating it'.[3]

In one respect, of course, this supposed distinction between separate artistic traditions is misconceived. The Athenian tradition presupposes the existence of a widely and well educated populace to observe and appreciate artistic display; the Greeks perhaps even more than the Romans scorned the barbarians beyond the gates. In like manner, no artist of today could expect or would want to get *any* response from the ignorant, the prejudiced, the deluded or the misinformed. Art and artists necessarily have to have an informed, an educated audience: that is an indispensable precondition of the languages in which they express themselves and try to communicate, for these are necessarily 'public' in character. Even Horace was aware of this when he requested his hearers to consent to receive his utterances — 'Favete linguis!' — 'Give me leave to speak'. It will therefore be one of the first tasks of educators in the Arts to bring about conditions in which this consent can be given and this receptivity erected and deployed: audiences for the arts must be presumed to have an informed and prepared predisposition to understand and respond to the utterances of an artist (to whichever tradition he sees himself as belonging) if any sort of communication and interaction is to take place. It is with the idea of that preparation and the fostering and promoting of that receptivity and capacity for responding that I am concerned, and in particular, with the role and function of the teacher of the Arts in those institutions where such processes are typically, though not exclusively, intended to occur. For these will constitute that part of the education of its future generations upon which a certain kind of value is placed by the whole community: and a value not of an instrumental or technical kind, but of a regard for and pursuit of objects and activities that are held to exhibit 'final' value.

The Nature of Community

'Community' is, of course, a concept of which there are many 'conceptions'[4] and I had better indicate that with which I am here working. I derive it from a Winchian kind of account of human social development.[5] The actual 'how' and 'why' of man's development as an animal that lives in groups is philosophically quite uninteresting; whether, as Aristotle averred,[6] man is such 'by nature' is something that we may tentatively argue about, though never in principle settle. It may be thought simpler and safer merely to advance the view that man could never have achieved his present degree of civilized development and cognitive sophistication without having entered into relations with others whom he recognized as being of the same class of entity as himself. At some time in history — what time is philosophically irrelevant — human beings began, fumblingly and haltingly at first, to communicate with each other. What they communicated we know little about and the significance of some of their communicative expressions (such as Cave paintings, for example) can often be no more than a subject for speculation. But the main point is this: at the moment at which one human being uttered or in some other way published to another a string of phonemes, images or marks, that was regarded by the other as well-formed and meaningful, language and linguistic communities came into being. Communication constituted a community. And the story of the progressive sophistication and diversification of languages and communication is at the same time the story of the development and differentiation of various diverse cultural communities. Experience of what such communities saw as the world they shared was, from those earliest moments, articulated and expressed in terms of those units or sequences of phoneme, image or gesture, the conventional but strictly rule-governed nature of which determined but also made possible communicative interchange between individual constituent members of those cultural communities — and *only* in terms of those.

Two points follow from this. The first is that linguistic communities are neither accidental agglomerations of individuals nor purposeful creations: they are evolutionary entities of an organic and strictly conventional kind. They are the effects of the development of groups of beings into self-conscious centres of social organization and interchange, arising from and resting on bases that alone make this development possible. The second must be that they are not single, uniform or homogeneous; the number and diversity of natural languages in the world, and the number of cultural communities of which they are embodiments, is eloquent demonstration of this. And this is true not only in the case of the languages that we call our mother-tongues; it is also true of the multiplicity of artificial systems of rules and conventions which mankind has invented and developed in order to transmit meanings and to expand and enrich his understandings of the world and to render it intelligible, in some form, to others: such non-natural languages as those of mathematics, science, religion — and the Arts.

Each of these various languages will have its own employing community of discourse, the identity of which becomes discernible in the various particularized forms in which its members publish and render objective their experience in it and so make it amenable to elucidation and appraisal. The story of the evolution and progressive refinement of the world of the Arts and all its diverse forms is the story of the evolution and increasing sophistication of such a cultural community. The artefacts and activities of artists are public objectifications of the experiences and imaginative conceptions of the members of this community, embodied and transmitted in the various different constituent languages and in accordance with the canons of their proper logics. By 'logic' here I mean the various forms and criteria of significance and sense that will function so as to structure and determine the intelligibility of utterances within the form of communication in question — if you like, the grammar and syntax, the coinage and common currency of any cultural community. Naturally, too, each such community will generate its own 'literature',[7] that will reflect and embody the growth and state of the culture and the increasing range and innovation of and in its products. All that remains now is to add the crucial point that, in some linguistic communities, meaningful communicative interchange need not be restricted to the discursive model only. The idea of nonlinguistic communication is (*pace* Michael Argyle)[8] incoherent; that of nonverbal communication, far from being so. Indeed it is perhaps the variety of its modes of linguistic interchange — the languages of poetry, music, painting, drama and the dance, in which highly complex and variegated layers of meaning are embodied and expressed — which makes that particular community, the language of which is seen in the Arts, one of the most prolific and multifarious that we can conceive of. It is perhaps, in this respect, equalled only by that other cultural community that we call the world of science.

The Function of the School in the Community

So far, not so good; for although I may have delineated my version of the context within which the artist works and communicates, I have still said nothing of the relationship of any of these communities to 'schools'. What I now have to do is to elucidate my notion of 'school'. Instead of any other model 'school' — Driving, Cookery, poker or pre-Raphaelite — I wish to signify by my use of this term that particular form, agency and setting, in and by means of which our society chooses to institutionalize its child-rearing practices. What, I am asking, is the nature of schools, conceived of and operating as educating institutions and what are their purposes? What is the relationship between such places and the society in which they function — and especially with that particular part of it in which we choose to live, as the *locale* in which our sense of identity and cultural aspirations find readiest and nearest expression — the 'Community'?

In our society the processes of induction, socialization and acculturation are relatively complex and long-lasting, and the reasons for this are not hard to find: the constantly changing and expanding character and store of knowledge; the proliferation of social institutions and practices; the heterogeneity of the subcultures constituting the social whole; the pluralization and conflicts of values; the diversification of needs and interests; changes in attitudes on matters considered important; mobility in and between classes; and differences in language and culture. All of these have led to a state of affairs in our community in which one man could not completely socialize and acculturate his young, even if he would — nor would he, if he could. He and his fellows have agreed that the task of imparting all the various kinds of knowledge and skill which they value and wish to see institutionalized and re-inforced has to be handed over to the agency and ministration of another set of individuals who will act in this capacity in their stead. This is part though not the whole of what I see as the tasks of schools as educating institutions: the transmission of our valued knowledge from one generation to the next;[9] the attempt to induct the young into those modes of discourse in and through which such knowledge can be created and communicated; the inculcation of an awareness of those attitudes, beliefs and values, habits, skills and achievements in which a society's identity is recognized and expressed; and — to use a phrase of Professor Peters'[10] — the 'initiation' of the young into those traditions of thought and action, imagination and creation, feeling and expression in which the character and preferred direction of that society is exemplified and developed. In order that these processes shall take place with what is hoped will be the greatest efficiency for the greatest number, the community makes provision for access to these 'goods' to be available in centres for all to attend, the structure and programmes of which will open such access to its young — and sometimes to its not so young members — brought together by it for the common pursuit of activities and ends that are held by it to be worthwhile, and under the supervision of those whom it believes qualify as authorities in the skills of imparting this kind of information and of its valued procedures and dispositions.

It follows, then, that in schools thus conceived of, our society will want to arrange to have, functioning as its agents of transmission, induction and innovation, representatives of all the linguistic and cultural communities that make up the determinant traditions of its identity *and* which it wishes to be taken up, engaged in and perpetuated by its young. Members of such communities will serve as the teachers of their language and literature. It will be their assigned task to get young people started on the various 'modes of thought and awareness', and activity and achievement, by means of which it seeks to stabilize their cultural identity, expand their consciousness and offer them an acquaintance with the various alternatives from among which an individual may proceed to make an informed choice as to the pattern of life options that he himself prefers. [11] Clearly, some activities and ways of looking at the world — exemplified in the activities of the Great Train Robber, the necromancer and the pornographer — our society disvalues and seeks to inhibit or eradicate; others it values and promotes. Among these, I believe, our society places the pursuits and achievements of those cultural communities that we call mathematics, science, the humanities, morality — and that world for which Professor Hirst used the denotative title of 'literature and the fine arts'. [12] For these are basic to its existence — not only in the sense of providing means by which its members may earn their daily bread and ways in which they may regulate their interpersonal conduct (though those are certainly crucial, too), but also in the sense that they are the chief strands in the fabric of its identity and are thus the very foundations on which the research for sources of satisfaction and enrichment must necessarily rest. In all of these worlds, the teacher will have a dual function: that of imparting, or seeking to impart, a regard for what counts as the best in it and of endeavouring to secure its survival; and that of teaching by creating, of showing pupils how to produce new kinds of hypotheses for the future, of introducing them to ways of conceiving of alternative possible worlds that can stand the test of criticism and thus constitute new, though provisional, data in the world of 'objective knowledge'. [13] In this endeavour the mathematician will have a different role to play from that of the scientist or historian — though both will be of equal significance. And different again, though equally significant — and, some people would say, more important and valuable — will be the activity and presence of teachers of the Arts, in as many of their sub-disciplines (dramatic and mimetic, plastic and graphic, expressive and kinetic) as considerations of time, space, personnel and finance will allow. I am thus aligning myself firmly with those who aver that the Arts should be regarded as one of the indispensable elements in any core curriculum. My reasons for this are admirably summed up in W. D. Hudson's aphorism that someone who had no appreciation of beauty or morality we should surely regard as, to that extent, sub-human.[14]

The Characteristics of the Arts

This arises from a consideration of the character of activity — both performative and appreciative — in the arts and of the value placed on it by our community. The first and most obviously unique characteristic of works in the Arts is their emphasis on creator and spectator enjoyments of a *disinterested* kind. By this I mean that appraisals of works of art may be independent of all other considerations — technical, scientific, economic, moral or religious; in the Arts one learns to recognize and savour beauty (however expressed) in and for itself, apart from utilitarian purposes of any kind. The second characteristic of the Arts is their concern with ends or pursuits that 'bring delight and hurt not' — the giving and experiencing of joys and pleasures in artefacts and activities in and for themselves, expressed in judgments of an informed and deliberative kind resulting from the application of criteria that serve to define, in a certain class of comparison, what counts as pre-eminent and exemplary, and what as trivial, shoddy or second-rate. Then, too, we should probably also note another distinguishing feature of works that we regard as constituting 'great art' and of our various perceptions of it — their ephemeral character. On the one hand, great works of Art and outstanding performances in them tend to be inimitable and unrepeatable; on the other, the gradual accretion of experiences and increasingly informed and heightened awareness and growth in aesthetic understanding sensitizes us and makes possible fresh insights and more variegated enrichments on each occasion that we perceive aesthetically. So that, as our experience grows and we turn again to the 'same' work, it is as though we find new kinds of meaning and levels of communication in it that transform the work and our percipience and make them new to us.

These are among the prime features of the aesthetic mode of discourse operating in our activities and appreciation of the Arts.[15] In and by these ways, their objects are made intelligible: differentially conceived and responded to by someone who has been taught to perceive, judge and appreciate in this way, and can thus extend his awareness and add to his capacity for enriched understanding and enjoyment of some of the significant objects he sees in the world about him, as presented and mediated by the artist. At the end of such a period of tuition and immersion in it, he too, we may hope, will look, like Miranda, with transformed vision and exclaim, with the same excitement, 'Oh brave new world, that hath such creatures in it!'

Two further points in the logic of the Arts are important in this attempted justification of educational activity in it. One is that characteristic of this form of communication and creation that Ehrenzweig termed its function of 'de-different-iation'.[16] It has been regarded by him and others as a fundamental 'truth' in and about Art that in any art work there will be whole layers and kinds of meaning, embodied in it[17] and so inextricably intertwined and connected that they all fuse into one complete organic unity. The various kinds and intensities of meaning of *Guernica*, for example, like that of Blake's *Sick Rose* or Brahms' *3rd Symphony*, can only be fully understood and savoured by attending to the totality of the work and 'letting it be'. The activity of 'stripping away the layers' of meaning[18] brings about effects in the perceiver that illuminates and transforms his vision of the truths about the world he sees about him as a result of the disclosures that his receptivity to the work precipitates. This process — which Broudy described as 'enlightened cherishing'[19] — has other deeply transformative effects too: for attending to works of art and letting their meanings emerge and suffuse our insights with their own fresh illuminations of the world and of our perceptions and judgments of our own situation in it, is to engage, as it were, in what Professor Arnaud Reid has called a 'process of conversation'.[20] To see this and learn to do it one has to undertake the task of learning to *address* the individual work of art, almost as though it were a person, in what Martin Buber called the I-Thou relationship.

In this respect the Arts can act as powerful agents of a real integration, in the sense that wide varieties of meaning and value are brought together and reconciled, presented for understanding and appreciation, in one harmonious manifestation. So far as I can think, this characteristic of syncretization and unification is to be found in no other mode of discourse; all that we find elsewhere is analysis, differentiation and dissection. The Arts are a model for our being open to the many-sidedness of things, for flexibility and the capacity to re-integrate and fuse infinite possibilities of significance and utility. And this flexibility and many-sidedness have a social value and applicability too, for it is in their harmonizations, reconciliations and enlightenments of newer and possibly better worlds that artists, through their work, can bring about transformations in a society that dignify the daily struggle for survival, add tone to the whole atmosphere and environment, and transcend the brute facts of mere existence.

These features invest the artist and the teacher in the Arts with a considerable power. He is an artificer and illustrator of innumerable possible worlds, a synthesizer of discrete parts and often warring factions, a reconciler and a harmonist. One recent critic went beyond this and spoke of the function of the artist as that of 'prophet and healer'.[21] Fusion and reconciliation, maybe: but prophesy? This has to do, I think, with one further feature of artists' work which I wish to lay bare — its commitment to the world of the imagination, what I have called the 'expansion of consciousness'. For perhaps the key trait that is characteristic of this cultural community is its dynamism and creativity. Members of it are typically preoccupied with the exercise of their imaginations, not only to perceive and judge in the forms and according to the criteria subsisting in and defining their own part of the aesthetic realm, but also in the attempt to restructure that realm and redefine it, by adding novel creations, alternative conjunctions of forms and concepts — perhaps even proposing entirely new forms, concepts or categories that enable us to reinterpret or add substantially to the store of meanings in that world.[22] In this, the Arts provide us with ways of not only re-experiencing the richness of others' visions for ourselves (and thus to extend our own store of meanings) but also of conceiving of alternative possible worlds and thus adding further increments to the whole community's limits of consciousness and cultural inheritance. In this respect the Artist is different from the teacher who transmits and inducts; he innovates and makes advances. He is a smith and his work an anvil upon which culture is forged. And in so far as some of his proposals will either add to or call into question existing practices, structures or institutions, he will also be seen as being, in quite a decided sense, a revolutionary. For the artist is concerned not so much to understand and appreciate the creations or interpretations of others but more to criticize them and in his own work to show how they may be ameliorated or amended. No one who has been present at or party to the often fierce discussions of some artists in their judgments of each other's works — though of course, in this, as any moralist or theologian would tell us, artists are far from being alone — can be in any doubt that the world of the Arts is also an exemplar of what Popper[23] called an 'open' society — one in which there are no superior authorities, in which every man's view counts and is treated impartially on its merits, in which every performance or artefact becomes a hypothesis to be examined, tested and, if possible, knocked down. In this respect products or performances in the Arts are no different from propositions, theories or judgments in mathematics, science or morals.[24] They are, in a significant sense, communications published and proposed for inspection, adjudication and, if possible, falsification. They constitute the valid parts along with the rest of that objective world of one of our most valued 'forms of life'.[25]

Art and the Open Society

In this way and for this reason, the teacher of the Arts is one of those whom some people view with alarm. For he deliberately seeks to get his pupils started on that activity of exploring, questioning, criticizing and maybe even subverting existing concepts, structures and categories that constitute the cores and define the limits of the languages of those communities, being and doing in which is regarded by their constituents as being the best guarantee of a life of any tolerable quality or acceptability. Their forms of procedure and institutions are in this way paradigms of a liberal society and democratic way of life. Both the artist as practitioner and the arts teacher as initiator are lauded variously as liberal democrats or dangerous revolutionaries; for the one engages in, and the other demonstrates the value of, those activities that define a form of existence which all who value or fear autonomy desire or deplore. For they require and promote the development of patterns of social relations in which each participant is an equal and in which anything that smacks of totalitarianism, appeals to authority and inauthenticity is anathema.

Perhaps that is the reason why artists and educators are feared, often mistrusted, sometimes derided. As Keith Sagar remarked:

> The prophets are never heeded; their healing powers are spurned. ... All have been persecuted, mocked, mistrusted, or, at best, ignored...

and this experience is no stranger to the artist or the teacher, perhaps especially in a time when Lawrence was banned, Stravinsky howled down and Solzhenitsyn put into a psychiatric ward. Small wonder when some people speak of artists as being 'enormously conceited and full of contempt for others', of their being 'Totally unfitted for *normal* life', of the experience of the artist as being disabling;[26] when politicians dismiss educationalists' expression of concern at their proposals for recension as a 'knee-jerk of the left'; and when the media make money out of the disenchantment of a few who caricature education as making our children 'just another brick in the wall'. Such are the sentiments of those who, for one reason or another, seek to close the open society into which our community desires its young to be admitted, and to subvert the very institutions in which the articulation of such views is made possible; such is the spirit of those who fear the criticism and creative endeavours of those who have benefitted from engagement in activities devoted to the asking of such questions and caring that answers should be found to them; such are those who yearn for comfort, conformity and acceptance, who would have people say 'Enfin ça suffit: je crois!' And that attitude, as Bronowski noted, leads ultimately to the mentality and practices of the concentration camp, wherein men seek to stifle and suffocate the aspirations of those spirits who would don wings and fly to the sun.[27]

It is against that possibility that any community that values openness and progress must secure its future. And leaders in that undertaking will be the proponents of those communities which exemplify the virtues of the open society: the pursuit of truth in all its various forms and the struggle to serve the interests of all men impartially and to promote their welfare and flourishing. I wish to argue that one of the communities of discourse and activity upon which for all those reasons and valued outcomes, our society lays greatest value, is the world of the Arts. The Arts are part of the fabric of our culture and of the environment in which it is developed and by which it is being continually uplifted and enriched. The Secretary of the Arts Council went further than this, when he wrote: 'The Arts — stories, pictures, music and dance — are indeed as much a human need as food and drink'.[28] And just as basic a 'need' — if our lives are not to be lived at the minimum level of mere survival, to be bereft of quality and elevation, and unenhanced by any of those conventions and traditions by which men have transmuted their world from brutishness to civilization — is the indispensable necessity of that mode of institutionalization that we call 'education', however formal or informal and in whatever form. Failure to come to terms with this and to make provision for induction into culture in our educating institutions would, in a marked sense, be irreparably to impoverish ourselves and our society. We should become troglodytes, Caliban-like figures, stunted and distorted members of the family of creatures on earth, unable to have a fully-informed power to appreciate or create the goods of society and the products of the 'great human traditions of critico-creative thought'.[29] We should become what some anti-educationalists want us to be: complaisant inhabitants of a dreary, soulless, technocratic, robot-run world, easily persuaded, controlled and exploited, mollified and pacified by a soma-like diet of the trivial, the shoddy and the second-rate — a culture of Page 3, Top Twenty and Crossroads.

There is a risk of that now, in these times of recension and 'rationalization'. Schools may not replace resigning Arts teachers so that a subject dies; or, through lack of support or funds for a teacher's efforts at continued personal development in his subject, or restrictions on resources and materials, an ossification of culture in the Arts sets in. Another way of defusing or ignoring the Arts is to patronize them and turn them into 'classics and examination fodder'. One sure way of controverting such endeavours is to demonstrate the vitality and dynamism of the Arts, their unique contribution to enriching the quality of a nation's way by its stress on that greatest of a society's resources — the powers of the creative imagination. We must lay open and be prepared to expatiate on the value of the Arts as sources of satisfaction, personal growth and community reconciliation, but also, and crucially, their dialectical character, in which there is no gulf between participation and appreciation, process and product, form and content (all the antinomies which bedevil much talk about the arts), and in which the interaction between art-work and environment serves to uplift the tone of all — as many industrialists, both in this country and abroad, have long realized. For Maecenas has his counterpart today in figures such as Sir Robert Mayer: *now* we see that the so-called 'Roman' tradition of a secret citadel for the cultivated, a 'private language' for insiders only, is mistaken — indeed incoherent.[30] Artists are *necessarily* interested in and committed to dialogue: they use the concepts, criteria and forms of expression that are public, because they are communicative and communicated. And though their profundities and complexities may make them initially seem esoteric, this does not mean that their products or performances can be in any way private or idiosyncratic. Artists communicate; and the obviousness of this entails that they have to have audiences and that these audiences have to learn the languages in which they speak. Where else can they learn this but in some educating institution, of which the most informal example is a mother's knee and the more formal a school?

The Development of Aesthetic Intelligence and the Life of Civilization

If we value the induction of our young into this — or any other — universe of discourse, then we must have instruction and demonstration in it. And, given that art is essentially concerned with skills and activities, it will have to be taught and shown in two processes that are distinct: doing or making, or demonstrating or performing; and teaching about and in such activities. It may be that, in order to secure the most effective induction and immersion, we shall need to expose our young to excellence in both — art *and* teaching; it may be too that one who is an outstanding artist will also be an outstanding teacher of the arts. As often, however, the artist will be a poor teacher and the teacher an artist whose products he himself knows are no more than merely competent. In such cases the teacher will be the first to show examples of artistic excellence to his charges, that will function as living proofs of what he is so assiduously, albeit imperfectly, trying to get them 'on the inside of'. But since art *is* a fusion of process and product, form and function, and, above all, the work of personal consciousness acting within and reacting to a socio-historical context, he will bring before his pupils, not only poems, pictures and passacaglias, but writers, painters, composers, actors and dancers.[31] The making and creating of art being a dynamic process, in educational institutions the practice of and teaching in the arts will have to go hand in hand — sometimes fused in the work of one person (who will have to have a clearly differentiated awareness of when he is teaching and when he is doing his art); and sometimes presented by two persons or more, each working according to the highest standards of precision and according to the demands of his own particular art and function.

One can think of a number of reasons, of course, why teachers might want access to the work of a plethora of other professionals: the desirability of variety; the need for fresh thinking and new ideas; expertise in other fields or radically different views in the same field. But above all these I should want to stress the point that, by making the experience of other people at work in the Arts accessible to my pupils, I should be demonstrating to them the unity-in-diversity, the shared sense of excitement and the readiness for discovery that characterizes and coalesces this community, into which, by encouraging their own efforts and inviting their participation, I was thus offering them an *entrée*. Indeed the vital importance of a partnership between the Arts and schools as agents of the community's educating endeavours was well expressed in the policy statement of 1965, *A Policy for the Arts*:[32]

> The place that the Arts occupy in the life of a nation is largely a reflection
> of the time and effort devoted to them in schools and colleges.

This view was put forward by a government committed to a radical reappraisal of social institutions and cultural traditions in an age of the 'white heat of the technological revolution', relatively full employment, and a booming economy. How different times are now, fifteen years on, in a period of recession, stagnation, increasing unemployment and financial stringency; yet how much more important now than then it is to give men a reassurance of the creative capacities of human intelligence, a revivified awareness of the richness of that greatest of our resources — man's creative imagination. To say this is not, of course, to imply that there cannot be creativity in other subjects, such as the sciences or mathematics — far from it; nor is it to belittle the power and inventiveness that can be found in the exercise of the imagination in history, philosophy and economic planning. It is simply to underline the point that in the Arts we are centrally concerned with creativity and the life of the imagination, in and for themselves alone. For we hold that in them we can find, as against the starkly utilitarian concerns of a bleak present and a bleaker future, springs of satisfaction that are indifferent to and independent of the low-level concerns of living a life in increasingly restrictive circumstances, sources of inspiration for asserting our own sense of worth, by trying to create and learning to appreciate works which express basic truths about the human condition and in their embodiments of these truths represent final value. It is, we may say, the perceived task of artists and teachers to endeavour to implant and evoke in man, faced with education for an enforced leisure, some visions of greatness and intimations of immortality. A recent writer to the newspapers put this thought well, if pessimistically:

> Looking round at the God-awful mess man has made of this planet, I am increasingly convinced that, were I faced with an omnipotent visitor from Outer Space asking me for one good reason why this world should not be wiped out tomorrow, I should reply by asking him to see *Hamlet*, to watch Ashton's 'Symphonic Variations', to listen to the 'Meistersinger' quintet and to look at Vermeer's 'Head of a Girl'. Basically all forms of activity other than Art are inspired by self-interest and it is only in Art that humanity can justify its miserable existence.

This spirit is not new; it is as old as civilization itself. For a common concern among developed states is to go beyond the minimum exigencies and resources required for securing livelihood and economic viability; to transcend the pragmatic preoccupations of the struggle for existence; to dignify their cities and beautify their environments; and to transform and add vividness, intensity and untold possibilities of personal advancement to the lives of all their people. The principal pride of that great statesman Pericles lay in the knowledge that in Athens the Arts were public agencies of the instruction and edification of the populace and the adornment and enrichment of the City's surroundings. It was the work and hope of such statesmen that the activities of the drama, poetry, sculpture, painting and the dance should be the preferred pursuits and chief joys of all the community, once life itself and the minimum conditions necessary for survival had been secured.

The sentiments of Pericles' *Funeral Oration* would surely be echoed now by artists, of whatever persuasion, and teachers, of whatever background and subject concerns — and all members of our community who have an interest in and a care for the preservation and continuance of the valued elements in its culture: that, in not providing for and encouraging the practice of the Arts and instruction in them, we should be abandoning both our heritage and our future; that in following the dictates of the technocrats and the political ideologues, of either left or right, we should be abdicating the kind of autonomy and authenticity that is the stock in trade of both the artist and the educated man; that in putting economic self-sufficiency and the control of the money supply before any other ends, we should be deciding upon and fostering a climate in which any other form of excellence, creativity and imagination might well be suspected and stifled, and

David Aspin

in which the sensitivity and the capacity for enlightened cherishing that is brought to bear on all things by aesthetic intelligence and understanding may well stagnate and die.

As a bulwark against this awful possibility, as a reincarnation of the past, as a synthesis and reconciliation of all that is best in the present, as a projection of a better, more refined, civilized and exciting tomorrow, we must, or so I believe, do all we can to make the Arts more widely accessible, 'to develop and improve the knowledge and understanding of the Arts'.[33] And this requires the best efforts and initiatives of a combined contribution from the Arts, Education and the Community.

It will take brave spirits to embark upon this task, in *these* daunting times and against all the odds. Indeed, as Sagar remarks,

The battle, even if it is doomed, has to be fought again every generation by the bravest men.

But artists and teachers have never lacked courage. Even in the darkest days,

... brave men are forever born, and nothing else is worth having.[34]

Notes and References

1. HORACE, *Odes*, I xxxii.
2. Cf. THUCYDIDES, *Histories*, II.43.
3. EDWARD BOND, 'An Introduction to The Fool', in *Theatre Quarterly* (London) 1976 (Spring).
4. For this distinction see J. RAWLS, *A Theory of Justice*, Oxford, Clarendon Press, 1973. Also RAYMOND PLANT, *Community and Ideology*, London, Routledge and Kegan Paul, 1973.
5. See PETER WINCH, *The Idea of a Social Science*, London, Routledge, 1958.
6. ARISTOTLE, *Politics*, 1253 a.1–4 ἄνθρωπος φύσει πολίτικον ζῷον ἐστι. Cf. PETER WINCH, 'Nature and Convention' in *Proceedings of the Aristotelian Society*, 1959–1960.
7. For the idea of a 'language' and its 'literature' cf. M. OAKESHOTT, 'The Study of "Politics" in a University' in his *Rationalism in Politics and Other Essays*, London, Methuen, 1962.
8. MICHAEL ARGYLE, *Bodily Communication*, London, Methuen, 1975. For a refutation of his argument cf. DAVID BEST, *Philosophy and Human Movement*, London, Allen and Unwin, 1978, Ch. 9.
9. On this cf Ch. 1 of KEVIN HARRIS, *Knowledge and Education*, London, Routledge, 1979.
10. See R. S. PETERS, 'Education as Initiation', in R. D. ARCHAMBAULT (Ed), *Philosophical Analysis and Education*, London, Routledge, 1965. It is an idea that has not been without its critics: cf. K. E. ROBINSON, 'Education and Initiation', in *Educational Philosophy and Theory*, 2, 2, October 1970.
11. This might be thought to be a defensible principle of curriculum choice: cf. J. P. WHITE, *Towards a Compulsory Curriculum*, London, Routledge, 1973.
12. See P. H. HIRST, 'Liberal Education and the Nature of Knowledge', in R. D. ARCHAMBAULT, *op.cit.*
13. K. R. POPPER, *Objective Knowledge*, Oxford, Clarendon Press, 1972.

14. So W. D. Hudson, 'Is Religious Education Possible?', pp. 194–5, in Glenn Langford and D. J. O'Connor, *New Essays in Philosophy of Education*, London, Routledge, 1973.
15. See P. F. Strawson, 'Aesthetic Appraisal and Works of Art', in his *Freedom and Resentment and Other Essays*, London, Methuen, 1974.
16. A. Ehrenzweig, *The Hidden Order of Art: A Study in the Psychology of Artistic Imagination*, University of California Press, 1976.
17. For the idea of works of Art as 'embodiments' of meaning cf. L. Arnaud Reid, *Meaning in the Arts*, London, Allen and Unwin, 1969.
18. On this see Sonia Greger, 'Aesthetic Meaning', in *Proceedings of the Philosophy of Education Society of Great Britain*, VI, 2, July 1972.
19. H. S. Broudy, 'Enlightened Preference and Justification' in R. A. Smith (Ed), *Aesthetics and Problems of Education*, Urbana, Ill., University of Illinois Press, 1971.
20. L. Arnaud Reid, 'The Philosophy of Education through The Arts', in *Conference Report*: 'A Consideration of Humanity, Technology and Education in our time', London, Joint Council for Education through Art, 1957.
21. Keith Sagar, 'A Lawrence for today: art for life's sake', in *The Times Higher Education Supplement*, February 1980.
22. See Mary Warnock, *Imagination*, London, Faber and Faber.
23. K. R. Popper, *The Open Society and Its Enemies*, I and II, London, Routledge, 1943.
24. Cf. P. H. Hirst, 'Literature and the Fine Arts', in his *Knowledge and the Curriculum*, London, Routledge, 1973.
25. L. Wittgenstein, *Philosophical Investigation*, (trs. G. E. M. Anscombe), Oxford, Blackwell, 1953, p.226e.
26. So F. Musgrove, *Margins of the Mind*, London, Methuen, 1977, pp. 67ff.
27. J. Bronowski, 'Knowledge and Certainty', Ch. 11, in his *The Ascent of Man*, London, BBC Publications, 1973.
28. Sir Roy Shaw, *Report of the Arts Council of Great Britain: Progress and Renewal*, 35th Annual Report, London, Arts Council, 1980.
29. So J. Passmore, 'On Teaching to Be Critical' in R. S. Peters (Ed), *The Concept of Education*, London, Routledge, 1966.
30. On the 'private language' argument see papers by R. Rhees, A. J. Ayer, *et al.* in G. Pitcher (Ed), *Wittgenstein*, London, Macmillan, 1966.
31. Cf. Irene Macdonald, *Professional Arts and Schools*, London, Arts Council.
32. *A Policy for the Arts: The First Steps*, London, HMSO, Cmnd 2601, 1965.
33. One of the chief aims in the Charter of the Arts Council.
34. Keith Sagar, *loc. cit., ad fin.*

PART X
Art as Affirmation

In the final chapter George Steiner returns to many of the
issues raised in the section on 'The Demise of Modernism'.
He analyzes the present crisis in the interpretation of the
arts and concludes that our answer to it must be to affirm
meaning and the possibility of meaning.

The conclusions of George Steiner's 'Real Presences'
are remarkably close to the claims made by Iris Murdoch at
the opening of this volume. Both insist on the need to
reclaim and honour 'the background', both insist on the
recognition of values and realities which transcend us; and
both these propositions are fundamental to this symposium on the arts.

Chapter 22

Real Presences

George Steiner

The Modern Crisis in Understanding

The turn of the century witnessed a philosophic crisis in the foundation of mathematics. Logicians, philosophers of mathematics and formal semantics, such as Frege and Russell, investigated the axiomatic fabric of mathematical reasoning and proof. Ancient logical and metaphysical disputes as to the true nature of mathematics — is it arbitrarily conventional? Is it 'a natural' construct corresponding to realities in the empirical order of the world? — were revived and given rigorous philosophical and technical expression. Gödel's celebrated proof of the necessity for an 'outside' addition to all self-consistent mathematical systems and operational rules, took on formal and applied significance far beyond the strictly mathematical domain. It is, at the same time, fair to say that certain of the questions raised in the late nineteenth and early twentieth centuries as to the logical foundations, internal coherence and psychological or existential sources of mathematical reasoning and proof, remain open.

A comparable crisis is occurring in the concept and understanding of language. Again, the far sources of questioning and disputation are those of Platonic, Aristotelian and Stoic thought. Grammatology, semantics, the study of the interpretation of meaning and actual interpretative practice (hermeneutics), models of the possible origins of human speech, the formal and pragmatic analysis and description of linguistic acts and performance — have their precedent in Plato's *Cratylus* and *Theaetetus*, in Aristotelian logic, in the classical and post-classical arts and anatomies of rhetoric. Nonetheless, the current 'language turn', as it affects not only linguistics, the logical investigations of grammar, theories of semantics and semiology, but also philosophy at large, poetics and literary studies, psychology and political theory, is a radical break with traditional sensibility and assumptions. The historical sources of the 'crises of sense' are themselves complicated and fascinating. I can, here, allude to them only summarily.

Though in many respects conservative, the Kantian revolution carried within it the seeds of a fundamental re-examination and critique of the relations between word and world. The logical and psychological location by Kant of fundamental perceptions within human reason, Kant's conviction that the 'thing in itself', the ultimate reality-substance 'out there' could not be analytically defined or demonstrated, let alone articulated, laid the ground for solipsism and doubt. A dissociation of language from reality, of designation from perception, is alien to Kant's idealism of common sense; but it is an implicit potential. This potential will be seized upon, at first, not by linguistics or philosophic logic, but by poetry and poetics. Our current debates on transformational generative grammars, on speech-acts, on structuralist and deconstructive modes of textual reading, our present-day focus, in short, on 'the meaning of meaning' — derive from the poetics and experimental practice of Mallarmé and of Rimbaud. It is the period from the 1870s to the mid-1890s which generates our present agenda for debate, which situates the problem of the nature of language at the very centre of the philosophic and applied *sciences de l'homme*. Coming after Mallarmé and Rimbaud we know that a serious anthropology has at its formal and substantive core a theory or pragmatics of the *logos*.

It is from Mallarmé that stems the programmatic attempt to dissociate poetic language from external reference, to fix the otherwise undefinable, unrecapturable texture and odour of the rose in the word 'rose' and not in some fiction of external correspondence and validation. Poetic discourse, which is, in fact, discourse made essential and maximally *meaning-ful*, constitutes an internally coherent, infinitely connotative and innovative, structure or set. It is richer than that of largely indeterminate and illusory sensory experience. Its logic and dynamics are internalized: words refer to other words; the 'naming of the world' — that Adamic conceit which is the primal myth and metaphor of all western theories of language — is not a descriptive or analytic mapping of the world 'out there', but a literal construction, animation, unfolding of conceptual possibilities. (Poetic) speech is creation. Rimbaud's *Je est un autre* lies at the base of all subsequent histories and theories of the dispersal of individuality, of the historical and epistemological eclipse of the *ego*. When Foucault heralds the end of the classical or Judaeo-Christian 'self', when deconstructionists refuse the notion of personal *auctoritas*, when Heidegger bids 'language speak' from an ontological well-spring prior to man, who is only the medium, the more or less opaque instrument of autonomous meaning — they are, each in their own framework of tactical intent, developing and systematizing Rimbaud's anarchic manifesto, his ecstatic *dérèglement* of traditional and innocent realism.

This scattering, this dissemination of the self, this subversion of naive correspondence between the word and the empirical world, between public enunciation and what is actually being said, is accentuated by psychoanalysis. The Freudian view and use of human speech, of written texts (with its unmistakable analogues to Talmudic and to Kabbalistic techniques of decipherment in depths, of revelatory descent into hidden levels of etymology and verbal association), radically dislocates and undermines the old stabilities of language. The common sense — observe that phrase — of our spoken or written words, the visible orderings and values of our syntax, are shown to be a masking surface. Beneath each stratum of conscious, lexical meaning, lie further strata of more or less realized, avowed, intended meanings. The impulses of intentionality, of declared and covert significance, extend from the brittle surface to the unfathomable nocturnal deep structures or prestructures of the unconscious. No ascription of meaning is ever final, no associative sequence or field of possible resonance ever end-stopped. (Wittgenstein's dissent from Freud seizes upon this very point.) Meanings and the psychic energies which enunciate or, more exactly, which encode them, are in perpetual motion. 'Must we mean what we say?' asks the epistemologist: 'can we mean what we say?' asks the psychoanalyst. And what, after Rimbaud, is that fiction of stable identity we label 'I' or 'we'?

Logical positivism and linguistic philosophy, as they arise in Central Europe at the turn of the century and are institutionalized in Anglo-American practice, are exercises in demarcation: between sense and nonsense, between what can be said reasonably and what cannot, between truth-functions and metaphor. The endeavour to 'purge language' of its metaphysical impurities, of its facile fantasms of unexamined inference, is undertaken in the name of logic, of transparent formalization and systematic scepticism. But the *kathartic*-therapeutic image, the ideal of cleansing and restoration to ascetic clarity so vivid in the Vienna Circle, in Frege, in Wittgenstein and their inheritors, relates obviously to Mallarmé's famous imperative: let us 'cleanse the words of the tribe', let language be made translucent to itself.

The fourth principal area of the language-critique and deconstructions of classical innocence as to word and world, is historical and cultural. Here also, and with few exceptions, the source is Central European and Judaic. (One need hardly stress the Judaic character of the entire movement, philosophic, psychological, literary, cultural-political which I am addressing, or the tensed overlap between this movement and the tragic destiny of European Judaism. From Roman Jakobson, Freud, Wittgenstein, Karl Kraus, Kafka or Walter Benjamin to Lévi-Strauss, Jacques Derrida and Saul Kripke, the *dramatis personae* of our enquiry declare a larger logic.) This fourth area is that of the critique of language as an inadequate instrument and as an instrument not merely of political-social falsehood but of potential barbarism. Hofmannsthal's 'Letter of Lord Chandos', the parables of Franz Kafka, the reflections on language of Mauthner (a cardinal, hence unavowed source of Wittgenstein's *Tractatus*), tell of man's incapacity to express in words his innermost truths, his sensory experiences, his moral and transcendent intuitions. This despair before the limitations of language will climax in the final cry in Schoenberg's *Moses und Aron*: 'O Word, of Word which is lacking to me'. Or in Kafka's inexhaustible parable on the mortal silence of the Sirens. The political-aesthetic assault on language is that of Karl Kraus, of his auditor, Canetti, or George Orwell (a more pallid but rationally usable version of Kraus). Political rhetoric, the tidal mendacity of journalism and the mass media, the trivializing cant of public and socially approved modes of discourse, have made of almost everything modern urban men and women say or hear or read an empty jargon, a cancerous loquacity (Heidegger's term is *Gerede*). Language has lost the very capacity for truth, for political or personal honesty. It has marketed and mass-marketed its mysteries of prophetic intuition, its answerabilities to accurate remembrance. In Kafka's prose, in the poetry of Paul Celan or of Mandelstam, in the messianic linguistics of Benjamin and in the aesthetics and political sociology of Adorno, language operates, self-doubtingly on the sharp edge of silence. We know now that if the Word 'was in the beginning', it can also be in at the end: that there is a vocabulary and a grammar of the death camps, that thermo-nuclear detonations can be designated as 'Operation sunshine'. It were as if the quintessential, the identifying attribute of man — the *Logos*, the organon of language — had broken in our mouths.

The consequences and correlatives of these great philosophical-psychological underminings and of the western experience of uttermost political inhumanity, are ubiquitous. They are too numerous and various to designate accurately. Much of classical literacy, of *litterae humaniores* as understood, taught and practised from the Hellenistic age to the two world wars, is eroded. The retreat from the word is drastic in the special and increasingly numerate or symbolic codes of not only the exact and applied sciences, but in philosophy and logic, in the social sciences. The picture and the caption dominate ever-expanding spheres of information and communication. The values implicit in rhetoric, in citation, in the canonic body of texts, are under severe pressure. It is more than likely that the performance and personal reception of music are now moving to that cultural pivot once occupied by the cultivation of discourse and of letters. The methodical devaluation of speech in political propaganda and in the *esperanto* of the mass-market are too powerful and diffuse to be readily defined. At decisive points, ours is today a civilization 'after the word'.

What I want to look at is a more specific ground of crisis and debate.

The Plight of Interpretation

The act and art of serious reading comport two principal motions of spirit; that of interpretation (hermeneutics) and that of valuation (criticism, aesthetic judgment). The two are strictly inseparable. To interpret is to judge. No decipherment, however philological, however textual in the most technical sense, is value-free. Correspondingly, no critical assessment, no aesthetic commentary is not, at the same time, interpretative. The very word 'interpretation', encompassing as it does concepts of explication, of translation and of enactment (as in the interpretation of a dramatic part or musical score) tells us of this manifold interplay.

The relativity, the arbitrariness of *all* aesthetic propositions, of *all* value-judgments is inherent in human consciousness and in human speech. *Anything can be said about anything*. The assertion that Shakespeare's *King Lear* 'is beneath serious criticism' (Tolstoy), the finding that Mozart composes mere trivia, are *totally irrefutable*. They can be falsified neither on formal (logical) grounds, nor in existential substance. Aesthetic philosophies, critical theories, constructs of the 'classic' or the 'canonic' can never be anything but more or less persuasive, more or less comprehensive, more or less consequent descriptions of this or that process of preference. A critical theory, an aesthetic, is a *politics of taste*. It seeks to systematize, to make visibly applicable and pedagogic an intuitive 'set', a bent of sensibility, the conservative or radical bias of a master perceiver or alliance of opinions. There can neither be proof nor disproof. Aristotle's readings and Pope's, Coleridge's and Sainte-Beuve's, T. S. Eliot's and Croce's, do not constitute a science of judgment and disproof, of experimental advance and confirmation or falsification. They constitute the metamorphic play and counter-play of individual response, of (to borrow Quine's teasing phrase) 'blameless intuition'. The difference between the judgment of a great critic and that of a semi-literate or censorious fool lies in its range of inferred or cited reference, in the lucidity and rhetorical strength of articulation (the critic's style) or in the accidental *addendum* which is that of the critic who is also a creator in his own right. But it is not a scientifically or logically demonstrable difference. No aesthetic proposition can be termed either 'right' or 'wrong'. The sole appropriate response is personal assent or dissent.

How, in actual practice, do we handle the anarchic nature of value-judgments, the formal and pragmatic equality of all critical findings? We count heads and, in particular, what we take to be qualified and laurelled heads. We observe that, over the centuries, a great majority of writers, critics, professors and honourable men have judged Shakespeare to be a poet and dramatist of genius and have found Mozart's music to be both emotionally enriching and technically inspired. Reciprocally, we observe that those who judge otherwise are in a tiny, literally eccentric minority, that their critiques carry little weight and that the motives we make out behind their dissent are psychologically suspect (Jeffrey on Wordsworth, Hanslick on Wagner, Tolstoy on Shakespeare). After which perfectly valid observations we get on with the business of literate commentary and appreciation.

Now and again, as out of an irritant twilight, we sense the partial circularity and the contingency of the whole argument. We realize that there can be no ballot on aesthetic values, that a majority vote, however constant and massive, can never refute, can never disprove the refusal, the abstention, the counter-statement of the solitary or denier. We realize, more or less clearly, the degree to which 'literate common sense', the acceptable limits of debate, the transmission of the generally agreed syllabus of major texts and works of art and of music, is an ideological process, a reflection of power-relations within a culture and society. The literate person is one who concurs with the reflexes of approval and aesthetic enjoyment which have been suggested and exemplified to him by the dominant legacy. But we dismiss such worries. We accept as inevitable and as adequate the merely statistical weight of 'institutional consensus', of common-sense authority. How else could we marshal our cultural choices and be at home in our pleasures?

It is at this precise juncture that a distinction has, traditionally, been drawn between aesthetic criticism on the one hand and interpretation or analysis strictly considered on the other. The ontological indeterminacy of all value-judgments, the impossibility of any probative, logically consistent 'decision procedure' as between conflicting aesthetic views, have been conceded. *De gustibus non disputandum*. The determination of a true or most probable meaning in a text has, in contrast, been held to be the reasonable aim and merit of informed reading or philology.

Linguistic, formal, historical factors may impede such determination and documented analysis. The context in which the poem or fable was composed may elude us. The stylistic conventions may have become esoteric. We may, simply, not have the requisite critical density of information, of controlling comparisons, needed to arrive at a secure choice between variant readings, between differing glosses and *explications du texte*. But these are accidental, empirical problems. In the case of ancient writings, new lexical, grammatical or contextual material may come to light. Where the inhibitions to understanding are more modern, further biographical or referential data may turn up and help elucidate the author's intentions and field of assumed echo. Unlike criticism and asethetic valuation, which are always synchronic (Aristotle's 'Oedipus' is not negated or made obsolete by Hölderlin's, Hölderlin's is neither improved nor cancelled out by Freud's), the process of textual interpretation is cumulative. Our readings become better informed, evidence progresses, substantiation grows. Ideally — though not, to be sure, in actual practice — the corpus of lexical knowledge, of grammatical analysis, of semantic and contextual matter, of historical and biographical fact, will finally suffice to arrive at a demonstrable determination of what the passage means. This determination need not claim exhaustiveness; it will know itself to be susceptible to amendment, to revision, even to rejection as fresh knowledge becomes available, as linguistic or stylistic insights are sharpened. But at any given point in the long history of disciplined understanding, a decision as to the better reading, as to the more plausible paraphrase, as to the more reasonable grasp of the author's purpose, will be a rational and demonstrable one. At the end of the philological road, now or tomorrow, there *is* a best reading, there is a meaning or constellation of meanings to be perceived, analyzed and chosen over others. In its authentic sense, philology is, indeed, the working passage, via the arts of scrupulous observance and trust (*philein*) from the uncertainties of the word to the stability of the *Logos*.

It is the rational credibility and practice of this passage, of this cumulative advance towards textual understanding, which is today in sharp doubt. It is the hermeneutic possibility itself which the 'crises of sense', as I sketched them at the outset, have put in question.

Let me contract, and thus radicalize, the claims of the new semantics. The post-structuralist, the deconstructionist remind us (justly) that there is no difference in substance between primary text and commentary, between the poem and the explication or critique. All propositions and enunciations, be they primary, secondary or tertiary (the commentary on the commentary, the interpretation of previous interpretations, the criticism of criticism, so familiar to our current Byzantine culture), are part of an encompassing *intertexuality*. They are equivalent as *écriture*. It follows in a profoundly challenging play on words (and is not all discourse and writing a play on words?) that a primary text and each and every text it gives rise or occasion to is no more and no less than a *pre-text*. It happens to become before, temporally, by accident of chronology. It is the occasion, more or less contingent, more or less random, of the commentary, critique, variant on, pastiche, parody, citation of itself. It has no privilege of canonic originality — if only because language always precedes its user and always imposes on his usage rules, conventions, opacities for which he is not responsible and over which his control is minimal. No sentence spoken or composed in any intelligible language is, in the rigorous sense of the concept, original. It is merely one among the formal unbounded set of transformational possibilities within a rule-bound grammar. The poem or play or novel is, strictly considered, anonymous. It belongs to the topological space of the underlying grammatical and lexical structures and availabilities. We do not need to know the name of the poet to read the poem. That very name, moreover, is a naive and obtrusive ascription of identity where, in the philosophic and logical sense, there is no demonstrable identity. The 'ego', the *moi*, after Freud, Foucault or Lacan, is not only, as in Rimbaud, *un autre*, but a kind of Magellanic cloud of interactive and changing energies, partial introspections, moments of compacted consciousness, mobile, unstable, as it were, around an even more indeterminate central region or black hole of the sub-conscious, of the unconscious or the pre-conscious. The notion that we can grasp an author's intentionality, that we should attend to what he would tell us of his own purpose in or understanding of his text, is utterly naive. What does he know of the meanings hidden by or projected from the interplay of semantic potentialities which he has momentarily circumscribed and formalized? Why should we trust in his own self-delusions, in the suppressions of the psychic impulses, which most likely have impelled him to produce a 'text' in the first place? The adage had it: 'do not trust the teller but the tale'. Deconstruction asks: why trust either? Confidence is not the relevant hermeneutic note.

Invoking the commonplace but cardinal verity that in all interpretation, in all statements of understanding, language is simply being used about language in an infinitely self-multiplying series (the mirror arcade), the deconstructive reader defines the act of reading as follows. The ascription of sense, the preference of one possible reading over another, the choice of this explication and paraphrase and not that, is no more than the playful, unstable, undemonstrable option or fiction of a subjective scanner who constructs and deconstructs purely semiotic markers as his own momentary pleasures, politics, psychic needs or self-deceptions bid him do. There are no rational or falsifiable decision-procedures as between a multitude of differing interpretations or 'constructs of proposal'. At best, we will select (for a time, at least) the one which strikes us as the more ingenious, the richer in surprise, the more powerfully decompositional and re-creative of the original or *pre-text*. Derrida on Rousseau is richer *fun* than, say, an old literalist and historicist such as Lanson. Why labour through philological-historical exegeses of the Lurianic Kabbala when one can read the constructs of the semioticians at Yale? No *auctoritas* external to the game can legislate between these alternatives. *Gaudeamus igitur*.

Let me say at once that I do not perceive any adequate logical or epistemological refutation of deconstructive semiotics. It is evident that the playful abolition of the stable subject contains a logical circularity, for it is an ego which observes or intends its own dissolution. And there is an infinite regress of intentionality in the mere denial of intent. But these formal fallacies or petitions of principle do not really cripple the deconstructive language-game or the fundamental claim that there are no valid procedures of decision as between competing and even antithetical ascriptions of meaning.

The common sense (but what, challenges the deconstructionist, is 'a common sense'?) and liberal move is one of more or less unworried circumvention. The carnival and saturnalia of post-structuralism, of Barthe's *jouissance*, or Lacan's and Derrida's endless punning and wilful etymologizing, will pass as have so many other rhetorics of reading. 'Fashion', as Leopardi reassures us, 'is the mother of death'. The 'common reader', Virginia Woolf's positive rubric, the serious scholar, editor and critic will get on, as they always have, with the work in hand, with the elucidation of what is taken to be an authentic, though often polysemic and even ambiguous sense, and will enunciate what are taken to be informed, rationally arguable, though always provisional and self-questioning, preferences and value-judgments. Across the millennia, a decisive majority of informed receivers have not only arrived at a manifold but broadly coherent view of what the *Iliad* or *King Lear* or *The Marriage of Figaro* are about (the meanings of their meaning), but have concurred in judging Homer, Shakespeare, Mozart to be supreme artists in a hierarchy of recognitions which extends from the classical summits to the trivial and the mendacious. This broad concordance, with its undeniable residue of dissent, or hermeneutic and critical disputes, with its margins of uncertainty and altering 'placement' (F. R. Leavis's word), constitutes an 'institutional consensus', a syllabus of agreed reference and exemplariness across the ages. This general concurrence provides culture with its energies of remembrance, and furnishes the 'touchstones' (Matthew Arnold) whereby to test new literature, new art, new music.

So robust and fertile a pragmatism is seductive. It allows one, indeed it authorizes one, to 'get on the with the job'. It bids one acknowledge, as out of the corner of a clear eye, that all determinations of textual meaning are probabilistic, that all critical assessments are ultimately uncertain; but to draw confident re-insurance from the cumulative — that is to say statistical — weight of historical agreement and practical persuasion. The bark and ironies of deconstruction resound in the night but the caravan of 'good sense' passes on.

Responding to Nihilism

I know that this *praxis* of liberal consensus satisfies most readers. I know that it is the general guarantor of our literacies and common pursuits of understanding. Nevertheless, the current 'crises of sense', the current equation of text and pre-text, the abolitions of *auctoritas*, seem to me so radical as to challenge a response other than pragmatic, statistical or professional (as in the protectionism of the academy). If counter-moves are worth exploring, they will be of an order no less radical than are those of the anarchic and even 'terrorist' grammatologists and masters of mirrors. The summons of nihilism demand answer.

The initial move is one away from the autistic echo-chambers of deconstruction, from a theory and practice of games which — this is the very point and *ingenium* of the thing — subvert and alter their own rules in the course of play. It is a move palpably indebted to the Kierkegaardian triad of the aesthetic, the ethical and the religious. But the resort to certain ethical postulates or categories in respect of our interpretations and valuations of literature and the arts is older than Kierkegaard. The belief that the moral imagination relates to the analytic and the critical imaginations is at least as ancient as the poetics of Aristotle. These are, themselves, an attempt to refute Plato's dissociation between aesthetics and morality. A move towards the ethical rejoins the hermeneutics of Aquinas and Dante and the aesthetics of disinterestedness in Kant (himself an obligatory and representative target of recent deconstruction). It is, I think, the abandonment of this high and rigorous ground, in the name of nineteenth-century positivism and twentieth-century secular psychology, which has brought on much of the (intensely stimulating) anarchy in which we now find ourselves.

If we wish to transcend the merely pragmatic, if we wish to meet the challenge of autistic textuality or, more accurately, 'anti-textuality' on grounds as radical as its own, we must bring to bear on the act of meaning, on the understanding of meaning, the full force of moral intuition. The vitally concentrated agencies are those of tact, of courtesy of heart, of good taste, in a sense not decorous or civil, but inward and ethical. Such focus and agencies cannot be logically formalized. They are existential modes. Their underwriting is, as we shall be compelled to propose, of a transcendent kind. This makes them utterly vulnerable. But also 'of the essence', this is to say, essential.

I take the ethical inference to entail the following, to make the following *morally*, not logically, not empirically, self-evident.

The poem comes before the commentary. The primary text is first not only temporally. It is not a pre-text, an occasion for subsequent exegetic or metamorphic treatment. Its priority is one of essence, of ontological need and self-sufficiency. Even the greatest critique or commentary, be it that of a writer or painter or composer on his own work, is *accidental* (the cardinal Aristotelian distinction). It is dependent, secondary, contingent. The poem embodies and bodies forth through a singular enactment its own *raison d'être*. The secondary text does not contain an imperative of being. Again the Aristotelian and Thomist differentiations between essence and accident are clarifying. The poem *is*; the commentary *signifies*. Meaning is an attribute of being. Both phenomenologies are, in the nature of the case, 'textual'. But to equate and confound their respective textualities is to confound *poiesis*, the act of creation, of bringing into autonomous being, with the derivative, secondary ratio of interpretation or adaptation. (We know that the violinist, however gifted and penetrating, 'interprets' the Beethoven sonata; he does not compose it. To keep our knowledge of this difference at risk, we do remind ourselves that the existential status of an unperformed work, an unread text, an unseen painting *is* philosophically and psychologically problematic.)

It follows from these intuitive and ethical postulates that the present-day inflation of commentary and criticism, that the equalities of weight and force which deconstruction assigns to the primary and the secondary texts, are spurious. They represent that reversal in the natural order of values and interest which characterize an Alexandrine or Byzantine period in the history of the arts and of thought. It follows also that the statement propounded by an academic leader of the new semantics — 'It is more interesting to read Derrida on Rousseau than to read Rousseau' — is a perversion not only of the calling of the teacher, but of common sense where common sense is a lucid, concentrated expression of moral imagining. Such a perversion of values and receptive practice, however playful, is not only wasteful and confusing *per se*: it is potentially corrosive of the strengths of creation, of true invention in literature and the arts. The current crisis of meaning does appear to coincide with a spell of enervation and profound self-doubt in art and letters. Where cats are sovereign, tigers do not burn.

But liberating as I believe it to be, the ethical inference does not engage finality. It does not confront in immediacy the nihilistic supposition. It is formally conceivable and arguable that every discourse and text is idiolectic, this is to say that it is a 'one-time' cryptogram whose rules of usage and decipherment are non-repeatable. If Saul Kripke is right, this would be the strong version of Wittgenstein's view of rules and language. 'There can be no such thing as meaning anything by the word. Each new application we make is a leap in the dark; any present criterion could be interpreted so as to accord with anything we may choose to do. So there can be neither accord nor conflict.'

Equally, it is conceivable and arguable that every assignment and experience of value is not only undemonstrable, is not only susceptible of statistical derision (on a free vote, mankind will choose bingo over Aeschylus), but is empty, is meaningless in the logical positivist use of the concept.

We know of Descartes' axiomatic solution to such possibility. He postulates the *sine qua non* that God will not systematically confuse or falsify our perception and understanding of the world, that He will not arbitrarily alter the rules of reality (as these govern nature and as these are accessible to rational deduction and application). Without some such fundamental presupposition in regard to the existence of sense and of value, there can be no responsible response, no answering answerability to either the act of speech or to that ordering of and selections from this act which we call the text. Without some axiomatic leap towards a postulate of *meaning-fulness*, there can be no striving towards intelligibility or value-judgment however provisional (and note the part of 'vision' in the provisional). Where it elides the 'radical' root — the etymological and conceptual root — of the *Logos*, logic is indeed vacant play.

We must read *as if*.

The Supposition of Meaning

We must read as if the text before us had meaning. This will not be a single meaning if the text is a serious one, if it makes us answerable to its force of life. It will not be a meaning or *figura* (structure, complex) of meanings isolated from the transformative and reinterpretative pressures of historical and cultural change. It will not be a meaning arrived at by any determinant or automatic process of cumulation and consensus. The true understanding(s) of the text or music or painting may, during a briefer or longer time-spell, be in the custody of a few, indeed of one witness and respondent. Above all, the meaning striven towards will never be one which exegesis, commentary, translation, paraphrase, psychoanalytic or sociological decoding, can ever exhaust, can ever define as total. Only weak poems can be exhaustively interpreted or understood. Only in trivial or opportunistic texts is the sum of significance that of the parts.

We must read as if the temporal and executive setting of a text do matter. The historical surroundings, the cultural and formal circumstances, the biographical stratum, what we can construe or conjecture of an author's intentions, constitute vulnerable aids. We know that they ought to be stringently ironized and examined for what there is in them of subjective hazard. They matter none the less. They enrich the levels of awareness and enjoyment; they generate constraints on the complacencies and licence of interpretative anarchy.

This 'as if', this axiomatic conditionality, is our Cartesian-Kantian wager, our leap into sense. Without it, literacy becomes transient Narcissism. But this wager is itself in need of a clear foundation. Let me spell out summarily the risks of finality, the assumptions of transcendence which, at the first and at the last, underlie the reading of the word as I conceive it.

Where we read truly, where the experience is to be that of meaning, we do so as if the text (the piece of music, the work of art) *incarnates* (the notion is grounded in the sacramental) *a real presence of significant being*. This real presence, as in an icon, as in the enacted metaphor of the sacramental bread and wine, is, finally, irreducible to any other formal articulation, to any analytic deconstruction or paraphrase. It is a singularity in which concept and form constitute a tautology, coincide point to point, energy to energy, in that excess of significance over all discrete elements and codes of meaning which we call the symbol or the agency of transparence.

These are not occult notions. They are of the immensity of the commonplace. They are perfectly pragmatic, experiential, repetitive, each and every time a melody comes to inhabit us, to possess us even unbidden, each and every time a poem, a passage of prose seizes upon our thought and feelings, enters into the sinews of our remembrance and sense of the future, each and every time a painting transmutes the landscape of our previous perceptions (poplars are on fire after Van Gogh, viaducts walk after Klee). To be 'indwelt' by music, art, literature, to be made responsible, answerable to such habitation as a host is to a guest — perhaps unknown, unexpected — at evening, is to experience the *commonplace mystery of a real presence.* Not many of us feel compelled to, have the expressive means to, register the mastering quality of this experience — as does Proust when he crystallizes the sense of the world and of the word in the little yellow spot which is the real presence of a riverside door in Vermeer's *View of Delft*, or as does Thomas Mann when he enacts in word and metaphor the coming over us, the 'overcoming of us', in Beethoven's *Opus* 111. No matter. The experience itself is one we are thoroughly *at home* with — an informing idiom — each and every time we live a text, a sonata, a painting.

Moreover, though we have largely forgotten it, this experience of, the underwriting by, a real presence is the source of the history, methods and practice of hermeneutics and criticism, of interpretation and value-judgment in the western inheritance.

The disciplines of reading, the very idea of close commentary and interpretation, textual criticism as we know it, derive from the study of Holy Scripture or, more accurately, from the incorporation and development in that study of older practices of Hellenistic grammar, recension and rhetoric. Our grammars, our explications, our criticisms of texts, our endeavours to pass from letter to spirit, are the immediate heirs to the textualities of western Judaeo-Christian theology and biblical-patristic exegetics. What we have done since the masked scepticism of Spinoza, since the critiques of the rationalist Enlightenment and since the positivism of the nineteenth century, is to borrow vital currency, vital investments and contracts of trust from the bank or treasure-house of theology. It is from there that we have borrowed our theories of the symbol, our use of the iconic, our idiom of poetic creation and aura. It is loans of terminology and reference from the reserves of theology which provide the master readers in our time (such as Walter Benjamin and Martin Heidegger) with their licence to practise. We have borrowed, traded upon, made small change of the reserves of transcendent authority. Very few of us have made any return deposit. At its key points of discourse and inference, hermeneutics and aesthetics in our secular, agnostic civilization are a more or less conscious, a more or less embarrassed act of larceny (it is just this embarrassment which makes resonant and tensely illuminating Benjamin on Kafka or Heidegger on Trakl and on Sophocles).

What would it mean to acknowledge, indeed to repay these massive loans?

For Plato the rhapsode is one possessed by the god. Inspiration is literal; the *daimon* enters into the artist, mastering and overreaching the bounds of his natural person. Seeking a reinsurance for the imperious obscurity, for the great burst into the inordinate of his poems, Gerard Manley Hopkins reckoned neither on the perception of a few elect spirits nor on the pedagogic authority of time. He did not know whether his language and prosody would *ever* be understood by other men and women. But such understanding was not of the essence. Reception and validation, said Hopkins, lay with Christ, 'the only true critic'. As set out in *Clio*, Péguy's analysis and description of the complete act of reading, or the *lecture bien faite*, remains the most incisive, the most indispensable we have. Here is the classic statement of the symbiosis between writer and reader, of the collaborative and organic generation of textual meaning, of the dynamics of necessity and hope which knit discourse to the life-giving response of the reader and 'remembrancer'. In Péguy, the pre-emptions and logic of the argument are explicitly religious; the mystery of poetic, artistic creation and that of vital reception are never wholly secular. A dread sense of blasphemy in regard to the primal act of creation, of illegitimacy in the face of God, inhabits every motion of spirit and of composition in Kafka's work. The breath of inspiration, against which the true artist would seek to close his terrified lips, is that of those paradoxically animate winds which blow from 'the nether regions of death' in the final sentence of Kafka's *The Hunter Gracchus*. They too are not of secular, rational provenance.

In the main, western art, music and literature have, from the time of Homer and Pindar to that of Eliot's *Four Quartets*, of Pasternak's *Doctor Zhivago* or the poetry of Paul Celan, spoken immediately either to the presence or absence of the god. Often, that address has been agonistic and polemic. The great artist has had Jacob for his patron, wrestling with the terrible precedent and power of original creation. The poem, the symphony, the Sistine ceiling are acts of counter-creation. 'I am God', said Matisse when he completed painting the chapel at Vence. 'God, the other craftsman', said Picasso, in open rivalry. Indeed it may well be that modernism can best be defined as that form of music, literature and art which no longer experiences God as a competitor, a predecessor, an antagonist in the long night (that of St John of the Cross which is every true poet's). There may well be in atonal or aleatory music, in non-representational art, in certain modes of surrealist, automatic or concrete writing, a sort of shadow-boxing. The adversary is now the form itself. Shadow-boxing can be technically dazzling and formative. But like so much of modern art it remains solipsistic. The sovereign challenger is gone. And much of the audience.

I do not imagine that He can be summoned back to our agnostic and positivist condition. I do not suppose that a theory of hermeneutics and of criticism whose underwriting is theological, or a practice of poetry and the arts which implies, which implicates the real presence of the transcendent or its 'substantive absence' from a new solitude of man, can command general assent. What I have wanted to make clear is the spiritual and existential duplicity in so much of our current models of meaning and of aesthetic value. Consciously or not, with embarrassment or indifference, these models draw upon, they meta-phorize crucially, the abandoned, the unpaid-for-idiom, imaginings and guaran-tees of a theology or, at the least, of a transcendent metaphysics. The astute trivializations, the playful nihilism of deconstruction do have the merits of their honesty. They instruct us that 'nothing shall come of nothing'.

Personally, I do not see how a secular, statistically based theory of meaning and of value can, over time, withstand either the deconstructionist challenge or its own fragmentation into liberal eclecticism. I cannot arrive at any rigorous conception of a possible determination of either sense or stature which does not wager on a transcendence, on a real presence, in the act and product of serious art, be it verbal, musical, or that of material forms.

Such a conviction leads to logical suppositions which are exceedingly difficult to express clearly, let alone to demonstrate. But the possible confusion and, in our present climate of approved sentiment, the inevitable embarrassment which must accompany any public avowal of mystery, seem to be preferable to the slippery evasions and conceptual deficits in contemporary hermeneutics and criticism. It is these which strike me as false to common experience, as incapable of bearing witness to such manifest phenomena as the creation of a literary persona who will endure far beyond the life of the creator (Flaubert's dying cry against 'that whore' Emma Bovary), as incapable of insight into the invention of melody or the evident transmutations of our experiences of space, of light, of the planes and volumes of our own being, brought about by a Mantegna, a Turner or a Cézanne.

It may be the case that nothing more is available to us than the absence of God. Wholly felt and lived, that absence is an agency and *mysterium tremendum* (without which a Racine, a Dostoevsky, a Kafka are, indeed, nonsense or food for deconstruction). To infer such terms of reference, to apprehend something of the cost one must be prepared to pay in declaring them, is to be left naked to unknowing. I believe that one must take the risk if one is to have the right to strive towards the perennial, never-fully-to-be-realized ideal of all interpretation and valuation: which is that, one day, Orpheus will not turn around, and that the truth of the poem will return to the light of understanding, whole, inviolate, life-giving, even out of the dark of omission and of death.

Notes on Contributors

PETER ABBS is Lecturer in Education at the University of Sussex where he directs the Master of Arts Course, *Language, the Arts and Education*. He is the author of a number of books on education and culture.

DAVID ASPIN is Professor of Education at Macquarie University, New South Wales, Australia. He was co-author of the influential Gulbenkian Report *The Arts in Schools* (1982).

G. R. BANTOCK is Emeritus Professor of Education, University of Leicester, and author of a number of volumes on education including *Education, Culture and the Emotions, Education in an Industrial Society* and *The Parochialism of the Present*.

DAVID BEST is Leverhulme Fellow in the Department of Philosophy at the University College of Swansea. He is the author of a number of highly regarded books on the arts in education: *Expression and Movement in the Arts, Philosophy and Human Movement* and *Feeling and Reason in the Arts*.

PETER BROOK is a distinguished British theatre and film director, author of *The Empty Space* and *The Shifting Point*, now directing theatre productions in Paris.

JEROME BRUNER is one of America's leading educationists whose work has always been highly regarded in Britain. His publications include *Towards a Theory of Instruction On Knowing. Essays for the Left Hand* and *The Process of Education*.

ARTHUR DANTO is president of the American Philosophical Association and author of a number of influential books including *The Transfiguration of the Commonplace* and *The State of the Art*.

DENIS DONOGHUE is Professor of Literature in the Department of English and American Letters at New York University. He is the author of many volumes including *The Third Voice, Connoisseurs of Chaos* and *Ferocious Alphabets*. In 1982 he gave the BBC Reith Lectures, *The Arts Without Mystery*.

PETER FULLER is editor of *Modern Painters* and author of a number of influential books on art and art criticism including *Images of God* and *Theoria*.

REX GIBSON is a tutor at the Cambridge Institute of Education and Director of the Shakespeare and Schools Project. He is the author of *Structuralism and Education* and *Critical Theory and Education*.

ERNST GOMBRICH is a distinguished British art historian and critic. His publications include *The Story of Art, Art and Illusion, Norm and Form, The Sense of Order* and *Tributes*.

MAXINE GREENE is Professor of Philosophy and Education and the William F. Russell Professor in the Foundations of Education at Teachers College, Columbia University, New York. She is author of *Teacher as Stranger, Landscapes of Learning and the Dialectic of Freedom*.

TED HUGHES is Britain's Poet Laureate.

L. C. KNIGHTS was until his retirement King Edward VII Professor of English Literature at the University of Cambridge. His works include *Some Shakespearian Themes, Drama and Society in the Age of Johnson, An Approach to Hamlet* and *Selected Essays in Criticism*.

LOUIS ARNAUD REID was Professor Emeritus of Philosophy and Education at the University of London. He held the Chair of Philosophy and Education at the Institute of Education from 1947 till 1962. His last work, introduced by Harold Osborne, *Ways of Understanding and Education*, was published in 1986. During the last decade of his life he exerted a broad and positive influence on the formation of a common aesthetic for British education.

ROGER SCRUTON is Professor of Aesthetics at Birkbeck College, the University of London. He is the author of a number of books on aesthetic understanding. These include *Art and Imagination, The Aesthetics of Architecture* and *The Aesthetic Understanding*.

GEORGE STEINER is Professor of English and Comparative Literature at the University of Geneva. His publications include *Tolstoy or Dostoevsky, The Death of Tragedy, Language and Silence, After Babel* and *Heidegger*.

ANTHONY STORR is consultant in Psychotherapy for Oxfordshire, a Fellow of Green College and Clinical Lecturer in Psychiatry. He is the author of many books including *The Dynamics of Creation, The Art of Psychotherapy* and *Schools of Genius*.

KEITH SWANWICK is Professor of Music Education at the Institute of Education, and Chairman of the National Association for Education in the Arts. Recent books include *A Basis for Music Education* and *Discovering Music* (with Dorothy Taylor).

DOROTHY TAYLOR is Lecturer in Music at the Institute of Education, London. She is editor of the International Society for Music Education's Yearbook and the author of *Music Now* and, with Professor Swanwick, *Discovering Music*.

MICHAEL TIPPETT is one of Britain's most distinguished living composers.

GEORGE WHALLEY was Professor of English at Queens University, Ontario, Canada. He is author of *Poetic Process* and *Coleridge and Sarah Hutchinson*.

Bibliography

The editor is indebted to Edwin Webb, Marian Metcalfe, Robert Watson, Anna Haynes, Christopher Havell and Robin Morris for the bibliographies on English, Music, Film, Dance, Drama and Art.

Arts and Education

ABBS, P. (1975) *Reclamations: Essays on Culture, Mass Culture and the Curriculum*, Gryphon Press.

ABBS, P. (Ed.) (1987) *Living Powers: The Arts in Education*, Falmer Press.

ABBS, P. (1988) *A Is for Aesthetic: Essays on Creative and Aesthetic Education*, Falmer Press.

ASPIN, D. (1984) *Objectivity and Assessment in the Arts: The Problem of Aesthetic Education*, NAEA.

BANTOCK, G. H. (1967) *Education, Culture and the Emotions*, Faber and Faber.

BANTOCK, G. H. (1981) *The Parochialism of the Present*, Routledge and Kegan Paul.

BERLEANT, A. (1970) *The Aesthetic Field*, Charles C. Thomas.

BEST, D. (1985) *Feeling and Reason in the Arts*, Allen and Unwin.

BLOOMFIELD, A. (Ed.) *Creative and Aesthetic Education Aspects*, 34, University of Hull.

BROOK, P. (1987) *The Shifting Point*, Harper and Row.

BROUDY, H. (1972) *Enlightened Cherishing: An Essay in Aesthetic Education*, University of Illinois Press.

BRUNER, J. (1962) *On Knowing: Essays for the Left Hand*, Harvard University Press.

CASSIRER, E. (1944) *An Essay on Man*, Bantam Books.

CASSIRER, E. (1955–8) *The Philosophy of Symbolic Forms* (in three volumes), Yale University Press.

COLLINGWOOD, R. G. (1958) *The Principles of Art*, Oxford University Press.

DANTO, A. (1987) *The State of the Art*, Prentice Hall.

DEWEY, J. (1934) *Art as Experience*, Minton Balch and Company.

DONOGHUE, D. (1985) *The Arts Without Mystery*, BBC.

EAGLETON, T. (1983) *Literary Theory*, Basil Blackwell.

ELIOT, T. S. (1975) *Selected Prose of TS Eliot*, edited Frank Kermode, Faber and Faber.

FREUD, S. (1973) *Introductory Lectures on Psychoanalysis*, Penguin.

FREUD, S. (1973) *New Introductory Lectures on Psychoanalysis*, Penguin.

FRYE, N. (1957) *The Anatomy of Criticism*, Princeton University Press.

FULLER, P. (1980a) *Art and Psycho-Analysis*, Writers and Readers.

FULLER, P. (1980b) *Beyond the Crisis in Art*, Writers and Readers.

FULLER, P. (1982) *Aesthetics after Modernism*, Writers and Readers.
FULLER, P. (1985) *Images of God*, Chatto and Windus.
FULLER, P. (1988) *Theoria*, Chatto and Windus.
GIBSON, R. (1986) *Structuralism and Education*, Pergamon.
GOMBRICH, E. (1960) *Art and Illusion*, Phaidon.
GOMBRICH, E. (1966) *Norm and Form*, Phaidon.
GOMBRICH, E. (1979) *The Sense of Order*, Phaidon.
GOMBRICH, E. (1978) *The Story of Art*, Phaidon.
GOMBRICH, E. (1984) *Tributes: Interpreters of our Cultural Tradition*, Phaidon.
GREENE, M. (1988) *The Dialectic of Freedom*, Teachers College Press.
GULBENKIAN FOUNDATION (1982) *The Arts in Schools*, Gulbenkian Foundation.
HARGREAVES, D. (1982) *The Challenge of the Comprehensive School*, Routledge and Kegan Paul.
HOSPERS, J. (1969) *Introductory Readings in Aesthetics*, Collier Macmillan.
JONES, D. (1973) *Epoch and Artist*, Faber and Faber.
JUNG, C. *et al.* (1964) *Man and His Symbols*, Aldus Books.
JUNG, C. (1967) *The Spirit in Man, Art and Literature*, Routledge and Kegan Paul.
KANT, I. (1952) *Critique of Pure Reason*, Oxford University Press.
KANT, I. (1952) *Critique of Judgement*, Oxford University Press.
KNIGHTS, L. C. (1960) *Selected Essays in Criticism*, Chatto and Windus.
KOESTLER, A. (1975) *The Act of Creation*, Picador.
LANGER, S. (1953) *Feling and Form*, Routledge and Kegan Paul.
LANGER, S. (1957) *Philosophy in a New Key*, Harvard University Press.
LANGER, S. (1957) *Problems of Art*, Routledge and Kegan Paul.
LANGER, S. (1974) *Mind: An Essay on Human Feeling*, Johns Hopkins University Press.
LIPMAN, M. (Ed.) (1973) *Contemporary Aesthetics*, Allyn and Bacon.
LODGE, D. (1981) *Working with Structuralism*, Routledge and Kegan Paul.
MARCUSE, H. (1978) *The Aesthetic Dimension*, Macmillan.
MORDAUNT CROOK, J. (1987) *The Dilemma of Style*, John Murray.
MUMFORD, L. (1971) *The Myth of the Machine*, Secker and Warburg.
PHENIX, P. (1964) *Realms of Meaning*, McGraw Hill.
POLANYI, M. (1973) *Personal Knowledge*, Routledge and Kegan Paul.
READ, H. (1943) *Education through Art*, Faber and Faber.
READ, H. (1955) *Ikon and Idea*, Faber and Faber.
REDFERN, H. B. (1986) *Questions in Aesthetic Education*, Allen and Unwin.
REID, L. A. (1961) *Ways of Knowledge and Experience*, Allen and Unwin.
REID, L. A. (1970) *Meaning in the Arts*, Allen and Unwin.
REID, L. A. (1986) *Ways of Understanding and Education*, Heinemann Educational Books.
ROBERTSON, S. (1982) *Rosegarden and Labyrinth: Art in Education*, Gryphon Press.
ROSS, M. (1975) *Arts and the Adolescent*, Schools Council, Evans.
ROSS, M. (1978) *The Creative Arts*, Heinemann Educational Books.
ROSS, M. (Ed.) (1983) *The Arts in Education*, Falmer Press.
ROSS, M. (1984) *The Aesthetic Impulse*, Pergamon.
SCHILLER, (1974) *On the Aesthetic Education of Man*, Clarendon Press.
SCRUTON, R. (1974) *Art and Imagination*, Methuen.
SCRUTON, R. (1979) *The Aesthetics of Architecture*, Methuen.
SCRUTON, R. (1983) *The Aesthetic Understanding*, Methuen.
STEINER, G. (1967) *Language and Silence*, Penguin.
STEINER, G. (1975) *After Babel*, Cambridge University Press.
STOKES, A. (1965) *The Invitation in Art*, Tavistock.
STORR, A. (1972) *Dynamics of Creation*, Penguin.
TIPPETT, M. (1974) *Moving into Aquarius*, Picador.
VALERY, P. (1964) *Aesthetics*, Routledge and Kegan Paul.
WARNOCK, M. (1980) *Imagination*, Faber and Faber.

Bibliography

WHALLEY, G. (1953) *Poetic Process*, Greenwood Press.
WINNICOT, D. W. (1971) *Playing and Reality*, Tavistock.
WITKIN, R. (1974) *The Intelligence of Feeling*, Heinemann Educational Books.
WITTGENSTEIN, L. (1966) *Lectures and Conversations on Aesthetics, Psychology and Religious Belief*, Oxford University Press.
WOLLHEIM, R. (1970) *Art and Its Objects: An Introduction to Aesthetics*, Harper and Row.

English

ABBS, P. (1982) *English within the Arts*, Hodder and Stoughton.
ABBS, P. (1985) *English as an Arts Discipline*, Take up No 2, National Association for Education in the Arts.
ALLEN, D. (1980) *English Teaching Since 1965*, Heinemann Educational Books.
BARNES, D. (1969) *From Communication to Curriculum*, Penguin.
BARNES, D. and TODD, (1969) *Language, the Learner and the School*, Penguin.
BRITTON, J. (1972) *Language and Learning*, Penguin.
COOK, C. (1917) *The Play Way*, Heinemann.
CREBER, J. (1965) *Sense and Sensitivity*, University of London Press.
DIXON, J. (1975) *Growth through English*, Oxford University Press.
HARRISON, B. (1982) *An Arts-based Approach to English*, Hodder and Stoughton.
HOLBROOK, D. *English for Maturity*, Cambridge University Press.
HOLBROOK, D. (1979) *English for Meaning*, NFER.
HOURD, M. (1949) *The Education of the Poetic Spirit*, Heinemann Educational Books.
ROSENBLATT, L. (1970) *Literature as Exploration*, Heinemann Educational Books.
SAMPSON, G. (1975) *English for the English*, Cambridge University Press.
SCHAYER, D. (1972) *The Teaching of English in Schools* 1900–1970, Routledge and Kegan Paul.
WHITEHEAD, F. (1971) *The Disappearing Dais*, Chatto and Windus.
WILKINSON, A. (1971) *The Foundations of Language*, Oxford University Press.

Music

BROCKLEHURST, B. (1971) *Response to Music: Principles of Music Education*, Routledge and Kegan Paul.
FLETCHER, R. D. (1985) 'New forms of examination in music: The assessment of listening: A discussion paper', unpublished paper generally available from the Secondary Examinations Council, Newcombe House, 45 Notting Hill Gate, London, W11 3JB, or from the author at 8 Olivers Battery Gardens, Winchester, Hants SO22 4HF.
DES (1985) *General Certificate of Secondary Education: The National Criteria: Music*, HMSO.
DES (1985) *Music from 5–16*, Curriculum Matters 4, an HMI Series, HMSO.
HALE, N. V. (1974) *Education for Music: A Skeleton Plan of Research into the Development of the Study of Music as Part of the Organized Plan of General Education*, Oxford University Press.
LONG, N. (1959) *Music in English Education*, Faber and Faber.
NETTEL, R. (1952) *The Englishman Makes Music*, Dennis Dobson.
PAYNTER, J. (1972) *Hear and Now: An Introduction to Modern Music in Schools*, Universal Edition.
PAYNTER, J. (1982) *Music in the Secondary School Curriculum: Trends and Developments in Class Music Teaching*, Cambridge University Press.
PAYNTER, J. and ASTON, P. (1970) *Sound and Silence: Classroom Projects in Creative Music*, Cambridge University Press.

PLUMMERIDGE, C. *et al.* (1981) *Issues in Music Education*, University of London Institute of Education, Bedford Way Papers 3.

PRESTON, G. H. H. (1986) 'A new approach to music examinations', *International Journal of Music Education*, May.

REIMER, B. (1970) *A Philosophy of Music Education*, Prentice-Hall.

SMALL, C. (1977) *Music, Society, Education*, 2nd ed., John Calder.

SWANWICK, K. (1979) *A Basis for Music Education*, NFER, Nelson Publishing.

SWANWICK, K. and TAYLOR, D. (1982) *Discovering Music: Developing the Music Curriculum in Secondary Schools*, Batsford Academic and Educational.

TAYLOR, D. (1979) *Music Now: A Guide to Recent Developments and Current Opportunities in Music Education*, Open University Press.

Film (with notes by Rob Watson)

Almost every aspect of film has its own immense bibliography. The following suggestions are simply introductions to a few relevant areas.

Courses Combining Theory and Practice

HERBERT, F. MARGOLIS (1947) 'The American scene and the problems of film education', *The Penguin Film Review*, January.

WILLIAMS, C. (1981) *Film-making and Film Theory*. This paper gives a detailed outline of a degree course and is the most persuasive short account of film teaching I have found, especially taken in its context.

See also:

ALVARADO, M. 'Practical work in television studies', BFI pamphlet.

BOBKER, L. R. (1969) *Elements of Film*, Harcourt Brace.

DICKINSON, T. (1921) *A Discovery of Cinema*, Oxford University Press.

HORNSBY, J. 'The case for practical studies in media education', BFI pamphlet.

LINDGREN, E. (1948) *The Art of the Film*, Allen and Unwin.

Practical Teaching Ideas

LOWNDES, D. (1968) *Film Making in Schools*, Batsford — highly recommended.

WALL, I. and KRUGER, S. (1986) *Reading a Film*. This pack of materials is available free, as part of British Film Year, from Film Education, 12 St. George's Avenue, London W5.

Literary Adaptations, Screenplays, etc.

BLUESTONE, G. (1957) *Novels into Film*, Johns Hopkins University Press — American cinema.

CORLISS, R. (1975) *Talking Pictures*, David and Charles.

COULOURIS and HERRMANN (1972) 'The Citizen Kane Book', *Sight and Sound*, spring.

KAEL, P. (1971) *The Citizen Kane Book*, Secker and Warburg.

McFARLANE, B. (1984) *Words and Images*, Secker and Warburg — Australian cinema.

Bibliography

Auteurism, Structuralism, etc.

BRITTON, A. (1978/79) 'The Ideology of Screen,' *Movies 26*, winter — fairly impenetrable but effective critique of theories derived from Althusser, Lacan and Barthes.

CAUGHIE, J. (Ed.) (1981) *Theories of Authorship*, RKP — recommended.

COOK, P. (Ed.) (1985) *The Cinema Book*, BFI — thorough summaries, but written in the deadly style of the new academicism.

NICHOLS, B. (Ed.) (1976) *Movies and Methods*, University of California Press — highly recommended.

WOLLEN, P. (1969) *Signs and Meaning in the Cinema*, Secker and Warburg.

Critical Studies of Directors

ANDERSON, L. (1981) *About John Ford Plexus* — this is the most intelligent study of any body of work in films. Anyone more interested in theory than film should perhaps consult the sections on Ford in *Theories of Authorship* and *Movies and Methods*.

ARANDA, F. (1975) *Luis Buñuel: A Critical Biography*, Secker and Warburg.

BAZIN, A. (1974) *Jean Renoir*, W. H. Allen.

BJÖRKMAN, MANNS, SIMA, (1973) *Bergman on Bergman*, Secker and Warburg — interviews.

BOGDANOVITCH, P. (1978) *John Ford*, University of California Press — interviews.

DURGNAT, R. (1973) *Jean Renoir*, University of California Press.

MCBRIDE, W. (1974) *John Ford*, Secker and Warburg.

PLACE, J. A. (1974) *The Western Films of John Ford*, Citadel Press.

PLACE, J. A. (1979) *The Non-Western Films of John Ford*, Citadel Press.

RENOIR, J. (1974) *My Life and My Films*, Collins.

ROUD, R. (Ed.) (1980) *Cinema, A Critical Dictionary*, Secker and Warburg.

SALLES GOMES, P. E. (1972) *Jean Vigo*, Secker and Warburg — recommended.

SARRIS, A. (1976) *The John Ford Movie Mystery*, Secker and Warburg.

SESONSKE, A. (1980) *Jean Renoir, the French Films, 1924–1939*, Harvard University Press — highly recommended.

SIMON, J. (1973) *Ingmar Bergman Directs*, Davis-Poynter.

TRUFFAUT, F. (1968) *Hitchcock*, Secker and Warburg — interviews.

WOOD, R. (1965) *Hitchcock's Films*, Zwemmer — highly recommended.

WOOD, R. (1968) *Howard Hawks*, Secker and Warburg — recommended.

Historical Development of Film

BROWNLOW, K. (1968) *The Parade's Gone By...*, Secker and Warburg.

CERAM, C. W. (1965) *Archaeology of the Cinema*, Thames and Hudson.

COE, B. (1981) *The History of Movie Photography*, Ash and Grant.

DICKINSON, T. (1971) *A Discovery of Cinema*, Oxford University Press.

MONTAGUE, I. (1964) *Film World*, Penguin.

SALT, B. (1983) *Film Style and Technology: History and Analysis* — highly recommended.

WENDEN, D. J. (1975) *The Birth of the Movies*, Macdonald and Jane's.

Dance

ADSHEAD, J. (1981) *The Study of Dance*, Dance Books Ltd.

ADSHEAD, J. and LAYSON, J. (Eds) (1984) *Dance History*, Dance Books Ltd.

BANES, S. (1980) *Terpsichore in Sneakers: Post Modern Dance*, Houghton Mifflin.

BEST, D. (1974) *Expression in Movement and the Arts*, Lepus Books.
BEST, D. (1978) *Philosophy and Human Movement*, Unwin Educational Books.
GULBENKIAN FOUNDATION (1980) *Dance Education and Training in Britain*, Oyez Press.
HUMPHREY, D. (1959) *The Art of Making Dances*, Dance Books Ltd.
KRAUS, R. (1969) *History of the Dance*, Prentice Hall.
LABAN, R. (1960) *The Mastery of Movement*, MacDonald and Evans.
LANGER, S. K. (1953) *Feeling and Form*, chapters 11 and 12, Routledge and Kegan Paul.
MYERS, G. and FANCHER, G. (Eds) (1981) *Philosophical Essays on Dance*, Dance Horizons.
PRESTON-DUNLOP, V. (1980) *A Handbook for Dance in Education*, MacDonald and Evans.
REDFERN, B. (1982) *Concepts in Modern Educational Dance*, Dance Books Ltd.
REDFERN, B. (1983) *Dance, Art and Aesthetics*, Dance Books Ltd.
SMITH, J. M. (1976) *Dance Composition*, Lepus Books.
SORELL, W. (1981) *Dance in Its Time: The Emergence of an Art Form*, Anchor Press.
ULLMANN, L. (1984) *A Vision of Dynamic Space*, Falmer Press.

Drama

ALLEN, J. (1979) *Drama in Schools: Its Theory and Practice*, Heinemann.
BOLTON, G. (1979) *Towards a Theory of Drama in Education*, Longman.
BOLTON, G. (1983) *Bolton at the Barbican*, National Association for Teachers of Drama.
BOLTON, G. (1984) *Drama as Education*, Longman.
DAY, C. (1975) *Drama for Middle and Upper Schools*, Batsford.
HEATHCOTE, D. (1980) *Drama as Context*, NATE.
HEATHCOTE, D. (1982) 'Signs and portents?', SCYPT *Journal*, 9 April.
HORNBROOK, D. (1989) *Education and Dramatic Art*, Basil Blackwell.
JOHNSON, L. and O'NEILL, C. (Eds) (1983) *Selected Writings of Dorothy Heathcote*, Hutchinson.
LINNELL, R. (1982) *Approaching Classroom Drama*, Edward Arnold.
MCGREGOR, L., TATE, M. and ROBINSON, K. (1977) *Learning through Drama*, Schools Council Drama Teaching Project (10–11), Heinemann.
O'NEILL, C. and LAMBERT, A. (1982) *Drama Structures*, Hutchinson.
ROBINSON, K. (1980) *Exploring Theatre and Education*, Heinemann.
SLADE, P. (1954) *Child Drama*, University of London Press.
WAGNER, B. J. (1978) *Dorothy Heathcote: Drama as a Learning Medium*, National Education Association.
WATKINS, B. (1981) *Drama and Education*, Batsford Academic and Educational.
WAY, B. (1967) *Development through Drama*, Longman.

Visual Arts

ADAMS, E. (1982) *Art and the Built Environment*, Schools Council, Longman.
ART ADVISERS ASSOCIATION (1978) *Learning through Drawing*, Art Advisers Association, North East Region.
BARRATT, M. (1979) *Art Education: A Strategy for Course Design*, Heinemann Educational Books.
BAYNES, K. (1976) *About Design*, Heinemann Educational Books.
BERGER, J. (1972) *Ways of Seeing*, Penguin.
EISNER, E. (1972) *Educating Artistic Vision*, Macmillan.
FRY, R. (1920) *Vision and Design*, Chatto and Windus.
GENTLE, K. (1985) *Children and Art Teaching*, Croom Helm.
GREEN, P. (1974) *Design Education: Problem Solving and Visual Experience*, Batsford.
LOWENFIELD, V. (1947) *Creative and Mental Growth*, Collier Macmillan.

Bibliography

READ, H. (1943) *Education through Art*, Faber.
RICHARDSON, M. (1948) *Art and the Child*, University of London Press.
ROBERTSON, S. (1982) *Rosegarden and Labyrinth*, Gryphon Press.
ROWLAND, K. (1968) *Learning to See*, Ginn and Co.
SAUSMAREZ, M. DE (1964) *Basic Design: The Dynamics of Visual Form*.
TAYLOR, R. (1986) *Educating for Art*, Longman.
VIOLA, W. (1936) *Child Art*, Simpkin Marshall.

Index

Lightning Source UK Ltd.
Milton Keynes UK
UKOW030630020512

191822UK00002B/26/A